LIBRARY OF HEBREW BIBLE/
OLD TESTAMENT STUDIES

714

Formerly Journal for the Study of the Old Testament Supplement Series

Editors
Laura Quick, Oxford University, UK
Jacqueline Vayntrub, Yale University, USA

Founding Editors
David J. A. Clines, Philip R. Davies and David M. Gunn

Editorial Board
Sonja Ammann, Alan Cooper, Steed Davidson, Susan Gillingham,
Rachelle Gilmour, John Goldingay, Rhiannon Graybill, Anne Katrine Gudme,
Norman K. Gottwald, James E. Harding, John Jarick, Tracy Lemos,
Carol Meyers, Eva Mroczek, Daniel L. Smith-Christopher,
Francesca Stavrakopoulou, James W. Watts

READING LAMENTATIONS
INTERTEXTUALLY

Edited by

Heath A. Thomas and Brittany N. Melton

LONDON • NEW YORK • OXFORD • NEW DELHI • SYDNEY

T&T CLARK
Bloomsbury Publishing Plc
50 Bedford Square, London, WC1B 3DP, UK
1385 Broadway, New York, NY 10018, USA
29 Earlsfort Terrace, Dublin 2, Ireland

BLOOMSBURY, T&T CLARK and the T&T Clark logo
are trademarks of Bloomsbury Publishing Plc

First published in Great Britain 2021
This paperback edition published 2023

Copyright © Heath A. Thomas, Brittany N. Melton and contributors, 2021

Heath A. Thomas, Brittany N. Melton and contributors have asserted their right under the Copyright, Designs and Patents Act, 1988, to be identified as Authors of this work.

All rights reserved. No part of this publication may be reproduced or transmitted in any form or by any means, electronic or mechanical, including photocopying, recording, or any information storage or retrieval system, without prior permission in writing from the publishers.

Bloomsbury Publishing Plc does not have any control over, or responsibility for, any third-party websites referred to or in this book. All internet addresses given in this book were correct at the time of going to press. The author and publisher regret any inconvenience caused if addresses have changed or sites have ceased to exist, but can accept no responsibility for any such changes.

A catalogue record for this book is available from the British Library.
Library of Congress Control Number: 2021945665.

ISBN: HB: 978-0-5676-9958-9
PB: 978-0-5676-9961-9
ePDF: 978-0-5676-9959-6

Series: Library of Hebrew Bible/Old Testament Studies, volume 714
ISSN 2513-8758

To find out more about our authors and books visit www.bloomsbury.com
and sign up for our newsletters.

Contents

List of Tables and Figures ... ix
List of Contributors ... xi
Preface ... xiii
Abbreviations ... xv

A SEA OF INTERTEXTS:
INTRODUCTION TO *READING LAMENTATIONS INTERTEXTUALLY*
  Brittany N. Melton and Heath A. Thomas ... 1

Part I
LAMENTATIONS IN DIALOGUE WITH THE TORAH

Chapter 1
EXODUS 32–34 AND LAMENTATIONS: COMPARISON OF SIN, PUNISHMENT, AND CONFESSION
  Alison Lo ... 17

Chapter 2
"AWAY! UNCLEAN! DO NOT TOUCH!":
DEFILED AND DEFILING PRIESTS IN LAMENTATIONS
  Samuel E. Balentine ... 29

Chapter 3
THE OSTRICH AND THE SWORD: READING THE CITY-LAMENT OF LAMENTATIONS INTERTEXTUALLY WITH THE WILDERNESS WANDERINGS OF THE BOOK OF NUMBERS
  Richard S. Briggs ... 43

Chapter 4
CHAOS AND ORDER: LAMENTATIONS AND DEUTERONOMY AS RESPONSES TO DESTRUCTION AND EXILE
  Elizabeth Boase ... 55

Part II
LAMENTATIONS IN DIALOGUE WITH THE PROPHETS

Chapter 5
OUT OF SIGHT, BUT NOT OUT OF MIND (2 KINGS 23:27):
READING 1–2 KINGS WITH LAMENTATIONS
J. Andrew Dearman   73

Chapter 6
"I AM HE, YOUR COMFORTER": SECOND ISAIAH'S PERVASIVE DIVINE VOICE
AS INTERTEXTUAL "ANSWER" TO LAMENTATIONS' DIVINE SILENCE
Katie M. Heffelfinger   85

Chapter 7
THE AFFLICTED MAN IN LAMENTATIONS 3 AS COMRADE TO JEREMIAH
Christl M. Maier   97

Chapter 8
THE SOUND AND THE FURY: WOMEN AND SUFFERING IN EZEKIEL
AND LAMENTATIONS
Amy Kalmanofsky   110

Chapter 9
ZECHARIAH'S INTERTEXTUAL REVERSAL OF LAMENTATIONS
Michael R. Stead   123

Part III
LAMENTATIONS IN DIALOGUE WITH THE WRITINGS

Chapter 10
MODELS FOR PRAYER IN LAMENTATIONS AND PSALMS
John Goldingay   139

Chapter 11
VERSE AND VOICE IN LAMENTATIONS 3 AND PSALM 119
David J. Reimer   152

Chapter 12
DEBATING SUFFERING:
THE VOICES OF LAMENTATIONS PERSONIFIED IN JOB'S DIALOGUE
Will Kynes   170

Chapter 13
ALL IS DECAY: INTERTEXTUAL LINKS BETWEEN LAMENTATIONS 5
AND ECCLESIASTES 12:1-7
Katharine J. Dell   183

Chapter 14
CONSPICUOUS FEMALES AND AN INCONSPICUOUS GOD:
THE DISTINCTIVE CHARACTERIZATION OF WOMEN AND GOD
IN THE *MEGILLOTH*
   Brittany N. Melton   193

Part IV
LAMENTATIONS IN DIALOGUE BEYOND THE HEBREW BIBLE

Chapter 15
LAMENTATIONS AT QUMRAN
   Gideon R. Kotzé   207

Chapter 16
FROM ANONYMITY TO BIOGRAPHY:
JEREMIAH AS A CHARACTER MEMORIZING THE PAST
IN THE SEPTUAGINT VERSION OF LAMENTATIONS
   Antje Labahn   219

Chapter 17
"LET US TEST AND EXAMINE OUR WAYS, AND RETURN TO THE LORD":
JOSEPHUS' INTERPRETATIONS OF LAMENTATIONS
   Honora Howell Chapman   242

Chapter 18
JESUS AND JERUSALEM: CHRISTOLOGICAL INTERPRETATION
OF LAMENTATIONS IN THE CHURCH
   Robin A. Parry   252

Chapter 19
THE RABBIS TALK BACK THROUGH THE PROPHETS:
INTERTEXTUALITY, LAMENTATIONS, AND DIVINE MOURNING
   Heath A. Thomas   266

Chapter 20
READING LAMENTATIONS AFTER THE *SHOAH*: A MANDATE TO QUESTION
   Hemchand Gossai   279

Bibliography   290
Index of References   312
Index of Authors   326

List of Tables and Figures

Table 1	Kinds of Intertextuality in the Volume	12
Figure 9.1	Intertextuality Spectrum	123
Figure 9.2	Lam. 2:17a and Zech. 1:6b	125
Figure 9.3	Lam. 2:17, Zech. 1:6b and Zech. 8:14-15	126
Figure 12.1	Job 19:6-8 and Lam. 3:6-9	175
Figure 12.2	Job 16:12-13 and Lam. 3:11-13	177
Figure 15.1	4Q179 and Lamentations 1 and 4	210
Figure 15.2	4Q501 and Lamentations 5	213
Figure 18.1	The Valiant Man and Jesus	261
Figure 19.1	Correlating God and Zion	272

Contributors

Dr. Samuel E. Balentine, Professor of Old Testament and Director of Graduate Studies, Union Presbyterian Seminary (VA, USA).

Dr. Elizabeth Boase, Dean of the School of Graduate Research, University of Divinity (Australia); Previously with Flinders University.

Dr. Richard S. Briggs, Lecturer in Old Testament and Director of Biblical Studies at St John's College, Durham University (United Kingdom).

Dr. Honora Howell Chapman, Professor of Classics and Humanities and Interim Dean of the College of Arts and Humanities, California State University, Fresno (CA, USA).

Rev. Dr. J. Andrew Dearman, Professor of Old Testament, Fuller Theological Seminary (CA, USA).

Dr. Katharine J. Dell, Reader in Old Testament Literature and Theology, University of Cambridge and Fellow of St Catharine's College, Cambridge (United Kingdom).

Professor John Goldingay, David Allan Hubbard Professor Emeritus of Old Testament, Fuller Theological Seminary (CA, USA).

Dr. Hemchand Gossai, Professor of Hebrew and Religious Studies and Associate Dean of Humanities and Social Sciences, Northern Virginia Community College (VA, USA).

Dr. Katie M. Heffelfinger, Lecturer in Biblical Studies and Hermeneutics, Church of Ireland Theological Institute (Ireland).

Dr. Amy Kalmanofsky, Blanche and Romie Shapiro Associate Professor of Bible, Jewish Theological Seminary and Dean of Albert A. List College of Jewish Studies (NY, USA).

Professor Gideon R. Kotzé, Research Professor, Focus Area: Ancient Texts, Faculty of Theology, North-West University (South Africa).

Dr. Will Kynes, Associate Professor of Hebrew Bible/Old Testament, Samford University (AL, USA).

Professor Dr. Antje Labahn, Extraordinary Associate Professor, North-West University (South Africa) and Privatdozentin at College of Theology Wuppertal/Bethel (Germany).

Dr. Alison Lo, Associate Professor of Old Testament, Bethel Seminary (MN, USA).

Professor Dr. Christl M. Maier, Professor of Old Testament, Philipps-Universität Marburg (Germany) and Professor Extraordinary of the Disciplinary Group Old and New Testament, Stellenbosch University (South Africa).

Dr. Brittany N. Melton, Assistant Professor of Biblical and Theological Studies, Palm Beach Atlantic University (FL, USA) and Research Fellow, University of the Free State (South Africa).

Rev. Dr. Robin A. Parry, Commissioning Editor for Wipf and Stock Publishers.

Dr. David J. Reimer, Academic Dean, Faith Mission Bible College and Honorary Senior Lecturer, University of St Andrews (United Kingdom).

Rt. Rev. Dr. Michael R. Stead, Bishop of South Sydney and Visiting Lecturer in Old Testament, Moore Theological College, Sydney (Australia).

Dr. Heath A. Thomas, Professor of Old Testament and University President, Oklahoma Baptist University (OK, USA).

Preface

We, the editors, are indebted to the fine work of Katharine Dell and Will Kynes on the previous volumes in this *Reading Intertextually* series. They graciously entrusted the continuation of the series to us once the traditional wisdom books had been completed. We would also like to thank them especially for the contributions they made to the present volume to maintain continuity with the other volumes. The remaining contributors to the volume we would like to warmly thank for their time and insights. We are grateful to Andrew Mein and Claudia Camp, the previous co-editors for the LHBOTS series, for their enthusiasm to continue the series and patience while we composed the present volume, and to Laura Quick and Jacqueline Vayntrub for bringing it to completion as the current co-editors. Finally, special thanks should be given to Dylan Watson for his careful editing assistance. The book of Lamentations has engendered many responsive texts, those referred to within this book, those composed for this book, and it is hoped those produced as a result of reading this book.

In dedication to our supervisors, Gordon McConville, Katharine Dell, and Paul Joyce, for their inspiration and friendship.

Brittany N. Melton
Heath A. Thomas

Abbreviations

AB	The Anchor Bible
ABR	*Australian Biblical Review*
ABRL	Anchor Bible Reference Library
AcBib	Academia Biblica
ActJut	Acta Jutlandica XLVIII Theology Series
AGJU	Arbeiten zur Geschichte des antiken Judentums und des Urchristentums
AIL	Ancient Israel and Its Literature
APB	*Acta Patristica et Byzantina*
ApOTC	Apollos Old Testament Commentary
ASB	*Austin Seminary Bulletin*
ATANT	Abhandlungen zur Theologie des Alten und Neuen Testaments
BDB	Brown, Francis, S. R. Driver, and Charles A. Briggs. *A Hebrew and English Lexicon of the Old Testament*
BE	Biblische Enzyklopädie
BEATAJ	Beiträge zur Erforschung des Alten Testaments und des antiken Judentums
BETL	Bibliotheca Ephemeridum Theologicarum Lovaniensium
BG	Beiträge zur Geschichtskultur
Bib	*Biblica*
BibInt	*Biblical Interpretation*
BibInt	Biblical Interpretation Series
BJS	Brown Judaic Studies
BKAT	Biblischer Kommentar, Altes Testament
BO	Berit Olam: Studies in Hebrew Narrative and Poetry
BRLA	Brill Reference Library of Judaism
BThSt	Biblisch-Theologische Studien
BZ	*Biblische Zeitschrift*
BZAW	Beihefte zur Zeitschrift für die alttestamentliche Wissenschaft
CBS	Core Biblical Studies
CSLL	*Cardoza Studies in Law and Literature*
CurBR	*Currents in Biblical Research*
CurBS	*Currents in Research: Biblical Studies*
DJD	Discoveries in the Judaean Desert
DSD	*Dead Sea Discoveries*
EBib	*Etudes bibliques*

EBR	Encyclopedia of the Bible and its Reception. Edited by Hans-Josef Klauck et al. Berlin: de Gruyter, 2009–
ECDSS	*Eerdmans Commentaries on the Dead Sea Scrolls*
EGI	Erinnerung, Geschichte, Identität
EuroJ	*European Judaism*
EuroJTh	*European Journal of Theology*
FAT	Forschungen zum Alten Testament
FOTL	Forms of the Old Testament Literature
FRLANT	Forschungen zur Religion und Literatur des Alten und Neuen Testaments
GS	Geistliche Schriftlesung
HB	Hebrew Bible
HBM	Hebrew Bible Monographs
HBS	History of Biblical Studies
HBT	*Horizons in Biblical Theology*
HCOT	Historical Commentary on the Old Testament
HistTh	*History and Theory*
HThKAT	Herders Theologischer Kommentar zum Alten Testament
IB	Interpreter's Bible. Edited by George A. Buttrick et al. 12 vols. New York, 1951–1957
IBC	*Interpretation: A Bible Commentary for Teaching and Preaching*
IBMR	*International Bulletin of Missionary Research*
ICC	International Critical Commentary
Int	*Interpretation*
JAAR	*Journal of the American Academy of Religion*
JAB	*Journal for the Aramaic Bible*
JAJSup	Supplements to the Journal of Ancient Judaism
JANES	*Journal of the Ancient Near Eastern Society*
JBL	*Journal of Biblical Literature*
JFSR	*Journal of Feminist Studies in Religion*
JJS	*Journal of Jewish Studies*
JPS	*Jewish Publication Society*
JR	*Journal of Religion*
JR&H	*Journal of Religion and Health*
JSem	*Journal of Semitics*
JSJSup	Journal for the Study of Judaism Supplement Series
JSOT	*Journal for the Study of the Old Testament*
JSOTSup	Journal for the Study of the Old Testament Supplement Series
JSRI	*Journal for the Study of Religions and Ideologies*
JSS	*Journal of Semitic Studies*
KAT	Kommentar zum Alten Testament
L&T	*Literature and Theology*
LCL	Loeb Classical Library
LHBOTS	The Library of Hebrew Bible/Old Testament Studies
LJLE	The Library of Jewish Law and Ethics
NCB	New Century Bible

NIB	The New Interpreter's Bible. Edited by Leander E. Keck. 12 vols. Nashville: Abingdon, 1994–2004
NIBCOT	New International Commentary on the Old Testament
NIVAC	The NIV Application Commentary
NSKAT	Neuer Stuttgarter Kommentar, Altes Testament
NT	New Testament
OBO	Orbis Biblicus et Orientalis
ÖBS	Österreichische Biblische Studien
OBT	Overtures to Biblical Theology
OT	Old Testament
OTE	Old Testament Essays
OTG	Old Testament Guides
OTL	Old Testament Library
OTS	Oudtestamentische Studiën / Old Testament Studies
PT	Poetics Today
Proof	Prooftexts: A Journal of Jewish Literary History
R&E	Review and Expositor
RevQ	Revue de Qumran
RTS	Reading the Scriptures
SAIS	Studies in Aramaic Interpretation of Scripture
SBAB	Stuttgarter biblische Aufsatzbände
SBLDS	Society of Biblical Literature Dissertation Series
SBLSCS	Society of Biblical Literature Septuagint and Cognate Studies
SBLSymS	Society of Biblical Literature Symposium Series
SBT	Studies in Biblical Theology
SCS	Septuagint and Cognate Studies
SemeiaSt	Semeia Studies
SJOT	Scandinavian Journal of the Old Testament
SJT	*Scottish Journal of Theology*
SOSup	*Symbolae Osloensis Fasc. Suppl.*
SSN	*Studia Semitica Neerlandica*
STDJ	Studies on the Texts of the Desert of Judah
StJ	*Studies in Judaism*
STL	*Studia Theologica Lundensia*
SubBi	Subsidia Biblica
THL	Theory and History of Literature
THOTC	Two Horizons Old Testament Commentary
ThWAT	*Theologisches Wörterbuch zum Alten Testament.* Edited by G. Johannes Botterweck and Helmer Ringgren. Stuttgart: Kohlhammer, 1970–
TThSt	Trierer theologische Studien
TynBul	*Tyndale Bulletin*
VEc	*Verbum et Ecclesia*
VT	*Vetus Testamentum*
VTSup	Supplements to Vetus Testamentum
WBBC	Wiley-Blackwell Bible Commentaries

WBC	*The Women's Bible Commentary*. Edited by Carol A. Newsom, Sharon H. Ringe, and Jacqueline E. Lapsley. London: SPCK, 1992
WBC	Word Biblical Commentary
WMANT	Wissenschaftliche Monographien zum Alten und Neuen Testament
WTJ	*Westminster Theological Journal*
WUNT	Wissenschaftliche Untersuchungen zum Neuen Testament
ZAW	*Zeitschrift für die alttestamentliche Wissenschaft*

A Sea of Intertexts: Introduction to *Reading Lamentations Intertextually*

Brittany N. Melton and Heath A. Thomas

Introduction

For centuries Bible scholars have negotiated intersections between biblical texts and assessed reception of traditions of the Hebrew Bible. In the light of these interactions, de Moor (1998: ix) drolly avers: "To the Bible scholar, intertextuality is nothing new." And yet fresh research on "intertextuality" persists. Carr (2012: 506) programmatically affirms that "this issue of intertextuality in biblical literature is a strategic and widespread issue for study of the Hebrew Bible." And Kwon (2016a: 33) characterizes intertextuality in biblical studies as a "burgeoning" field. If it is "nothing new," as de Moor maintains, what explains the continuing fascination for biblical scholars, even to the present day?

One reason for its persistence in biblical studies no doubt stems from the way intertextuality resources different interpretative impulses among biblical scholars. Moore and Sherwood (2011: 34) argue that when intertextuality hit the biblical studies scene in the 1980s, the concept was filtered, diluted, or reduced so that it was normalized into a method or means of discourse whereby scholars could explore historical relationships between texts, fitting to patterns of historicist concerns in biblical studies, namely, "Pentateuchal source-paternity, inter-Isaianic textual intercourse, Synoptic *ménages à trois*, and all the other intensely inter-subjective authorial exchanges that elicit quiet excitement in the average biblical scholar." While the language remains provocative, they rightly touch upon the historical impulse that funds some scholars' vision of intertextuality.

Despite the ubiquity of historically grounded intertextual study in biblical scholarship, in its originating coinage, intertextuality's reach was broader than historicist aspirations. A term introduced in literary studies in the late 1960s by Julia Kristeva (1941–), "intertextuality" was not a literary *topic* (in the sense that one understands other literary topics like metaphor, metonymy, antanaclasis, or the like) or a historical *method* (in the sense of text-criticism, inner-biblical exegesis, or *Fortschriebungen*). By coining this neologism, Kristeva, rather, attempted to describe a phenomenon of human meaning-making: humans create by interacting with a field of influences. As such, intertextuality marks a reality of the human condition. Humans make meaning through a sea of intertexts, whether intentionally or unintentionally. The present volume will make good on Kristeva's vision by exemplifying how scholars employ intertextuality in diverse ways: historical relationships, canonical relationships, and readerly interests.

For Kristeva, intertextuality identifies how works of art and "utterances, taken from other texts" "intersect and neutralize one another" (1989: 989). Her notion of intertextuality emerges from her engagement with Russian formalist Mikhail Bakhtin (1895–1975), who thought that texts speak with many voices (which he terms *polyphony*) because latent influences (social, economic, geographical, historical) interact with other texts and readers who are also penetrated by a multitude of influences. Although he never used the term "intertextuality," this nascent concept can be observed in one of his later essays: "The text lives only by coming into contact with another text (with context). Only at the point of this contact between texts does a light flash, illuminating both the posterior and anterior, joining a given text to a dialogue" (Bakhtin 1986: 162). Dialogue between texts is a reality to be celebrated, as the interaction, both of posterior and anterior texts, creates "light" and "life."

Turning back to Kristeva, she argues that texts cannot be hermetically sealed (semantically, historically, culturally) from other texts. Instead, cross-contamination occurs because texts emerge in varied contexts (historical, linguistic, cultural) and necessarily interact with others from different contexts; in this process, intertextuality is not a method of interpretation as much as it is a reality of the human creative process.[1]

---

1. "The term *intertextuality* denotes this transposition of one (or several) sign-system(s) into another; but since the term has often been understood in the banal sense of a 'study of sources', we prefer the term *transposition* because it specifies that the passage from one signifying system to another demands a new articulation of the thetic—enunciative and denotative positionality. If one grants that every signifying practice is a field of transpositions of various signifying systems (an intertextuality),

In Kristeva's broad vision, intertextuality should not be domesticated by a method of textual use (or re-use) of earlier texts in later texts, which is a common domain of research: differentiation of intertextuality into categories of allusions, echoes, inner-biblical exegesis, intra-textuality, etc. to differentiate later uses of earlier traditions.[2] But in Kristeva's conception, intertextuality as a phenomenon of human creativity stands out, rather than the concept becoming instrumentalized as a historical tool from the biblical scholars' methodological toolbox. Historicist conceptions of intertextuality as well as broader visions coexist in this volume. And, to be fair, our readers should be commended for noting a latent tension therein. Is intertextuality a study in historical relationships or a study in broader concerns that emerge between texts and cultures? In her classic work, Susan Handelman (1982: 47) avers: "Texts echo, interact, and interpenetrate. In the world of the text, rigid temporal and spatial distinctions collapse." Is Handelman's position true to the field of biblical studies?

Our contributors do not adjudicate one way or another but rather surface the ways in which scholars engage the question. Temporal and spatial relationships between Lamentations and earlier tradition stands as a worthy focus of study as much as the ways canon and culture receive or appropriate Lamentations in a generative meaning-making move. The concept (and phenomenon) of intertextuality encompasses both impulses, and both impulses emerge in the present study on Lamentations.

This volume serves as a companion to other works in this series devoted to intertextuality and the Hebrew Bible by Dell and Kynes: *Reading Job Intertextually* (2013), *Reading Ecclesiastes Intertextually* (2014), and *Reading Proverbs Intertextually* (2018). Our focus is the book of Lamentations and the worlds which receive and interact with it. This five-poem masterpiece of ancient Hebrew poetry comprises some of the most forlorn pages in the Hebrew Bible and, as such, it invites rejoinder to its cries.

---

then one understands that its 'place' of enunciation and its denoted 'object' are never single, complete and identical to themselves, but always plural, shattered, capable of being tabulated" (Kristeva 1986: 111).

2. See, for example, the classic work of Richard Hays (1989). Or in Hebrew Bible studies, how Fishbane (1985) identified the ways tradition (*traditum*) re-uses earlier materials in the long and multifaceted process of transmission (*traditio*). Fishbane never uses the term "intertextuality" in this classic work and only later uses the language to describe his understanding of inner-biblical exegesis, for example in Fishbane 2000: 39: "Intertextuality is a form that creativity takes when innovation is grounded in a tradition."

The Present Volume

The contributors work through the intersections between Lamentations and the Hebrew Bible (Torah, Prophets, and Writings). This is followed by a set of receptions of Lamentations in later texts in Jewish and Christian tradition, including LXX, Qumran, Josephus, Midrash Rabbah, early and Medieval Christian writings, and post-*Shoah* literature.

Alison Lo explores connections between Exodus tradition (particularly language of lament in Exodus) and Lamentations. Lo sets these texts in dialogue with one another instead of claiming historical dependence, as Thomas has done (2013b: 133). As a result, Lo does not specify an intentionally designed intertextual resonance between Lamentations and Exodus. The canon of the Hebrew Bible may set the context that invites the interchange as a result of a common body of authoritative text (canonical intertextuality), or perhaps this is simply the interaction that Lo evinces between two disparate texts. That is, when Lo reads Lamentations with Exodus, her reading emerges. Intertextuality as a concept allows all three dimensions of readings.

Samuel Balentine assesses the relationship between Leviticus (Priestly Tradition) and Lamentations, noting that purity paradigms from priestly sources and the concept of the *niddah* in priestly tradition reappear in Lam. 1 and 4. Different from previous research, Balentine's reading does not base his intertextual analysis on diachronic concerns. The intertextual connection emerges from his scholarly expertise but also from his intentional setting of the two texts into dialogue with one another. Balentine's reading generates engagement between the two texts (Leviticus and Lamentations) and yields a way of reviewing Lamentations.

Richard Briggs correlates Numbers and Lamentations, drawing upon complaint tradition found in Numbers and visaging its reception in Lam. 2 and 3. For Briggs, the placement of both Lamentations and Numbers within the canon of the Hebrew Bible enables the reader to read them as co-texts rather than claiming Lamentations' historical dependence upon Numbers. As he says, "Reading them intertextually is therefore a decision to let their co-existence in the Hebrew/OT canon create resonance and mutual illumination even where or if none existed in the minds of authors and editors of either book." In this way, Briggs activates a broader conception of intertextuality than a purely historical concern or interpretative practice in the case of Lamentations' poets in their reception of Numbers.

Elizabeth Boase utilizes a comparative and diachronic intertextual strategy to read Lamentations and Deuteronomy together as complementary, and at points competing, responses to catastrophe and exile. She explores the paradigm of covenant curse in Deuteronomy, which has been a significant scholarly point of discussion since the foundational research of Gottwald over 60 years ago. Boase provides a different valence to the discussion by assessing how both texts provide divergent responses to trauma. Boase explores the ways the books envisage the divine, with Lamentations' divine portrait vacillating between positive and negative poles, resonant with a community coming to grips with their corporate pain. Deuteronomy provides a normalizing portrait of God, where the people of God experience his positive characteristics as they serve YHWH faithfully. When read together, these texts do not conflict but rather provide varied responses to the trauma of exile. Neither text or response, in Boase's estimation, is better than the other but represent divergent responses to the vagaries and traumas of the communities that embraced them. Lamentations counters Deuteronomy's vision whilst Deuteronomy provides grounds for future hope in the character of God.

Andrew Dearman explores connections between Kings and Lamentations, recognizing that both texts present rationales for the disaster of exile and the concomitant disruption of the "triad" of both texts: Davidic monarchy, Jerusalem, and the temple located there. Similar to Boase, Dearman's reading is comparative and diachronic. However, he admits that the two texts show little evidence of "literary interaction," by which Dearman means conscious drawing of 1–2 Kings by the poets of Lamentations. His concern, then, is not primarily diachronic but rather a fertile reading based upon the presence of both texts in the Hebrew Bible. He focuses particularly upon the allusive manner in which Lamentations echoes the demise of the Judahite state reflected in 2 Kgs 24–25, a view of multi-generational sin and corporate punishment in both texts, and the shedding of innocent blood. Both texts reflect upon the memory of Babylonian destruction of the Judahite state and resonate with key theological themes. Neither text, however, betrays knowledge of the other. The intertextuality at play, then, is due to their shared reflection on an exilic reality that befell the people of God.

Katie Heffelfinger assesses connections between Isa. 40–66 and Lamentations, particularly building on previous research between the corpora. In her analysis, which is constructed on historical foundations of intertextual study, Heffelfinger traces the distinctive figure of the broken and redeemed Zion and her body. She argues that Second Isaiah meets Lamentations' cry for divine comfort, with the preponderance of the divine voice in its oracles and the unique vision of YHWH as a nursing mother who cares for his/her children. Second Isaiah's poetry re-deploys images from Lamentations and inverts them to answer Zion's complaints. In so doing, Heffelfinger provides a fresh perspective on the reading of Second Isaiah.

Christl Maier examines the reception of the Jeremiah tradition in Lam. 3 in order give further specificity to the "afflicted man" of Lam. 3:1-19. Her discussion naturally evokes other suffering male figures in the Hebrew Bible, including Job and the Servant of YHWH in Second Isaiah, along with the suffering prophet, Jeremiah. In her intertextual analysis of shared language and vocabulary between the texts, Maier believes that the "afflicted man" of Lam. 3 and the figure of Jeremiah resonate most strongly, offering further clarity on the literary identity of the figure in Lam. 3. He is the comrade of Jeremiah, a prophet who suffers on behalf of the people of Judah. Her analysis gives rationale as to why Jeremiah and Lamentations have been linked in the history of interpretation of Lamentations. Maier is not content to stop with this observation, however, noting that the complexity of the presentation of pain in Lamentations evokes Davidic suffering, Job, and indeed readers today.

Amy Kalmanofsky offers a dialogic reading of Ezek. 19 and 24 with Lam. 1 and 2, in the vein of Bakhtinian dialogism. Rather than making an historicist argument in the sense that Ezekiel predates Lamentations or vice-versa, she argues that the texts work as the first and second stage in an emotional continuum. Whereas the texts of Ezekiel represent an early response to the shock of exile, Lamentations presents a later response of pain. Lamentations' response is one in which the people have found their voice and they contend with the divine. Notably, however, in her reading Kalmanofsky points out how the presentation of women predominates both texts. In this way, she uniquely provides a way to perceive gender and suffering in the conversation between texts.

Building upon previous intertextual study between Zechariah and Lamentations, Michael Stead argues that Zechariah receives and re-interprets metaphors of destruction from Lam. 2, transforming them into images of restoration and hope. Stead argues that eight sustained allusions exist between Lam. 1–2 and Zech. 1–2; he identifies an allusion as a partial re-use of an earlier text's sequence of words or ideas. Zechariah's use of Lamentations provides a way for the prophetic work to open an avenue of hope, answering the cries of Lamentations in a way akin to Second Isaiah's response to Lamentations.

John Goldingay does not envisage historical connections between Lamentations and the psalms of lament, but rather productively sets the texts into conversation with one another. He correlates the texts partly because of their participation in the canon of the Hebrew Bible, but more directly because both texts are concerned with the experience of prayer and canonized as a result of that spiritual insight. As such, Goldingay explores how particular psalms of lament and Lamentations negotiate prayer and the human experiences of guilt, navigating divine anger, voicing protest, expressing trust, navigating disappointment, and expressing hopelessness. In this way, Lamentations and Psalms provide avenues to walk through the human condition before God, both in ancient and modern contexts.

David Reimer draws together Lam. 3 and Ps. 119 as the longest acrostic poems in the Hebrew Bible. On the face of it, he argues that little connects the poems beyond their acrostic form; however, upon more careful investigation, the formal connection of the acrostic structure enables the texts to be set into a closer conversation. This "readerly" exercise of intertextual engagement between the poems leads Reimer to note correspondence between lines in the acrostic; for instance, the *dalet* lines in each poem that both use *derek* language; the *zayin* lines in each poem that employ the concept and language of memory; and the *ḥet* lines in the poems both draw upon the concept of the steadfast love of YHWH. These and other correspondences between them lead Reimer to note that the poems converge at key points. However, he notes the differences between the poems as well. Reimer shows the ways that Lam. 3 focuses upon the voice of the sufferer and Ps. 119 focuses upon the voice of the learner of Torah, whose own voice recedes so that one only hears the Torah of God. In Reimer's reading, Lam. 3 informs Ps. 119 and vice-versa. The one enriches the reading of the other.

Recognizing scholarly tendency to note general similarities between the suffering expressed in the book of Job and Lamentations (Berlin 2002: 85), Will Kynes rightly notes that little work explicitly assesses whether these surface similarities are warranted. Kynes rectifies the lacuna by reading Job alongside Lam. 3. Kynes explores the voices present in Lam. 3 and the divergent speeches in the book of Job (Job's friends, Job, and God) and marks connections and differences between them. Without committing fully to the notion, Kynes provocatively suggests the possibility that Job's poet may be interacting with Lamentations by providing the divine speeches in Job to "answer" the missing voice of God in Lamentations. Whether these connections between texts are intentional or not, treating them as co-texts deepens the reading of both.

Katharine Dell draws Lamentations and Ecclesiastes together in an intertextual reading of the cityscape: Jerusalem bereaved and destroyed in exile in Lamentations; the city busy with business and social affairs in Ecclesiastes. Both descriptions of the city in the texts, however, present cities of death, or as Dell avers, cities in which "all is decay." Her reading draws the presentation of Jerusalem in Lam. 5 together with the enigmatic presentation of the city in Eccl. 12:1-7. As in Reimer's correlated reading of Ps. 119 and Lam. 3, Dell finds reading Lam. 5 and Eccl. 12:1-7 as co-texts mutually enriches the interpretation of both.

Brittany Melton continues her previous work on divine presence and absence in the *Megilloth*, exploring the interface between divine absence and female roles in the books of Esther, Ruth, Song of Songs, and Lamentations. She finds that conspicuous females predominate in the exploration, counterbalanced with a presentation of an inconspicuous God. Her approach is compatible with, but not identical to, the approach of early twentieth-century Russian formalist Mikhail Bakhtin, who esteemed the multi-voiced nature of literature (specifically in narrative). The multiple, varied, and conspicuous voices of females in the *Megilloth* present pathways for the community of faith to understand their relationship with their God.

Gideon Kotzé explores the various ways in which the Qumran texts receive and employ the biblical book of Lamentations. Kotzé surveys the landscape of Qumran texts of Lamentations (3QLam, 4QLam, 5QLam^a, and 5QLam^b) as well as what scholars sometimes call "Apocryphal Lamentations" A and B (4Q179 and 4Q501). These latter two texts utilize phrases and ideas of Lamentations, but are not of the same kind as 3QLam, 4QLam, 5QLam^a, and 5QLam^b. He explores 4Q179 briefly but then focuses upon 4Q501, offering a fresh reading of possible (inter)textual connections between 4Q501 and Lam. 5, which provides a different valence on how scribes utilized material from Lamentations. In so doing, Kotzé breaks new ground in the study of 4Q501, Lamentations, and scribal activity at Qumran.

Antje Labahn treats the Greek version of Lamentations (LamLXX) as a reception of a previous Hebrew text and, therefore, as an intertextual reading. She shows how the Greek translator received the Hebrew text of Lamentations, all the while influenced by the figure in another biblical text: the prophet Jeremiah. As a result, the intertextuality at play, and the translation of LamLXX, leads the reader of the Greek text to Jeremiah where his portrait may be less prominent in the Hebrew text. In this way, Labahn presents a fresh reading of the scribal vision at work in LamLXX, reinforcing a Jeremianic understanding of history through the reception and translation of its parent text.

Honora Howell Chapman explores how Josephus' *Jewish Wars* possibly receives Lamentations, informing how the historian tells the story of the destruction of the temple in 70 CE. She assesses potential intertextual connections between Lamentations and *Jewish Wars*, including the presentation of a mother's cannibalism as well as the fall of the temple itself in Josephus' account. Chapman then turns to Christian reception of Josephus, especially Origen, who makes connections between Lamentations and *Jewish Wars* to reinforce God's supposed repudiation of the Jews. In this way, Josephus strangely became a tool for Christian polemic against Judaism. Chapman concludes that although Josephus wrote of the fall of Jerusalem's temple to exonerate most of his Jewish people, Christians later used Josephus' *Jewish Wars* to condemn them. In this way, she exposes a dark afterlife of a biblical book.

Robin Parry reviews a litany of past Christological readings of Lamentations from Christian church history to assess whether he deems them to be "hermeneutically responsible, theologically fruitful, and spiritually enriching," irrespective of authorial intention. To begin, Parry explores the gospel of Matthew's presentation of the crucifixion scene with intertexts from Lamentations. He finds that LamLXX illumines Matthew's characterization of Jesus' suffering. He then turns to the Church Fathers' reading of Lam. 3:53 and 4:20 as well as the ways Lamentations appears in the Medieval Christian Tenebrae liturgical tradition. In the light of these discussions, Parry concludes with other avenues of Christological readings of Lamentations (the valiant man of Lam. 3:1 and Jesus; the Narrator of Lamentations and Jesus; Jerusalem and Jesus). Parry's essay highlights one of the tension points in the volume regarding the scope and limits of intertextuality in biblical studies.

Heath Thomas explores how intertextuality at work in *Lamentations Rabbah* disrupts previous tradition, particularly the silence and distance of God and the sinfulness of the Daughter of Zion in Lamentations. Although it disrupts this tradition, intertextuality in the work also preserves and advances Jewish tradition by providing fresh ways to explore relationship between God and God's people through divine pathos in mourning. *Lamentations Rabbah* incorporates prophetic speech to negotiate the radicality of divine mourning, insisting that God's mourning of the destruction of his city is fitting to the prophetic word. Because divine mourning has been prophetically decreed, the audacity of God's association with death is somehow ameliorated. Instead of undermining Jewish tradition, intertextuality in *Lamentations Rabbah* innovates to open another relational horizon between God and God's people.

In his intertextual reading of Lamentations and select post-*Shoah* literature, Hemchand Gossai illumines the ways in which Lamentations mandates questioning God, memorializing individual and communal trauma, and envisioning a kind of future hope in the face of disaster. In so doing he invites readers to remember the texts of the past in order to engage with present pain and injustice. Although Zachary Braiterman (2011) has read Lamentations through Jewish post-*Shoah* literature, Gossai draws other unrecognized connections between Lamentations and *Shoah* literature and exposes Lamentations' afterlife in post-*Shoah* Jewish experience.

Summarizing the contents of the volume as we have done up to this point takes the reader only so far. After all, one notes divergent deployments of intertextuality throughout. Previous attempts to categorize different types of intertextuality have either worked on a spectrum of (a) synchronic and diachronic, or (b) traditional and postmodern approaches to intertextuality.[3] We will mention these briefly and then turn to the triad with which we began: historical relationships, canonical relationships, and readerly interests.

Understanding intertextuality on a synchronic to diachronic spectrum is a commonplace among studies of the concept; these studies reveal how diachronic studies of intertextuality tend towards use/re-use of previous text traditions (and how one might demonstrate the use/re-use), translation technique and scribal practices, textual criticism and text-traditions, and even the afterlife of biblical books in later culture and history (broadly conceived). By contrast, synchronic studies on intertextuality, then, feature how texts might be read together, regardless of intentional correlation. Repetition structures in rhetorical criticism or synchronic readings of biblical texts in literary criticism afford less of an emphasis upon historical relationships and instead focus upon the textual surface and texture to comprise the fabric of meaning.

John Barton (2013: 1–18) has exposed the deficiency of diachronic/synchronic to categorize intertextuality. He argues that synchronic reading of biblical intertexts may lead to diachronic explanations of intertexts, and vice-versa. Asserting a binary construction of either synchronic or diachronic does not satisfy because it is not true to the deployments of intertextual study present in this volume, much less the broader guild of biblical studies.

Another possibility has been to describe intertextuality in terms of more traditional or postmodern approaches (A. Wilson 2018: 22–3). In this construction, intertextuality represents a modern innovation in interpretation that moves beyond traditional, historical approaches to texts.

---

3. We note Barton's "hard" and "soft" intertextuality, with the hard version being the phenomenon of human culture and the soft version being the methodological variety. In his analysis, he also distinguishes between spatial and temporal forms of intertextuality (Barton 2013: 1–18).

This approach takes due account of the reality that intertextual approaches to biblical interpretation emerge after the literary turn in biblical studies in the 1970s and 1980s. However, it does not satisfy because the approach treats intertextuality as a modern phenomenon, which it patently is not. For example, Boyarin reveals the phenomenon of intertextuality at the very heart of midrashic explorations of biblical texts (Boyarin 1987). Although the *study* of intertextuality is a modern phenomenon born out of French literary theory funded by French political impulses of the 1960s (Barton 2013), intertextuality as a phenomenon of human culture extends throughout the ancient world to the present, as explorations in the present volume demonstrate.

It would do well for us to consider that intertextuality finds horizon in yet another way of seeing. In this volume, studies in both Jewish and Christian reception of the book of Lamentations aver that the biblical canon (Jewish or Christian, as the case may be) provides the necessary context from which new readings of Lamentations might emerge. Studies in Jewish literature particularly engage the question of how the sacred canon of Hebrew Scripture funds integrated readings across the tradition. Shaye J. D. Cohen (1983: 48–63) notes that texts in Jewish tradition (such as the Mishnah) need to be read in the light of other texts in the tradition; interactions between texts create webs of meaning within the tradition. Webs of meaning comprise the fabric of rabbinic thought. It is the sacredness of the Jewish Scriptures that creates the fertile context from which varied connections between biblical books and later Jewish traditions find their birth. Boyarin (1987: 546) recognizes the ways that rabbinic literature sets texts into conversation regardless of historical connection: "Midrashic reading is discovery of meaning through the interanimation of recontexted verses." Boyarin (1987: 547) further states:

> Midrash is interpretation because it shows how meaning is created in the (nearly) infinite dialogical relations of text to text within the Torah and of the readers' discourse to that of the Other. As opposed to the hermeneutic model, such as Schleiermacher's and its descendants, which pictures the reader as going back into the past and becoming one somehow with it, midrash figures interpretation as digging into the past and appropriating its treasures for the present and it achieves this appropriation via textual recombination and recontexting.

Previous studies of intertextuality have collapsed, in our view, the sacred canon to "readerly" responses to biblical texts. This is too reductionistic, at least from the perspective of those Jewish or Christian traditions that receive earlier texts; Jewish and Christian receptions of Lamentations, then, do not expose "readerly" interests as much as they expose the interest in the "Other" whose gift of the biblical text demands continued answering. In this understanding, charting the sea of intertexts remains fundamental to the life of faith and responsive to the cues of the canonical Scriptures.

Once the sacredness of the canon is taken into proper account, then one notes three kinds of intertextual readings represented in the volume. One finds the kinds of historical relations between texts where Lamentations' connections with biblical texts or text traditions are viewed in terms of their diachronic relationship. The other approach to intertextuality is found in the readerly responses to Lamentations and other texts. These literary approaches are found in this volume, as noted below. But finally, one finds the kind of studies on intertextuality that take the notion of the sacred canon as the fertile literary *and* theological context that necessarily invites intertextual readings between Lamentations, other texts, and later traditions. It is the sacredness of the text that demands the continued engagement between texts rather than an historical or readerly necessity. As Alkier (2009: 12) has already noted: "All canonical texts have an intertextual disposition independent from their intertextually perceptible references to other texts. The canon itself established this hermeneutical possibility. The biblical canon sets the individual writings in new relationships, and it is precisely this intertextual connection that alters the meaning potential of the individual writings."

In light of these three kinds of intertextuality, the approaches of our contributors have been categorized as such, as seen in Figure 1, below:

Table 1. Kinds of Intertextuality in the Volume

Intertextuality as an Historical Phenomenon between Texts
(Dearman), Boase, Heffelfinger, Stead, Chapman, Labahn, Kotzé, (Kynes), Maier
Intertextuality as a Mode of Response to Texts
(Lo), Balentine, Briggs, Kalmanofsky, Gossai
Intertextuality as a Phenomenon in the Sacred Canon
(Lo), (Dearman), Thomas, Parry, Melton, Dell, (Kynes), Reimer, Goldingay

Contributors in parentheses represent "fuzzy boundaries" between kinds of intertextual readings. Dearman, Lo, and Kynes remain elusive, not easily set within a schema of intertextual approaches. At the heart of the volume, then, is a demonstration of the varieties of intertextuality on display in the engagement of the book of Lamentations. As readers of this volume explore the book of Lamentations and its intertexts (whether readerly, historical, or canonical), our hope is that all the studies enrich the reading and interaction with these resplendent biblical laments.

Part I

LAMENTATIONS IN DIALOGUE WITH THE TORAH

Chapter 1

EXODUS 32–34 AND LAMENTATIONS: COMPARISON OF SIN, PUNISHMENT, AND CONFESSION

Alison Lo

The golden calf episode in Exod. 32–34 takes place suddenly after Moses' presence on Mount Sinai has been in the spotlight for a considerable length of time (Exod. 24:18–31:18). Along with Moses, the reader is informed of how Yahweh wants to live among his people and associate with them. The abrupt move from the final instructions for the tabernacle and the handing over of the tablets to Moses (Exod. 31) "on the mountain" to the rebellion "at the foot of the mountain" (Exod. 32) is a shocking development (Houtman 2000: 610). The five poems of Lamentations appear soon after the destruction of Jerusalem by the Babylonians in 586 BCE, and they are probably the work of the Judean community who remained in Palestine after the catastrophe (Hillers 1992: 15; Dobbs-Allsopp 2002: 4). Focusing on the fate of the survivors in Palestine, the book shows no "special interest in the plight of exiles in Babylon or Egypt" (Hillers 1992: 15). Despite their different historical backdrops, the motifs of sin, punishment, and confession emerge in both Exod. 32–34 and Lamentations. Taking a synchronic (reader-oriented) approach, this paper sets out to read Exod. 32–34 and Lamentations intertextually, comparing the aspects of sin, punishment, and confession between the two texts.

The Motif of Sin

Sin in Exodus 32–34

The rebellion in Exod. 32–34 is considered as Israel's "paradigmatic apostasy" (Moberly 2002: 193). Requested by the Israelites to act as a buffer, Moses is the only means of contact that the people have with God

(Exod. 20:19). Out of "spiritual void" (Sarna 1986: 215) and "frightened impatience" (Durham 1987: 419) caused by Moses' long stay on Mount Sinai, the Israelites press Aaron to make a golden calf to lead their journey (Exod. 32:1). Since Aaron calls the image "god" and proclaims a feast for "Yahweh," most probably the golden calf is an image representing Yahweh (Exod. 32:4-5).[1] The image-less Yahweh worship is replaced by a pagan syncretistic worship (Houtman 2000: 611). As Moberly (2002: 198) puts it, Israel's sin with the golden calf while still at Sinai, a violation of the first two commandments (Exod. 20:2-6; Deut. 5:6-10), is likened to "adultery on one's wedding night." The predominance of Israel's wrong-doing in Exod. 32–34 is reflected by the frequency of חטא "sin," "to sin" (32:21, 30 [×3], 31, 32, 33, 34; 34:7, 9), עון "iniquity" (34:7 [×2], 9), and פשע "transgression" (34:7). Its severity is indicated in Moses' emphatic expression: "You have sinned a great sin" (חטאתם חטאה גדלה, 32:30; cf. 32:21, 31).[2]

As the golden calf event reveals, the Israelites seem to have totally forgotten their solemn promise to Yahweh (Exod. 19:8; 24:3) made only a short while previously. As they rebelled before, the Israelites' stiff-necked behavior has not changed over time (cf. Exod. 14:11-12; 15:24; 16:2-3; 17:2-4). They have lost their trust in God's care for them soon after having witnessed Yahweh's majestic appearance (Exod. 19). Instead of antici-pating the tablets (the constitution of the divine covenant), they act against God's commandments (Exod. 32:1; cf. 20:4, 23). No wonder this event is seen as the "quintessential example of rebellion in the Old Testament" (Enns 2000: 568), which reflects the severity of the golden calf rebellion and the stiff-neckedness of the Israelites.

Sin in Lamentations

Regarding the sin motif in Lamentations, 16 verses refer to sin (1:5, 8, 9, 14, 18, 20, 22; 2:14; 3:39, 42, 64; 4:6, 13, 22; 5:7, 16). Among these, 1:22, 3:64, and 4:22 refer to the sins of Jerusalem's enemies, whereas the remaining 13 references relate to the sins of Jerusalem and/or the people (Boase 2006: 141; 2008a: 457–8). The reference to sin occurs most frequently in ch. 1 (1:5, 8, 9, 14, 18, 20, 22). Here Yahweh's action is considered as the consequence of Jerusalem's sin (1:5, 18). It points out Jerusalem's sinning grievously (1:8), Zion's impurity (1:9), Jerusalem's transgression (1:14), and her rebellion (1:20). Lamentations 1:20-22

---

1. For the three possible functions of the golden calf, see Van Dam 2003: 369.
2. Unless otherwise noted, all biblical quotations are from the NRSV.

calls for Yahweh to deal with the enemy as he has dealt with Jerusalem's transgression (Boase 2008a: 459). Despite the use of common terms for sin (פשע, vv. 5, 14, 21-22; חטא, v. 8; מרה, vv. 18, 20), no specific sin is mentioned in ch. 1 (Boase 2008a: 460).

In Lam. 2, any reference to the sin of Zion drops away. There is only one reference to sin in v. 14, which highlights the failure of the prophets to expose the iniquity (עון) of Jerusalem/the people. Lamentations 2:1-8 extensively describes Yahweh's actions against Jerusalem, which leads the narrator to lament the plight of the city (2:9-12). The poet attributes the destruction to Yahweh. No direct link between sin and God's action is seen, although the sin of the people is undeniable (Boase 2008a: 460). In Lam. 3, even though v. 39 does link sin with Yahweh's punishment and v. 42a contains a confession—"We have transgressed (פשע) and rebelled (מרה)"—there is a lack of specificity in terms of people's sin. Lamentations 3:64 is a plea for God's retaliation against Jerusalem's enemy according to their deeds. It is not focused on Jerusalem's sin. All in all, the infrequency and vagueness with reference to sin are evident in both chs. 2 and 3.

In Lam. 4:6, though עון and חטא carry the notions of both sin and punishment, the context of comparing the nature of punishment befalling Jerusalem and Sodom suggests that "chastisement" (RSV; NRSV; ESV; NIV) rather than "sin" (NASV; NLT; NJPS) is a much more preferable translation.[3] Whereas 4:13 deals with the sin of the priests and prophets, 4:22 highlights the sin of Jerusalem's enemy, Edom. Finally, Lam. 5:7 refers to the sin of the previous generations while 5:16 is placed amidst the extended description of the horrendous suffering, which overpowers the vague reference to sin. Again, Jerusalem's sin and its specificity are not a major concern in chs 4 and 5.

Comparative Reading

Comparatively speaking, Exod. 32–34 and Lamentations deal with the issue of sin differently. The Israelites' specific sin of apostasy is clearly pointed out in the former passage. In stark contrast, Lamentations does not focus on the specificity of the people's sin even though sin is undeniable. Gottwald (1962: 68) clearly comments, "As to the specific sins which constitute the great iniquity of Judah, we are surprised that more detail is

---

3. KJV and NKJV render עון and חטא as "the punishment of the iniquity" and "the punishment of the sin" respectively, which places the notions of sin and punishment alongside each other. See also Boase 2008a: 461.

not given."[4] For the ordinary people, their responsibility for the downfall of Judah is only partial. After all, the priests, prophets, and ancestors (who incur Yahweh's wrath) as well as the foreign enemies (who cause Jerusalem's unbearable agony) should be held accountable. The next section proceeds to examine the aspect of punishment in these two texts.

The Motif of Punishment

Punishment in Exodus 32–34

The golden calf event kindles Yahweh's immediate and totally consuming wrath. His "anger burns hot" against the Israelites (32:10). As Davis (1982: 75–9) observes, the coherence and progression in Moses' intercession (32:9-14, 30-34; 33:12-17, 18-23; 34:5-10a) binds all three chapters (Exod. 32–34) together. In order to fully understand the extent of Yahweh's punishment and forgiveness, Moses' five intercession passages will be examined below.

Yahweh's intention to utterly destroy his people and begin all over again with Moses (32:9-10) is overturned after Moses' first reasoned and passionate plea (32:11-14). Firstly, Moses reminds God that Israel is his people, whom he brought out of Egypt (32:11). Secondly, he reminds God that his divine honor is at stake as the Egyptians will rejoice in his defeat (32:12). Thirdly, he reminds God not to forget his promise to the patriarchs (32:13; cf. Gen. 12:7; 15:5). Yahweh changes his mind about the disaster (הרעה, literally "the evil") that he planned to bring on his people (32:14). With his anger burning hot against his people, Moses smashes the two tablets (32:19), which symbolizes the breaking of the divine covenant. The Levites volunteer to mete out punishment, killing 3,000 people with their swords (32:25-28). Enns (2000: 576) appropriately comments, "The death penalty is not extreme, at least in the context of Exodus." At this point, no word of forgiveness is mentioned (Davis 1982: 75).

Moses' attempt to go up the mountain to make atonement for the people (32:30) has two implications: (1) those who have been killed by the Levites are the guiltier party; and (2) the remaining people are also guilty collectively in some sense, otherwise no atonement would be needed. In his second intercession (32:30-34), Moses pleads for Israel's forgiveness in exchange for his own life, but Yahweh rejects Moses' offer. God tells Moses to carry on the journey with an angel leading them (32:34). After Moses' plea Yahweh strikes the Israelites with a plague, which does not

---

4. See also Mintz 1984: 25; Greenstein 2004: 34; Renkema 1998: 476; Provan 1991: 23.

seem to be on a grand scale though it is not specific (Enns 2000: 577–8). The Hebrew of v. 35 reads, "Then the LORD sent a plague on the people because they made (עשׂה) the calf—the one that Aaron made (עשׂה)." Both the people and Aaron are equally held accountable (Enns 2000: 578). Until now, God's forgiveness is still held in suspense.

Intending to send an angel to lead their journey (33:2), Yahweh refuses to go to the promised land with his people because they are stiff-necked and God is afraid that he might destroy them on the way (33:3). In his third intercession (33:12-17), Moses pleads for Yahweh's favor to include the whole people with himself, which is clearly reflected in 33:13—"consider that this nation is your people"—and 33:16—"I and your people" (×2). Moses maintains that Yahweh's "going with us" makes them distinct among the nations (33:16), which is granted in 33:17. In this plea Moses wants to make sure the people will not be left behind. However, no word of forgiveness is mentioned yet (Davis 1982: 77).

Moses' request to see God's glory in 33:18-23 (the fourth intercession), which serves as an introduction to 34:5-10a (the last intercession), should be understood within its context. Yahweh's presence and Israel's forgiveness are interrelated (Davis 1982: 76). Moses wants to prompt God to fulfil the promise of his presence, which means the assurance of his forgiveness. Yahweh answers his prayer, promising to show Moses his goodness by letting him see his back but not his face (33:20-23). The revelation in 34:5-10a, especially the climactic proclamation of 34:6-7, offers a perfect answer to Moses' utmost concern—the covenant breakers are finally ensured forgiveness by this God who takes away/forgives (נשׂא) iniquity (עון), transgression (פשׁע), and sin (חטא, 34:7) (Davis 1982: 78). Moses' prayer for God's presence and forgiveness in 34:9 is answered and the covenant is restored in the end (34:10-28).

As Moberly (2002: 198) points out, Moses' persistent intercession prepares the way for Yahweh's self-revelation. His five intercession passages demonstrate a coherent progression, which reaches its climax when God's forgiveness is finally granted and his presence is fully restored. The punishment of total extinction is reversed, although the execution of 3,000 people and the strike of a plague are inevitable. The tension between God's wrath and his forgiveness is resolved in the end.

Punishment in Lamentations

In contrast to the references to Jerusalem's wrongdoing (as discussed above), the overwhelming majority of the verses in Lamentations contain images of suffering, which significantly play down the sin theme (Dobbs-Allsopp 1997: 37; Stiebert 2003: 197). Contrary to those scholars who understand Judah's suffering as the deserved consequence of Yahweh's just punishment, Dobbs-Allsopp (1997: 36) rightly suggests that the sin of Judah is not equal to her suffering, which can be seen by studying divine punishment and its consequences as follows.

God's punishment in Lamentations reveals two main features: (1) divine violence and (2) divine absence. Yahweh appears to be brutal and ruthless when he is present in Lamentations. To study the connection between victims and perpetrators of violence helps to demonstrate the scale of punishment and parameters of forgiveness by God. Whereas Lam. 1:1-11 focuses on the human agents of destruction (foes, enemies, pursuers, betrayers, despisers, and invaders), from 1:12 onward Yahweh is frequently pinpointed as the subject of affliction. It is clear that Yahweh is the primary agent of Jerusalem's punishment (e.g., 1:5, 12, 13, 14, 15, 17; 2:1-9, 17, 21), and is ultimately responsible for its destruction (Linafelt 2000b: 271, 275; Stiebert 2003: 197–8). As Dobbs-Allsopp (1997: 38) states, "the enemy and the divine warrior are two sides of the same coin." The threefold depiction of divine violence is highlighted in Lam. 1:12-15; 2:1-9; and 3:1-18 (Dobbs-Allsopp 2002: 44–6), where active verbs of violence are attributed to Yahweh (for instance: "hurl backward" [*hiphil* of שוב, 1:13]; "tread" [דרך, 1:15]; "cast down" [שלך, 2:1]; "tear down" [הרס, 2:2, 17]; "cut down" [גדע, 2:3]; "kill" [הרג, 2:4, 21; 3:43]; "treat violently"/"strip" [חמס, 2:6]; "destroy"/"bring ruin" [שחת, 2:6, 8]; "slaughter" [טבח, 2:21]; "shatter"/"smash" [רשב, 1:15; 3:4]; "tear in pieces" [פשח, 3:11]; "crush" [גרס, 3:16], and so on) (Stiebert 2003: 198; Linafelt 2000b: 275). These verbs portray God as a perpetrator of violence.

In addition, Yahweh is compared to a fierce hunter stalking and ensnaring his people (1:13); a predatory bear and lion lying in ambush (3:10); and an archer stringing his bow against the victims (2:4; 3:12-13). God as an enemy warrior serves as the predominant metaphor to underscore God's aggression against his people. Take 2:1-9, for example. The devastating inferno unleashed by Yahweh's wrath in 2:1-4 is vividly portrayed by a cluster of similar terms: "in his anger" (באפו, 2:1); "on the day of his anger" (ביום אפו, 2:1); "in his wrath" (בעברתו, 2:1); "in blazing anger" (בחרי־אף, 2:3); "burns (יבער)...like a flaming fire (כאש להבה)" (2:3); and "his fury like fire" (כאש חמתו, 2:4). In his wrath, Yahweh dismantles Zion by destroying her military bases (fortified palaces, fortresses; 2:5), eradicating all means of access to God (booth, tabernacle, festival, sabbath, altar, sanctuary, the house of the LORD; 2:6-7), demolishing the city structures (wall, rampart, gates, bar, 2:8-9a), executing, and taking political and religious leaders into exile (king, princes, teachers of Torah, prophets; 2:9b) (Linafelt 2000b: 278–9).

Dobbs-Allsopp (1997: 45) rightly points out, "The absence of Yahweh is as oppressive as was his hostile presence. This absence is most effectively communicated through the deity's silence." Yahweh is not given a voice in Lamentations. God is relentlessly requested to "look" and "see" Zion's destruction and suffering (1:9, 11, 12, 20; 2:20; 3:49-50, 59-60, 63; 5:1), as God is questioned whether he sees his people's plight (3:36). In addition, the poet finds his pleas unheard by God as he complains: "though I call and cry for help, he shuts out my prayer" (3:8). The same experience is voiced again in 3:44 ("you have wrapped yourself with a cloud so that no prayer can pass through") and 3:56 ("Hear my plea. Do not shut your ear to my groan, to my cry!"). As Yahweh's voice never sounds, the final appeal in 5:20-22, like the earlier ones, remains unanswered. The despairing refrain "there is no comforter for her" is repeated five times with slight variations in ch. 1 (1:2, 9, 16, 17, 21). The fact that Yahweh is addressed in the immediate context of vv. 9, 17, and 21 demonstrates the desperate urge for his comfort. The desire for a comforter indicates Yahweh's absence, which is implied by the poet's rhetorical questions in 2:13—Daughter Zion's devastation is so great that no one could possibly comfort her except Yahweh (Dobbs-Allsopp 1997: 56–7). God's absence and silence in terms of not seeing, not hearing, and not comforting are in fact a harsh punishment for his people. His abandonment of Jerusalem can be traced throughout (1:1; 2:1, 3, 6, 7, 8; 5:20, 22) (Dobbs-Allsopp 1997: 50; 2002: 31).

The scale of Yahweh's punishment can be seen through the description of the victims' suffering. Jerusalem is personified and speaks "as a particular woman whose specific feelings are embodied in a certain texture of imagery" (Lanahan 1974: 41). She is most remembered as "Daughter Zion" (1:6; 2:1, 4, 8, 10, 18) with other variants.[5] She was once a princess (1:1), but is now a widow and a slave (1:1; cf. 5:3, 8), who suffers invasion (1:15), exile (1:3, 7, 18), hard servitude (1:3; 5:5, 8, 13), starvation (1:11, 19; 2:11-12, 19-20; 4:3-5, 9-10; 5:10), mocking (1:21; 2:15-17; 4:14-15), and betrayal by her lovers and friends (1:2, 19). Most insulting of all, she is humiliated by sexual violence (1:8-9; cf. 5:11). Her nakedness (ערוה) exposed to the nations (1:8) implies the foreign invaders entering her sanctuary (1:10) (Mintz 1982: 4; 1984: 25; Stiebert 2003: 200). Despite the references to her sins (1:5, 8), the text shows no evidence of her committing adultery. Greenstein (2004: 35) rightly comments, "The city can explain her afflictions only as punishment for her rebelliousness; but this is at most a subjective impression, not

---

5. Virgin Daughter Judah (1:15); Virgin Daughter Zion (2:13); Daughter Jerusalem (2:13, 15); Daughter Judah (2:2, 5).

unlike the guilt that is sometimes felt by a battered woman..." (see also O'Connor 1992: 180; 2001: 1032–3). The reader's attention is drawn to Daughter Zion's suffering more than her sins as she appears to be a victim of forcible defilement. The plight of such a victimized woman calls forth empathy from any onlooker.

Apart from being a widow, Daughter Zion is a mother grieving for her children (1:16; 2:21). As Bosworth (2013: 228) puts it, Daughter Zion's pain mirrors the pain of the bereaved mothers in Jerusalem. Knowing the pain of losing a child to death (2:21) or exile (1:5, 18), she stands in solidarity with these devastated mothers (1:16; 2:11-12, 19-22) whom she represents. Famine is mentioned frequently in Lamentations (1:11, 19; 2:11-12, 19-20; 4:3-5, 9-10; 5:10). The picture of starving infants (2:11-12; 4:3-4) slowly dying in their mothers' arms elicits the empathetic tears of the narrator, whose liver (the center of emotion) "is poured out" (נשפך, 2:11) just as the children's lives "are poured out" (בהשתפך) into their mothers' bosom (2:12).[6] Those who were killed by the sword are considered to be better off than those enduring the hunger (4:9). Most distressing of all is the image of mothers eating their children as food (2:19-20; 4:10).

The Hebrew verb of violence עלל "inflict" is repeated strategically to highlight Yahweh's cruel treatment against his people (1:12, 22; 2:20). During the portrayal of the cannibalism of children, the wordplay between the verb עלל "inflict" (2:20a) and the noun עולל "child" (2:20b) indeed brings out a horrific pun and a strong irony (Renkema 1998: 319; Dobbs-Allsopp 2002: 99; Greenstein 2004: 37–8; Bosworth 2013: 235). Renkema (1998: 319) states well, Daughter Zion intends to challenge Yahweh that innocent children cannot be held responsible for the present calamity. There is a good reason to mention twice the starvation of children (2:11-12; 4:3-4) and the cannibalism of these young victims (2:20; 4:10) in Lamentations. As they stand as "paradigms of innocent suffering" (Dobbs-Allsopp 1997: 38), it raises the question about the rightness of Yahweh's wrath. His punishment appears to be completely out of proportion (Dobbs-Allsopp 1997: 38; Greenstein 2004: 37).

The extent of divine wrath can also be assessed by tracing Yahweh's response toward the suffering of his afflicted victims. His utter lack of compassion is accentuated by the fourfold repetition of לא חמל "has shown no mercy" (2:2a, 17b, 21c; 3:43). In Lam. 3 the poet, as a defeated

---

6. As Mintz (1982: 6) states, the wordplay of שפך establishes "an empathetic vibration" between the children and the narrator. See also Mintz 1984: 28; Bosworth 2013: 233; Stiebert 2003: 201.

soldier (גבר) who witnesses the affliction and violence under the rod of God's wrath (3:1-18), expresses his sorrow over his failure to prevent the catastrophe from happening (Owens 1990: 83, 85). Despite his two claims of divine compassion (3:22, 32), these vague assertions are soon undermined by his complaint of לא חמלת "you have shown no mercy" (3:43). There is no evidence to substantiate God's capacity for pity. Owens (1990: 85) vividly points out the poet's real struggle of faith in the face of God's excessive brutality.

Yahweh's disproportionate punishment is fully expressed when Jerusalem's chastisement is considered to be far greater than that of "the sinner *par excellence*" (Stiebert 2003: 204)—Sodom, which was destroyed quickly with no hand laid on it (4:6). Rapid destruction means less torment. Compared with Sodom, Zion's ordeal outweighs her crime. No wonder Daughter Zion cries out to the passer-by (1:12), "Is there any sorrow like my sorrow which he brought upon me, which the LORD inflicted on the day of his fierce anger?" The poet also echoes (2:13), "What can I say for you, to what compare you, O daughter Jerusalem? To what can I liken you, that I may comfort you, O virgin daughter Zion? For vast as the sea is your ruin; who can heal you?" Daughter Zion's tremendous trauma is incomparable and her ocean-vast devastation is immeasurable. "Even where there is sin and guilt, there can be suffering that goes too far, that is evil," as Dobbs-Allsopp (1997: 44) puts it.

Comparative Reading

In the golden calf incident, God's original intention to completely destroy Israel is overturned by Moses' persistent intercession. Such a grand scale of annihilation is reduced to the execution of 3,000 people and the strike of a plague. Compared with the sin of "paradigmatic apostasy" in Exod. 32–34, Daughter Zion's unspecific sin is excessively punished far beyond what she deserves. The magnitude of Jerusalem's suffering is unprecedented. Yahweh listens to Moses when he pleads for the Israelites, but he turns his deaf ears to the prayers in Lamentations. After all, forgiveness is granted to Israel during Yahweh's revelation to Moses (Exod. 34:5-10a). However, the poet in Lamentations cries out to God, "We have transgressed and rebelled, and you have not forgiven" (Lam. 3:42). In the golden calf event, although God's presence is withdrawn at the beginning, it is fully restored in the end. Divine presence means Israel's forgiveness, as both of them are interrelated. However, Yahweh's voice never sounds in Lamentations, which is overshadowed by his complete silence and absence, showing no sign of his forgiveness throughout.

The Motif of Confession

Confession in Exodus

Exodus 33:1-6 records the Israelites' communal confession after the golden calf incident. In light of their acknowledgment of Yahweh refusing his presence in their midst (33:1-3), the Israelites deeply mourn (*hithpael* of אבל) and spontaneously strip themselves of their jewelry (33:4). It becomes a permanent custom imposed by God as a symbol of grief and repentance (33:5-6). The people obey heartily (*hithpael* of נצל) from Mount Horeb onward, which involves a long-term obedience (Timmer 2007: 93). Despite the genuine confession, their relationship with God has not yet been restored. Whereas Moses is able to meet God "face to face" at the tent of meeting outside the camp, Israel is suffering the forfeiture of the divine presence (33:7-11). At this point the people's forgiveness still hangs in the balance until it is completely granted later in 34:5-10a.

Confession in Lamentations

There is confession and repentance in Lamentations. In Lam. 1 Daughter Zion does acknowledge Yahweh's justice and her own rebelliousness: "Yahweh is in the right, for I have rebelled against his word" (1:18a). Admissions of her wrongdoing occur again in v. 20, "I have been very rebellious," and v. 22, "you have dealt with me because of all my transgressions." Linafelt (1995: 47) rightly maintains, "We should note that the character of Zion, for all her challenging of YHWH, never claims complete innocence. But she does shift the rhetoric to the experience and extent of pain...." Despite her acknowledgment of God's righteousness and her own transgression (1:18, 20, 22), Daughter Zion's utterance in the nearest context seems to be at odds with her confession. Her accusation against God's infliction on her (1:12-15, 22), her lament about the loss of her children (1:16), her grieving over the betrayal by her allies and the strike of hunger (1:19), her command for God to see her distress (1:20), her complaint against the absent comforter (1:16, 17, 21), and her call for a similar affliction on her enemies (1:22) raise doubts about the sincerity of her confession. Zion's brief confession of guilt simply gives way to further extended expressions of affliction, grief, and challenge to God. Linafelt (2000b: 278) further claims, "Yet rather than making her sins the primary concern of her speeches, she admits them flatly and not altogether wholeheartedly."

Brief confessions are found in Lam. 3. Witnessing affliction and brutality (3:1), the poet as a defeated soldier (גבר) does acknowledge Yahweh's steadfast love (חסד, 3:22), compassion (רחם, 3:22), faithfulness

(אמונה, 3:23), goodness (טוב, 3:25), and salvation (תשועה, 3:26). He then declares his hope that Yahweh will not abandon his people forever (3:31) and that he will show his compassion (רחם, 3:32) and steadfast love (חסד, 3:32). These admissions come right after the lengthy description of divine violence in 3:1-16. It begs the question about the genuineness of the poet's confessions in the light of Yahweh's excessive cruelty. Even more oddly, a series of protests are uttered soon after the confessions. The poet does admit "We have transgressed and rebelled" (3:42a), but he immediately complains "and you have not forgiven" (3:42b). Then he continues to accuse God of not listening to prayers (3:43-45, 56) and tormenting his people by sending the enemies (3:46, 52-53, 60-63). The poet's admissions are effectively dismantled by the preceding and subsequent accusations against God.

In the final chapter of Lamentations, Jerusalem once again acknowledges her guilt "we have sinned" (5:16). However, she points out that it is the sin of her ancestors that leads to the present generation's misery: "Our ancestors sinned; they are no more, and we bear their iniquities" (5:7). Jerusalem's vague confession in 5:16, which seems to be contradictory to the preceding complaint in 5:7, is then overturned by the subsequent protest in 5:20: "Why have you forgotten us completely? Why have you forsaken us these many days?" After all there is no evidence of reaching reconciliation with God. The communal plea for restoration in the end (5:21) casts some doubt on whether Yahweh's anger is limitless and he has utterly rejected them (5:22). The book ends on the highest note of doubt and protest.

Comparative Reading

In the golden calf event, confessions are made by both the community and Moses. Despite their genuine repentance, the Israelites' corporate confession (Exod. 33:1-6) after the incident does not bring about immediate forgiveness by God. It is only through Moses' persistent intercession that full restoration with God is finally achieved. Moses makes confessions collectively on behalf of the whole nation. His diplomatic skill, passionate urgency, selfless sacrifice, relentless plea, intimate relationship with God, and deep love for his people finally change God's mind. For the sake of his servant Moses, divine presence and forgiveness are granted in the end. In Lamentations, brief confession and repentance are evident. Despite the acknowledgment of guilt, the major concern of the book is the sheer magnitude of suffering Jerusalem is facing. Confession most often gives way to extended expression of grief, suffering, and anger, which illuminates the issue of God's justness of punishment. In light of

Jerusalem's unspecific sin and her protest against Yahweh's excessive cruelty, confession appears to be vague with a lack of wholeheartedness throughout the book of Lamentations.

Conclusion

The specific sin of apostasy, limited scale of sentence, forgiveness of guilt, and renewal of covenant in the golden calf event contrast diametrically with the un-specificity of sin, unprecedented scale of punishment, unforgiveness of God, and brokenness of covenant in Lamentations. The tension between divine wrath and forgiveness in the golden calf episode is finally resolved when Yahweh makes this self-proclamation: "The LORD, the LORD, a God merciful and gracious, slow to anger, and abounding in steadfast love and faithfulness, keeping steadfast love for the thousandth generation, forgiving iniquity and transgression and sin, yet by no means clearing the guilty, but visiting the iniquity of the parents upon the children and the children's children, to the third and the fourth generation" (Exod. 34:6-7). For the people in Lamentations, however, what they experience is simply this section—"but visiting the iniquity of the parents upon the children and the children's children, to the third and the fourth generation" (Exod. 34:7b).

Chapter 2

"Away! Unclean! Do Not Touch!": Defiled and Defiling Priests in Lamentations

Samuel E. Balentine

Lamentations provides the Hebrew Bible's most gruesome and grievous account of the fall of Jerusalem. Its description of the corpses strewn in the city streets, the famine and starvation that ravaged survivors, and the indifferent silence of heaven and earth strains with hyperbole to say the unsayable. The acrostic form of the book's first four poems summons every letter of the alphabet to the task, but the syntactic pause after the opening groan (אֵיכָה, 1:1; cf. 2:1; 4:1) is the sound of someone choking on their words.

For all its visceral effect on readers, however, the gist of Lamentations is an axiom about divine justice that was conventional in the ancient world from Mesopotamia to Greece: God (the gods) visits destruction on cities as divine punishment for sin.[1] The narrator in ch. 1 states the matter succinctly: "the Lord made her [Zion] suffer for her many transgressions" (1:5). As a text that rationalizes human suffering as divine punishment, Lamentations is therefore generally indistinguishable from a wide range of similar theodic texts in the ancient world. Such texts typically democratize guilt by indicting both the city (or city-state) and its inhabitants, both its wayward leaders (kings, prophets, priests) and their errant

---

1. See, for example, Homer's account of the pestilence (*miasma*) that falls on the camp of the Aecheans (*Iliad* 1.50-52) or Hesiod's description of the pestilence and famine Zeus ordains: "Often even a whole city suffers for a bad man who sins…and the son of Chronos lays great trouble upon the people, famine and plague together, so that the men perish away, and the women do not bear children, and their houses become few, through the contriving of Olympian Zeus" (*Works and Days* 238–47).

followers. Lamentations follows this general template—Israel's kings, prophets, elders, and princes are targets of God's anger—but it gives disproportionate attention to the priests, who are described as both defiled and defiling. Lamentations 4:11-16 stands at the center of this indictment.

"Away! Unclean! Do Not Touch!"

The anonymous narrator who speaks in Lam. 1 and 2 returns in ch. 4, now to provide a third-person account of the effects of the siege of Jerusalem on its inhabitants (vv. 1-10) and to spell out the divine rationale for effecting such horrific ruin on a place and a people God had once treasured (vv. 11-16). The siege destroys one world and creates another in which the impossible and the incomprehensible become the new norms: gold that does not naturally tarnish loses its luster; valuable gems, once secured in safe places, are scattered in the streets; children more precious than gold are thrown aside like cheap pottery; infants die of starvation because they are not nursed; those who enjoyed prosperity and success now live on garbage dumps (4:1-5). Jerusalem has been transformed—deformed—in unimaginable ways. The narrator recalls the destruction of Sodom (v. 6; cf. Gen. 19:23-25), the conventional yardstick in the Old Testament for measuring the severity of a city's destruction,[2] but the comparison fails because Jerusalem's plight exceeds the worst-case scenario. Imagine something "purer than snow," "whiter than milk," "blacker than soot," something worse than being stabbed to death (vv. 7-9). Or, as the narrator puts it in the last of these futile attempts to find anything that compares with the utterly inconceivable devastation in Jerusalem, imagine compassionate mothers cannibalizing their own children (v. 10). What has happened in Jerusalem goes against (mother) nature; it defies comprehension. Commentators note that the narrator seems exhausted in Lam. 4, "as if the tragedy has left him stunned and depleted."[3] To adapt the words of the American poet Wallace Stevens, the narrator has come to the end of imagination.[4]

It is clear from the emotional tenor of ch. 1 that there is ample sadness and sorrow in Jerusalem. It is also clear that this sadness, incomparably heavy as it is, is not "without cause." The one who has made Jerusalem grieve is God (1:5, 12; cf. 3:32, 33), who does so with a burning anger that

---

2. Cf. Deut. 29:23; Isa. 1:9, 10; 13:19; Jer. 23:14; 49:18; 50:40; Amos 4:11; Zeph. 2:9.

3. O'Connor 2002: 58.

4. Stevens 1982a: 502.

divine compassion cannot (apparently) restrain (3:32-33).[5] In 4:11-16, the narrator sharpens the focus on God's anger, now honing in on the match that lit the fuse. The stones "poured out" (תִּשְׁתַּפֵּכְנָה; 4:1) into Jerusalem's streets come from God, who "poured out" (שָׁפַךְ; v. 11) burning anger on Zion because of "the sins (חַטֹּאת) of her prophets and the iniquities (עֲוֺנוֹת) of her priests" (v. 13). The narrator has previously spoken of the sins of the people that triggered God's punishment (1:5, 8), and Zion herself has confessed culpability (1:18, 22). Similarly, the poet has previously assigned blame to the prophets, who have either prophesied falsely or not at all (2:9, 14). To this point, however, there has been no specific mention of priestly guilt. Priests groan in the streets (1:4), die of starvation (1:19), and experience the wrath of God's anger (2:6) like their fellow citizens, presumably because they share a collective guilt; but they have not thus far been charged with responsibility for Jerusalem's destruction. Now, the narrator points the finger of blame directly at the priests, who "pour out" (הַשֹּׁפְכִים; v. 13) the blood of the righteous in the city.[6]

The repetition of the verb "pour out" (שָׁפַךְ; 4:1, 11, 13) points to the principle of retributive justice that provides the rationale for the destruction of Jerusalem. The measure of the anger God pours out on the city is roughly proportional to the blood the priests pour out. The narrator provides no evidence in support of the charge that the priests have literally shed innocent blood, although there may be at least a memory of past times when they were accused of such acts.[7] The accusation is more likely directed broadly against the priestly establishment, which has as its primary responsibility the obligation "to distinguish between the holy (הַקֹּדֶשׁ) and the common (הַחֹל), and between the unclean (הַטָּמֵא) and clean (הַטָּהוֹר)" (Lev. 10:10). To be "holy" is to be in the realm of God, whose intrinsic holiness provides the reference point for all "common" or

---

5. The "man" who speaks in Lam. 3:32-33 affirms that even when God causes grief, God does not do so "willingly" (מִלִּבּוֹ, "from the heart"), because God is compassionate (רחם). The apparent objective of the affirmation is to explain the affliction that God has in fact brought on Zion (3:1-20), when compassion was insufficient to restrain God from acting against the divine will (cf. O'Connor 2002: 51).

6. Lam. 4:13 indicts priests *and* prophets. The prophets are no doubt guilty of a range of offenses (2:9, 14) and are severely punished for them (2:20; 4:13), but the emphasis in 4:13-16 on the shedding of blood in relation to ritual uncleanness suggests the priests are the primary focus (cf. Thomas 2013b: 222).

7. Jer. 26:7-24 reports that priests and prophets are among those who threaten Jeremiah with death, but no text in the Old Testament states that priests and prophets actually committed murder (cf. Rudolph 1962: 252).

"profane" persons or objects that may, under certain conditions, refract the special status that God alone possesses fully. Persons or objects that are "unclean" or "impure" are prohibited from contact with the holy; only that which is "clean" or "pure" can come near the holy. The narrator charges that the priests who must guard against defilement have themselves become defiled. The ones who ritually manipulate the blood of sacrificial offerings to purge the sins of the people, thereby maintaining the ritual purity that makes proximity to God possible, are themselves now agents of pollution.

There are two consequences of the priests' failure, according to the narrator, one restricted to the priests themselves, another that has far greater ramifications. At a base level, the priests become the ritual equivalent of lepers; the blood on their garments, like the skin disease that mars the leper's body, renders them unfit for contact with others and more importantly with God.[8] Leviticus 13 stipulates that when a priest diagnoses a case of skin disease, he is to instruct the person to wear torn clothes, dishevel their hair, cover their upper lip, and "cry out, 'Unclean! Unclean!' (וְטָמֵא טָמֵא יִקְרָא)." For as long as this skin condition remains, the person must live alone, outside the camp (13:45-46; cf. Num. 16:26). Lamentations' narrator appropriates this priestly ritual but reverses its function. Instead of the priest diagnosing the leper, the people now diagnose the priests,[9] warning others to stay away lest the priests contaminate them with their own impurity: "Get away! Unclean (טָמֵא)! the people say about them. Away! Away! Do not touch!" (Lam. 4:15).[10] The defiled priests are now defiling agents. The people announce that they are

---

8. On the metaphorical representation of sin as a stain or impurity, see Lam 2016: 179–216.

9. There is disagreement about the identity of those who wander through the streets with blood-stained garments. Some commentators understand the subject to be the people of Jerusalem as a whole (e.g., Provan 1991: 118; Hillers 1972: 82–3). There are, however, strong contextual indicators that the priests and prophets of Lam. 4:13 are the blind wanderers in 4:14 (e.g., Berlin 2002: 111; Berges 2012: 254).

10. The only other occurrence of the word "unclean" (טָמֵ) in Lamentations is 1:9, with reference to the "uncleanness" in Daughter Zion's skirts. The nature of the woman's uncleanness may be debated—perhaps the reference is to menstrual blood, a ritual impurity, not a moral one, or perhaps the reference is metaphorical—but the context permits a suggestive parallel between the uncleanness of the priests and woman Zion. Both are shunned; in the world of this text, they are regarded as unfit for proximity to God. Inasmuch as priestly theology itself is under close scrutiny in Lamentations (see further below), we may ask whether either the woman or the priests deserve the punishment—from God—they have received.

no longer welcomed in their community. God himself scatters them and no longer pays them any attention (Lam. 4:16). Indeed, in the final form of the book of Lamentations, the priests are never mentioned again.

A second consequence of the priests' failure is far more serious. The narrator implicitly maps their guilt on to the priestly understanding of sin as a dynamic miasma. Like a modern-day virus that invades and progressively diminishes the body, impurity invades the realm of the holy, physically manifest in the temple and its accouterments. The degradation process may be schematized in three stages: (1) An individual's inadvertent sins defile the outer altar and courtyard area, thus requiring the priest to cleanse the altar by daubing its sides with the blood of the purification offering (Lev. 4:25, 30). (2) More serious are the unintentional sins of the high priest or of the entire community, because they extend their reach beyond the outer courtyard to the inner sanctum. The ritual of purification requires the priest to respond by placing the blood of the offering on the inner altar of incense and to sprinkle it seven times before the curtain that separates the inner sanctum from the Holy of Holies (Lev. 4:5-7, 16-18). (3) Most severe of all are intentional unrepentant sins. They defile not only the outer altar and the inner shrine but also the Holy of Holies, which houses the very throne of God. Because intentional unrepentant sinners are barred from bringing an offering to the sanctuary (Num. 15:27-31), the defilement their sins cause can be rectified only on the annual Day of Purification, when the high priest cleanses the entire sanctuary, from the outer court to the Holy of Holies (Lev. 16:14, 16, 19).[11] The inference in Lam. 4:13-15 is that the priests' defilement constitutes a "level-three" danger. They have contaminated the innermost sanctum, the holiest of the holy places that permits the most intimate proximity to God that is humanly possible. A holy God will not abide in a defiled sanctuary, an axiomatic truth of priestly theology that now confirms, *ex post facto* as it were, what Lam. 2:7 has already made clear: "The Lord has scorned his altar, disowned his sanctuary; he has delivered into the hands of the enemy the walls of her palaces."[12]

Adele Berlin has discerned that the priestly paradigm of purity/impurity is at the center of the theology of Lamentations. Moreover, she rightly notes that the priests were concerned with both ritual and moral impurity.[13] Ritual impurities, such as defilement by blood, semen, skin

---

11. Milgrom 1991: 257.
12. Ibid., 258.
13. Berlin 2002: 19–21. On discussion and debate about the properties that distinguish moral impurity from ritual impurity, see Klawans 2002: 21–42 and Feinstein 2014: 11–41.

disease, or other physical afflictions that signaled encroaching death, could be expiated by purification offerings (Lev. 11–15), unless of course the priests who administer the offerings are themselves defiled, as noted above. Moral impurities, however—unethical behavior in everyday life outside the sanctuary—offend God *and* defile the community. There is no ritual remedy for moral impurity, which is regarded as a capital crime against both God and God's creation. If individuals defile themselves by committing immoral acts, they will be "cut off," that is, excised from the community (e.g., Lev. 18:29). But if the entire community defiles itself with immoral and unethical behavior, it pollutes the very land that provides the resources for its life. Like a sensate human being, the land will be so sickened by what it has ingested from its inhabitants that it will automatically vomit them out in order to cleanse itself (e.g., Lev. 18:25, 28; 20:22).[14] Interpreted through this priestly paradigm of purity, Lev. 4:16 signals not only the banishment of the unclean priests but also the exile from the land of an unclean people: "The Lord himself has scattered them; he will regard them no more."

"Should Priest and Prophet Be Killed in the Sanctuary of the Lord?"

The purity/impurity paradigm provides the foundation for priestly theodicy, the rationale meant to sustain trust and confidence in divine justice.[15] Unlike its neighbors, Israel's priests uncoupled impurity from its putative origin in demonic, metadivine forces, which posed a threat even to the gods, and located its source instead in human behavior. In priestly theology, "man is demonized," as Jacob Milgrom puts it. Although not a demon strictly speaking, "he is capable of the demonic. He alone is the cause of the world's ills. He alone can contaminate the sanctuary and force God out."[16] The priestly antidote is the cultic system of ritual purification, which provides a pragmatic means of maintaining and, when necessary, restoring the sanctity of the temple, thus securing God's presence in the midst of the people. To be sure, prophets and sages also constructed theodicies in defense of God's justice, but apart from the prophets' summons to repentance (e.g., "return to the Lord," Isa. 19:22; Jer. 18:11; Ezek. 18:21) and the sages' exhortation to piety (the "fear of the Lord," e.g., Prov. 1:9; 9:10; Job 28:28; Sir. 1:16; 19:20;

---

14. Milgrom 2000: 1573; cf. Balentine 2002: 152–5.
15. See further Gane 2005: 324–33.
16. Milgrom 1991: 260.

21:11; 23:27),[17] they offered no tangible ways to remove the corruption that precipitated divine punishment.

With the destruction of the temple, all cultic rituals cease and priestly theodicy becomes irrelevant. If the priests who administer the rituals are themselves disqualified from cultic service, then they bear direct responsibility not only for the punishment that falls on Jerusalem but also for the corruption of the rites that may have prevented the catastrophe or repaired its damage. The priests are therefore doubly accountable. On first read, Lamentations gives no reason to be sympathetic with the priests, no reason to believe they should be excluded from the list of those who are culpable—perhaps especially culpable—for Jerusalem's demise. But several indicators suggest that Lamentations regards God as the principal defiling agent in Jerusalem, that God, from a ritual perspective, is as unclean as the priests who serve God.

(1) A first clue may be the verb יָעִיב that introduces God's anger in 2:1. The form is a *hapax legomenon* whose meaning is uncertain. Commentators often treat it as denominative verb associated with the noun עָב "cloud" (the root presumably עוב), thus yielding the translation, "The Lord has *darkened/put under a cloud* Daughter Zion in anger."[18] Others associate the verb with the Arabic root, *'yb*, "to revile, disgrace," thus rendering the line, "The Lord has *disgraced/humiliated* Daughter Zion in anger."[19] A third option that fits well with a priestly context is to understand the verb as derived from the root ועב, which is related to the noun תּוֹעֵבָה, "abomination," a word used to signify cultic impurity (e.g., Ezek. 22:2; 23:36; 33:26, all with reference to bloodshed),[20] thus: "The Lord made Daughter Zion an *abomination* (literally, 'the Lord abominated/defiled') in anger."[21] Such a reading conveys a paradox: a holy God creates the very defilement that defiles a holy God. In essence, God's own

---

17. For an overview of theodic responses, see Crenshaw 2005; Bier 2015. For discussion of the emergence and evolution of the prophetic concept of repentance, see Lambert 2016: 71–118. On the advocacy of and resistance to piety as theodicy in sapiential literature, see Balentine 2018.

18. E.g., Albrektson 1963: 85–6; Provan 1991: 58–9; O'Connor 2001: 1038; Dobbs-Allsopp 2002: 80; Berges 2012: 124, 128; Salters 2010: 111–12.

19. E.g., Rudolph 1962: 136–7.

20. McDaniel 1968: 34–5; followed by, for example, Berlin 2002: 61, 66; cf. Hillers 1972: 31, 35. On תּוֹעֵבָה as a primary signifier of impurity, see Paschen 1970: 28–30.

21. "Abomination" (תּוֹעֵבָה), although not limited to priestly texts (note its frequency in Deuteronomy and Proverbs to describe a variety of things that are morally offensive to God), occurs 22 times in Ezekiel, including multiple references

actions defile God. Perhaps such a thought was as unthinkable for the narrator in Lam. 2 as it has been for some commentators.²² Or, perhaps it is precisely such an unthinkable idea that catches in the narrator's throat, the unsayable that sounds like the groan at the beginning of this chapter, אֵיכָה (2:1).

(2) Lamentations 1:4 is the first mention of "Zion," the name that conjures the idea of Jerusalem, not simply as the capital of the nation-state, but as the city of God, a conviction made visible in the temple, the cultic center of God's residence. At the center of the lament that ch. 1 initiates is the collapse of the priestly cult that makes Zion Zion. Its festivals and sabbaths, occasions for celebrating the presence of God that makes ordinary time and space sacred, have ceased. In their place, around the altar that God has rejected and in the sanctuary that God has repudiated,²³ the enemy celebrates its victory (2:5-7).

In the place of a beautiful city that was once full of people, there sits now a widow, metaphorized as an object to be shunned because of her "uncleanness" (טֻמְאָתָהּ, 1:9) and "impurity" (נִדָּה, 1:17). The terms, however, describe only the ritual degradation of menstruation, which renders a woman temporarily unable to come into contact with the sancta (Lev. 15:19-24).²⁴ Within priestly legislation, there is no inference of moral failure, no requirement that the community break off social contact with her. Among Israel's contemporaries, the menstruant was widely regarded not only as a metaphor for impurity but also for that which society regarded as repulsive. Apart from Lam. 1:17 and a few other non-Priestly texts, there is little evidence that Israel shared this otherwise common fear of a woman's uncleanness.²⁵ To the contrary, despite the obvious limitations of a patriarchal system that privileged men, Israel's priestly laws may be viewed as a culturally atypical effort to protect

---

to abominations that defile the sanctuary and drive God away (e.g., Ezek. 8:6, 9, 13, 15, 17). On תּוֹעֵבָה as a primary signifier of moral impurity, see Klawans 2002: 21–42; Feinstein 2014: 21–2.

22. Renkema 1998: 216: "Such an interpretation, however, implies a theological *contradictio in terminis*: the Holy one makes somebody or something תּוֹעֵבָה. Such an idea is never expressed so directly. We opt, therefore, for the traditional interpretation 'to engulf with a cloud'."

23. The verb נֵאֵר ("repudiate") occurs only in Lam. 2:7 and Ps. 89:40, where it is used in parallel with חִלֵּל, "defile," a common cultic term; cf. Lam. 2:2: "The Lord has defiled (חִלֵּל) the kingdom and its rulers."

24. Cf. Feinstein 2014: 12–22, 38–57; on the term נִדָּה, see Appendix G: 181–4.

25. See the discussion in Milgrom 1991: 948–53. On cross-cultural comparisons, see Feinstein 2014: 23–37.

women from the very abuse Lam. 1 describes as being heaped on Zion. The question rumbling just underneath this pained introduction of Zion's plight is, "Why?" Why have priestly rituals intended to create ritual space for the menstruating woman been turned into reasons to destroy that space and cast her aside? The answer that begins to emerge is that the priests are themselves responsible, because they have failed to measure up to their own moral standards. But how can "the Lord be in the right" (1:18) to punish Zion—and her priests and prophets—for their "uncleanness" (1:9; 4:15) and "impurity" (1:17) if God himself is the one who made Zion such a defiling "abomination" (2:1; cf. 2:2, with the verb חָלַל, "defile")?

(3) Lamentations 2 frames the destruction of the temple as the "day of the Lord's anger" (2:1, 22). The opening section (2:1-8) emphasizes God's agency[26] as the "enemy" (2:3, 5) who executes a careful plan to kill and destroy his opponent without mercy (2:2; repeated in 2:17, 21). Verbs of violence pile up verse by verse, none more horrifying than the one that introduces God's assault on the temple: "He has violated (וַיַּחְמֹס) his booth like a garden" (2:6a). At one level, the narrator may only be correlating God's behavior with that of the priests, who elsewhere are accused of doing violence (חָמַס) to God's instructions and defiling (חָלַל) holy things (Ezek. 22:26; Zeph. 3:4).[27] But the violence typically associated with the verb חָמַס is especially brutal. In view of the violent imagery associated with Daughter Zion in Lam. 1, it is especially telling that חָמַס conveys the semantic equivalent of rape (Jer. 13:22; cf. Jer. 6:7).[28] That such violence should be unthinkable with respect to God may be indicated by the fact that the verb is never used with God as the grammatical subject, except in Lam. 2:6.

To both the narrator and Zion, God's anger and violence is incomprehensible. The narrator looks at Zion's ruination and asks three questions (2:13): What can I say on your behalf?[29] What can I compare to you? Who can heal you? Each question assumes there is no conceivable answer that

---

26. Dobbs-Allsopp (2002: 82) notes that God is the subject of 29 of the first 31 verbs in 2:1-8.

27. Berges 2012: 141.

28. Dobbs-Allsopp 2002: 85; cf. Holladay 1986: 414. See also Zion's lament in 2:20, "Look, Lord, to whom you have done [עוֹלַלְתָּ] this." The verb עָלַל, "to afflict," signifies a level of abuse that may be consonant with sexual violence, as in Judg. 19:25, where it occurs parallel to the verb "rape" (cf. Linafelt 2000a: 57). See further below.

29. The verb אֲעִידֵךְ in 2:13a is difficult. I follow the *kĕtîb* in deriving the verb from the Hebrew root עוּד, "testify" or "witness" (cf. LXX: *ti martureso soi ē ti omoiōsō*, "What witness shall I bear of you?").

would be adequate. There are no words that can restore what Zion has lost. There is no similar situation in history that offers sufficient perspective to understand what has happened in Zion. There is no one who can cure what is incurable (cf. Jer. 30:12, 15)—neither the prophets, the passersby, the enemy, nor God, who "has done what he had planned…destroyed without compassion…made your enemy happy" (2:17). The priests are not included in this list; presumably, they do not merit consideration at all. O'Connor's summation is apt:

> At last, the narrator confronts her [Zion's] suffering in its totality, its incomparability, and in the inability of his words to bear witness to it. He needs a "language of the unsayable," but such a language of direct speech that can express and encompass her suffering does not exist, for her suffering is "as vast as the sea." The narrator and the poet behind him confront the limits of language. Language "breaks" on account of her "breaking" [שֶׁבֶר; 2:13].[30]

When Zion speaks, she summons God to pay attention to her own questions (2:20). The first is surely rhetorical: "Against whom have you acted so violently (עוֹלַלְתָּ)?" Zion has no doubt that she has been God's target, but she is at a loss to understand *why* God would be so abusive, even if she has sinned. The verb עָלַל, "to treat violently," can signify an assault that may be consonant with sexual violence, as in Judg. 19:25, where it occurs parallel to the verb "rape." Associative language and imagery in Lamentations suggests violence associated not with rape but instead with the trauma of cannibalism. The same verbal root equates the violence done to Zion (1:12, 22) and to her inhabitants (2:20) with the victims of this violence, the children (עוֹלְלֵי, 2:19) who "faint for hunger at the head of very street," the violence that forces mothers (עֹלְלֵי, 2:20) to cannibalize their own children.[31] Two additional questions (2:20b-c) presuppose answers that compel thinking the unthinkable. Should mothers eat the children they have birthed? The answer presupposed is "No," but since they do, what possible reason justifies such unbelievable behavior?[32]

---

30. O'Connor 2001: 1041. Linafelt (2000b: 54) draws upon the words of Wiesel (1978: 235) to offer a similar observation: "But how is one to say, how is one to communicate that which by its very nature defies language? How is one to tell without betraying the dead, without betraying oneself?"

31. Dobbs-Allsopp 2002: 99; cf. Thomas 2013b: 160–1.

32. Deut. 28:53-57 cites cannibalism as one of the curses enacted by God as a consequence of covenantal disobedience, but it is likely that this explanation of cannibalism is itself part of the *ex post facto* theodic *responses* to the horrors of the Babylonian siege of Jerusalem that the book of Lamentations challenges.

Should priests and prophets be killed in the sanctuary of God?[33] Again, the presupposed answer is "No." Only in a world where mothers eat their own children would a God who kills his own priests and prophets be thought righteous and just. Berlin notes the cultic backdrop for the parallel between the killing (הָרֹגְתָּ) in the sanctuary and the butchering (טָבַחְתָּ) of meat for sacrificial offering. She concludes: "God who slaughters his people is no less a cannibal than the mothers who eat their children."[34]

(4) One additional indicator of divine culpability may be considered. Blood (דָּם) is the principal defiling agent in Lam. 4:13-15, specifically the spilt blood of the righteous that splatters on the garments of the priests and prophets, who stagger blindly through the streets. Befouled garments convey miasmic pollution (Lev. 13:47-58), and as noted above, the community responds with the warning that priestly instructions associate with those afflicted by skin disease: "Away! Unclean!... Away! Away! Do not touch!" (4:13). The verb describing the defiling of the garments is an odd hybrid of *Nip'al* and *Pu'al* forms (4:14, נְגֹאֲלוּ) that occurs only here and in Isa. 63:3.

The Isaiah poem describes a bloodbath in Edom, the paradigmatic stand-in for all who are God's opponents (63:1-6). The poet metaphorizes blood as the blood-red juice of grapes being crushed in a wine press. In response to the poem's opening question, "Who is this coming from Edom...in bright red garments?" (63:1, CEB), the poet supplies the following answer:

---

33. The verb form in 2:20 is passive (יֵהָרֵג, "be killed"), which leaves it grammatically unclear who is responsible for the action. Kaiser (1987: 179), however, argues that the singular form of the verb should be read as active, with God as the inferred subject, "Should YHWH slay" (cited in Mandolfo 1990: 99). The active form of the same verb in the following verse, which clearly attributes the action to God—"you [God] have killed (הָרַגְתָּ) them" (2:21)—supports Kaiser's reading. The LXX also translates 2:20 as an active verb but attributes agency to an unnamed other person, implicitly pointing the finger of guilt at the people of Jerusalem themselves: "Will you kill (*apekteinas*) in the holy precinct of the Lord priest and prophet?" *Targum Lam.* 2:20 takes a more explicit step in the direction of exonerating God and indicting Israel for the killing by introducing a response to Zion from the "Attribute of Justice," God himself: "Is it right to kill priest and prophet in the temple of the Lord, as when you killed Zechariah son of Iddo, the High Priest and faithful prophet in the Temple of the Lord on the Day of Atonement because he told you not to do evil before the Lord?" (Thomas 2013b: 161, referencing Brady 2001: 34–5).

34. Berlin 2002: 76; cf. Mandolfo 2007b: 99: "The children are being 'sacrificed' by YHWH in order to serve the 'festival day' that he has called (v. 22)."

I have pressed out in the vat by myself—
from the peoples, no one was with me.
I stomped on them in my anger,
trampled them in my wrath.

Their blood splashed on my garments,
and stained [אֶגְאָלְתִּי]³⁵ all my clothing,
because I intended a day of vengeance;
the year of my deliverance had arrived....

I trampled down nations in my anger and made them drunk on my wrath;
I spilled their blood on the ground. (63:3-4, 6, CEB)

The language and imagery in this poem, especially the accents on defiling blood, anger, and punishment, are consonant with Lam. 4:13-14, although in Isaiah the one whose garments are stained with blood is God, not the priests. If one reads Isaiah through the lens of priestly theology, then the blood that stains God's garments makes God no less ritually impure than the blood that stains the priests' garments in Lamentations. We may ask whether the consonance extends to Lam. 4:15. Might the warning to stay away from defiled and defiling priests also be a warning to stay away from a defiled and defiling God? "Away! Away! people shouted [at God]. Away! Away! Do not touch!" The thought is jarring from multiple perspectives, not least because of the tension it creates (or accentuates) within the book of Lamentations itself.³⁶ For all its attention to Zion's complaint about God's unbearable silence and absence, God's excessive anger and violence, the book never completely detaches itself from the hope and expectation that someday God will once again "come near" when Zion calls for help, and say, "Do not fear!" (Lam. 3:57).³⁷ One of the ironies of Zion's residual hope, however, is that with the absent temple, which creates ritual space for God's presence, there is no

---

35. The form in MT is irregular, combining a first person singular Imperfect preformative with a first person masculine singular Perfect ending. English translations typically render it as if it were a third person form, "their blood...stained my garments," but the form might just as well be rendered as a first person verb, thus, "I stained all my garments."

36. Renkema (1998: 534) recognizes the similarities between Lam. 4:14 and Isa. 63:3 and briefly considers the theological ramifications before dismissing them: "How is it possible, however, for YHWH to make himself ritually impure? In order to avoid such an association, the author of Isa. 63 opted for an alternative term for blood, namely נֵצַח, a rare synonym for דָּם."

37. On God's silence and absence in Lamentations, see Melton 2018.

tangible way in which God can come near to Zion. Moreover, if God's presence is itself defiling, then perhaps the only recourse for Zion is to quarantine God like a leper and wait…and hope that after a period of time the community can welcome a "healed" God back into the community.[38]

Imagining the Unimaginable

This essay began where the book of Lamentations itself begins, with the אֵיכָה that catches in the throat when one looks at the fall of Jerusalem through the eyes of the poet and tries to say the unsayable or think the unthinkable. The decimation of the city is virtually beyond words; the poet must summon all his rhetorical skills even to approximate emotional overload. The idea that defiled and defiling priests are culpable is bewildering but not unprecedented, for priests are often included in the list of those responsible for Jerusalem's downfall (e.g., Isa. 1:10-20; Jer. 2:4-9; Amos 5:21-27; Mic. 3:11). But the notion that a holy God would ritually defile himself, inviting (requiring) the community to protect itself from contamination by shouting "Away! Unclean! Do not touch!" is unimaginable. Even if there were only intimations of such thoughts in Lamentations, what would a poet hope to accomplish by including them?

In pondering this question, I look to the reflections of a modern poet to help me understand an ancient one. The lines cited at the beginning of this essay are from Wallace Steven's poem, "The Plain Sense of Things."[39] Stevens describes the changes that come in the autumn of the year, when the leaves "that do not transcend themselves"[40] fall from the trees, and the trees become less than they were. It is a time when "we return to a plain sense of things," a time when nature strips itself to an essential bareness—and barrenness—that anticipates the arrival of winter. Like the trees that lose their foliage, like the clear and glistening waters of the pond now overlaid with mud, "water like a dirty glass," we come to an end of things. Everything is reduced, destitute, dislocated, dying. We know that in the grand scheme of things autumnal death is the necessary, inevitable, precursor of spring's rebirth, but the fulfillment of the promise is far beyond any horizon we can see. It is "as if," the poet says, we have

---

38. Priestly instructions specify a fourteen-day quarantine for the skin-diseased, with priestly follow-up inspections on each seventh day (Lev. 13:4-8). When the priest verifies that the skin disease is no longer present, the person's return to the community is ritually enacted in an eight-day process (Lev. 14:1-32).

39. Unless otherwise noted, all citations from Stevens in this paragraph are from Stevens 1982a.

40. Stevens 2009.

come to the end of imagination, when all mental capacities fall into a deep sleep, "inanimate in an inert savoir," a knowing that makes no difference in life. Or does it? Stevens suggests that when the absence of imagination itself has to be imagined, we come as close to the plain truth about life as we can, even the ugly, which is an inevitable part of the real. As he puts it in one of his winter poems, we see the "Nothing that is not there and the nothing that is."[41]

I "imagine" that the poet in Lam. 4 looks on Daughter Zion and sees through her eyes only what is there and "Nothing that is not there." He is clear eyed about defiled and defiling priests. He flinches, perhaps, but does not turn away from Zion's wonderment about a God more soiled by the spilt blood of the righteous than the priests. He hears the words "Away!" Unclean!"—can they possibly be addressed to God?—and he discerns that Zion has imagined the unimaginable. The poet only sees what is there, nothing that is not there.

But the poet also sees the "nothing that is," the nothing that might become something, the something that for an uncertain period of time is inaccessible, unborn, unreal, a promise of life wrapped in the shroud of certain death. Stevens describes the imagination of this blank, cold "nothing that is" as the "inevitable knowledge" the plain sense of life teaches. I imagine the plain sense of life in Zion causes the poet in Lamentations to gag when trying to speak of this "inevitable knowledge." And I imagine it is the poet's task and our burden as readers to sit with Zion in the midst of all that is defiled and defiling until or "unless"—as Zion puts it in the last words attributed to her in this book (5:22a)—we come to the end of our imaginations about what God is doing in Lamentations.

41. "The Snow Man," in Stevens 1982b: 10.

Chapter 3

THE OSTRICH AND THE SWORD: READING THE CITY-LAMENT OF LAMENTATIONS INTERTEXTUALLY WITH THE WILDERNESS WANDERINGS OF THE BOOK OF NUMBERS

Richard S. Briggs

Numbers and Lamentations are not books that naturally invite cross-comparison, and their canonical locations are relatively well isolated from each other on any construction of the canon. Reading them intertextually is therefore a decision to let their co-existence in the Hebrew/OT canon create resonance and mutual illumination even where or if none existed in the minds of authors and editors of either book. The book of Numbers is now widely held to be a late, post-exilic production drawing on materials that stretch back in time for a long and indeterminate period. Most likely Lamentations would have been composed with awareness of many of the textual elements that now make up Numbers, while the finished product of Numbers would have been composed with an awareness both of the fall of Jerusalem and the book of Lamentations that it doubtless provoked.[1] An analysis of the texts of the two books does not suggest any particular evidence of conscious indebtedness of one to the other. I will rehearse the minor suggestions of such allusion or reference, before falling back in the remainder of this piece to a more literary-critical form of intertextuality that operates regardless of authorial intention.

---

1. The present state of the scholarly settlement on Numbers is well represented by Frevel 2013. This settlement will most likely prove to be a way-station en route to a land not settled in our lifetimes.

Conscious Echoes?

Generic Indebtedness?

The genre of the book of Numbers is notoriously difficult to determine. It is clearly, on some level, a compendium of resources and literary works: legal prescriptions, narratives, and priestly texts, all edited into a narrative context that seems to serve the need to propel the reader from Sinai to the plains of Moab. Although it ends up being called the "junk room of the priestly code," I have argued elsewhere that one might reorientate such a description as a store-house of treasured (but otherwise homeless) texts.[2] Lamentations is a poem and/or a collection of poems: laments of some sort, arguably city-laments indebted to Mesopotamian exemplars of the genre.[3] The most that one could look for here, then, would be elements of the lament genre in the book of Numbers.

The presence of a ballad aimed at Heshbon in Num. 21:27-30 is indeed sometimes noted by commentators on Lamentations as a parallel phenomenon to the taunt songs of others that are referenced in various places in Lamentations.[4] Rabbinic traditions saw Num. 21 as making constructive use of Amorite poetry rather than singing their own taunt, because thereby the prohibition of Deut. 2:9 ("Do not harass Moab") would be upheld in Israel, who instead profited from someone else having first taken the land of Moab.[5]

Other than this there is little direct comparison between the two books on this level. But note that if Lamentations does indeed consist of some form of city-lament(s), then it is in turn not surprising that a book that seeks a home while travelling through the wilderness bears little formal similarity to it. It is this contrast in substance that will occupy us below.

Specific Links

By virtue of being in the canon, any scriptural verse can be cross-compared to another one for the sake of mutual illumination, but in practice even this is rare with regard to these two books. Vocabulary links between the

---

2. See Briggs 2018: 119–31. The "junk room" phrase may be found in Seybold 1977: 54.

3. The emphasis on city-lament is indebted to the work of F. W. Dobbs-Allsopp, summarized in his 2002: 6–12.

4. Noted already by Gottwald 1954: 79.

5. There is a wide range of biblical cross-referencing to this point; cf. the full discussion of Milgrom 1990: 462–3. All biblical quotations are from the NRSV translation.

two books are not conspicuous. There may be one occasion of significance when a term is limited to appearances in just these two books.

Numbers 11:1 ("Now when the people complained in the hearing of the LORD") uses the rare verb אנן, in a construction most likely to mean that the people were "like those who complain" (כמתאננים) about evil, and which occurs elsewhere only in Lam. 3:39, "Why should any who draw breath complain (יתאונן)."[6] The two verses both point to grumbling: both instances are rendered in Greek with the standard LXX verb of grumbling (γογγύζω), and the thematic links between the two contexts are arguably thereby highlighted. I will argue below that one can indeed probe this link to develop insight into the dynamics of the text(s), but that this works effectively as a reading strategy prompted by the coincidence of vocabulary. On the level of seeing how either one text is drawing consciously on the other, no judgment seems secure.

Conscious Reception?

Finally, in terms of conscious echoes of mutual dependence or illumination, one might in principle look for evidence that the books have been received in subsequent times as mutually illuminating, but here the largely distinct nature and roles of the books seem to have mitigated against this. Academic specialization is one obvious factor here, where Pentateuchal scholars do not often write on Lamentations and vice versa, but the relative obscurity of Numbers in Christian terms, and its generally low profile even in Jewish worship, is another. Although Numbers is read every year on the cycle of Torah readings, at least one Jewish scholar pondering how its rough-edged texts are received notes that "Jews read these passages every summer in the synagogue and, it is safe to say, pay almost no attention to them" (Kellner 2014: 153–4).

Only on the broadest levels—both books being scripture—is there any degree of interaction. Perhaps the most notable case of this occurs on a liturgical level, with the sung response to the read Torah portion in the weekly Sabbath service or on other festival occasions. When the torah scroll is processed back to its resting place, a collection of verses is proclaimed that begins with Num. 10:36 and ends with Lam. 5:21.[7] Both verses draw attention to the presence (or longed-for presence) of the LORD as it is understood through the presence of the torah scrolls. There

---

6. In both cases it is a *hithpolel* of אנן, to complain or murmur (BDB: 59). Levine (2000: 320) offers discussion of the oddities of the term in Numbers (cf. Renkema 1998: 423; Thomas 2013b: 192–3).

7. Described in Joyce and Lipton 2013: 188.

is clearly much here that could be discussed in terms of how Numbers and Lamentations as books relate to the theme of divine presence and absence, but such text-focused enquiry is not really what is in view in the liturgical practice in question.

Intertextual Resonances for Readers of the Canon: The Wilderness and the City

On all three of these levels of conscious echo, then—questions of genre, of lexical cross-referencing, and of subsequent uptake of mutual illumination—we have discovered some small ways in which there might be deliberate intertextual interplay between Numbers and Lamentations. I now proceed to argue that what insight is thereby afforded is more productively recast in a literary reading strategy that takes as given the two finished books, and asks what light is shed for the reader who is able to read both one and then the other. This is in any case the natural habitat of "inter-textuality," which is not in general about references from one text to another, but is rather the rejoicing in the interpretative possibilities that arise out of placing two texts alongside one another and seeing what happens: "Every text—as an intersection of other textual surfaces—suggests an indeterminate *surplus* of meaningful possibilities" (Beal 1992: 31). There are obvious points of contact here with aspects of Rabbinic interpretation, and the possibilities opened up by rejoicing in the "literary simultaneity" of the canonical texts (Levenson 1993: 62–81).

For each of our two focal books, the points we have been considering take purchase in a wider reading scheme that seeks symbolic value in the cross-comparison of wilderness and lamented city. On this broader conceptual and theological level, the two books offer an interesting dialogue.

Locating the Wilderness

Where would readers of scripture aspire to live? For readers of the Torah, the answer seems relatively clear: the land promised to Abraham and his descendants. The whole narrative of the five books of the Torah presses ineluctably towards that promised land, although of course ending just short of it, perhaps to inculcate in later readers the permanent longing for a home not yet attained, or a rest not yet entered into.[8]

---

8. Cf. Heb. 4:1-11. The ending of the torah short of the land is put to constructive theological and hermeneutical use by Sanders 1972/2005: xvii (xiii), 15 (20), and especially 52–3.

The book of Numbers narrates the failure to enter the land. After breaking camp in ch. 10, the people arrive within scouting distance of the land of Canaan in time for ch. 13's account of the distrustful and easily overwhelmed expedition to the land over-flowing with milk and honey. Their unwillingness to enter in is described by the LORD as a failure of trust (14:11), and met with punishment (14:28-35). Forty years shall they wander, and "in this wilderness they shall come to a full end, and there they shall die" (14:35). The rest of the book, insofar as it has a narrative development, describes precisely such wandering and death. The reader of Numbers, who is perforce a reader of Numbers as it is now found in the Torah since it never had an independent existence as a separate book, will experience the denial of the land as a privation of the life-support that YHWH intended to offer his people. It is particularly striking that Numbers ends with two chapters that are concerned with the use of certain towns (or cities; ערים) as cities of refuge, and with land inheritance among the daughters of Zelophehad. Of course it is true that the strange collection of texts that make up Numbers comes from a wide range of times and specific places, but rhetorically it is arguably poignant to some degree that this book of wilderness wanderings ends with attention to the appropriate disposition of towns and land.

In a broader perspective, the narration of the five books of the Torah locates the wilderness as one of a number of alternatives for the unfolding action. In his thoughtful reading of wilderness in Christian spiritual tradition, Andrew Louth (2003: 25–6) notes that in the Bible "the desert is not an ultimate symbol: the desert is encountered in the course of the story many times, but the story neither begins there, nor does it end there.... It is between the garden and the city that we find the desert." The sense in which this is true in the Pentateuch requires one to notice certain nuances.

Although the conceptual map is not yet fully drawn in Genesis, it is helpful to note that only the marginalized are described as in the wilderness (מדבר) in Genesis: the abandoned Hagar is found in the wilderness in 16:7, and then sent again to wander in the wilderness in 21:14, where in turn Ishmael (unnamed in this particular story) grows and lives (21:20, 21). When Joseph is thrown into the pit by his brothers, it is into "this pit here in the wilderness" in Reuben's words (37:22), which may perhaps connote a sense of local contextual weakness, rather than a physical description of wilderness *per se*. Otherwise there is only a passing reference to Anah son of Zibeon who found springs in the wilderness (36:24) and the location of some of the military action of Gen. 14 on the edge of the wilderness (14:6). In other words, while the mainline narrative may well be taking place in wide and spacious sparsely populated places, the language of the מדבר is reserved for those removed from its focus.

With the arrival of Egypt, as a nation engaged in the physical building of empire in the book of Exodus, the wilderness can become a positive alternative, starting as early as 3:1, with Moses coming across the burning bush, not just in, but beyond (אחר) the wilderness. In time the request to Pharaoh is to leave the hard labour in order to enter into the wilderness to worship "the God of the Hebrews" (5:3, cf. 5:1). This is perhaps where the tradition of desert spirituality finds its earliest purchase, as an alternative to the foreign requirements of Egypt. But the Israelites have not even crossed the sea before they are worrying about the wilderness's fragile capacity to sustain life: still on the wrong side of the Red Sea they complain to Moses: "Was it because there were no graves in Egypt that you have taken us away to die in the wilderness?" (14:11), and in the very next verse they add: "It would have been better for us to serve the Egyptians than to die in the wilderness" (14:12).

This is the perspective that we find in the book of Numbers, only now compounded on the brink of the promised land, as the complaint grows still further to be: "Would that we had died in the land of Egypt! Or would that we had died in this wilderness!" (Num. 14:2). Tragically, this latter lament foreshadows the deaths that will follow in the wilderness as a result of failing to enter the land.

The rhetorical function of the wilderness in the Pentateuch thus seems to be a matter of emphasising the alternative to whatever is currently the predominant space in the narrative. In the first twelve or so chapters of Exodus the מדבר therefore acquires a positive overlay as the alternative to the place of forced labour in Egypt. But in Genesis the "wilderness" was the absence of being at the centre of God's then-present action. In neither case is it helpfully understood as the return to the lost "garden" state of Eden.[9] In Numbers, all these elements come together so that the wilderness is the place where all God's people find themselves, and yet it remains not the place where God's provision is intending to operate: that was the land that they rejected in ch. 14.

In short, readers of Numbers do not aspire to live in the wilderness. It is instead the place of death, as forewarned in Num. 14 and as played out in dispiriting detail through the rest of the book. What is interesting about this reading of wilderness and Numbers is that it highlights how ch. 14 clearly articulates a sense that they should have entered the land (hence 14:40, the immediate recognition that "we have sinned" when the divine judgment is relayed to them). Thus the text attests to a self-understanding

---

9. The "romanticised" sense of a lost paradise is found rather in prophetic texts like Jer. 2.

of disobedience. "Wilderness" can only function positively when one's self-understanding does not assume that God wants you elsewhere (or to put the point with fewer negatives: the default understanding of "wilderness" is that it is the negative alternative to where God wants you, but it can function as a positive alternative to being in a place of oppression). So, for instance, if you have had to depart the city for the sake of maintaining a holy life, then the wilderness can be positive. We may note, therefore, that in the Dead Sea Scrolls the wilderness has a range of positive connotations that fits entirely with the location of the scrolls communities as those who have come apart precisely out of a sense of obedience or faithfulness: the wilderness as a place of withdrawal for subsequent purification, or as the locus of revelation, as Hindy Najman (2006: 99–113) has shown.[10]

The Wilderness in the Book of Lamentations

The book of Lamentations, by way of contrast, knows precisely where God would have wished his people to be: in Jerusalem. The desolation of the city is a result of the exile, on one level, but is construed as the result of the judgment of God, on the more profound level of theological self-analysis. Readers may anticipate, therefore, that when the book portrays the collapse of Jerusalem as the collapse of life, the particular dimension of this collapse highlighted by the wilderness theme will be the return to the death-dealing traditions of Numbers, where such hope as there was had been vested in future settlement.

Lamentations offers three references to the wilderness (מדבר). The first is with reference to God's people in 4:3: in contrast with the תנין who know how to look after their young. The תנין (so the *Kethib*) are the KJV's "sea monsters," followed by the LXX as "dragons" (NETS), and arguably there is mileage in pondering the incongruity of sea dragons' care of their young as a spur to the shortcomings of the people of God, but even so most follow the *Qere* and amend to תנים, "jackals." Either way, unlike them, the lament is that "my people [lit. 'the daughter of my people'] has become cruel," which is then further parsed as "like the ostriches in the wilderness." Ostriches and jackals often appear together in prophetic texts.[11] "The cry of the ostrich," says Renkema, "is quite similar to that of

---

10. These are the second and third of her three categories: the other is the wilderness as exile, but this too can be read more positively than exile is straightforwardly read in the Bible.

11. So Berlin 2002: 106; noting Isa. 34:13; Mic. 1:8; Job 30:29.

human lament." More significantly: "Since it lives in uninhabited regions, the ostrich constitutes a sign of devastation and abandonment" (Renkema 1998: 503). This nicely picks up on the rhetorical sense of "wilderness" here: a cruel place marked by the absence of appropriate care, and the collapse of life.

The second reference occurs towards the end of ch. 4, in a passage that seems to imagine Jerusalem as being hunted by a human enemy, "pursuers" (קלם) in the word of 4:19. In some form this is presumably a reflection on the events of the fall of Jerusalem: "our pursuers were swifter than the eagles in the sky; they chased us on the mountains, they lay in wait for us in the wilderness." As the next verse goes on to talk of the taking of the LORD's anointed in the pits, this section of Lam. 4 is often related to the failed flight of King Zedekiah at the height of the siege (2 Kgs 25:1-7, esp. vv. 4-5) (Berlin 2002: 112). As Renkema notes, "the question remains, however, whether the pursuit mentioned in the present verse is exclusively related to [these] historical events," and concludes rightly that "the capture of Zedekiah did not bring an end to the enemy pursuit" (1998: 554, cf. 558 also). One might add that poetry is rarely best read as a puzzle of historical reference that awaits solving before there can be illumination. If it were the king in view, then the resonance of the wilderness language extends to the collapse of the (Davidic) monarchy; but even without that degree of specificity, the poem still says that fleeing to the wilderness did not bring safety, or more poetically, that the collapse of life in the city could not be escaped by running away, and death pursued them into the wilderness.

The third reference comes from ch. 5, now reflecting on the dangers of the resultant life outside the city: "We get our bread at the peril of our lives (בנפשנו), because of the sword in the wilderness" (5:9). Especially if one has not read 4:19 over-specifically, then it is easy to relate this to the pursuers who lay in wait for them outside the city. Now the wilderness is understood as a threat to food provision, a threat symbolized with a sword.

Because the book of Lamentations presumes that the city of Jerusalem was where God's people had been supposed to be, the wilderness is a place of unremitting hostility and the threat of death. It is characterized as the haunt of the ostrich and the domain of the sword. There is no hint of withdrawal for spiritual resourcing, or to receive revelation. The collapse of the city is not a covert gift of the opportunity to recover refreshed forms of the simple life. Rather, Lamentations operates with the same sense that we noted earlier with Numbers: with a self-understanding of disobedience.

Intertextual Resonances

What is added to this reading of Lamentations by such intertextual reference, and conversely to our appreciation of Numbers in light of Lamentations' emphases? I suggest three angles from which the rhetorical power of these texts may be perceived more sharply, or with a greater sense of what is at stake.

First, Numbers brooks no sympathy for the failure to enter the land. This failure is parsed as lack of trust (14:11), regardless of the complex specifics of how the military operation of entering it might have proceeded. It turned out to be a choice for death over life. Does this highlight for readers of Lamentations the sense of culpability for what has gone wrong in Jerusalem? Readers of Lamentations can feel torn between sympathy and indignation for what God has done to the city, alternately acknowledging God's justice and then criticising God's own involvement in the suffering (e.g., Lam. 2:20).[12] But readers fresh from Numbers are less likely to be sympathetic, and more likely to discern God's judgment as deserved. The resultant reading of Lamentations seems more likely to emphasise moral dimensions of the failure involved in terms of the city-society's failure to protect its people. To have seen the promised land and not to have entered was bad enough; to have occupied that land, and fortified its capital city, and then to have lost it through inability to live out the requisite justice and righteousness is then culpable failure.

Secondly, the failure to go up as instructed in Num. 13–14 was not a choice that could be overturned by the recognition that they had made the wrong decision. When the people regroup for an ill-advised, post-rejection attempt on entering the land, in 14:39-45, it is doomed, and the inhabitants of the hill country come down and defeat them, "pursuing them as far as Hormah" (14:45). Hormah appears to have been somewhere south-west of their starting place, though commentators regularly note the odd detail that it has a definite article here and a root from חרם ("destruction"), perhaps suggesting that they were pursued to "the annihilation." In any case, does this turn of events underline for readers of Lamentations that it is no part of the purpose of the lament to presume upon God turning back the clock and giving them another chance? The nearest the book gets to such a move is in the recalling to self-examination, to return (שוב) to the LORD, in 3:40 and in the general tone of much of the latter part of ch. 3, which appeals to the steadfast love (חסד) of the LORD (3:22). There was a time, in the mid–late twentieth century, when readings of ch. 3 would typically build on this to push all the way to saying that it offered hope, and swayed

---

12. For a thoughtful theological reflection on this tension see Parry 2010: 201–6.

the whole book's interpretation that way too, though surely subsequent interpreters have the edge here, such as with Iain Provan's (1991: 23) summation that "to characterise Lamentations as a hopeful book is…to mislead." But just as Num. 14 spells out clearly that the judgment on their disobedience is going to take a long time to work through, though it will not be endless (14:26-35), perhaps the point is that Lamentations can do no more than hope that God has not "utterly rejected" Jerusalem (5:22), which is the note on which the book ends.

The reader of Lamentations, in other words, is not left seeking the restoration of social structure, the rebuilding of the city as such. Rather, they are required to relocate the focus of God's action consequent upon the judgment. The wilderness is now experienced as the domain of death again. In the face of the ostrich and the sword, rehabilitation involves recognizing judgment upon failure as life-giving intervention, and finding a new home, "located" in the practice of repentance. Only in this somewhat limited sense is the book a book of hope.

A third aspect, that follows on from this, returns us to our earlier discussion of grumbling, pursued above with reference to the lexical links between Num. 11:1 and Lam. 3:39. But absent an attempt to locate this in conscious authorial echo, what is the net result of the intertextual reading of Lamentations and Numbers with regard to how those who suffer should respond to divine judgment? The book of Lamentations seems poised between complaint and repentance, as 3:39-40 says explicitly: "Why should any who draw breath complain about the punishment of their sins? Let us test and examine our ways, and return to the LORD." Whereas the beginning of Lam. 3 rehearsed its complaint somewhat against God, the turn at 3:39 is that the complaint "is directed *towards* God with the goal of persuading him to forgive" (Parry 2010: 116). This same distinction, I suggest, is interwoven through the narratives of Numbers, a book that also seems poised between willingness to accept God's judgment, and the desire to complain. In Numbers, arguably, the distinction is more pointedly between the people, who complain, and Moses, who addresses the complaints directly to God with the hope of securing divine forgiveness, with 14:19 being perhaps the most obvious example.

In each case, we seem to have a difference between a form of complaint that bewails the situation the complainer finds themselves in (call it a self-focused complaint) and a form of complaint that addresses itself more openly to God, with or without hope of specific transformation. One of the hardest things to do when beset with trouble is to see beyond one's immediate pressing (and distressing) horizons. One simple intertextual resource afforded by reading Numbers and Lamentations together is the transportation of the troubled reader to a different textual world where the implications of complaint and judgment may be considered a little less personally. Interestingly, *Targum Lamentations* already makes such a move, when it inserts into Lam. 1:2 a mention of the bad report brought back to Moses by the messengers sent to spy out the land (Num. 13:25-33), locating this on the 9th of Ab, and in a sense reading "the people of the house of Israel wept that night" as linking Num. 14 and Lam. 1:2: "She weeps bitterly in the night."[13] As the Targum has perhaps perceived, both books defer the realization of hope beyond their own limits. Readers of both books in the canon may thereby be drawn to see that their present darkness is both recognized and also not the last word. In the evocative analysis of Tod Linafelt (2000a), readers find ways to "survive Lamentations," just as Lamentations itself has survived the trials of its readers down through the ages.[14] There is probably scope for thinking about "surviving Numbers" in the same way, and my contention is that each book may be part of the resource for surviving the other.

Conclusions

We have explored a three-fold result of the intertextual reading of Numbers and Lamentations. It involves a tendency, first, to reduce the reader's sympathy for the loss of Jerusalem by pointing to ways that the city should have been life-giving, emphasising the moral dimensions of the failure involved. Secondly, it highlights that the loss of Jerusalem demands something other than the rebuilding of Jerusalem. That it may lead to that rebuilding is good news in the long run, but like the death of the wilderness generation in Numbers, it is not a promise of good news directly for those now cast out into the wilderness. Thirdly, it offers mutually reinforcing readings of each text in terms of the transformation of the self-focus of complaint into the life-giving hope of lament to God.

---

13. See briefly (and indeed with the intention of focusing a different attention on the Targum), Linafelt 2000a: 89. *Targum Lamentations* offers extended expansions of the opening verses of ch. 1, but gradually simplifies down to translating the text. I am indebted to the translation of Targum provided as Appendix 3 by Brady (2003: 155–67). For his online translation, see his "Targum Lamentations," http://targum.info/meg/tglam.htm.

14. For his reading of survival as the "hermeneutical key" to chs 1–2 especially, see p. 18.

It is part of the productive capacity of the canon to generate such prompts for rich re-reading. If such re-readings incorporate the uncovering of matters intended in the production of the texts concerned, then that is a bonus, although with regard to most of the OT, how would one ever know? Perhaps the wilderness path of the identifying of such historical specificity is an approach that operates under the bleak signs of the ostrich and the sword? Though whether intertextuality is the hermeneutical promised land, or just one way-marker on the journey towards it, must await other discussions and wider considerations.

As a rather delightful coda, I can report that after finishing a draft of this paper I was pointed to the strange phenomenon of the portrait of Lady Justice in Raphael's mural of *The Battle of Milvian Bridge* in the Sala di Costantino (the Hall of Constantine) in the Vatican. This mural of the battle of 312, completed by Raphael's followers after his death in 1520, includes an oil-painted insert of Lady Justice (perhaps by Raphael himself) depicting her with the expected scales of justice in her left hand. Her right hand, however, does not hold a sword, but rather she has draped it around the shadowy figure of an ostrich. According to the wonderful study of Una Roman D'Elia, to which I am entirely indebted for this final paragraph, the ostrich had acquired by the Renaissance a symbolic sense of challenging one's interpretation of the world by way of reflecting God's own delight in creating hybrid creatures.[15] Trace it further back to ancient Egypt, says D'Elia, and the ostrich was once a symbol of justice. Raphael doubtless had certain (subversive?) intentions in painting an ostrich in for a sword in the context of the Vatican's honouring of Constantine. It is altogether a more serendipitous matter that he thereby illustrates some of the strange resonances between Numbers and Lamentations: a fitting conclusion, one might suggest, for an intertextual exploration.

---

15. See D'Elia 2015. It was a lively discussion of a draft of this paper at the Durham University Old Testament Research seminar that alerted me to this painting, the book, and its strange appropriateness.

Chapter 4

CHAOS AND ORDER:
LAMENTATIONS AND DEUTERONOMY AS RESPONSES TO DESTRUCTION AND EXILE

Elizabeth Boase

Two texts.
Two liminal moments.

In the book of Deuteronomy the community stands at the edge of the land, looking towards a bright new future full of promise and hope. In the book of Lamentations the community sits in the rubble of that dream, the land decimated and hope seemingly destroyed. As texts that frame the narrative of Israel's time in the land, these two texts occupy seemingly incompatible narrative worlds.[1] Deuteronomy constructs a world which "delights in singularity, clarity, predictability, and stability,"[2] a world in which divine activity, whether for blessing or curse, is predicated on human behavior. Lamentations, in contrast, portrays a world in which all sense of reason and order has collapsed, a world in which divine action and divine justice no longer make sense. How, then, could one read these texts together, and to what end?

Drawing on aspects of trauma theory, this essay seeks to read Lamentations and Deuteronomy intertextually in order to explore the way that these seemingly disparate texts might converse, collude, collide, disrupt, and disturb. My aim is to unsettle conventional readings which preference order over chaos, sin over suffering, while at the same time

---

1. I am making a distinction here between narrative context and historical context, dating the earliest edition of Deuteronomy no earlier than the late eighth century, and arguing that the text took its final form in the exilic or even post-exilic period.

2. To quote Stulman's (2016: 131) discussion of the Deuteronomic material in Jeremiah.

refusing the temptation to valorize expressions of suffering and pain at the expense of the genuine attempts to find moral coherence. I will argue that although Lamentations and Deuteronomy inhabit "different symbolic and literary terrains,"[3] when read together these texts speak not only into each other's worlds, but create new worlds of meaning for readers, both old and new.

Previous Readings of Lamentations and Deuteronomy

There is a long and distinguished tradition of reading Lamentations and Deuteronomy together.[4] In the field of Lamentations' research, Lamentations has been linked with Deuteronomy through its supposed expression of a Deuteronomic theology of sin and punishment, seen primarily in the references to sin (1:5, 8, 9, 14, 18, 20, 22; 2:14; 3:39, 42, 64; 4:6, 13, 22; 5:7, 16) and on the basis of the didactic material in Lam. 3:22-39. Deuteronomy has been identified as either being the theological tradition against which Lamentations reacts (Gottwald 1954: 48–67), or as the theological solution to the problems addressed within the poems (Albrektson 2010). The occurrence of similar descriptions of suffering between Lamentations and Deut. 28 has further reinforced the association between these texts, with Deut. 28 frequently, but not exclusively, identified as the source text.[5]

In identifying Deuteronomy as a source text for Lamentations it is argued that a Deuteronomic worldview shaped the cultural and theological framework of the text. Authorial and communal knowledge is often assumed, with the Deuteronomistic correlation between sin and punishment identified as common knowledge for the producing community. So, for example, Bertil Albrektson (2010: 31) argues that within Lamentations there is "a conscious reminiscence of Deuteronomy's descriptions of punishment."

A number of literary studies, especially those in more recent years, focus less on the literary traditions which lie behind Lamentations, and more on the literary associations between Lamentations and Deuteronomy, with a view to exploring the contribution that Lamentations makes to a

---

3. Ibid.

4. In identifying trends in the history of Lamentations research there is no attempt here to provide a comprehensive overview. For a fuller discussion of the literature up to 2003 see Boase 2006: 6–23.

5. See, for example, Westermann 1994: 116, 122, 135–6; Mintz 1982: 9; House 2004: 316–29; Berlin 2002: 18.

theology of exile (Smith-Christopher 2002: 75–105; Berlin 2002; Rainer 2003). Adele Berlin (2002: 18), for example, who, on the whole, eschews historical-critical questions, includes a discussion of the worldview of Lamentations, which she states "assumes the 'theology of destruction' in which destruction and exile are the punishment for sin (Deut. 4:26-27; 28:32-67; 29:33-27; 30:17-18). The sin that warranted such severe punishment is idolatry, the code word for the rejection of God and his [*sic*] commandments."[6] Although Berlin does not claim that Deuteronomy is a source text for Lamentations, she does make some assumptions about the dominance or at least the priority of the Deuteronomic school of thought. The worldview of the Deuteronomic school, with its retributive theology and its naming of idolatry as the prime cause for exile, is identified as central to the theology of Lamentations. Although Berlin discusses the causal link between sin and punishment as central to a theology of exile, to which Lamentations contributes, she is careful to not limit the purpose of Lamentations to an exploration of the meaning of the destruction. Rather, the book recreates and commemorates the suffering within a framework of an ongoing covenant relationship between God and Israel, as is expressed in Deut. 30:1-5 (Berlin 2002: 18).

In their recent commentary in the Wiley-Blackwell Commentary Series, Paul Joyce and Diana Lipton (2013) approach Lamentations from the perspective of reception history. In a brief discussion of the curses in Lamentations, which has a focus on the engagement with Deut. 28, Joyce and Lipton (2013: 114) state that both Lamentations and Deuteronomy "represent two sets of responses to the same eternally relevant question—why do bad things happen to good people?" They suggest that reading Deuteronomy and Lamentations together, without regard to chronology, opens new perspectives on the "complex, sensitive question of divine and human responsibility for the destruction of Jerusalem and the Babylonian exile" (2013: 114). This insight occurs in the context of the discussion of a specific text (Lam. 3:15), but opens up evocative possibilities for a more extended intertextual reading.

In the intertextual reading which follows, I will explore the way that both Lamentations and Deuteronomy might have functioned as responses to the events of 597–87 as distinct yet inter-related responses to communal trauma. Building on these insights, I will then explore the way that these two texts, when considered in dialogue, might redefine the way the theology of exile is read.

---

6. Berlin (2002: 18) makes no absolute claims as to relative dating with regard to Lamentations, and is silent on the issue of chronology with regard to the two books.

Divergent Responses to Trauma

Both Lamentations and Deuteronomy are texts located at liminal moments of Israel's history, situated either side of Israel's occupation of the land. There is scholarly consensus that Lamentations emerges out of, and in response to, the Babylonian destruction of Jerusalem, mourning the desolation of place and the human losses which resulted from siege, warfare, disease, famine, and exile.[7] Less certain, however, is the relationship of Deuteronomy to these same events, with there being considerable debate as to whether any of the book has its origins during the exilic period. It is widely argued that the book of Deuteronomy has a lengthy redactional history, with the seventh-century reform movement and the period of the exile identified as significant moments in the book's growth. As such, despite its narrative location at the edge of the land, the book, in its final form, is best read in response to moments of crisis in subsequent time periods—as a response to questions which arose from the Assyrian conquest of Israel, and in response to the trauma of the Babylonian destruction and exile.[8] While not trying to solve the complex issues around the dating of Deuteronomy, when read in conjunction with the well-accepted theory that the final edition of the Deuteronomistic History (DtrH) emerges in response to the events of the exile, a history for which Deuteronomy provides the opening "chapter," it is a reasonable working assumption that Deuteronomy can be read as one of the possible responses to the experience of destruction and exile.

If, as I am arguing, Lamentations and Deuteronomy both entered into the rhetorical context of the exilic period, and continued to engage in the dialogues of the post-exilic period where these books were read and re-read, how might these contrasting books be understood as responses to the traumatic experiences of this period? Given the dramatic contrasts between the two, is it possible to read them together in a way that seeks to neither prioritize the expression of one over the other, but recognizes the contribution that both together might have made within these settings?

---

7. For detailed discussion see Dobbs-Allsopp 1998; Berlin 2002: 30–6.

8. For a discussion of the literary evidence for a complex redactional history of Deuteronomy see Nelson 2002: 4–9 (Nelson himself identifies the book with the seventh century). Nicholson (2014: 10), by contrast, argues that provenance within the exilic period, and specifically amongst the exiles in Babylon, best explains the character and features of the book (e.g., the urgent style, the preoccupation with encroachment, the focus on worship of other gods, and the emphasis on remembering/not forgetting, and meditation on law). For another detailed discussion see Lundbom 2013: 6–20, 73–92.

Lamentations and Deuteronomy stand, in many ways, in sharp contrast. At the literary level, one is poetry, the other prose; one is full of propositional statements, the other of evocative poetry. One looks to the future, exhorting the community to choose life in obedience to the law, the other portrays the present in terms of death, destruction, and lawlessness. Deuteronomy creates a world of causal predictability, allowing no exceptions to the consequences of the failure to adhere to the terms of the covenant. Within Lamentations, with its focus on portrayals of suffering, there is no order or predictability, with established frameworks of causality, divine justice, and human agency in tatters. Deuteronomy, seemingly, stands as a monolith of monologic "truth," proposing a retributive framework of predictable and predicted consequences,[9] while Lamentations is thoroughly polyphonic, voicing varied and contrasting viewpoints and perspectives on the unpredictable and unpredicted lived experience of the people.[10]

Despite their contrasts, both books can be seen to be valid, and, I would suggest, expected responses to the trauma of destruction and exile. Read through the lens of trauma theory it can be seen that both books grapple with a crisis of meaning. Lamentations provides a much-needed expression of pain and suffering, giving witness to violence, loss, suffering, and death, mirroring the collapsed frameworks of meaning and assumptions. Deuteronomy, by contrast, is an alternate but equally essential voice, which provides an explanatory framework in which human agency is reinstated, and the possibility of future order and control offered as a beacon of hope. To draw on Louis Stulman's discussion of the prose and poetry in Jeremiah, Lamentations and Deuteronomy "represent two radically different social and symbolic worlds," both of which help those who experienced the violence of war and destruction construct meaning (Stulman 2016: 135–6).

These two literary reflexes, naming the pain and providing explanatory frameworks, arguably correspond to what Judith Herman (1997: 3, 155) has identified as major stages in the recovery from trauma: remembering

---

9. See Janzen (2012: 76–91) for a discussion of the way that the master narrative is subverted in Deuteronomy.

10. For discussions of the polyphonic nature of Lamentations see Dobbs-Allsopp 2002; Boase 2006; O'Connor 2002; Bier 2015; C. W. Miller 2001; Mandolfo 2007b. The terms monologic and polyphonic are drawn from the work of Mikhail Bakhtin (1984: 78–100) and can be broadly defined in terms of texts in which one ideological viewpoint controls meaning (monologic) versus texts in which a multiplicity of viewpoints (dialogic or polyphonic) are present.

and mourning the traumatic event, and reconnecting with normal life.[11] One of the primary functions of Lamentations is to name the suffering experienced and in so doing give voice to the mourning of the community. The retributive theology developed in Deuteronomy, and indeed in parts of Lamentations, helps to facilitate the process of reconnecting to ordinary life.

Psychological studies of trauma suggest that in the wake of traumatic violence and loss (where trauma is defined as an event which is perceived as an overwhelming threat and which exceeds the individual's ability to cope[12]), individuals experience a collapse of meaning predicated on the shattering of core beliefs or assumptions. Core beliefs are "the assumptions or beliefs that ground, secure, or orient people, that give a sense of reality, meaning or purpose to life" (Kauffman 2002: 1). As humans, we live in an assumptive world, "which include(s) our interpretation of the past and our expectations of the future, our plans and our prejudices" (2002: 2). At the core of the assumptive world are "beliefs about ourselves, the external world, and the relationship between the two" (Janoff-Bulman 1992: 6).[13] Core beliefs frequently include concepts of justice and control in which outcomes are assumed to be contingent upon behavior. As such, the world is believed to be neither random nor chaotic and is therefore meaningful. In such a worldview, humans have both agency and control.

One of the consequences of traumatic suffering is the disruption of core beliefs. Disruptions may occur in relation to assumptions about the benevolence of the world, about concepts of justice and control, and about self-worth. In addition, assumptions about the nature and character of God/gods, and the relationship of the divine to the contingencies of life, may also be disrupted or shattered. One of the tasks of post-traumatic recovery is the reconstruction of a meaningful world which addresses the emotional and existential losses associated with the traumatic experience (Smith-Landsman 2002: 13).

In entering into the rhetorical context of the exilic and post-exilic periods, Lamentations and Deuteronomy give voice to the two stages of recovery suggested by Herman (1997: 3, 155). Lamentations gives voice

---

11. Note that Herman's first stage in recovery is to establish safety, a stage which is not pertinent to the current discussion.
12. Frechette and Boase 2016: 4.
13. See Janoff-Bulman (1992: 6–8)—who notes that while not everyone holds these beliefs, most do—for a discussion of the preponderance of these assumptions, even in the face of contradictory or counter evidence.

to the suffering experienced by the community, with the poetry reflecting the shattered assumptions about the world and about God. The dominant voice of Deuteronomy provides one framework through which shattered assumptions about human agency, justice, and divine character can be restored. Both texts engage with issues of justice, sin, divine character and power, failures of leadership, suffering, exile, hope, repentance, and restoration. Both speak into the "narrative wreckage" (O'Connor 2002: 7) of sixth-century Judah, one by documenting the trauma, the other by constructing a dominant master narrative. An intertextual reading against the backdrop of trauma leads to the conclusion that neither text constructs a permanent, monolithic narrative world, but that each is responsive to the needs of the community in the face of crisis.

In the discussion which follows I will focus on one particular aspect common to both books, the image of God. While a case could be made to discuss each of the aspects listed above, space prevents this fuller discussion. In focusing on the image of God, questions of justice, sin, agency, human responsibility, and divine power will also be touched upon.

Images of God

Both Lamentations and Deuteronomy are deeply concerned with the nature and character of God. Neither presentation is monolithic, with Lamentations portraying God as a violent (and perhaps capricious) destroyer, a longed-for absence, a God of steadfast love, and as the hope for the future (Boase 2008b). The portrayal of God within the master-narrative of Deuteronomy can be defined through God's various attributes and actions. God is a holy god, who loves Israel and demands love in return. God has elected Israel and has entered into a covenant relationship with them in faithfulness to the promises made to the ancestors. God is portrayed as an impartial judge whose righteousness can be assumed through the various descriptions of those things that God either hates, or declares as an "abomination" (Lundbom 2013: 59–63; Nelson 2004: 9–12).[14] As will be seen below, despite the dominant expression of the character of God in Deuteronomy, the characterization is not without its contradictions (Janzen 2012: 76–91).

---

14. Things considered an abomination to God include "worship of other gods (17:3-4), idols and idolatrous rites (7:25-26; 12:31; 13:15[13:14]; 20:18; 27:15; 32:16), magic and divination (18:12), immoral customs (22:5; 23:19[23:18]; 24:4), blemished sacrifices (17:1), and commercial injustice (25:16)" (Lundbom 2013: 62).

The characterization of God in Lamentations occurs primarily within the descriptions of suffering, with God most frequently identified as the causal agent behind that suffering. God acts in burning anger and wrath (1:12; 2:1, 2, 3, 4, 6, 21, 22), without mercy (2:2, 21), with determination (2:8, 17), and with seeming excess (2:1-10[15]). In the symbolic world of Lamentations (with the exception of 3:21-39) God acts with overarching and dominant power, a destructive force that leaves the recipients of the violence feeling overwhelmed and powerless, as is evident in the speeches of the city-woman (Lam. 1:11-16, 18-22; 2:20-22) and the *geber* (3:1-18). Previous conceptions of God's responsiveness have been overturned, evident as the people bemoan God's absence and God's unresponsiveness. In Lam. 1, multiple references are made to the absence of a comforter for the city (vv. 2, 9, 16, 17, 21), with the city-woman calling on God to look and see her plight (vv. 9, 11, 20). God is described as having destroyed the temple, the site of God's dwelling amongst the people (2:1, 6-7). Although the people petition God (3:42), God does not respond, described as being wrapped in anger, in an impenetrable cloud (3:43-44). The collapse of trust and confidence in God and God's ways is expressed in the book's final question, which raises the possibility that God has abandoned the people permanently and will no longer be present to them (5:19-22).[16]

Within this characterization there are theodic elements which describe God's actions as either retributive (1:5, 8, 9, 14, 18, 20, 22; 3:34-39, 64; 4:6, 21-22; 5:7 [possibly], 16) or educative (3:22-39). Although the description of suffering far exceeds references to sin within Lamentations, a causal framework for the suffering is seen in those places where the city-woman is either described as sinning or herself names her own rebelliousness and transgression as cause for her suffering (1:5, 8, 14, 18, 20, 22). In addition, priests and prophets are identified as failing in their leadership (2:14; 4:13), and the community both confesses their sin (3:42; 5:16) and names the sin of past generations (5:7).

Alongside this theodic element, there is also a (perhaps) stronger antitheodic voice which refuses "to justify, explain or accept as somehow meaningful the relationship between God and suffering" (Dobbs-Allsopp 2002: 29). God is certainly implicated in the suffering through both violent presence and ongoing absence, but the suffering is not uniformly

---

15. Over thirty verbs are used of God in these nine verses, depicting a relentless torrent of destruction. In v. 6 the verb חמם is used. This is the only time this verb is used of God, with its general sense being the wrongful application of violence (see Gottlieb 1978: 27).

16. For a full discussion see Boase 2008b.

seen as retributive nor educative. God's actions are described, but not always explained, thus breaking open the link between suffering and sin. So, for example, in the vivid description of God's destruction in 2:1-8 no reference to sin is made, with the only reference in the whole chapter being to the failure of the prophets (2:14).[17]

Lamentations 3 also evokes the tradition of God as a God of justice, steadfast love, and compassion. In language reminiscent of Exod. 34:6, as the *geber* turns from despair to hope, he recalls God's steadfast love (חסד), faithfulness (אמונה), and endless mercies (רחמים) (3:22-23). As this wisdom-like section continues, God is described as good (טוב) to those who wait and endure their suffering in silence (vv. 25-30). The speaker acknowledges that the grief and rejection come from God, albeit not willingly (vv. 31-33), however, rejection and grief are not a permanent state of affairs, as God will have compassion (רחם) "according to the abundance of his steadfast love (חסד)" (v. 32).[18] The "bad" (הרעות, v. 38) that comes from God is named as punishment for sin (חטא, v. 39), and the community is called to refrain from complaint, and to confess their sins.

The image of God in Lamentations is, therefore, varied. God's power and the fact that God's hand is present in the suffering is evident, yet the portrayal, in its fragmentation, witnesses to a loss of confidence as to the nature of God, and in the nature of God's justice. Established understandings of God's attributes and the ways of God in the world are juxtaposed against descriptions of God's actions which defy explanation, all of which are named alongside the awful possibility that God has permanently abandoned the people (5:20-22). The poems give voice to the struggle of the community to understand God in the midst of the extremities of suffering.

If read intertextually with Deuteronomy, however, Deuteronomy can be seen to provide a concrete expression of the character of God which serves to reorient the community through an expression of God as a God who is responsive and who acts in just measure to Israel's behavior. Deuteronomy provides a strong theodic statement, identifying sin as being the causal impetus for divine action. The sin which results in destruction and exile is identified as being either idolatry and/or disobedience to the law (see, for example, Deut. 4:26-27; 28:32-67; 29:33-27; 30:17-18). The God of Deuteronomy, at least in the master-narrative, is neither absent nor capricious.

---

17. For a discussion of theodicy in Lamentations see Boase 2008a.
18. All biblical quotations are from the NRSV.

Reading for intentional authorial associations first, the most direct intertextual links (here reading for the possibility of "double-voicing"[19]) occur between Lamentations and Deut. 28. There is much shared language with regard to the nature of the suffering that either is (Lamentations), or may be (Deuteronomy) experienced. Common elements include references to the captivity of sons and daughters (Lam. 1:5, 18/Deut. 28:41, 32), serving the enemies (Lam. 1:5/Deut. 28:13, 42, 44, 47), famine (Lam. 5:9-10/Deut. 28:22), disinheritance (Lam. 5:2/Deut. 28:30-33), becoming a mockery (Lam. 2:15/Deut. 28:37), disregard for the young and the old (Lam. 5:12/Deut. 28:50), physical destruction of the city (Lam. 2:1-9/Deut. 28:52), and to cannibalism (Lam. 2:20; 4:10/Deut. 28:52-57[20]). Unlike Lamentations, sin in Deuteronomy is defined. Reading intertextually, Deuteronomy provides a specificity missing within Lamentations, providing the exilic and post-exilic communities both a reason for the divine wrath experienced, and, potentially, the possibility of future agency. If the past sin could be named and identified, the possibility for future security is present.

The didactic voice of Lam. 3 is reinforced in an intertextual reading, with the wider divine characterization of a God of love, justice, election, and covenant being portrayed as a God of consistency and reason. God's behavior in the destruction of the city and, in particular, the exile of the people, becomes both predicted and predictable.

In this way Deuteronomy can be argued as providing a means, to use Herman's framework, of reconnecting to normal life. The narrative world of Deuteronomy (and indeed of the DtrH) asserts that God had made known from before the time the people took possession of the land what was required: worship only God and obey the law. Even as it is set in the past, Deuteronomy addresses all Israelites, collapsing the past sinful generation addressed in Moses' speech with all generations. A normative world of meaning is in this way established, with each subsequent generation given the guidance required to live well in the land (Nelson 2002: 11–12; Janzen 2012: 71–3). Deuteronomy functions to reconnect the generation(s) which experienced destruction and exile with a meaningful

---

19. A term used by Bakhtin (1984: 189) who defines double-voiced discourse as the intentional co-option of another's voice within an utterance. An author makes use "of someone else's discourse for his own purposes by inserting a new semantic intention into a discourse which already has, and which retains, an intention of its own."

20. The Deuteronomy reference is more detailed, longer and more explicit than those found in Lamentations.

framework of order and predictability, a world where divine behavior arises out of principles of justice, righteousness, and mercy.[21]

In addition, the promises of God's presence and God's compassion can be read as a response to the uncertain future expressed in Lamentations. Lamentations 5 gropes for hope in an ongoing relationship with God, but concludes with uncertainty and the possibility that the relationship with God might be over (Lam. 5:19-22), with v. 19 imploring God to restore (שוב) the people to God's-self.

Both Deut. 4:25-31 and 30:1-10 look to the future and name exile as an inevitable outcome of Israel's time in the land, but do not see the condition of exile as being the end of the relationship between God and Israel. Deuteronomy 4:28-31 outlines the means by which the people will be restored to the land. The people will seek and find God, if their search is from the heart, and in their distress will return (שוב) to God. Because of who God is (רחום, merciful), the people will not be abandoned or destroyed, and God will not forget (שכח) the covenant (note that Lam. 5 begins with a call for God to remember [זכר] God's people, a cry that recurs throughout the book[22]). Deuteronomy 30:2 similarly calls on the people, when they find themselves in exile, to return (שוב) to God in order to be restored (שוב, v. 3), this time predicated on God's compassion (רחם). The promise of return is followed by a renewal of the promises to the ancestors (vv. 4-5).

There is an interesting dynamic when these verses are read together. In Lamentations the people cry to God, asking God to bring about the restoration. In Deuteronomy, the onus is on the people. In part this is due to the speaking voice and the context of each of the texts. In Lamentations it is the people who are speaking to God, calling on God, in lament form, to bring an end to the current suffering. Arising out of a context of powerlessness and loss, it is God who holds the power, and God alone who is able to bring about change. In the midst of the destruction the people name God as the destroyer of the city and, arguably, of the relationship. As such it is God who has the power to bring about the longed-for restoration. After all, it is God who has failed to see, to remember, to listen. In Deuteronomy, the speaker is Moses, who addresses the people with divine authority. The perspective is from the one in power, from God, and from that perspective, the ones who have behaved in such a way as to cause

---

21. See Assmann (2006: 14–21, 51–6) for an important discussion of Deuteronomy and cultural memory in the context of trauma. So also Nicholson 2014: 62–6.

22. Lam. 1:9, 11, 12, 20; 2:20; 3:50; 5:1, 20-22.

the destruction and who have failed in their obligations, who have not remembered, are the people themselves. Responsibility looks different depending on where you stand.

But wider circles of meaning resonate here. Taken together, the books of Lamentations and Deuteronomy do, as Joyce and Lipton (2013: 114) suggest, open up the "complex, sensitive question of divine and human responsibility for the destruction of Jerusalem and the Babylonian exile." The cause of the suffering and the solution to the suffering are articulated differently, with the emphasis variously placed at the feet of one or both parties in the covenant relationship. From the perspective of trauma theory, Lamentations articulates the severity of the suffering and the collapse of the assumptive world, giving voice to the loss of confidence in the nature and character of God, but also attributing responsibility for the suffering to the one who is the ultimate power. In this voice the designation of responsibility for both the suffering and the hope for change witness to the sense of disenfranchisement and powerlessness of the community. Simply speaking of the suffering is task enough on its own.

Deuteronomy, however, speaks into a different symbolic world, and addresses a different need within the community. Whilst powerlessness might be a reality for the traumatized community, new possibilities remain beyond the scope when the world is viewed only through this lens. Deuteronomy returns to the community a sense of hope through placing agency back into the hands of the people. Whilst "blaming the victims" might seem counter-intuitive, the possibility that something might have been done to avert disaster, and that something can be done to change the future, in its own way provides agency and hope. We see here a transition from hopelessness to hopefulness, a hope that can be achieved through human response to God and God's commands.

Read together, Lamentations and Deuteronomy wrestle with questions of innocent and deserved suffering, divine control and power, human agency and responsibility. In many subsequent readings of these texts precedence has been given to the voice of Deuteronomy, advocating divine righteousness, even to the point of holding those innocent sufferers within the Jerusalem community responsible for their own fate. But to read intertextually, consideration can be given to the way that Lamentations is not only "answered" by Deuteronomy, but also becomes an answer to Deuteronomy. In a predictable world of inevitable consequences and divine retribution, the voice of the innocent sufferer is silenced. Lamentations provides the voice that protests the ordered world of Deuteronomy, allowing for life to be more than the inevitable unfolding of the consequences of human sinfulness.

This voice is not completely devoid from Deuteronomy itself. In a reading of Deuteronomy which looks for those places where the master-narrative is itself subverted, thus witnessing to the traumatization of the exilic community, Janzen argues that narrative ambiguity breaks open the seemingly stable framework of the narrative. He argues, for example, that there is ambiguity as to the sin which caused Moses to die outside the land. According to Janzen, Deuteronomy does not clearly identify Moses' sin, with it being "only obliquely" linked to the people's desire to send spies into the land. What's more, Caleb, one of the spies, is allowed to enter the land whilst Moses is not. To quote Janzen (2012: 79): "Right at the point where Moses' punishment—death outside the land—paralleled that of the exiles, whose punishment the narrative is trying to explain, we find ambiguity in the explanation." He (2012: 81) goes on to argue:

> The master narrative's pictures of God, justice, and punishment simply fail as parts of a totalizing, airtight explanation at this point; narrative explanation has become unexplained ambiguity that subverts the logic of just divine punishment that attempts to make sense of the exiles' trauma.

Janzen also suggests that the rhetorical strategy, which sees the present generation (both the conquest generation and the generations of subsequent readers) being addressed as if they were the sinful generation precluded from the land, also functions to subvert the master narrative:

> When trauma presents Israel as a single generation constantly committing and suffering the same act of disloyalty, it subverts the master narrative's concepts of Israel, history, punishment, and justice.... Unlike the case of Deut 28, which claims that the trauma of siege, famine, and destruction that the exiles suffered can be explained through the ethical choice of the nation, Moses' comments that conflate the exodus and conquest generations suggest that God can confuse the ethical choices of one generation with those of the next. (Janzen 2012: 85)

That this was a live issue for the exilic and post-exilic communities is found also in Lam. 5:7, which states, "Our ancestors sinned; they are no more, and we bear their iniquities."[23] If Janzen's argument is accepted, neither Deuteronomy nor Lamentations is monolithic in their perspectives of God and justice, both voicing uncertainty about the nature of divine justice. Both texts give voice to the collapse of meaning associated with the disasters of the sixth century, raising questions about the nature of

---

23. See also Jer. 31:29 and Ezek. 18:2.

divine justice and righteousness. Both texts also offer an alternate vision of God as just and righteous. The balance between the two texts varies markedly, but there is, arguably, more in common between the two than is usually recognized.

The difference in balance and perspective can be attributed to the different needs being addressed. Lamentations provides a means by which the community can give voice to its pain and suffering, memorializing that suffering for present and future generations. Deuteronomy, by contrast, seeks to assert a narrative which helps the community to connect with a larger narrative, enabling a sense of hope and a future trajectory. Each in their own way, therefore, speak to the traumatized community.

Conclusion: Breaking the Hold of Retributive Theology

Too often Deuteronomy, with its propositional statements of divine justice and mercy, has been given precedence as a normative expression of the nature of God, and as an explanation for the destruction of Jerusalem and the experience of exile. As an extension of this, a retributive theology which associates suffering with sin has become something of a clichéd understanding of OT theology. When discussed in association with Lamentations, the voice of Deuteronomy has been used to explain away and silence the more problematic images of God that are present within Lamentations.

I have argued, however, that both Lamentations and Deuteronomy are shaped by their rhetorical context. Each, in their own way, responds to the needs of the community/communities which experienced the trauma of the destruction of Jerusalem and the exile to Babylon. As such, these are not competing voices but are responding to the contingencies of their time. To preference one over the other is a failure to recognize that both texts are provisional, seeking to respond to the needs of their communities. Neither text says all there is to say about God. Neither text says the last word about God.

Reading Lamentations and Deuteronomy intertextually through the lens of trauma highlights the provisional nature of both texts. As a response to the need to express pain and suffering, Lamentations gives voice to the shattering of assumptions about the world and the nature of God. Deuteronomy seeks to reconstruct a meaningful world where the character of God is reaffirmed and human agency is again made possible.

Stulman notes a parallel dynamic in the book of Jeremiah. He states (2016: 136):

The Deuteronomistic prose, no less than the poetry, attempts to help victims of violence survive the collapse of their worlds of meaning. It creates order amid social and symbolic chaos. It translates the ravages of war into discursive language and provides solutions; it teaches lessons and brings clarity and recognition to a world that is fractured seemingly beyond repair. The Deuteronomistic prose literature creates a metanarrative of a once seemingly unshakable world on the brink of destruction. The cumulative effect is to transform a victimized community into a community of active meaning-makers, albeit in terms starkly different from those employed in the poetry.

Read together, Lamentations provides a counter-voice to the retributive world of the book of Deuteronomy, a voice which refuses to accept the conclusion that the destruction and exile were the result of divine punishment for human sin. Conversely, the book of Deuteronomy (re)constructs a world where divine predictability, which is predicated on the divine characteristics of covenant loyalty, loving-kindness, faithfulness, and mercy, are again reinforced. Neither text is completely monolithic in perspective, and taken together they do provide a discursive space where the "complex, sensitive question of divine and human responsibility" (Joyce and Lipton 2013: 114) can be addressed.

Within our contemporary context, where war, terrorism, natural disaster, genocide, and myriad other suffering is so prevalent, there is a place for both voices. Lamentations continues to speak into moments of suffering and pain, giving voice to the doubts, uncertainties, and sheer horror of trauma. Alongside that, Deuteronomy continues to offer a voice of certainty and stability, a way of reconnecting to the larger narrative of God. Occupying their different symbolic worlds, each text is enriched by the juxtaposition of the other's counter-narrative.

Part II

LAMENTATIONS IN DIALOGUE
WITH THE PROPHETS

Chapter 5

OUT OF SIGHT, BUT NOT OUT OF MIND (2 KINGS 23:27): READING 1–2 KINGS WITH LAMENTATIONS

J. Andrew Dearman

The poems in Lamentations present the suffering of Jerusalem and Judah at the hands of the Babylonians and their allies in the early sixth century BCE. The historical narratives in 1–2 Kings, correspondingly, present Jerusalem and Judah as attacked on several occasions, including the catastrophic defeat at the hands of the Babylonians and their allies. Three central institutions (henceforth the triad) are common to both presentations: Davidic monarchy, Jerusalem, and the temple located there. This triad, therefore, offers viable ways to examine intersections between reading the two independent works, both of which likely took their essential form in the exilic period, and which are decisively shaped by the demise of Judah, even as they reflect little evidence of literary interaction with one another.

The Triad in 1–2 Kings

Following the tenets of Deuteronomy, Kings evaluates the monarchical history of Israel and Judah from David's last days in Jerusalem to Jehoiachin's last days in Babylonian exile. According to the compilers, YHWH chose a triad of institutions for the edification and preservation of Israel.[1] They are the Davidic dynasty, the city of Jerusalem, and the temple-for-his-name located there. Solomon conveniently presents the triad in his temple dedication speech (1 Kgs 8:15-21). The theological

---

1. Assuming an exilic date for the penultimate and/or final form of the Deuteronomistic History. For discussion see Halpern and Lemaire (2010) and Knoppers (2010).

underpinnings of the triad in Kings are both Israelite and Judahite (cf. Ps. 78). The theology is foremost Israelite in the sense that all of Israel is in its purview as the people YHWH redeemed from Egypt and brought to the promised land; even foreigners who worship at the temple in Jerusalem have access to YHWH (1 Kgs 8:41-43). After the demise of separatist Israel at the hands of the Assyrians, the institutions continued in Judah, from which the final compilers of the Deuteronomistic History (DtrH) likely originated. We might even think of Judah as the fourth institution that the Lord chose (cf. 1 Kgs 11:26-40). Of the triad, Jerusalem receives the least attention in Solomon's dedication speech. Note, for example, the oblique reference to a "city" in 8:16. It does identify Jerusalem as the "place" which the Lord has chosen for his name to dwell (cf. Deut. 12:5, 11, 13; 2 Kgs 21:7).

In the Kings narratives, YHWH holds these elect institutions accountable. In another word to Solomon after the completion of the temple (1 Kgs 9:1-9), the rule of the Davidic dynasty is contingent on the existence of Israel as a kingdom. In response to the failures of the ruling house and people, YHWH threatens to cut off Israel from the land and to cast the temple out of his sight. Israel would then become a taunt among peoples and those who pass by would "hiss" at the ruined temple. After the failures during the time of Manasseh, YHWH's threat becomes a promise to remove Judah from his sight, as happened earlier with Israel, and to reject the chosen city of Jerusalem and the temple (2 Kgs 23:26-27; cf. 21:10-15; 24:3). These things come to pass with the Babylonian onslaughts narrated in 2 Kgs 24–25.

How the narrators of 1–2 Kings reckoned the fate of the Davidic dynasty is difficult to summarize adequately. Kings is, after all, a layered work incorporating traditions of various origins. On the one hand, the narrators acknowledge that YHWH had promised to undergird the dynasty (1 Kgs 11:36; 15:4; 2 Kgs 8:19). On the other hand, in the final, exilic edition they reckon with the fact that Davidic rule had come to an end in Jerusalem.

The monarchs of Israel and Judah are individually assessed in Kings, often with formulaic statements. Apart from David and the reforming kings, Hezekiah and Josiah, they are variously judged and found wanting. Ahab and Manasseh come in for withering criticism. As noted, the failures of Manasseh are judged as particularly heinous and the consequences for them are placed corporately on Judah and Jerusalem. Nevertheless, there is no rejection of the dynasty *per se* in 2 Kgs 23:26-27, or anywhere else in Kings. The continuation of the family/dynasty as such is addressed specifically at the conclusion of 2 Kings, where "King Jehoiachin" is released from prison in Babylon after decades of incarceration (25:27-30). Thus, in Kings the triad comes to a historical end, with the Davidic dynasty's fate left open-ended. Jehoiachin is neither out-of-sight nor out-of-mind.[2]

The Triad in Lamentations

The triad is Judahite in Lamentations, although an Israelite identity for the intended audience is also recognized (2:1-3). Jerusalem/Zion is a central character and subject in the poetry and thus bears the brunt of judgment for the triad. She has a speaking voice and is portrayed metaphorically in ways used elsewhere in Hebrew poetry and the royal court, but rarely in Kings. The city is represented by Daughter Zion (2:1, 8, 10, 18; 4:22), Daughter Jerusalem (2:13, 15), and Virgin Daughter Zion (2:13). There are similar appositional phrases to represent Judah (1:15; 2:2), the people (2:11; 3:48; 4:3, 6, 10), and Edom (4:21-22). In the poetry Jerusalem moves from princess and perfection of beauty among nations to humiliated widow and filth among them (1:1, 17; 2:15).[3]

There are a few direct references to a Judahite king (2:6, 9; 4:20) in Lamentations and none are explicitly named. There are also several references to leaders, some of which may include the monarch or members of the royal house (2:2, 9). All bear YHWH's judgment. In 4:20 YHWH's unnamed "anointed" is "captured in the pits" of Judah's oppressors.

The temple is referred to as both YHWH's and Jerusalem's "sanctuary" (מקדש; 1:10; 2:7, 20). It is also called YHWH's "place" (מקום) and house, and the location of his altar (2:6-7). The temple and "Mount Zion" (5:18) have been violated by foreigners and reside under YHWH's judgment. The sanctuary, and likely the city as well, are metaphorically YHWH's footstool (הדם־רגלים; 2:1), which he has angrily rejected. Whatever the failures of temple and priesthood, their Yahwistic identities are assumed.

One of the striking things about the triad in Lamentations is the difference in terminology and characterization with that in Kings, given the commonality of divine judgment on these institutions in each work. Here quickly are some examples. There is only one place in Kings where an appositional phrase—Virgin Daughter Zion—is used for the city (2 Kgs 19:21). She is not otherwise personified in Kings. There is only one mention of Mount Zion (2 Kgs 19:31) in all the references to Jerusalem

---

2. See bibliography and discussion in Janzen 2008.
3. On Daughter Zion/Jerusalem and her personification, see Boda, Dempsey, and Flesher 2012; Kartveit 2013.

and to the temple in Kings. Indeed, the term Zion occurs only three times in all of Kings (1 Kgs 8:1; 2 Kgs 19:21, 31), so pronounced is the preference for "Jerusalem." Kings does not use the adjective "anointed" to describe the Davidic ruler. Kings does not employ the term מקדש for the Jerusalem temple. Lamentations does not use the Deuteronomic name formula for the temple.

There is no reason to assume that the compilers of Kings disliked the name Zion or opposed the personification of Jerusalem. The fact that at one point they incorporated material with these characteristics argues against it. Similarly, there is no reason to assume that the poet of Lamentations rejected the name theology for the temple in Kings. In the case of the adjective "anointed," its lack in Kings is likely a coincidence, as it is used elsewhere in the DtrH. These select data do suggest, however, that the compilers of Kings and Lamentations did not draw handily on the other. Perhaps the phenomenon at hand can be explained as a matter of genre, with lament poetry as performance and historical narrative as explanation rooted in different *Sitze im Leben*.

Virgin Daughter Zion (VDZ), David and Mount Zion in 2 Kings 19:20-34

The data summarized above also shows lexical connections between Lamentations' portrayal of Zion and Isaiah's prophecy to Hezekiah. The prophecy begins with VDZ's word to Sennacherib (19:21):

> Virgin Daughter Zion has contempt for you,
> She holds you up to ridicule,
> Daughter Jerusalem shakes her head after you.[4]

The prophecy continues with a sarcastic rendering of Sennacherib's pretensions and upholds YHWH's resolve to vindicate his own. Although the Assyrian king has conquered elsewhere, the Holy One of Israel, a phrase used only here in Kings, will thwart his overconfidence (vv. 22-28). Isaiah's word to Hezekiah also includes the claims that a remnant shall go forth from "Mount Zion" (v. 31), a term also occurring only here in Kings, and that the Lord will defend the city for his own sake and that of David his servant (v. 34).

Isaiah's words are part of the segment in 2 Kings devoted to the reign of King Hezekiah (18:1–20:19), incorporating material very closely paralleled in Isa. 36–39. Common sources underlie the two segments. This

---

4. All translations are the author's unless otherwise noted.

does not necessarily mean that the Deuteronomistic Historians drew their material from an emerging Isaiah book—although that is a possibility. It is more likely that both they and the compilers of an Isaiah book adopted coalescing traditions about Hezekiah and Jerusalem and that both shaped them for their respective presentations.[5] In any case, 2 Kgs 19:20-34 employs unique vocabulary and personification for Kings, but found elsewhere in Lamentations and Isaiah. The text in 2 Kgs 19:21 and its parallel in Isa. 37:22 are two of the three texts in the HB that characterize Jerusalem as VDZ. The other is Lam. 2:3. All three verses contain the parallel appositional phrase Daughter Jerusalem for VDZ.

Just how do Isaiah's words to Hezekiah in 2 Kgs 19:20-34 intersect with Lamentations' poetry? One way is that VDZ is a counter-posed figure in comparison, or what might be called a mirror image.

2 Kgs 19:21	Lam. 2:15
Jerusalem ridicules Sennacherib	Passers-by shake their head at Jerusalem
She shakes her head at his folly	They mock her prior beauty and renown

In Lamentations she is a pitied royal figure; in 2 Kgs 19:21 she is a daughter-princess, who speaks for YHWH and heaps scorn on her unsuccessful attacker. In Isaiah's words she represents YHWH's vindication of his elect institutions; in Lamentations she is the recipient of divine judgment and the object (not the proclaimer) of ridicule.

In 2 Kgs 19:21, VDZ uses two verbs in her scorn of Sennacherib. They are בוז and לעג. Noun cognates of these two verbs characterize verbal ridicule (Ps. 123:3-4), something common to her roles here and in Lamentations. The shaking (נוע) of her head physically illustrates her word to Sennacherib, even as the same act illustrates the verbal abuse she suffers in Lam. 2:15-16.

The triumphant theology of the triad in Hezekiah's day meets its opposite in the humiliation of Zion's fall. It is an interesting question—just how does the triumph of the triad in Hezekiah's day fit in the overall scheme of Kings and its narrated demise of Judah? That is discussion for another day.[6] In reading Isaiah's words through Lamentations, we might say that his portrait of VDZ comes from the cultural and theological matrix that the poet(s) of Lamentations inherited (4:12) and then found dismantled with Judah's demise.

---

5. See Evans 2009 for discussion on the origin and function of 2 Kgs 18–19.
6. For one perspective see Olley 1999.

Allusiveness in National Demise

The allusive poetry of Lamentations connects variously to the narrated summary of Judah's defeats in 2 Kgs 24–25. As one example, Lamentations does not offer the name of any attacker or enemies, except that of Edom (4:21-22). And no reason is given for addressing Edom, although Lamentations' antipathy toward it is part of a broader biblical tradition (Ps. 137:7-9; Isa. 34:5-17; Obadiah; Mal. 1:2-5). Its poetry is replete, however, with references to enemies, oppressive neighbors, aggressive foreigners, pursuers, those who humiliate, etc. Kings, on the other hand, mentions bands of Chaldeans, Aramaeans, Ammonites, and Moabites, who afflicted Judah during Jehoiakim's reign and the first siege of Jerusalem by the Babylonians (24:2). Occasionally, a commentator suggests that the reference to "Aramaeans" in 2 Kgs 24:2 should be emended to "Edomites," given the ease with which a *dalet* becomes a *resh* through copyist error, but this proposal seems more a harmonization than a necessity.

"Judah has gone into exile...among the nations" (גלה; Lam. 1:3). Although the poet does not mention Babylon explicitly, its subjugation of Judah and its agency in forced migration are surely presupposed in the portrayals of Judah's oppressive setting "among the nations" (1:10; 2:9). Kings repeatedly uses the same verb as the poet to describe the forced migrations imposed by Assyria and Babylon on Israel and Judah (e.g., 15:29; 17:6; 25:21). It is used also to describe the removal of Jehoiachin himself to Babylon (24:15).

According to the terse description in 2 Kgs 25:1-3, the Babylonian siege of Jerusalem during Zedekiah's reign lasted some 18 months and resulted in severe famine. The plaintive cry of Jerusalem in Lam. 2:19-20 and that of the poet in 4:4, 9-10, leave little to the imagination in describing the horrors of famine and cannibalism (cf. 2 Kgs 6:28-29). Here perhaps we see again the difference that genre makes in rendering a subject. In this instance the allusiveness is in the Kings account, not that of the poet.

Similar literary dynamics are at work in the narration of the city's and temple's violation. According to the Kings narrative, foreigners periodically stripped Jerusalem of resources after sieges or otherwise gained advantage over the city (1 Kgs 14:25-29; 2 Kgs 12:17-18; 16:7-8; 18:13-16). The Babylonians were the last in the line of looters, twice taking valuables from the palace and temple (2 Kgs 24:10-16; 25:8-17). The second time they burned portions of the city. Again, the Kings narrative is sparing on the details of suffering in these accounts, but provides some data on the treasures and sacred vessels taken from the temple.

Lamentations is allusive on the details of looting, even as it provides multiple voices for those violated. Plausibly the references to "precious items" (מחמד) in Lam. 1:7, 10, indicate the looting of temple and palace. The Kings account says nothing about the death of prophets and priests in the temple precincts, but it is easy enough to imagine the scenario (2:20). YHWH's metaphorical fire (1:13; 2:3; 4:11) possibly interprets the Babylonian destruction of the conquered city (2 Kgs 25:9). Zion's personification includes the voice of her walls (2:8, 18), a portrayal that intersects with the report in Kings that the Babylonian army broke down the city's walls (25:10).

YHWH's Anointed

The poet's lament over the capture of YHWH's "anointed" (משיח) describes the king in exalted, royal-court rhetoric (4:20), with imagery reaching back centuries in Egyptian texts (Salters 2010: 331). Although held by the enemy, he is:

> The breath of our countenance....
> In his shadow we thought to live among the nations.

As noted, it is likely a coincidence that the Kings narrative lacks references to the phrase "YHWH's anointed," for the compilers would certainly recognize its attribution to a Judahite king. One cannot tell, however, whether the poet refers to Jehoiachin or Zedekiah, both of whom were Babylonian prisoners. There is nothing comparable to this palace rhetoric in Kings. In 2:9 the presence of Jerusalem's king and leaders among the nations is lifted up as a detriment for the life of surviving Judahites, listed along with the lack of instruction and the absence of vision from prophets. Taken together these references represent support for the institution of monarchy and what it offered by way of stability and security. Although YHWH's judgment has fallen on it, the monarchy's failures are not enumerated, even in a summary or formulaic way. Perhaps they are included in Zion's corporate confession (1:14, 18)? This contrasts with the Kings narratives, which in several ways hold the monarchs of Israel and Judah responsible for national transgressions.

It is an interesting exercise to look more closely at the fate of Jehoiachin and Zedekiah in Kings in light of Lamentations' poetry. Jehoiachin surrendered the city to the Babylonians and was taken, along with his family and others, to Babylon (24:10-12, 15). He was incarcerated there for decades before being released by Amel-Marduk to finish his days in

Babylon (25:27-30). Zedekiah fled Jerusalem and was captured by the Babylonians near Jericho. Appearing before Nebuchadnezzar in Syria, Zedekiah was blinded after seeing his sons executed and he was then taken in chains to Babylon (25:4-7). Possibly there is an intersection between the Kings account of Zedekiah and the corporate voice in Lam. 4:19, where swift "pursuers" (רדף) lay in wait in the wilderness. In 2 Kgs 25:5, the Babylonian army "pursued" Zedekiah and caught him in the Jordan Valley.

Kings says nothing about the fate of Zedekiah, once taken to Babylon (cf. Jer. 52:11, which notes his death). In Lam. 4:20 it is not clear whether the poet laments the circumstance of a king who is currently held by oppressors, or remembers a tragic figure whose protection was lost and who is now deceased. As noted, the poet elsewhere laments that Zion's king and "princes" (שׂרים) are located among the nations (2:9). This is most naturally taken as a present reality at the time of composition. It could refer to Zedekiah or Jehoiachin and those deported with them. If the reference is to Jehoiachin, the term "princes" could include male relatives.

There is another voice in Lamentations to consider for Jehoiachin or Zedekiah, namely, the male who speaks in ch. 3. He is a representative figure for the fate of Judah, in some ways analogous to Zion/Jerusalem. She is a royal figure in representation, so why not this man as well?[7] He is constrained by darkness and chains (3:2-7). His glory is gone (3:18). He speaks on behalf of the people, acknowledges corporate guilt, and calls for a return to YHWH (3:40-42). He laments as one who suffers without cause (3:55-63). With this last characteristic, one understands the reason for the long-standing identity of the figure with Jeremiah, given the parallels with his prayers in the book by his name. A portrayal this allusive, finally, is also elusive regarding the speaker's historical identity, and the lack of a consensus among interpreters is understandable.

A possible connection in Lamentations to Jehoiachin turns, in part, on the significance attached to the report of his release from prison, after decades of incarceration, literally the last matter provided in the Kings narrative. Is it simply an epilogue, confirming the continuation of exile by noting an event near in time to the exilic edition of Kings? Or does the report undergird the continuation of YHWH's Davidic lamp, flickering as it were and *sans* a throne in Judah, when Jehoiachin takes his place above

---

7. For the possibility that a royal figure is portrayed in Lam. 3, or that he is Jehoiachin, see Porteous 1961: 244–5; Gottlieb 1987; Saebø 1993.

the seats of other captive rulers? Was his longevity in captivity a source of pride, respect, or hope for someone like the poet in 4:20?[8] In any case, possible connections between Kings and Lamentations with respect to Jehoiachin remain tantalizing.

A Rejected Sanctuary and Meeting Place

As with the king, YHWH's judgment has fallen on the temple, but its failures are not otherwise enumerated in Lamentations. Whereas the king and Judahites are in exile among the nations, the temple sits violated by nations who entered it (1:10). The allusiveness of the poet is such that hearers/readers get little detail on how the house has been physically compromised and more on the effects of violation. The sequence of destruction portrayed in 2:5-9 is citywide, including the temple.

Worship at the temple came to an end, at least as the poet had known the cult before the sanctuary's demise at the hand of the Babylonians. Festival and Sabbath were no more; the invading forces had also compromised the priesthood and prophecy (1:10; 2:6, 20). In the Kings account, the Babylonians took cultic elements from the temple and central priestly personnel were brought before Nebuchadnezzar and executed (25:13-21).

Sinfulness and Judgment

Various voices in Lamentations acknowledge corporate sinfulness and judgment. It is a staple subject in the ancient Near East and among the compilers of the HB. Personified Jerusalem has "uncleanness in her skirts," a metaphor of ritual impurity to indicate her disqualification from YHWH's presence (1:9). She rebelled against YHWH's word (1:18) with transgressions (1:22), sentiments also expressed in the plural voices of 3:42 and 5:16. And there is also this complaint in 5:7 regarding the correspondence between corporate sin and judgment:

> Our ancestors sinned—they are no more,
> But we bear their iniquities

---

8. A number of scholars think that Zedekiah is behind the description of the anointed one in the pits of the enemy in Lam. 4:20. See the discussion in Salters 2010: 330–2. A plausible case can also be made for Jehoiachin. He survived decades in captivity, and recognition of his status is reflected in the chronological scheme of the book of Ezekiel.

The tone of Lamentations reflects the voices of living memory regarding Judah's failure and fall—i.e. a lived experience of Judah's fall is portrayed in the book and not just a representative voice for subsequent generations. Moreover, the complainant of 5:7 is likely the confessor of 5:16, "woe to us, we've sinned!" The complaint, therefore, is not a denial of shared culpability with ancestors, but an acknowledgment of corporate judgment in multi-generational perspective, even as it sees that judgment as greater than a single generation brings upon itself. As the voice of survivors, the poet represents them as those to be pitied; they continue to bear accrued punishment in a way that the dead do not. As part of the final poem of Lamentations, the complaint is directed to YHWH in support of a plea for restoration.

The Kings narratives offer several points of comparison with the complaint in 5:7. In the presentation of Manasseh's reign, the ruler's enumerated sins result in a tipping point for Judah's fate. In listing his transgressions (2 Kgs 21:1-16), the narrators make the following charges:

1. His polytheistic religious practices were worse than the Canaanite nations whom YHWH previously expelled from the land.
2. He reversed the reforms of Hezekiah, his father.
3. He shed much innocent blood in Jerusalem.
4. He acted like Ahab, whose transgressions set the fall of Samaria in motion.

In response to these things, YHWH would stretch a measuring line over Jerusalem (cf. Lam. 2:8), wipe it like an overturned bowl, and cast the remnant of his heritage into the hands of enemies (21:13-14). As the account moves forward, the reforming efforts of Josiah were unable to turn the accumulated effects of Manasseh's failures (23:26-27), and YHWH confirmed a word of judgment from prophets to destroy Judah by sending marauding bands of enemies against it (24:2-4) (Sweeney 2005). The evaluative summaries for the last four Judahite kings are formulaic (23:32, 37; 24:9, 19-20) and confirm the connection already posited between culpability and national collapse. Each ruler did evil like his ancestor(s).

The Kings narratives and Lamentations thus overlap in their perspectives on corporate and multi-generational judgment.[9] Ahab set in motion the rebellious dynamics that ultimately swept Samaria away; correspondingly, Manasseh did so for Judah and Jerusalem. The poet laments the

---

9. On corporate and transgenerational judgment, see Schipper 2010.

burden of inherited guilt in 5:7, even while acknowledging its influence. In typical allusive style, Jerusalem's judgment is portrayed as the fulfillment of divine reckoning from an earlier time (2:17). This is not specifically the vocabulary of prophecy and fulfillment as in the Kings narrative (e.g. 24:2b). It seems rooted in the Day-of-YHWH traditions, where previously announced judgments against rebellion are enacted in Jerusalem's fall (1:12, 21; 2:1, 21-22) (Boase 2006: 105–39).

Kings and Lamentations intersect also in the concern for shed blood and its consequences for Judah and Jerusalem. Kings twice uses the phrase "innocent blood" (דם נקי) to describe murders in Jerusalem during Manasseh's reign (21:16; 24:4). For the narrator, whose viewpoint is rooted in Deuteronomic instruction, the connection between Manasseh's murders and the later punishment of Judah is a form of bloodguilt. Responsibility for murder accrues to the land and people where it takes place and that guilt must be expunged for the community to continue (Deut. 19:8-13; 21:1-9).

One of the odd elements in the presentation of Josiah's reign is that the king nowhere addresses the bloodguilt for the murders committed during his father's reign. His reforms cleansed the temple of practices supported by his father and the narrator commends him for adhering to the instruction in the book discovered in temple repairs and for turning to the Lord according to all the instruction of Moses (23:24-27). Whatever the historical circumstances, the narrator almost certainly intends readers to conclude that Josiah followed the tenets of Deuteronomy in reforming Judah's cultic life. "Nevertheless" (אך), the narrator concludes in v. 26, YHWH's anger against Manasseh (and thus Judah) was not assuaged. When this theme of Manasseh's iniquities is repeated during the presentation of Jehoiakim's reign, it is the shedding of innocent blood during Manasseh's reign that the Lord cannot forgive (24:4).

The poet laments that the city's formerly inviolable identity was overcome by the sins of prophets and priests (4:12-13). Indeed, the syntax of v. 13 indicates that it was "because" (causative מן) they shed the "blood of the righteous" (דם צדיקים). There is a functional equivalence between the phrase "innocent blood" in the Kings narrative and the "blood of the righteous" here in Lamentations. The two phrases are used in parallel in Ps. 94:21.

We've no other context in Lamentations for the poet's charge against prophets and priests, although prophets and priests are mentioned elsewhere, and thus no reason to attribute their failure to Manasseh's reign or that of Zedekiah, when the city fell. Their murderous activity in 4:13 may be one of responsibility rather than literal agency. Perhaps as guardians of YHWH's moral order they didn't prevent the death of innocent people when they should have. A similar dynamic is at work in the critique of prophets in 2:14. Had they done their job, they would have exposed iniquity in Jerusalem and thus helped preserve the city.

Conclusion

Both Lamentations and Kings have open-ended conclusions. Perhaps this common characteristic reflects the exilic setting of both compositions, as Jehoiachin, still in captivity, gets a better seat at the table, and the poet leads the performance of lament and asks the Lord to reconsider the duration of Judah's rejection.

Chapter 6

"I AM HE, YOUR COMFORTER": SECOND ISAIAH'S PERVASIVE DIVINE VOICE AS INTERTEXTUAL "ANSWER" TO LAMENTATIONS' DIVINE SILENCE

Katie M. Heffelfinger

In the words of Benjamin Sommer (1998: 166), Second Isaiah "invests the great labor necessary to inherit a tradition." The reader of this poetry, and even more intensely the ancient hearer of these words, cannot fail to hear rich and frequent echoes of familiar biblical language and imagery. Scholars such as Patricia Tull Willey (1997), Benjamin D. Sommer (1998), and Tod Linafelt (2000a) have produced careful and extensive studies of the exilic portions of Isaiah and its literary allusions. These useful studies demonstrate not only that Second Isaiah made considerable use of a number of biblical conversation partners, but that allusive echo achieves distinctive rhetorical aims in the work. While the details of their studies differ in many respects, these three scholars each consider the comforter theme to be an element of the allusive relationship between Lamentations and Second Isaiah.[1] Thus, the characterization of Lamentations as "a call to

---

1. Of the three scholars discussed, Sommer (1998) may be the most reticent about attributing a direct relationship to the comfort theme in Second Isaiah and the "comforterlessness" of Zion in Lamentations. He comments that "Isa 40.1-11...may allude to...Lamentations'" frequent refrain, "There is no comforter"' (165). However, he argues more directly for a case of "exact quotation" from Lamentations in Isa. 51:19, which also engages the comfort theme (130). Elsewhere he indicates the frequency of allusions to particular texts, highlighting Jeremiah and Isaiah [ben-Amoz] as Second Isaiah's most frequent sources, not mentioning Lamentations (168). Tod Linafelt (1995) ties together the call for a comforter (49), the silence of God in Lamentations (51), and the focus on the "lives of the children" as the "rhetorical move" designed by the poet to move Yhwh to comfort (50). Tull Willey (1997: 130) refers to the "motif

God to be Zion's comforter" resonates with one of the most central motifs of the "Book of Comfort."[2] Though the observation of this relationship is far from new, and was already commented upon by the authors of *Lamentations Rabbah*, this essay intends to incorporate recent work on the poetics of the two books to illustrate that the "answering" nature of Second Isaiah's response to Lamentations' complaint goes beyond the semantic correspondence highlighted in studies of literary allusion and extends to the poetic cohesion of Second Isaiah as a generically, thematically, and structurally fitting response.[3] Thus, this essay will argue that Second Isaiah presents itself as an "answer" to Lamentations' cry to Yhwh to be Zion's comforter. It is an answer that is complex and multifaceted. I will argue that Second Isaiah answers Lamentations' cry of "comforter-lessness" and its related critique of divine abandonment both structurally, through a particularly appropriate poetic mode of overwhelming the audience with the dominant speaking of the divine voice, and explicitly through literary allusion. These re-deployments demonstrate that Second Isaiah's response to Lamentations is appropriate to the mode by which the complaint is expressed and is inherently emotional and relational, as is the complaint itself.

Formal and Emotional Correspondence

Lamentations marshals its poetic devices toward the rhetorical aim of evoking a compassionate response from Yhwh.[4] It moves by a "rhythm of association" as images are juxtaposed with one another, creating a chaotic

---

of Zion's comfort…[as] both Second Isaiah's most prominently positioned message and its most frequently recurring allusion to Lamentations."

2. Adele Berlin (2002: 48) characterizes "Lam 1, and perhaps the entire book" in this way. On the motif of comfort or "consolation" in Second Isaiah see John L. McKenzie (1968: 16–17), who comments that "this is certainly a dominant theme," and James Muilenburg (1956: 403), whose comments are similar. Lena-Sofia Tiemeyer (2007: 373) highlights the connection between Lamentations and Second Isaiah's comforter themes.

3. *Lamentations Rabbah* 36:2, D, in Jacob Neusner (2007: 472). Linafelt (1995: 55) drew my attention to this matter.

4. As Dobbs-Allsopp (2002: 24) puts it, "mobilizing God, reactivating the Yahweh of old, and converting God's present fury into future favor." See also Boase (2016), whose position on what Lamentations accomplishes for the traumatized community is not inherently incompatible with my understanding of Lamentations' persuasive aims for its divine addressee as the text can accomplish different aims for different intended rhetorical targets.

and effective depiction of the multifaceted distress of destroyed Jerusalem, distress that demands a response.⁵ The acrostic serves as a structural form of cohesion which holds together conflicting metaphors and sudden shifts of speaker.⁶ This poetic structure gives a frame within which the chaos of the siege and its aftermath may be fully expressed and exposed.⁷ Yet, even the acrostic breaks down in the end, as if Lamentations' grief overflows the banks of its own poetic form.⁸ Zion's loquaciousness in Lamentations interrupts the anonymous "poet's" voice, expressing a sort of climax of emotion in the poems in which it occurs, breaking out in grief and over-stepping the poetic voice speaking on her behalf.⁹ The first chapter of Lamentations serves as a good example of this technique, where the repeated notice that Zion has no comforter (vv. 2, 9, 16, 17, 21) punctuates a complaint about the city's appalling condition (1:1-11a) followed by a mirror of that complaint in Zion's own voice (1:11b-21). By personifying the city as a woman, the poetry increases the pathos of its expression and opens up the metaphorical space for Zion to speak about her "children." As Linafelt (1995: 50) has amply demonstrated, the focus on Zion's children does powerful poetic and emotional work.

Given the numerous speakers and the unexplained transitions between them, as well as the recurrent addressing of the complaint to Yhwh (e.g., 1:20; 2:20; 3:55, 58, 59, 61; 5:1, 19, 21), it is striking that the divine voice does not speak at all in Lamentations.¹⁰ Indeed, commentators have

---

5. The phrase "rhythm of association" is one Dobbs-Allsopp (2015: 199) applies to parataxis quoting Northrop Frye. Parataxis is the formal poetic name for the technique I am describing here. The comments of Linafelt (1995: 47), that "The reader of [Lam.] 2:1-4 is confronted by a poetic whirlwind of wrath and fire," convey the characterization I am making of the poetry here quite well.

6. Thomas (2013b: 80) treats "the acrostic structure…as the most comprehensible structuring device for the book."

7. As Lanahan (1974: 45) comments, in the first four chapters the acrostic "offers the lamentations a movement of irreversible progression towards inevitable completion with the last letter of the alphabet. There is an inexorable certitude about the total fulfilment of God's punitive will."

8. Lanahan (1974: 49) helpfully comments, "The inevitable conclusion intended by the alphabetical sequence is inconceivable in the final moment of the book."

9. Barbara Bakke Kaiser (1987: 166) notes: "In each case [Lam. 1 and 2] the poet begins with a third-person narrator but changes to the female persona at the point of greatest tension." Linafelt (1995: 46–7) also observes these transitions. See also Boase 2016: 59. Lanahan (1974: 41) helpfully clarifies and defines the poetic *persona*.

10. Harris and Mandolfo (2013) explore this silence and discuss the possibility that Lam. 3:57 breaks this silence. They read these words attributed to the divine voice as "the traditions of Israel calling out to Daughter Zion" (138). While I agree

insightfully commented upon this feature as an example of Lamentations' poetic form mirroring its complaint (Linafelt 1995: 51; Dobbs-Allsopp 2002: 39; Berlin 2002: 49). The divine silence continues right to the end of Lamentations, culminating in the final "willful *non*ending...opening out into the emptiness of God's nonresponse" (Linafelt 2001: 343, emphasis original).

Second Isaiah's intertextual relationship with Lamentations takes up many of the themes and images I have highlighted—Zion and her children, comfort, fear, destruction and chaos—however, it responds within a poetic structure that is, in itself, a form of response. While the divine voice is strikingly absent in Lamentations, it dominates Second Isaiah.[11] So dominant is the Yhwh voice in Second Isaiah that it can be read as the poetic device which produces cohesion among the chapters.[12] The divine voice speaks from the first lines in Isa. 40: "Comfort, comfort my people, says your God" (v. 1).[13] The voice speaks, commanding the comfort demanded by Lamentations' complaint, and providing an element of that comfort by breaking the divine silence.[14] The poems that follow convey a juxtaposition of images of comfort and divine wrath. This apparent incongruity is not out of harmony with the chaotic world of Zion's complaint and responds to its emotional resonances as well as its poetic form.[15] That is, Second Isaiah answers Lamentations in its own terms.

with Harris' and Mandolfo's ultimate conclusion that Lam. 3:57 does not violate the divine silence in Lamentations, I read it as an embedded quotation spoken by the "man" reporting his experience. Even this one example serves as the exception that proves the rule (i.e., even the cited speech of Yhwh within another's speech is limited to the single phrase אל־תירא, carrying only one accent).

11. Tull Willey (1997: 89) notes the way Second Isaiah overturns Lamentations' divine silence. See also Linafelt (2000a: 79).

12. Further discussion of and argumentative support for this point may be found in Heffelfinger 2011: see especially 71–3, 161–74.

13. All translations of biblical texts, unless otherwise noted, are my own.

14. E.g., Alan Mintz (1984: 41), who writes, "Prophecy offers consolation not just in the promise of divine deliverance but in the very fact that through the prophet again God speaks."

15. I have argued (in 2011) that the juxtaposition, vivid metaphors, parataxis, and non-narrative nature of Second Isaiah can be helpfully illuminated by employing the comparison of lyric poetry drawn from poetic theory. Similarly, Lamentations can be described in this way; see the discussion of Dobbs-Allsopp 2002: 12–20. What I would call a "generic correspondence" adds to the sense that there is a suitability in the mode by which Second Isaiah conveys its intertextual answer to Lamentations. It is important to point out that I am not arguing that the authors of either Lamentations

Within the elements of response, divine voice, and emotional tenor that Second Isaiah expresses in its intertextual relationship with Lamentations, there are many examples of Second Isaiah taking up specific language, themes, and images which highlight and develop the ways in which it presents an emotional and poetic answer to Lamentations' cry for divine comfort. There is not space to explore all, or even many, such instances in this essay. Therefore, I have chosen Isa. 49:13-26 as a worked example of this phenomenon, because it illustrates the embedding of Zion's speech into the much more dominant speech of Yhwh in Second Isaiah, it signposts its own relationship to Lamentations' complaint, and it engages in some particularly potent poetic images shared between the two texts.[16] In this case, I think awareness of how Second Isaiah is employing Lamentations' imagery expands our understanding of the meaning of Second Isaiah's poem and the nature of its meaningful poetic response.

The Nursing Mother in Lamentations

Second Isaiah's distinctive use of the "love like a nursing mother" image for Yhwh has been heavily commented upon.[17] The poem presents the imagery as a counterpoint to personified Zion's quoted complaint. However, this insight into the context of the imagery can be expanded by attention to its source in the nursing mother imagery in Lamentations. Second Isaiah takes up the nursing mother image as a means of response to Lamentations, which conveys extreme tenderness, restoration from the overturned world of Lamentations, and a reversal of Zion's accusations through redirection of the neglectful mother image back onto Zion herself. Thus it carries both tender and indicting emotional freight, as is typical of the conflicted comfort offered by the dominant divine voice in Second Isaiah.

Isaiah 49:14 marks its connection to Lamentations through its embedded citation of Zion's speech (Linafelt 2000a: 72–3).[18] This speech, which was

---

or Second Isaiah wrote with a model of a category such as lyric poetry in mind, nor even that Second Isaiah's resonances with Lamentations' form were composed with deliberate poetic imitation. Rather, I find the comparison with the lyric poetic form an illuminating one, and one that explains the resonances that go beyond specific recurrence of motifs, metaphors, and language.

16. On embedded speech see Heffelfinger 2011: 237.
17. E.g., Roberts 2003: 59; Trible 1978: 51–2.
18. Tull Willey (1997: 189) notes in reference to עזב and שכח that the "two verbs…actually appear together rarely in biblical texts, and in no other instance in reference to YHWH's abandonment."

originally not Zion's but the people's, transforms and re-appropriates the language of Lamentations' concluding "near untranslatable trailing off" (Linafelt 2000a: 74).[19] In its re-deployment, Second Isaiah shifts the strength of the rhetorical questions to the divine voice (Linafelt 2000a: 74). Both the transition to Zion's speech being embedded in the overwhelming dominance of the divine voice, and the re-positioning of the rhetorical questions into the divine voice, cohere with Second Isaiah's poetic style as described above.[20] In addition, the imagery itself, with which the divine voice answers Zion's complaint, constitutes a dramatic poetic counterpoint to the book of Lamentations.[21]

Linafelt (2000a: 18) argues that Zion's children and particularly their survival are central and essential to Lamentations' concerns. He defends this claim with particular reference to chs. 1 and 2. Second Isaiah employs the imagery of Zion's children returning to her as one mode of leading its exilic audience to see themselves as a part of the divinely provided answer to Zion's complaint.[22] Within this overwhelmingly positive imagery of return and restoration in the guise of the exiles as personified Zion's children, lurks darker imagery that Second Isaiah also takes up and re-deploys. One of the ways in which Second Isaiah does this is by redirecting the image of maternal neglect to show that Yhwh is more compassionate than any human mother and to liken Zion to mothers who are plagued by forgetfulness and cruelty.[23]

The children of Zion in ch. 2 are not simply victims of Jerusalem's siege; they are victims of their mothers' victimization as well. They illustrate the loss of basic humanity that attends the siege, a loss in which the nurturers become predators. The Lamenter deploys powerful poetic tools, layering irony and wordplay to achieve maximum emotional impact.

---

19. Tiemeyer (2007: 375) also treats Zion's complaint in 49:14 as a quotation of Lam. 5:20.

20. Linafelt (2000a: 74) notes regarding the rhetorical question: "It is one of the poet's [Second Isaiah's] favorite literary techniques," and he observes that the poet gives the "power of a rhetorical question" to the divine voice here.

21. See further Tull Willey (1997: 190–1) on the ways the words about abandonment are "recontextualized" and "recast" in Second Isaiah.

22. See further discussion of this point in Heffelfinger 2011: 238. See also Linafelt (1995: 56), who claims "that Isaiah 49:14-26 is in fact a direct answer to Lamentations."

23. Regarding Isa. 49:15, Linafelt (2000a: 75) comments that "the poet chooses here the one metaphor for YHWH that can begin to answer the rhetoric of Lamentations: YHWH as a mother who also laments and hopes for the return of her children."

Visceral images deployed in Lamentations 2 and 4 seem to be the source of the "nursing mother" imagery that Second Isaiah employs to give voice to Yhwh's offer of comfort, an offer that carries a sting of accusation within it.[24] That is, the choice of nursing mother imagery to express divine fidelity is not random, nor is it purely motivated by the emotional freight of such tender imagery, though that freight is considerable. Rather, it is taken from the source of the complaint itself, and is transformed in reply into a complex iteration of overwhelming tenderness, restive aggravation, and persistent attentiveness.

In 2:20, the lamenting voice, apparently Zion's, responding to the imperative to cry out on behalf of her children, says

> Look, O Yhwh, and see to whom you have dealt harshly.
> Should women eat their fruit, children they have nurtured?
> Should priest and prophet be killed in the place of the Lord?

The word choice, "to whom you have dealt harshly" (עוללת), carries its own violent associations. The verb appears, for example, in Exod. 10:2 for God's harsh treatment of the Egyptians, and in Judg. 19:25 it is one of the verbs for the rape of a woman who dies as a result of her injuries. Lamentations develops this emotionally charged language, further deploying it ironically. As Dobbs-Allsopp (2002: 99) notes, "the poet matches the violence (ʽôlaltā 'you have acted violently,' 2:20a) and the victims of the violence, the children (ʽôlālayik, 2:19c; ʽōlălê, 2:20b) by a horrific pun." This juxtaposition of the violence and its victims underscores the incongruity of the world the poet evokes. It is a "possible world" in which reality has been perverted.[25] Employing the same poetic medium and producing the same effect, the second colon of this tricolon employs the rare form טפחים to elaborate the reference to children, and

---

24. Tull Willey (1997: 191) references Lam. 2:20 in connection with the divine response to Zion's complaint in Isa. 49. She helpfully comments, "Without more linguistic clues, it is not clear that cannibalism is the form of forgetting that is being recalled in this verse, nor that mention in Lamentations of this atrocity is being directly echoed." However, the nursing references, as discussed below, do at least present such a possibility. See also Linafelt (2000a: 75) on the possible connection between "even these" and Lam. 2:20. Additionally, Tull Willey (1997: 162–5) discusses "a high linguistic correspondence…between [Lam. 4] and the section concerning Zion's children in Isa 51:17-23" (1997: 126). That Second Isaiah appears to allude to Lam. 4 elsewhere, to my mind, supports the probability that Isa. 49 alludes to Lam. 4 by demonstrating that the text in question was known.

25. Ricoeur (2000: 92) notes that "meaning is the projection of a possible and inhabitable world."

the form reappears at the end of v. 22 (Dobbs-Allsopp 2002: 101). The word has been widely taken to refer to "child rearing," based on its contextual connection with children (e.g., Hillers 1992: 102). However, the word intersects with the language of the passage in at least two directions. It points backwards to the reference to the women devouring their fruit (i.e., their children) by punning "on the similar sounding...word for 'apple' (*tappûaḥ*; *tappûḥîm*...)" (Dobbs-Allsopp 2002: 15). It also points forward to the next poetic line in which the voice accuses Yhwh of "slaughtering" (טבחת) the people.²⁶ As Berlin (2002: 76) notes, "here it is not meat that is slaughtered, but people who are 'sacrificed' on the festival day." Each of these puns underscores the gruesome "reversal of the natural order in which women feed their children" and in which Yhwh's worshippers assemble to offer sacrifice (Berlin 2002: 75). As we will see, Second Isaiah's response to Lamentations' complaint overturns the upturned world, a poetic re-turning presented through juxtaposition of imageries and emotionally charged expressions.

Lamentations 4 adds to the picture of a desolate city, in which desperate mothers are transformed from those who give and nourish life into scavengers and cannibals. The hunger and thirst of Zion's inhabitants is a persistent theme in the book of Lamentations (1:11, 19; 2:12, 19; 4:4, 9; 5:4, 9, 10), and its full and final overturning is perhaps one reason that Isa. 55 presents restoration through abundance of water, wine, milk, and bread (Isa. 55:1-2). In a poignant presentation of this image, Lam. 4:4 describes the plight of the most vulnerable residents of the city:

> The tongue of the nursling sticks to his palate with thirst,
> children ask for a piece of bread, there is nothing for them.

The poetry underscores the tragedy of the children's plight. Dobbs-Allsopp (2002: 131) points out that the words translated "bread" and "for them," "assonate and alliterate (*leḥem/lāhem*), emphasizing that the children receive 'nothing' instead of the 'food' requested."

The language for children here echoes that of Lam. 2:20 where there is a similar wordplay as noted above. However, the children's plight is not just that nothing is given them, but that their mothers compare unfavorably to scavenger animals, not offering to nurse their young (Lam. 4:3). Indeed, the comparison with the scavenging jackal is heavily ironic. In the upturned world of fallen Jerusalem, the jackals, "carrion eaters who haunt deserted ruins," apparently eat plenty and have enough to

---

26. Berlin (2002: 76) notes the connection with טפחים calling it "wordplay." See also Dobbs-Allsopp 2002: 101.

nurse their young, while Judah's human mothers either lack milk through starvation, or lack the ability to care for their offspring (Hillers 1992: 146; Berlin 2002: 106).

In a third example of this poetry's depiction of the cruel impact of siege on mothers and their vulnerable children, Lam. 4:10 again employs heavily ironic wordplay, this time returning to the theme of mothers cannibalistically consuming their own children. The ironic language appears in the use of the adjective "compassionate" (רחמניות) for the women of this line. Clearly compassion has little to do with "boil[ing]" one's young, and the painful irony is further underscored by the sound play between this adjective and the noun "womb" (רחם) (Berlin 2002: 109). The shared root word implies that motherliness is somehow inherently connected to compassion, while the depiction of these women violates both the reader's expectations of motherhood and of compassion.[27]

As we have seen, the motif of nursing mothers and their children is a particularly dark set of images in the book of Lamentations. These poetic lines create shock and horror in their reader and seem designed to induce a compassionate response on the part of the hearer and particularly from the one to whom the cry is addressed, Yhwh. So, when Yhwh responds to Zion's complaint in Isa. 49:14-26, it is no surprise that these images appear. However, as we will see, awareness of their source in Lamentations helps the reader to hear both the immense comfort and righting of the overturned reality of the siege, but also the profound disquiet that accompanies the offer of comfort for Zion. Additionally, the poetic mode by which the divine voice responds shares techniques with Lamentations' complaint. Juxtaposition, wordplay, rhetorical questions, and emotionally charged imagery, along with the reversal of the trope of voicing, combine to produce poetry that is not only responsive to the content of Zion's complaint, but offered on its poetic and emotional terms as well.

Redeployment of the Nursing Mother Image in Second Isaiah

In response to the embedded, cited speech of Zion, echoing the words of Lamentations' conclusion, the divine voice explicitly introduces the nursing mother image.

---

27. Trible (1978: 33) discusses the relationship of the adjective "compassion" and the noun "womb" within Hebrew semantics as a metaphor that moves "from a physical organ of the female body to a psychic mode of being.... [T]his metaphor suggests the meaning of love as selfless participation in life."

> Can a woman forget her nursling,
> A mother the baby of her belly? (Isa. 49:15)

As is widely recognized, the obvious implied answer is "no."[28] The rhetorical question is structured in such a way as to underscore the incongruity of motherhood and forgetfulness. The poetic form of the line expresses this point well. The parallelism of the lines develops in the direction of explicit recognition of the child through expansion. The second colon leaves the verb "forget" gapped, expanding the reference to the child and explicitly linking the child to its mother. The heavily alliterated phrase "baby of her belly" (בן־בטנה), connects the child to its mother's body from whence it came. Also in this colon the general word for woman (אשה) of the first colon is particularized, employing a form of the word used in Lam. 4:10 (מרחם). There it ironically problematizes the connection between motherhood, wombed-ness, and compassion.[29] Here, in the process of presenting motherly forgetfulness of a nursling as unthinkable through the rhetorical question, the divine voice implicitly cites Lamentations' testimony that motherly/compassionate (רחמניות) women have "cooked" their own children, a profound form of parental forgetfulness that heavily tinges the response of comforting divine memory with stinging accusation. The unfavorable comparison with scavenging carrion-eaters from Lam. 4:3 may also be subtly at play. Certainly, the image of a mother and her nursing child in a context that has already referenced Lamentations draws the other references to breastfeeding in Lamentations to mind. In Lam. 4:3 "even jackals" (גם־תנים) offer to feed their young, while the "daughter of my people" does not.[30] The "even these" (גם־אלה) who may forget according to the divine voice (Isa. 49:15) faintly echoes that phrasing and calls to mind that it is not so terribly unheard of in the traditions Second Isaiah knows for mothers to neglect to feed their young, and even to feed upon them instead (Lam. 4:3-4, 10).[31] Thus, when later in the poem Zion appears to have forgotten her children, "who bore these for me…and these (מי ילד־לי את־אלה…ואלה), who raised them" (Isa. 49:21), the reader should not be entirely surprised. The "love

---

28. As Seitz (2001: 431) puts it, "Mothers are not given to forgetting their children." Roberts (2003: 59) underscores the biological imperative of remembering one's children, particularly if the reference is to a nursing child.

29. On the meaning of רחם, see further Trible 1978: 33.

30. I am reading the Qěrê: "jackals" rather than "sea monster" following Berlin 2002: 101.

31. Linafelt (2000a: 75) notes: "The acknowledgement that 'even these may forget' is perhaps an allusion to Lamentations 2:20."

like a nursing mother" metaphor is deployed to underscore the incomprehensibly surpassing level of steadfast commitment being expressed by the divine voice, as many have noted.[32] However, it is also deployed in a way that critiques the motherhood of Zion. Zion, who in Lamentations stood by synecdoche for the experience of the women of Jerusalem, now has the charges of her own complaint levelled against her. She is one who has forgotten. In re-deploying this imagery, Second Isaiah attempts to re-deploy his audience's allegiance, from Zion who could and apparently did forget her children, to Yhwh, accused of such forgetfulness, but expressing a fidelity beyond that of human mothers.[33]

The nursing mother imagery continues in the depiction of restoration, in which Yhwh presents "wet-nurses" for the people within the metaphorical world of the poetry. Here Zion, once "princess in the provinces" (Lam. 1:1), is supplanted by "kings" and "princesses" (Isa. 49:22-23), who "bring your sons in a bosom" and serve as "your nursemaids." The pair of bicola is clearly linked by parallelism.

> And I will bring your sons in a bosom,
> and your daughters upon shoulders will be carried.
> And kings will be your keepers,
> and princesses your nursemaids.

The patterning of these lines conveys restoration's fullness. Both male and female children will be brought, each time with reference to a part of the carrier's body (v. 22). In like fashion, both male and female regal figures will be employed for this purpose (v. 23). The connections to breastfeeding frame the pair of lines. The participle used for "nursemaids" (מיניקתיך) echoes Lamentations' complaint that "the tongue of the nursling (יונק) sticks to his palate" (Lam. 4:4), and its notice that the jackals "suckle" (היניקו) their young (Lam. 4:3).

Finally, connection to this alarming set of images for maternal behavior during the siege of Jerusalem may help to explain the particularly violent depiction of Yhwh's outpouring of wrath upon Zion's enemies in the concluding lines of this passage.[34] In v. 26 the divine voice proclaims:

> I will make your oppressors eat their own flesh,
> and they will drink their own blood like new wine.

---

32. E.g., Blocher 2002: 6; Roberts 2003: 59.
33. See Heffelfinger 2011: 235.
34. Tull Willey (1997: 191) notes the presence of this line as relevant.

The physical impossibility of such self-cannibalism is perhaps a means of underscoring the poetry's point (Heffelfinger 2011: 242). The incongruity, the overturned nature of Zion's world in Lamentations, is now to be visited upon her enemies.[35] More than that, Zion's connection of a woman's children with her own body, "their own fruit" (Lam. 2:20), is an extremity of the horrors of cannibalism in the siege, just as self-consumption turns that extremity upon those who afflicted Zion.[36] Just as sound play poetically develops the horror and incongruity of Zion's affliction, so also sound play underscores its reversal and re-deployment in Yhwh's response. The "oppressors" (מוניך) who are to "eat their own flesh" (בשרם) resonate through sound play with the "suckling children" (יונק) (Lam. 4:4) and the reference to the children Zion's women "boiled" (בשלו) in the "breaking" (בשבר) of the people (Lam. 4:10). The horror continues, but now it is turned around again, this time by Yhwh's "hand" (Isa. 49:22).[37]

Conclusion

This essay has treated one example of the ways in which Second Isaiah's poetry takes up and re-deploys the images of Lamentations for its rhetorical purposes. That example fits within Second Isaiah's larger structural and poetic response to Lamentations, which overcomes divine silence with a cohesion deployed largely through the presence of the divine voice. Second Isaiah also utilizes poetically parallel modes of engaging audience emotion through sound play, irony, and parallelism to achieve appropriately freighted lines which convey an alternative message to that of lament.[38] Bearing in mind the poetic form and mode of response, study of Second Isaiah's re-deployment of Lamentations' images presents itself as a valuable resource in the interpretation of Second Isaiah.

---

35. Linafelt (2000a: 78) reads this line as an indication that "The reversal of Zion's fortunes is complete."

36. Linafelt (2000a: 78) reads the reference to consumption of the enemies "own flesh" here as "offspring," noting "this same trope of the horrors of a besieged city was used in the book of Lamentations."

37. Berlin (2002: 109) notes an "ironic play on words" within Lamentations' own use of these terms, highlighting that "*šeber* also means 'food/grain provisions.'"

38. As Linafelt (2000a: 63) puts it, "To imagine a healing, a restoration, that is rooted in the rhetoric of destruction found in Lamentations is to imagine a rhetoric of survival that matches it in intensity. The poetry of Second Isaiah takes for itself exactly this task."

Chapter 7

THE AFFLICTED MAN IN LAMENTATIONS 3 AS COMRADE TO JEREMIAH

Christl M. Maier

As many scholars have observed, Lam. 3 sticks out among the dirges in the book with regard to form, speaker, and contents. First of all, ch. 3 provides a complex acrostic form: three successive short lines beginning with the same letter of the alphabet, many of which display the limping *qinah* meter, create "a staccato effect" (Middlemas 2006: 505). As a counterweight to this rigid structuring, some keywords and themes run across the alphabetical boundaries and thus keep the poem moving forward (cf. Berlin 2002: 85). Given this highly stylized form, the chapter is likely a literary unit written by a single hand (Bezzel 2011: 256). Whereas in Lam. 1–2 the voice of the poet can be easily distinguished from the utterances of Daughter Zion and Lam. 4–5 mostly present a plural voice, in Lam. 3 three voices alternate. As Claus Westermann (1990: 142) argues, the single voice of a male figure (גֶּבֶר, v. 1) frames (vv. 1-24 and 48-66) an impersonal reflection on the human condition (vv. 25-39) and a song of repentance in plural voice (vv. 40-47). Contrary to the bold laments of Daughter Zion and her accusations against God in Lam. 1–2, the speaker in Lam. 3 presents himself in self-abasement and withholds the identity of his persecutor. With regard to contents, Lam. 1 and 5 abound in describing the destruction of temple and city, Lam. 2 and 4 focus on God's wrath and the people's sin, while Lam. 3 depicts the emotional response of this single male figure. I take these different speakers in Lamentations as a literary device to present contesting voices that differ in perspective and theological reasoning and thus present Lamentations as a dialogic text (cf. Boase 2006: 223).

In terms of form, speaker, and topics, Lam. 3 is the center of the book of Lamentations. As Tod Linafelt (2000a: 5–13) has demonstrated, this structural centrality has been exploited by many, especially

Christian interpreters, to emphasize penitence and self-abasement as valuable human reactions to disaster. Yet, there are more ambiguities and differing perspectives within Lam. 3 and the rest of the book that prohibit foregrounding only one theological message (cf. O'Connor 2002: 44–5; Thomas 2013b: 247–8; Bier 2014). While I take Lam. 3 as the last editorial statement in the book's evolvement, it is, in my view, only one among several perspectives on Jerusalem's demise, human suffering, and the relationship to God.

Intertextuality is a wide topic that is variably defined and situated. In this essay, I refer to a narrow understanding of intertextuality as inner-biblical allusion or exegesis as discussed by Benjamin Sommer (1998: 8–31). In an attempt to reexamine suggested readings of Lam. 3 in light of other texts, I will distinguish different degrees of literary identifiable links on the basis of vocabulary, phrases, and motifs. Using this classification, I will explore the significant relations of Lam. 3 to three different textual traditions that have been proposed as intertexts, namely Jeremiah (Bezzel 2011), Job (Berlin 2002), and the servant songs in Second Isaiah (Tull Willey 1997; Middlemas 2006). As I will demonstrate, textually discernible links to the figure of Jeremiah are the strongest, which offers a reason for the widespread reception of this connection since antiquity. By way of conclusion, I will discuss the function of the literary figure in Lam. 3 for the entire book and similar personifications.

The Situation Described in Lamentations 3 and the Identity of the Speaker

As the structure of Lam. 3 is disputed, some reasoning for my delineation into four sections (vv. 1-24, 25-39, 40-47, and 48-66) is necessary. This structuring is based on verbal forms, suffixes, and pronouns as signs of relations. In vv. 1-21 the speaker describes his own dire situation caused by an unnamed "he" whose acts are reported in third person singular verbs. The unexpected turn to God's acts of faithfulness in v. 22, underlined by reference to God (אֱמוּנָתֶךָ, v. 23), still belongs to this section, as both vv. 20 and 24 refer to the speaker's inner self (נַפְשִׁי). In the Masoretic text (MT), there is a reference to God in v. 19 by an imperative masculine singular (זְכָר־עָנְיִי, "remember my affliction"), yet due to the following words, the form may alternatively be read as an infinitive; the Old Greek reads a first person singular (see Koenen 2015: 192). Moreover, in v. 22 MT has a first person plural verb (כִּי לֹא־תָמְנוּ, "that we are not consumed"). The lack of vv. 22-24 in the original Greek version is possibly due to *aberratio oculi* (cf. עַל־כֵּן אוֹחִיל in vv. 21, 24 and Bezzel 2011: 259 n. 30).

This ambiguity about speaker and addressee in vv. 17-21 may be intentional and, according to Beat Weber (2000: 114–15), indicates a transition in the poem's atmosphere.

The next section, vv. 25-39, does not contain first and second person forms, but offers a generalizing reflection about human fate and God's actions, which rehearses well-known statements about the divine–human relationship and thus lacks the concreteness of the framing laments. Therefore, in my view, it represents a different voice. The third section in vv. 40-47 uses first person plural forms and a direct address to God, thus representing a communal prayer of repentance. In the final section (vv. 48-66), the first speaker resumes the lament, which turns into a prayer to God starting in v. 55.

The speaker in Lam. 3:1-24, 48-66 introduces himself as a man (גֶּבֶר) with a specific experience: "I am the man who has seen affliction by the rod of his[1] wrath" (Lam. 3:1). The Hebrew root גבר connotes dominance and strength (cf. Lam. 1:16 and Kosmala 1973: 902), and the noun גֶּבֶר most often signifies an adult, virile man. Especially in psalms and the book of Job, גֶּבֶר denotes a god-fearing male person who trusts in God and follows divine orders (Pss. 34:9; 40:5; 94:12; Job 3:23; 14:14; 16:21, cf. Jer. 17:7 and Kosmala 1973: 915–18).

The speaker in Lam. 3 appears as a formerly strong man who now is crushed and distressed. Such reversal of fortune has a motif parallel in Jerusalem's fate as a former mother who has become a lonely widow lamenting her perishing children (Lam. 1:1-5). The afflicted man in Lam. 3 describes an assault on his body by an unnamed adversary, which resembles the attack on Daughter Zion's body in Lam. 1–2 (Maier 2008a). His flesh and skin are worn out, his bones broken (v. 4), and his body is smashed face down in the dust so that his teeth touch the gravel (v. 16). Lamentations 3:10-13 even envision deadly situations, with the body torn apart by a wild beast or struck down by the arrow of a hunter. These attacks are portrayed as physically brutal and violent.

In Lam. 3:1-20, the male figure laments a situation that oscillates between being led down an insecure road and imprisonment. The path is dark (v. 2), blocked (vv. 7, 9), crooked (v. 9), distorted (v. 11), and leads to nowhere. His detention is invoked by the verbs "to wall in" (גדר, vv. 7, 9), "to encircle" (נקף, v. 5), and by the nouns "dark places" (v. 6) and "chains" (v. 7). His food is bitter and tastes like wormwood (v. 15). The images of the rod (v. 1), the path (vv. 2, 9, 11), the bear and lion waiting for prey

---

1. Most modern translations insert "God" here, but the Hebrew only uses a suffix of the third person masculine singular. All translations of biblical verses are mine unless otherwise noted.

(v. 10), and the eating of bitter herbs (v. 15) invoke the motif of shepherd and flock in reversed form (Hillers 1992: 124). The body portrayed here is being imprisoned in a space that neither provides appropriate habitation nor proper food, a place that is life-threatening. The speaker sees no chance to escape and describes himself as downcast, miserable, and homeless (vv. 18-19). The recurrent motifs of capture and torture in vv. 1-20 describe the multiple terrors of war and deportation with a focus on incarceration rather than a "forced march into exile" (Berlin 2002: 86).

Although the afflicted man withholds the name of his adversary, its resemblance to the divine enemy in Zion's speech (Lam. 1–2) insinuates that the bad shepherd, who leads the man onto a dark and blocked road, or the hunter, who seeks his life, may be YHWH himself (cf. Berges 2000: 13). YHWH is mentioned in v. 18 only in passing, yet twice in vv. 22, 24, and more often from v. 25 onwards. The plural voice in vv. 40-47 directly addresses God as the one who intentionally chastised the community, and so explicitly confirms YHWH's agency as perpetrator. Thus, the initial ambiguity about the adversary's identity is resolved in the passages that follow the man's first words. In the second part of his speech, however, the afflicted man no longer mourns his own loss but the ruin of his people (v. 48). He names human adversaries who seek his life (vv. 52-53, 60-63) and asks YHWH to take revenge on these (vv. 64-66).

The often-discussed question of the speaker's identity has found many answers ranging from historical persons, like King Zedekiah or the prophet Jeremiah, to literary figures, like Job, the Suffering Servant in Second Isaiah, or "Everyman" (Hillers 1992; Dobbs-Allsopp 2002; cf. the overviews in Thomas 2013b: 172–3 and Koenen 2015: 214–21). The first part of the man's speech in Lam. 3:1-24 depicts the imprisonment of an individual in an unknown space, and thus is related to the situation after Jerusalem's fall conveyed in Lam. 1–2. The second part in Lam. 3:48-66, however, describes a rather unspecific situation of persecution and, like many psalms of individual lament, different situations may be inferred. These traits of "everyman" are emphasized in the reflection about decent human behavior in Lam. 3:25-39. This didactic part reasons what is good for the man and that he should not complain about the punishment of his sins (cf. גֶּבֶר in 3:27, 39). Thus, the afflicted man becomes a representative of all humans. However, the tension between lamenting one's suffering and silent endurance of one's fate is not resolved, as both the second part of the man's speech and the communal voice, which designates YHWH as angry and relentless, demonstrate. Thus, "the hope is neither accepted by the community nor maintained by the man, thus validating the ongoing suffering of individual and community alike" (Boase 2006: 231).

Read as a literary unit, Lam. 3 seems to portray a certain character rather than an individual person: The afflicted man appears as a personified role model like Job, Lady Wisdom, or the Suffering Servant, which all surface in post-exilic texts (cf. Berges 2000: 7). In other words, the chapter presents a literary male figure that can be interpreted both individually and collectively, depending on which traits the interpreter foregrounds. This observation concurs with Thomas's view of Lam. 3 as an "open" text, the poetry of which "opens up interpretative horizons for the reader" (2013b: 211).

Intertextual Links between Lamentations 3 and Jeremiah

In the following exploration of literary identifiable links I will distinguish between citation, allusion, motif parallel, and similar terminology in order to assess the degree of correspondence between texts—although I am aware of possible overlaps. The following definitions are meant to be descriptive working tools that do not imply a certain direction of dependency. Any diachronic relation is hard to establish and needs further reasoning with regard to the entire text of Lam. 3. Evaluating a link as citation requires a strict conformity of phrase (i.e., the use of the same verbal form, subject and/or object, plus an exclusive connection between two texts). An allusion can be detected in the use of the same verb, not necessarily of the same form, and another matching subject or object as well as a similar context. The third category, a motif parallel, does not require the same Hebrew wording but sameness of an idea or perspective on a given item and a certain keyword that would mark the connection. Finally, the use of similar terminology in a different context, in my view, does not comprise an identifiable intertextual link between two specific texts but simply refers to a shared topic or tradition.

Regarding the twofold speech of the afflicted man in Lam. 3:1-24, 49-66 the strongest intertextual links exist with the book of Jeremiah, and especially the figure of Jeremiah. This assessment is based on one citation, one allusion, and at least four motif parallels. I will start with the strongest links and proceed to the lesser ones.

The lament in Lam. 3:14 uses the same wording as Jer. 20:7, a verse in Jeremiah's last confession, and thus can be classified as a citation:

Lam. 3:14

הָיִיתִי שְּׂחֹק לְכָל־עַמִּי נְגִינָתָם כָּל־הַיּוֹם

I have become a laughingstock for all my people, their taunt-song all day long.

Jer. 20:7b

הָיִיתִי לִשְׂחוֹק כָּל־הַיּוֹם

I have become a laughingstock all day long.

Another strong link appears in Lam. 3:48 (cf. the parallel in Lam. 2:11), which alludes to several verses in the book of Jeremiah:

Lam. 3:48

פַּלְגֵי־מַיִם תֵּרַד עֵינִי עַל־שֶׁבֶר בַּת־עַמִּי׃

My eye runs down (with) rivers of water for the collapse of my dear[2] people.

Jer. 8:21, 23

עַל־שֶׁבֶר בַּת־עַמִּי הָשְׁבָּרְתִּי קָדַרְתִּי שַׁמָּה הֶחֱזִקָתְנִי
מִי־יִתֵּן רֹאשִׁי מַיִם וְעֵינִי מְקוֹר דִּמְעָה וְאֶבְכֶּה יוֹמָם וָלַיְלָה אֵת חַלְלֵי בַת־עַמִּי׃

[21] For the collapse of my dear people I have collapsed, I mourn, and dismay has taken hold of me.
[23] O that my head were water, and my eye a fountain of tears, so that I might weep day and night for the slain of my dear people!

Jer. 14:17

וְאָמַרְתָּ אֲלֵיהֶם אֶת־הַדָּבָר הַזֶּה תֵּרַדְנָה עֵינַי דִּמְעָה לַיְלָה וְיוֹמָם
וְאַל־תִּדְמֶינָה כִּי שֶׁבֶר גָּדוֹל נִשְׁבְּרָה בְּתוּלַת בַּת־עַמִּי מַכָּה נַחְלָה מְאֹד׃

You shall say to them this word: Let my eyes run down (with) tears night and day
and let them not cease, for the virgin, my dear people, has collapsed with a crushing blow, a very grievous wound.

The expression שֶׁבֶר בַּת־עַמִּי, "collapse of my dear people," occurs exclusively in Jer. 8:11, 21 and Lam. 2:11; 3:48; 4:10. The speaker of the lament in Jer. 8:18–9:1 is not identified, and thus the text is open for different identifications including Daughter Zion, Jeremiah, and God (cf. O'Connor 2011: 61–3). Beyond these verses, the motif of unceasing tears concerning the people's ruin is also used in the call to summon the women who sing dirges (Jer. 9:17) and in YHWH's announcement that he will weep bitterly when his flock is taken captive (Jer. 13:17). Thus, Lam. 3:48 alludes to the portrayals of both Jeremiah and God as lamenting over the devastated people of Judah.

2. Literally "the daughter of my people"; the title "daughter" for the people creates a metaphor that connotes the people's close relation to the speaker in the role of the "father" who would protect the "daughter." The expression occurs only in Jeremiah, Lamentations, and once in Isa. 22:4.

Another allusion that links the fates of the afflicted man and Jeremiah can be detected in Lam. 3:27-28, which is part of the general reflection about the human condition.

Lam. 3:27-28

טוֹב לַגֶּבֶר כִּי־יִשָּׂא עֹל בִּנְעוּרָיו׃
יֵשֵׁב בָּדָד וְיִדֹּם כִּי נָטַל עָלָיו׃

²⁷ It is good for a man to bear the yoke in his youth.
²⁸ He should sit alone³ and be still, for he laid it upon him.

In Jer. 15:17, the prophet laments "under your hand I sat alone (בָּדָד יָשַׁבְתִּי), for you had filled me with indignation." Thus, both figures are portrayed as isolated and lonely due to God's will. The motif of bearing the yoke⁴ evokes the story of Jeremiah's symbolic action with the yoke that signifies the submission under Babylon (Jer. 27–28). When Jeremiah's opponent Hananiah breaks the wooden yoke bar on his neck, Jeremiah goes his way without a word (Jer. 28:10-11).

Additionally, the similarity between the afflicted man in Lam. 3 and Jeremiah is reinforced by several motif parallels that use a key word or phrase. The strongest one is the notion of plotting adversaries by use of the key word מַחְשְׁבֹתָם, "plots, evil plans." While the afflicted man twice affirms that God has seen the plots of his enemies (Lam. 3:60, 61), the prophet informs God twice that his adversaries contrive plots against him (Jer. 11:19; 18:18).

A second motif is being thrown into the pit (keyword בּוֹר, "pit, cistern"); in the words of the afflicted man in Lam. 3:53-55: "They flung me alive into a pit and hurled stones on me; water closed over my head; I said, 'I am lost.' I called on your name, YHWH, from the depths of the pit." Jeremiah 38:1-13 narrates a similar story about Jeremiah: some officials of King Zedekiah throw him into an empty cistern so that he sinks into the mud and fears to die. Later, however, Jeremiah is rescued by the Cushite Ebed-Melech.

The third corresponding motif, the depiction of YHWH defending the afflicted, is based on the legal term רִיב, "to go to court, to defend." While the afflicted man asks God to take up his cause (Lam. 3:58), the lamenting Jeremiah hands his case over to YHWH (Jer. 11:20; 20:12) and names himself a man of strife (אִישׁ רִיב, Jer. 15:10).

---

3. The phrase "to sit alone" also describes the situation of Jerusalem (Lam. 1:1) and Hazor (Jer. 49:31).

4. Since different terms are used, the correspondence is classified here as a motif, not as an allusion.

Finally, a fourth motif links the fate of the afflicted man with the one of the people in the book of Jeremiah. In Lam. 3:15, the man laments: "He has filled me with bitterness, he has sated me with wormwood (לַעֲנָה)." In Lam. 3:19 he names his affliction and homelessness "wormwood and poison" (לַעֲנָה וָרֹאשׁ). In Jer. 9:14, YHWH announces that he will feed the people with wormwood, and give them poisonous water to drink.[5] In Jer. 23:15, the same announcement is addressed to the prophets who neglect God's words.

In sum, these intertextual links depict the afflicted man as a comrade to Jeremiah as portrayed in the story of Jer. 38, in lament passages, and in the confessions. Both figures appear as once strong and confident but then miserable and injured, persecuted by fellow humans, and struggling with God. Both Lam. 3 and the confessions in Jeremiah include statements of trust in God and perseverance, and in the end both speakers ask God to take revenge on their opponents (Lam. 3:64-66; Jer. 11:20; 15:15; 17:18; 20:12). Therefore, an intertextual reading that sees the afflicted man as an impersonation of the troubled Jeremiah figure has a strong literary verifiable basis in the text of Lam. 3. Additionally, these links support the traditional reception of Lamentations as composed by the prophet Jeremiah, which is attested in the book's Greek translation (LamLXX 1:1). As Antje Labahn (2005) demonstrates, the Greek text of Lam. 3:1-21 emphasizes the similarities with the Jeremiah figure by introducing further intertextual links and dramatizing the metaphors. If one looks for the direction of dependency, I would concur with Hannes Bezzel (2011: 264–5) that Lam. 3 is the receiving text, because it draws from different Jeremiah passages. Moreover, Lam. 3 includes further intertextual links to both Job and the Suffering Servant in Isaiah 50, although the latter ones are less strong than those to Jeremiah.

Intertextual Links to Job

In her Lamentations commentary, Adele Berlin (2002: 84–5) interprets the speaker of Lam. 3 as "the personified voice of the exile," a counterpart to the voice of female Zion and a "Job-like figure,…struggling to make sense of the awful tragedy that has befallen him." In order to substantiate the connection to Job, she lists several parallel motifs in both texts, among them being hunted by wild animals (Lam. 3:10; Job 10:16), targeted by God's arrows (Lam. 3:12; Job 16:12-13), cut off from access to God

---

5. This is not an allusion since the verbs are different in Lamentations and Jeremiah.

(Lam. 3:44; Job 3:23), and being sated with bitterness (Lam. 3:15; Job 9:18). While all these verses use different terminology, there are even two allusions that support Berlin's thesis.

Lam. 3:7

גָּדַר בַּעֲדִי וְלֹא אֵצֵא הִכְבִּיד נְחָשְׁתִּי

He has walled me in so that I cannot escape; he has weighed me down with bronze chains.

Lam. 3:9

גָּדַר דְּרָכַי בְּגָזִית נְתִיבֹתַי עִוָּה

He has walled in my ways with hewn stones, he has made my paths crooked.

Job 19:8

אָרְחִי גָדַר וְלֹא אֶעֱבוֹר וְעַל נְתִיבוֹתַי חֹשֶׁךְ יָשִׂים

He has walled in my trail so that I cannot pass, and he has set darkness upon my paths.

In Lam. 3:7, 9 the afflicted man feels encircled by God like Job. It is especially the experience that God is the speaker's enemy that links Lam. 3 to the Job tradition. This is underlined in Lam. 3:38, a verse on the general reflection about human destiny that shares a thought uttered by the Job figure:

Lam. 3:38

מִפִּי עֶלְיוֹן לֹא תֵצֵא הָרָעוֹת וְהַטּוֹב

Is it not from the mouth of the Most High that good and bad emerge?

Job 2:10

גַּם אֶת־הַטּוֹב נְקַבֵּל מֵאֵת הָאֱלֹהִים וְאֶת־הָרָע לֹא נְקַבֵּל

Shall we receive the good from God, and not receive the bad?

Although both lines only have the terms "the good" and "the bad" in common, while using different verbs, I consider their relation an allusion since the idea that humans accept both good and bad from God is exclusively used in these two verses and Job's answer is a highly memorable statement.

Interestingly, literary links between Job and Lam. 3 are stronger in the reflective passage (Lam. 3:25-39), which has already been deemed "sapiential" (Westermann 1990: 142; Boase 2006: 226–8). This general reflection on the human condition in Lam. 3 includes motif parallels to the arguments of Job's friends, e.g., the notion that it is good to bear chastisement from God (Lam. 3:25-27; Job 5:16-18) or that God would not pervert justice (Lam. 3:33-36; Job 8:3). In sum, it is not so much the lament part of Lam. 3 that offers literary identifiable links to the portrait of Job, but the reflection on the human condition. As readers perceive this connection, however, their overall impression is that the afflicted man in Lam. 3 is like Job, because he laments his fate (Lam. 3:1-21, 48-66) and still hopes for divine rescue (Lam. 3:22-24). A difference between these figures, however, remains with regard to the context of their portrayal. Whereas Job's calamity is individual and not explicitly tied to the fate of the people of Israel, the context of Lamentations renders the afflicted man a representative of the defeated Judeans who suffered from the national catastrophe of Jerusalem's fall by the Babylonians.

Intertextual Links to the Servant of YHWH in Second Isaiah

In her exploration of intertextuality in Second Isaiah, Patricia Tull Willey (1997: 216–17) argues that the servant songs in Isa. 50:4-11 and 52:13–53:12 draw from Lam. 3, "creating not a scribal exegesis from a manuscript, but an evocation of words and images remembered in association with the *geber* figure." While approving of the literary links noted by Tull Willey in general, Jill Middlemas pleads for the opposite direction of dependence, namely that "the characterisation in Lamentations iii has been informed by the figure of the suffering servant" (Middlemas 2006: 512).

Tull Willey (1997: 219) sees the closest connection in the reflection of Lam. 3:25-30, because this section contains hopeful statements and thus fits better to Second Isaiah's message of salvation. Her strongest argument is based on an allusion that interlinks the idea of "giving the cheek to the one who strikes."

Lam. 3:30

יִתֵּן לְמַכֵּהוּ לֶחִי

He shall give his cheek to the one who strikes him.

Isa. 50:6a

גֵּוִי נָתַתִּי לְמַכִּים וּלְחָיַי לְמֹרְטִים

I gave my back to those who struck me, and my cheeks to those who pulled out the beard.

Since the shared noun and participle is singular in Lam. 3:30 and plural in Isa. 50:6a, and the latter verse has two parallel sentences, this link is not a citation but an allusion, especially since the idea of voluntarily offering the cheek only appears in these two verses (cf. also Koenen 2013: 8).[6]

Tull Willey (1997: 217) detects another allusion in the verb מרה *qal*, "to be disobedient, rebellious," which is used only four times in the HB in first person perfect. The plural voice in Lam. 3:42 utters "we were rebellious" (מָרִינוּ)—comparable to Zion in Lam. 1:18, 20 (מָרִיתִי, "I was rebellious")—whereas the servant in Isa. 50:5 states the opposite "I was not rebellious" (לֹא מָרִיתִי). Compared to the first example, this allusion is rather weak. Moreover, it does not link the servant's words with the voice of the afflicted man but with the plural voice in Lam. 3. The other cases listed by Tull Willey are, in my view, only motif parallels, because they either describe quite different phenomena or employ rather common vocabulary.[7] As an example of the latter, I here comment on the use of the keywords קרב, "to come near," ריב, "to go to court, to defend," and מִשְׁפָּטִי, "my cause" in Lam. 3:57-59 and Isa. 50:8.

Lam. 3:57-59

קָרַבְתָּ בְּיוֹם אֶקְרָאֶךָּ אָמַרְתָּ אַל־תִּירָא׃
רַבְתָּ אֲדֹנָי רִיבֵי נַפְשִׁי גָּאַלְתָּ חַיָּי׃ [58]
רָאִיתָה יְהוָה עַוָּתָתִי שָׁפְטָה מִשְׁפָּטִי׃ [59]

[57] You came near the day I called you; you said, "Do not fear!"
[58] You took my case, my Lord, you redeemed my life.
[59] You saw the wrong done to me, YHWH; judge my cause.

Isa. 50:8

קָרוֹב מַצְדִּיקִי מִי־יָרִיב אִתִּי נַעַמְדָה יָּחַד מִי־בַעַל מִשְׁפָּטִי יִגַּשׁ אֵלָי׃

He who vindicates me is near. Who will go to court with me?
Let us stand up together. Who is the master of my cause? He shall approach me.

Although both passages employ the motif "God takes up the cause of the afflicted," the shared words are not specific enough to sustain an allusion between these two texts that readers would easily identify. Whereas in

---

6. There are more references to the action of striking somebody on the cheek, which seem to be shameful for the one who is beaten; cf. Ps. 3:8; Mic. 4:14.

7. Such as the terms "ear" and "listen" in Isa. 50:4, 5, 10 and Lam. 3:56 or the term "morning" in Isa. 50:4 and Lam. 3:23. The phrase "to go/lead into darkness and no light" in Isa. 50:10 and Lam. 3:2 uses different terms for darkness and light. Cf. Tull Willey 1997: 218–19.

Lam. 3:57-59 God is addressed in the role of both advocate and judge, the servant in Isa. 50:8 challenges his potential human opponents by relying on his divine advocate. Moreover, such juridical vocabulary is expected with regard to issues of judgment and vindication, as many similar verses demonstrate (cf., e.g., Pss. 9:5; 17:2; Isa. 49:4; Mic. 7:9). Thus, the intertextual links between the afflicted man and YHWH's servant are less strong than the ones to Jeremiah and even Job.

Tull Willey further argues (1997: 219–20) that the fourth servant song in Isa. 52:13–53:12 also draws terms and motifs from Lam. 3, although she concedes that these links are less obvious. In her reasoning, she refers to terms like נכה "strike," ענה pi. "afflict," דכא "crush," and נגזר "cut off" in both passages and to motifs that can be expected in a text about a person that is persecuted and vilified. In my view, the differences in the portraits of the two male figures outweigh the similarities. Whereas the afflicted man in Lam. 3 relates his suffering to a divine assault, has no specific commission, and still seeks God as his advocate, the Suffering Servant in Isa. 52–53 is granted a title and intimate relationship with God, suffers vicariously, and will be exalted in the end. Moreover, literarily detectable links connect Isa. 50:4-11 particularly to the sapiential reflection offered in Lam. 3:25-30, which evaluates the figure of the afflicted man and, as Middlemas (2006: 522) has rightly observed, even challenges the lament in foregrounding human sin and deserved punishment while pleading for silent submission in the face of tragedy. Therefore, I concur with Middlemas that Lam. 3 is the later text and its author different from the one who wrote the servant songs. When readers nevertheless see some common features in the afflicted man of Lam. 3 and YHWH's servant in Second Isaiah, this perception is based on rather common notions and the prominence of the Suffering Servant in Christian interpretation.

Conclusion

This reevaluation of literarily identifiable connections between the afflicted man in Lam. 3 and other suffering male figures discovered different degrees of intertextual links. It is no coincidence that the strongest links exist to the literary figure of the lamenting Jeremiah, especially since both the Jeremiah tradition and Lamentations focus on Jerusalem's violent destruction and the consequences for the Judean people and since both men are role models of individual suffering. The afflicted man can thus be called a comrade to Jeremiah, the persecuted prophet who is grief-stricken by the collapse of his dear people. The deplorable situation of both men is not resolved, and the man in Lam. 3:49-66 resumes his lament as does

Jeremiah in Jer. 20:14-18, a feature that provides both figures with a profound personality. These numerous links in the wording and imagery are the basis for a century-long tradition to see in Jeremiah the author of Lamentations.

In the context of the other songs of lament and protest in the book of Lamentations, however, Lam. 3 also offers some counter-arguments for how to react to the situation of distress and affliction, especially in the reflection on the human condition in Lam. 3:25-39 (cf. Middlemas 2006) and, to a lesser extent, in the communal prayer of repentance in Lam. 3:40-47. Based on these observations, it is highly probable that Lam. 3 is the latest text in the book and was placed in its middle to stress two ideas, namely that "God is good to those who trust in him and seek him" and that "it is good to wait quietly until rescue comes from God" (Lam. 3:25-26). Lamentations 3:25-39 evaluates the afflicted man who laments his fate and even sees God as his personal enemy—like Job—in sapiential terms, and thus renders the male figure a role model valid for every person who wrestles with God about any disturbing experience. This profiling of the afflicted man as "everyman" includes associations to other "afflicted men" like Job and the Suffering Servant. For ancient and modern readers, the afflicted man functions as a role model, like David in the psalms. They may see themselves in the tradition of all three of the great suffering men.

Yet, is this just another patriarchal image that takes man as representative for all humans? Or does the male voice also represent Daughter Zion, which now personifies the post-exilic community, as Berges (2000) argues? In my view, both the female collective and the male individual serve as representatives for both men and women, for all bodies injured in war and exile, for all minds afflicted by disturbing experience. The ways to pronounce such experience and to impersonate human–divine relations are different in antiquity and today. Yet, the figurations offered in Lamentations are so multi-layered and profound that modern readers may apply them to their own context and find even more intertexts.

Chapter 8

THE SOUND AND THE FURY: WOMEN AND SUFFERING IN EZEKIEL AND LAMENTATIONS

Amy Kalmanofsky

From Ezekiel to Lamentations

The HB is ripe for intertextual readings. Events are told and retold with new details and different characters as their focus;[1] texts quote other texts;[2] significant details from one story are found in another.[3] Intertextual readings most often are based on linguistic connections between texts. Using these connections, many scholars work to prove a direct relationship between texts in order to determine which text came first. Some scholars, like Carleen R. Mandolfo, create conversations among texts that are not clearly linguistically connected. In her book *Daughter Zion Talks Back to the Prophets: A Dialogic Theology of the Book of Lamentations* (2007b), Mandolfo places Lamentations in conversation with the prophetic books. She describes her methodology as "a type of intertextuality" that makes "connections between particular prophetic texts and Lamentations because in canonical and literary terms the texts themselves demand them" (10).[4]

Mandolfo offers an expansive model of intertextual interpretation that enables readers to bring texts together that are not intrinsically

---

1. E.g., the two creation narratives found in Gen. 1–2 and the wife–sister stories related in Gen. 12:10-20; 20; 26:6-11.
2. E.g., Isa. 40:6-8 offers a variation on Ps. 103:15-17.
3. Shared vocabulary connects the golden calf narrative in Exod. 32 to the flood narrative in Gen. 6–8.
4. Mandolfo's methodology is heavily influenced by the "dialogic philosophies" of Mikhail Bakhtin and Martin Buber (2007b: 1–3).

connected, in order to consider more broadly how different texts respond to similar historical realities and social trends. The books of Ezekiel and Lamentations are not usually read together. More often, ancient and contemporary scholars read Lamentations in relationship with the book of Jeremiah.[5] Daniel L. Smith-Christopher (2002: 75) makes a strong case for reading Ezekiel and Lamentations intertextually, since both books "claim to come directly from the experience of exile—one from Babylon and one back in Palestine." Both convey the trauma of communities "struggling with crises, personal and social, that include dealing with suddenly mobile identities and transnational culture and theology" (Smith-Christopher 2002: 76) For Smith-Christopher, Lamentations and Ezekiel preserve the "voices of traumatized communities" (76).

Lamentations was among the first biblical books to which scholars applied trauma theory as an interpretive lens. Scholars such as Tod Linafelt (2000a: 4) perceive Lamentations as "literature of survival," which "is more about the expression of suffering than the meaning behind it, more about the vicissitudes of *survival* than the abstractions of sin and guilt, and more about *protest* as a religious posture than capitulation or confession."[6]

David G. Garber argues that Ezekiel, like Lamentations, testifies to the trauma Israel experienced during exile. Garber (2014: 348) identifies a "commonality between trauma literatures," that is based not on structure, but rather on inception; trauma literature is "literature produced in the aftermath of a devastating or traumatic event that testifies to that event."

Although Garber does not identify common structural elements to trauma literature, it is interesting to observe that Ezekiel and Lamentations share a striking central feature. Both personify the community of Israel, Zion, as a suffering woman whose story conveys the drama and pain of Israel's experience leading up and in response to the Babylonian exile. The personification of Zion as a woman may be viewed as a convention reflecting the well-attested ancient phenomenon of personifying cities and lands as women (Maier 2008b: 60–74). Recently, feminist biblical scholars have looked beyond this convention to consider the rhetorical impact of the image, drawing attention to the ways in which it supports patriarchal assumptions and strategies within the biblical text.[7]

---

5. Berlin (2002: 30) observes: "The tradition linking Lamentations with Jeremiah is quite ancient and pervasive."

6. Scholars also examine Lamentations in the related context of the psychology of grief; see Reimer 1993; Joyce 1993.

7. See Van Dijk-Hemmes 1993; Shields 1998; Day 2000; Yee 2003: 111–34.

Mandolfo (2007b: 50–1) considers Ezekiel's portrayal of personified Zion to be "monologic to the extreme," presenting only the perspective that condemns Zion and justifies her punishment. Zion is silent and silenced in Ezekiel, unable to communicate her side of the story.[8] Through the prophet, God does all the talking in Ezekiel, accusing Zion of apostasy and infidelity.[9] According to Mandolfo, Lamentations resounds with Zion's voice and contains Zion's point of view. In Lamentations, Zion speaks back, challenging God and the prophets, and fighting for her life (Mandolfo 2007b: 83). Linafelt (2000a: 38) similarly suggests that Zion's first words in Lam. 1:9 initiate a transition in the text from dirge, or funeral song, to lament—a genre that Linafelt observes may respond to death, but whose "primary aim is life"; he writes:

> The scene of death implied by the dirge, already undercut by the presence of Zion, begins to open out toward life even more. Not only is the one who should be dead alive, but she is speaking, and speaking vigorously.

Mandolfo and Linafelt view Zion's presence and voice in Lamentations to be a form of protest. Mandolfo suggests that Zion protests her story and fate as told by the prophets. Linafelt (2000a: 50) asserts that Zion argues for her life and for the lives of her children before God. The silenced and condemned woman[10] lives and speaks in Lamentations. Like Mandolfo and Linafelt, I hear Zion shouting in Lamentations, and consider her first-person voice to be powerful. Like Mandolfo, I observe Zion's silence in Ezekiel. Yet, I offer in this essay a different interpretation of the transition from the silence of Ezekiel to the speech of Lamentations, and suggest viewing the Zion of Lamentations on a continuum with, as opposed to in tension with, the Zion of Ezekiel.

In my reading, the transition from the silence of Ezekiel to the sound and fury of Lamentations communicates personified Zion's experience of trauma, and indicates her healing from it. Ezekiel conveys the shocked silence experienced by Zion in the anticipation of the trauma of exile, or its immediate aftermath. In Lamentations, Zion finds her voice and is able to express her suffering. Like Linafelt, I consider the expression of Zion's suffering to be an embrace of life, which indicates a renewal of Zion's strength. Following Mandolfo's methodological example based on

---

8. Zion's shame silences her in Ezek. 16:62-63.
9. See Ezek. 16; 23. Mandolfo (2007b: 53) writes: "Ezekiel/YHWH tightly controls discourse from beginning to end."
10. Zion is condemned to death in Ezek. 16:38.

Bakhtin, I offer a dialogical reading. My analysis brings Ezek. 19 and 24 into conversation with Lam. 1 and 2, paying particular attention to how women represent and communicate suffering.

My goal is to present the silence conveyed by Ezekiel in these chapters not as an aggressive act of violence afflicted by a male prophet or God against a woman, but rather as first-stage response to trauma, in which Israel is at a loss for words. In this essay, I am not concerned with dating these texts, and making a text-critical argument. Rather, I suggest that Ezek. 19 and 24 precede Lam. 1 and 2 on an emotional continuum in which the community of Israel is coming to terms with the trauma of its exile. Although I argue that Ezek. 19 and 24 convey Israel's initial shocked and bleak response to exile, I also show how Ezek. 24:26-27 contains a glimmer of hope that may place these verses on the emotional continuum beside or after Lam. 1 and 2.[11]

From Silence to Tears: Ezekiel 19 and Lamentations 1 and 2

In her application of trauma theory to the book of Jeremiah, Kathleen M. O'Connor (2011: 3) writes about violence:

> It creates a kind of mental vacuum. It so overwhelms the capacities of victims to take in, that the violence cannot be absorbed as it is happening. Traumatic violence comes as a shocking blow, a terrifying disruption of normal mental processes, distorting reality, even as it becomes the only reality.

At first, traumatic violence shocks and wounds its victims who must respond to an incomprehensible and unfamiliar violent event.[12] Initially, the experience of this violence defies language (O'Connor 2011: 3). Yet, over time, traumatized individuals and communities find language to describe the violence that befell them. By recounting the trauma, they begin to integrate it into their lives and worldviews, as Garber (2015: 28) writes:

---

11. Emotional continuums are more variable and flexible than historical continuums, and are not tied neatly to historical events; as Garber (2015) observes: "While trauma may originate with particular and limited moments in history, the effects of trauma can last for years and have far-reaching implications."

12. The Greek word "trauma" means "wound" or "hurt."

While the initial experience is "missed", not fully integrated into the psyche of the victim, the experience perpetuates itself through recurrent manifestations of memory of the event. One way the survivor can testify to the experience is through literature—attempting to bear witness to the event through various literary forms.

I contend that Ezek. 19 and 24 convey an earlier stage in Israel's experience of the trauma of exile than do Lam. 1 and 2. Zion's silence in Ezekiel is the silence of a traumatized witness who has not yet integrated the event into her psyche. Zion's voice in Lamentations indicates that the community now is able to describe the trauma and to articulate its suffering. Judah has begun to integrate the trauma into its psyche, and to heal from it.[13]

Read in conversation with Lam. 1 and 2, Ezek. 19 illustrates this. Ezekiel 19 is framed as a dirge (קינה) over Israel's leaders, which connects it structurally with Lamentations.[14] Like Lamentations, Ezek. 19 begins with an interrogative exclamation,[15] proclaiming: "How like a lioness is your mother among the lions!"[16] The second half of the chapter compares this mother to a vine that is uprooted and cast into the wilderness. Commentators attempt to identify the mother, suggesting figures such as Hamutal, the mother of Kings Jehoahaz and Zedekiah. Although it may be possible that the mother refers to an historical figure, I view this figure as metaphorical, representing Judah.[17] Doing so aligns the mother in Ezekiel with the maternal Zion in Lamentations whose children have gone into captivity (Lam. 1:5). This alignment highlights a stark difference in the way Ezekiel and Lamentations portray these mothers. Whereas mother Zion witnesses her children's distress and cries out to God in Lamentations, the mother in Ezekiel witnesses her children's suffering and remains silent. In Ezek. 19:4-5, the lioness watches her strongest cub cast into a pit, chained, and then sent into exile in Egypt. She sees (ותרא), but says nothing. Without hope (אבדה תקותה), she accepts his fate, and places another cub in his place. Like his sibling, this cub is captured, chained, and brought into exile, this time in Babylon.

---

13. Herman (1997: 175) comments on the significant role personal narrative plays in healing from trauma.

14. I translate קינה as "dirge," intentionally reflecting Linafelt's distinction between dirge and lament, as my reading of Ezek. 19 will support.

15. The interrogative exclamation is typical of lament literature. See Lam. 1:1; 2:1; 4:1; Ezek. 26:17; Isa. 14:4, 12.

16. All biblical translations are my own.

17. In their commentaries, Greenberg (1983: 357) and Zimmerli (1979: 394) similarly perceive the mother figure.

In Lamentations, Zion does not silently watch her children suffer as they go into exile. Instead, she actively responds, weeping over her children in Lam. 1:16 and 2:11, and appealing to God on their behalf in Lam. 2:20-22. Zion's tears can be seen as a spontaneous emotional expression of her pain as she watches her children suffer. Zion weeps over her devastated and languishing children. Her tears also can be seen as a ritualized action that has a significant impact on how Israel/Zion experiences its trauma.

L. Juliana M. Claassens (2010: 65) observes "the well-documented phenomenon in both ancient and contemporary societies of public and communal lamentation, especially weeping at funerals, being associated with women." Biblical evidence of this phenomenon is found in Jer. 9:16-20. I contend that Zion's tears in Lamentations can be seen as a ritualized act of weeping. According to Claassens (2010: 66), wailing women served a significant purpose in shaping individual and communal expressions of suffering. Their tears gave expression to personal suffering, and were an invitation to others to share in the grief. In this way, weeping women enabled suffering individuals to find their voice within the community. As Claassens (2010: 68) notes, the personal expression and sharing of grief is essential to healing.

Viewed in this context, Zion's tears proactively work to heal Judah's trauma. Claassens's understanding of how weeping women enable communities to heal supports Linafelt's perception of Lamentations as survival literature. Just as Linafelt perceives Zion's voice in Lamentations to be a voice of protest that registers Zion's will to survive, Claassens considers ritual weeping to be "an act of resistance." Claassens (2010: 73) writes, "wailing women's tears...become a symbol of survival and a sign of hope, fostering the broader community's will to survive."

In contrast to weeping Zion in Lamentations, the mother figures in Ezek. 19 are silent. They accept the suffering of their children without protest. Ezekiel 19 embraces death, whereas Lamentations embraces life in the face of death. Garber (2014: 351) observes how "death imagery permeates the first twenty-four chapters of *Ezekiel*," and suggests that this imagery "has the rhetorical effect of bringing the audience—the exilic community—to a point of feeling 'dead.'" The mothers in Ezek. 19 cannot see beyond the suffering. Without hope, they accept the suffering, and even the death of their children. The comparison of the mother to the vine conveys this. Once tall and strong, the mother vine is plucked and cast into a parched wilderness. Fire consumes her children, the fruit of the vine (Ezek. 19:14), and she does not cry out. This is the last image of the chapter, which concludes: "This is a dirge, and it became a dirge." The chapter's frame conveys the acceptance of death. What may have been an opportunity for lament, an opportunity to plead for the children's lives, has become a formal and fixed dirge (ותהי לקינה) for all time.

The mothers' silence in Ezek. 19 is more notable when compared to Zion's desperate cries on behalf of her children, and to the general noise of Lam. 1 and 2. In Lamentations, Zion weeps and cries (1:2, 19; 2:11), people sigh (1:4, 8, 11, 21, 22), shout (2:7, 18), and clap (2:15). The narrator in Lamentations entreats Zion to shout to God on behalf of her children (2:19). Silence perhaps is seen and measured best when it follows loud sound, such as when a chattering audience falls silent before the start of a performance. This shift from sound to silence is captured in Ezek. 19, and provides further support for "hearing" silence in Ezekiel as a response to Israel's trauma. In Ezek. 19:7, the second lion cub to rise to power fills the world with the sound of his roars (ותשם ארץ ומלאה מקול שאגתו). His voice indicates his power. In response, the nations capture and exile him in Ezek. 19:9, in order to silence him (למען לא ישמע קולו עוד). The image of the silenced cub conveys how exile induces silence. Mother and son have no voice.

In light of O'Connor's observation that traumatic violence at first creates "a kind of mental vacuum," that disrupts "normal mental processes," I perceive the mothers' and the cub's silence in Ezek. 19 as indicative of their initial shock at the traumatic events that have occurred. They have not yet discovered the language with which to process and express the suffering of exile. Smith-Christopher (2002: 92) suggests that the prophet Ezekiel similarly is shocked and traumatized by exile, and may display symptoms of Post-Traumatic Stress Disorder (PTSD), such as a feeling of detachment—as "if one is an observer of one's own mental or bodily processes." In particular, Smith-Christopher (2002: 91–2) considers Ezekiel's silence as he performs various symbolic acts, like physically enacting the siege of Jerusalem (4:1-7), as symptomatic of PTSD. Strikingly, God renders the prophet mute (ונאלמת) in Ezek. 3:26, allowing the prophet to speak only when God opens Ezekiel's mouth to proclaim God's words.

From Defeat to Survival:
Ezekiel 24 and Lamentations 1 and 2

The prophet's silence is particularly striking in Ezek. 24. The chapter can be divided in two distinct parts. In the first, God commands the prophet to deliver an allegory to the people in which a pot of meat is brought to a brisk boil. The prophet must compare the pot with its bloody stew to impure Jerusalem, the "city of blood (עיר הדמים)." As this epithet conveys, the city's impurity is clearly connected to blood. Although the source of the blood is not specifically identified, use of the plural noun דמים suggests the shedding of innocent blood.[18] God accuses the community of Israel of murder, as well as of not following the proper burial ritual for blood.[19] Although Ezek. 24 does not personify Jerusalem as fully as Lam. 1 and 2 do, the city it describes is gendered female, and therefore can be seen alongside the maternal figures in Ezek. 19 as another figuration of female Zion. Throughout the passage, the city grammatically is referred to and addressed as a female.[20]

The biblical association of blood with impurity and women, found most prominently in the priestly strata of the Bible, further supports seeing the bloody city as personified female Zion. In this reading, the blood that fills and defiles the city evokes women's blood. According to the priestly material, women regularly encountered impurity through menstruation and childbirth.[21] Given this, women, particularly menstruating women, easily become symbols of impurity for the prophets.[22] Tarja S. Philip (2006: 73, 66) argues that Ezekiel reflects priestly ideology which accepts the "inherent nature of the impurity of menstrual blood," and presents the menstruant as a symbol of Israel's impurity, as Ezek. 36:17 illustrates:

> Human, when the house of Israel sat on their land, they defiled it through their ways and deeds; their ways were like the impurity of a menstruant before me.

I contend that the image of blood-filled Jerusalem in Ezek. 24 evokes the image of an impure, bloody woman, and invites a comparison with the image of blood-stained Zion found in Lam. 1:8-9:

> Jerusalem sinned a sin, and thus became a menstruant.[23]
> All who honored her, despise her for they have seen her nakedness.
> Indeed she moans, and turns around.
> Her impurity is upon her skirts, she cannot consider her future.

---

18. Other places where דמים refers to the bloodguilt accrued by the innocent shedding of blood are Gen. 4:10; Exod. 22:1; Lev. 20:9; Deut. 19:10; 2 Sam. 16:7; 21:1; Ezek. 9:9.

19. Leviticus 17:13 prescribes the burial of blood. Ezek. 24:7 reports that Israel shed blood without proper burial.

20. See Ezek. 24:13.

21. The priestly writers consider menstrual blood (Lev. 15:19-24) and the blood of childbirth (Lev. 12) as sources of impurity.

22. See Isa. 30:22 and 64:5.

23. Despite some orthographic differences, my translation of נידה as menstruant reflects the use of the word נדה in Lev. 15 to refer to menstruation and coheres with

She has fallen spectacularly; she has no comforter.
"Look, YHWH, at my humiliation, for the enemy has prevailed."

In comparison to this passage, Ezek. 24 offers a bloodier image of Zion. In Lamentations, Zion wears her impurity on her skirts. She is stained with blood, but not full of blood. I suggest that Ezek. 24 perceives Zion as a bloody object—one that is completely impure and beyond redemption.[24] Ezekiel's blood-filled Zion must be abandoned.[25] In contrast, there is hope for Lamentation's blood-stained Zion. Despite her impurity, or because of it, Zion still evokes pity. She does not avoid being seen. Rather, it is after the description of her impurity that she cries out, demanding God to look at her in her impure state. In Lamentations, Zion wants God to pity her, and, more importantly, to show compassion to her children.[26]

God has no pity on the blood-filled city in Ezekiel, as Ezek. 24:14 states:

> I, YHWH, have spoken. It comes. I will do it. I will not leave it unattended. I will have no pity. I will not relent. According to your ways and deeds you will be judged, says Lord YHWH.

In Ezek. 24, Zion is an abject object.[27] In essence, she functions as a dead object that must be removed, as Garber (2014: 351) observes:

> [I]n the metaphor of the filthy pot (Ezek 24:1-14), the inhabitants of Jerusalem are compared to cuts of meat in a pot.... The imagery of chopped meat accompanied by the intense focus on the impurity caused by the blood in the stew creates these death connotations.

The perception of female Zion as a dead object is more pronounced in the second half of Ezek. 24, in which God informs the prophet that he

---

the image of the impure skirts in this passage and the later reference to Zion as a menstruant in Lam. 1:17. Adele Berlin (2002: 54) translates this verse differently: "Grievously has Jerusalem sinned, therefore has she been banished," and notes that the orthography of נידה does not support the translation "menstruant" which would require a second *dālet* and no *yôd*.

24. Mandolfo (2007b: 46) offers a similar reading.
25. God's abandonment of the temple in Jerusalem is evident in Ezek. 8–10.
26. Linafelt (2000a: 50) writes: "Zion's first extended speech in 1:12-16, however, comes to a rhetorical, and one could say emotional, climax in her emphasis on the fate of her children."
27. I rely on French philosopher Julia Kristeva's (1982: 1) understanding of abjection as that which negates meaning, and therefore must be utterly rejected.

will take away something that Ezekiel treasures (מחמד עיניך, v. 16). The treasured object is Ezekiel's wife who dies in Ezek. 24:18. Although commentators often divide Ezek. 24 in two or three distinct units,[28] I consider the chapter to have on overarching coherence. The first half describes Jerusalem as a bloody impure object that is gendered female, and evokes death. The second half describes the death of a woman.

The passage clearly associates Ezekiel's dead wife with the temple in Jerusalem. Just as Ezekiel treasured his wife, the people treasured the temple (מחמד עיניכם, Ezek. 24:21). Similar language appears in Lamentations. Lamentations 1:7 describes how distraught Zion remembers her former treasures (מחמדיה). Lamentations 1:10 describes how her enemies took those treasures (מחמדיה), and Lam. 1:11 relates how her people exchanged Zion's treasures for food (מחמודיהם). Lamentations 2:4 accuses God of killing all the treasured ones (מחמדי עין). Read together, the passages in Lamentations and Ezekiel identify Zion—the people and things within her—as a treasured object. Yet, whereas Zion in Lamentations lives to speak, or, as Linafelt suggests speaks to live, Zion in Ezek. 24 is dead. She is a bloody pot filled with dismembered body parts, and she is also Ezekiel's treasured dead wife.

In Ezek. 24:16, God commands the prophet not to mourn for his wife. He may not cry out for her (לא תבכה), or weep for her (ולוא תבוא דמעתך). Ezekiel stands as an example (מופת, Ezek. 24:24) to the people. Just as Ezekiel must not mourn or cry for his treasured wife, the people must not mourn or cry (לא תבכו, Ezek. 24:23) for the loss of their treasured temple and city. Above, I suggested that Ezekiel's silence while performing symbolic acts was a symptom of PTSD, and that it is comparable to the mothers' silence in Ezek. 19. Ezekiel 24 supports this interpretation. Ezekiel's silence could be seen as an *inability* to mourn, which reflects the trauma Ezekiel experiences immediately following his wife's death. It is indicative of the "mental vacuum" that O'Connor suggests afflicts victims in the wake of traumatic events. Ezekiel's silence, like Zion's, communicates the immediate trauma of exile.

From Death to Resurrection

I have argued that Ezekiel and Lamentations are texts that respond to the trauma of exile, and that exist on an emotional continuum. Ezekiel 19 and 24 reflect an earlier stage in the trauma in which there are no words to express Israel's suffering, and in which the prophet and the people

---

28. See Zimmerli 1979: 504.

must come to terms with their exile. Lamentations 1 and 2 reflect a stage when the people have had time to process the trauma. They have found their voice, and are ready to fight for their lives. My readings of Ezek. 19 and 24 reveal how these chapters reflect silence and death, and reveal the earlier stage of Israel's trauma when the community experiences, as O'Connor describes, "a disruption of normal mental processes." In contrast to these chapters, Lam. 1 and 2 resound with shouts, cries, and moans. Like Linafelt and Mandolfo, I perceive Lam. 1 and 2 as a form of protest literature, and perceive Zion's voice as powerful. Whereas the maternal figures in Ezek. 19 silently watch their children suffer and die, mother Zion rages against God in Lamentations, and weeps on behalf of her children's lives. Ezekiel 24, in particular, presents a starkly different reality and perspective than Lam. 1 and 2. The widow Zion's cries in Lam. 1 and 2 ring louder next to the widower's silence in Ezekiel. Whereas Zion's cries in Lamentations testify to her survival and to her will to live, the prophet's silence testifies to his acceptance of death.

Although Ezekiel accepts the death of Zion, there is a glimmer of hope expressed in Ezek. 24:26-27:

> On that day, a survivor [פליט] will come to you to proclaim to you. On that day, your mouth shall be opened to the survivor, and you will speak, and no longer be dumb [לא תאלם]. You will be a sign [מופת] for them, and they will know that I am YHWH.

The devastation of exile is catastrophic, but a survivor remains. I suggest that this survivor provides hope that the community can and will survive, and even move on from its trauma. The survivor's ability to articulate the trauma implies some distance, whether physical or temporal, between the survivor, the prophet, and the traumatic events. The survivor is not struck dumb from the immediacy of his trauma. He has found the language to describe the devastation. In time, this passage ensures, the prophet also will be able to speak. Just as Ezekiel's silence was a sign for the people, so too is his voice. This suggests that, like the prophet, the people will be able to speak again as well.

Ezekiel's traumatized embrace of death, evident in Ezek. 19 and most of Ezek. 24, therefore, does not preclude a hope for Israel's future. Yet, in order to experience this future, there must be radical transformation—a miracle. Israel must be resurrected from the dead. The bloody stew must become pure, and the dead wife must come alive. Ezekiel 36 describes Israel's purification. God sprinkles purifying waters on Israel, the impure menstruant (בטמאת הנדה, v. 17). Ezekiel 37 describes Israel's resurrection. In Ezek. 37, God places the prophet in a valley filled with bones and commands the prophet to address the bones and to proclaim that God will revive them. Ezekiel then channels divine power in order to knit the bones together with sinews and flesh, and calls the wind to breathe life into the bodies so that the dead can live. The miraculous resurrection displays God's power, and is marked linguistically as a moment of re-creation. The mention of the "wind" (רוח) that "blows" (ופחי) life back into Israel in Ezek. 37:9, restoring its into a "great" (מאד מאד) army in Ezek. 37:10, evokes the language of the creation stories found in Gen. 1–2.[29] As Ezek. 37:9 and 11 make clear, Israel was dead (הרוגים), but now is revived (ויחיו). God opened their graves, and lifted the people up (אני פתח את קברותיכם והעליתי אתכם מקברותיכם). In this way, Ezek. 37's prophecy of hope does not negate the prophecy of doom in Ezek. 24. Like Ezekiel's wife, Zion *was* dead. Now, she is miraculously reborn. The body parts in the bloody stew are reassembled, and brought to life.

Notably, sound resounds in Ezek. 37. The prophet proclaims the word of God (שמעו דבר יהוה) in Ezek. 37:4, and describes the tremendous sound (ויהי קול ... והנה רעש) the bones make as they come together in Ezek. 37:7. The silence conveyed in Ezek. 19 and 24 is broken, suggesting that the prophet and the people have moved beyond the initial stages of their trauma, and perhaps even beyond the stage reflected by the depiction of Zion in Lam. 1 and 2. In Ezek. 37, God speaks (ויאמר, v. 4); the prophet speaks (ואמר, v. 3), and the people speak (הנה אמרים, v. 11). Remarkably, neither the prophet nor the people rage against God, as Zion does in Lamentations, suggesting that they have moved forward on the emotional continuum, and now are able to entertain hope for a future beyond the trauma.

Conclusions

Ezekiel and Lamentations use women to represent and articulate the suffering Israel/Judah experiences in response to its exile. Ezekiel 19 and 24 present female Zion as an impure object that must be rejected. She is like a dead woman. Lamentations 1 and 2 personify Zion as a stained woman who rages against God and fights for the life of her children. In this essay, I suggested that the Zion of Ezekiel and the Zion of Lamentations exist on an emotional continuum that reflects stages of Israel's coming to terms with the trauma of exile. In my reading, Ezek. 19 and 24 reflect

---

29. "Wind" (רוח) is among the primal elements in the creation narrative (see Gen. 1:2). In Gen. 1:31, God declares "all that he had done" to be "very" (מאד) good. In Gen. 2:7, God "breathes" (ויפח) life into the human creature.

an earlier stage than Lam. 1 and 2. In Ezek. 19 and 24, there is shocked silence and an embrace of despair and death. In Lam. 1 and 2, there is articulation of suffering and an embrace of hope and life. Zion fights for life in Lamentations. Her enraged voice indicates that she has not given up. She does not accept death. Read in relationship with Ezek. 37, Ezek. 24:26-27 also articulates hope and could reflect an even later stage on the emotional continuum, in which the community is able to move beyond its trauma and its rage and envision a new life.

Seeing Ezekiel and Lamentations on this continuum reveals a fuller range of the roles women play in representing and articulating suffering. Women are silent witnesses and victims of violence, whose bodies register its impact and testify to its purpose. They are symbols of impurity, sin, and death. Women also are vocal witnesses and resisters of violence, who use their bodies and voice to weep and rage in protest. Whether silent or vocal, their lives and bodies articulate Israel's suffering and testify to the trauma induced by exile. In Lamentations and Ezekiel, women give voice to Israel's suffering.

Chapter 9

Zechariah's Intertextual Reversal of Lamentations

Michael R. Stead

This essay examines the intertextual connections between Lamentations and the book of Zechariah. It will argue that Zechariah makes sustained allusions to Lamentations—especially Lam. 2—but with a twist. Metaphors of devastation and destruction from Lam. 2 are systematically reversed in Zechariah, to become images of rebuilding and restoration. The distressed lament of Daughter Zion in Lam. 1–2, which received no response from Yahweh in Lamentations, is answered by Yahweh's words of comfort, healing, and hope in the book of Zechariah.

I have elsewhere (2009: esp. §2.4) outlined my intertextual approach in more detail. I am using the term intertextuality as an umbrella term for approaches to textual interpretation that share three assumptions: that all texts are a "mosaic" of quotations of other texts, that textual meaning emerges from a "dialogue" between texts, and that the reader is necessarily involved in the production of meaning via the interplay of "texts in the mind." There is a range of intertextualities, because of the range of possible ways that these assumptions can be applied to particular texts. For example, the identifiability of the underlying "mosaic" lies on a spectrum from unknown to certain.

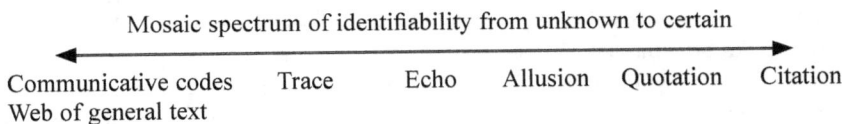

Mosaic spectrum of identifiability from unknown to certain

| Communicative codes | Trace | Echo | Allusion | Quotation | Citation |

Web of general text

Figure 9.1 Intertextuality Spectrum.

- A *citation* is an attributed quotation (i.e., acknowledging source).
- A *quotation* is an identifiable word-for-word repetition.
- An *allusion* is a partial re-use of a sequence of words or ideas.
- An *echo* is similar to an allusion, but where less identifiable elements are re-used.
- A *trace* is defined by Derrida as the indications of an absence that define a presence (Derrida 1997: 46–8). Any signifier contains "traces" of other signifiers which shape its meaning.

As we shall see, the intertextual connections between Lamentations and Zechariah do not qualify as "citation" or "quotation"—they are at best "allusions" and "echoes." For the purpose of this essay, I register an allusion where there are at least three verbal or thematic points of contact, to which is assigned a subjective assessment of likelihood based on the rarity of this combination elsewhere. I will identify eight "likely allusions" on the basis of *multiple* and *unusual* verbal and thematic connections. I register an "echo" where there are only one or two connections between texts.

It is commonly recognized that both Lamentations and Zechariah are highly intertextual works, in that each alludes to and echoes a range of other texts, some of which are readily identifiable. Furthermore, each text locates itself in an identifiable historical situation—Lamentations presupposes an exilic setting, and Zechariah is dated to the early post-exilic period.[1] Thus, the working assumption of this essay is that Lamentations is the earlier text, and that the intertextual connections between the texts are the result of the book of Lamentations being appropriated and applied to the later historical context of Zechariah.

The argument of this essay is that the book of Zechariah makes a "sustained allusion" to Lam. 1–2.[2] A sustained allusion consists of repeated references spanning multiple passages to the same source intertext. I argue that the following eight allusions make a compelling

---

1. It is generally accepted that Lam. 2 was written before Zech. 1–2. See Garrett and House (2004: 283–303) for a summary of the various positions on the dating of the book of Lamentations. House concludes that the majority of modern scholars agree that the book was written by 540–520 BCE, and perhaps even completed within a few decades after the fall of Jerusalem.

2. This essay synthesizes and develops material previously examined in Stead 2008 and 2009. In particular, it extends earlier work by exploring why the intertextual connections are focused almost exclusively in the first two chapters of each book, and posits that this is because Zech. 1–2 is Yahweh's response to Daughter Zion's lament in Lam. 1–2.

cumulative case for a deliberate and sustained allusion to Lam. 1–2 in the book of Zechariah. In each case, the intertexts have a similar rhetorical purpose—to give Yahweh's response to unanswered questions raised by Daughter Zion's lament in Lam. 1–2.

Zechariah's allusions to the book of Lamentations

Lamentations 2:17 and Zechariah 1:6 (and Zechariah 8:14-15)—What Yahweh has Purposed to Do

One of the clearest intertextual connections between the book of Lamentations and the book of Zechariah occurs in Zech. 1:6b and Lam. 2:17a.[3]

Lam. 2:17a	Zech. 1:6b
עשה יהוה אשר זמם Yahweh has done what he purposed	כאשר זמם יהוה צבאות לעשת...כן עשה אתנו Just as Yahweh of Hosts purposed to do, thus he has done to us

Figure 9.2 Lam. 2:17a and Zech. 1:6b.

The combination of "Yahweh" (יהוה), "purposing" (זמם), and "to do" (עשה) here is rare. Jer. 51:12 is the only other place where Yahweh is the subject of these two verbs, and in that instance God's purposes are directed against Babylon, rather than against his own people, as is the case in Lam. 2:17 and Zech. 1:6.[4] More broadly, the language of Yahweh's purpose (זמם) to bring judgment on his people is rare—outside of Zechariah, it only occurs in this sense in Jeremiah and Lamentations (see Jer. 4:28; 23:20; 30:24; Lam. 2:17). The Jeremian references are all declarations of God's (prospective) purposes to judge, whereas only Lam. 2:17 is (like Zech. 1:6b) an acknowledgment, by those who have been judged, that Yahweh has done what he purposed. This makes a strong case that Zech. 1:6 is an intentional allusion to Lam. 2:17.

The use of Lam. 2:17 in this opening section of Zech. 1 is an early signal to the reader that Lam. 2 is a key intertext for understanding the book of Zechariah. Furthermore, it also provides an intertextual pivot for the later reversal of this motif in Zech. 8:14-15.

---

3. Petitjean (1969: 51) connects Zech. 1:6 more broadly with the "Jeremian tradition," citing Jer. 51:12 and Lam. 2:17. All English translations are my own.

4. A related construction occurs in Jer. 23:20 and Jer. 30:24, which describes "Yahweh" (יהוה) "doing" (עשה) the "purposes of his heart" (מזמות לבו). מזמה is the cognate noun of the verb זמם.

Lam. 2:17a	Zech. 1:6b	Zech. 8:14-15
עשה יהוה אשר זמם Yahweh has done what he purposed	כאשר זמם יהוה צבאות לעשות...כן עשה אתנו Just as Yahweh of Hosts purposed to do thus he has done to us	כאשר זממתי להרע כן שבתי זממתי...להיטיב Just as I purposed to do evil, now I have turned; I purpose to do good

Figure 9.3 Lam. 2:17, Zech. 1:6b and Zech. 8:14-15.

Lamentations 2:17 declares that Yahweh has done what he purposed—overthrown his people without mercy. The intertextual echo of this in Zech. 1:6 acknowledges this as a past reality. However, the later echo and inversion of Zech. 1:6 in Zech. 8:14-15 also declares the reversal of God's purposes as originally expressed in Lam. 2:17, from "doing evil" to "doing good."

Lamentations 2 (esp. 2:6) and Zechariah 1:12—Yahweh's Anger at Jerusalem and the Cities of Judah

In Zech. 1:12, the angel laments that Yahweh has been *angry* (זעמתה) with *Jerusalem* and the cities of *Judah*. This is an intertextual echo of Lam. 2, which describes Yahweh's fierce anger (זעם־אפו, v. 2) towards "Daughter Jerusalem/Zion"[5] (vv. 1, 4, 8, 10, 13, 15, 18)[6] and the fortified cities of Daughter Judah (מבצרי בת־יהודה, v. 2).[7] Of the 34 instances of זעם and its cognates—and especially where this word is used of Yahweh's anger towards his people (Ezek. 22:31; Isa. 10:25; Lam. 2:6; Pss. 38:4; 78:49; 102:11; and Zech. 1:12)—only Lam. 2:6 and Zech. 1:12 refer to God's ongoing anger with the (post)exilic generation.

There is a further thematic (rather than verbal) connection between Zech. 1:12 and Lam. 2 based on the motif of "not showing mercy" (לא־תרחם, Zech. 1:12). Elsewhere, this phrase is only used in pre-exilic contexts related to Yahweh's withdrawal from his people (or a subset thereof) to punish their sin.[8] But if the search is widened to include

---

5. "Jerusalem" and "Zion" are synonymously paired in Zech. 1:14 and 1:17.
6. "Daughter Zion" (בת־ציון) is used in Zech. 2:14 (ET 2:10) and 9:9.
7. I understand מבצר in this context similarly to the more typical "city of fortification" (עיר מבצר). See especially Jer. 34:7, and the general usage in Josh. 10:20; 19:29, 35; 1 Sam. 6:8; 2 Kgs 3:19; 10:2; 17:9; 18:8; Jer. 1:18; 4:5; 5:17; 8:14; Ps. 108:11(MT); Dan. 11:15; 2 Chron. 17:19.
8. Yahweh not showing mercy (רחם + לא) towards his people (or a subset thereof) is elsewhere only attested in the pre-exilic prophets. In Hos. 1–2, this theme is a *leitmotif* in association with the name of Gomer's first daughter (לא־רחמה) (Hos. 1:6, 7, 8; 2:3, 6, 21, 25). Otherwise (apart from Zech. 1:12), the combination of רחם

synonymous phrases, then an exilic parallel can be found at several points in Lam. 2. Lamentations 2:2, 17 (לא חמל) and Lam. 2:21 (לא חמלת) are clear conceptual parallels to the phrase, which are applied (as in Zech. 1:12b) to the judgment of the exile.

The abbreviated lament expressed by the Angel of the Lord in Zech. 1:12 echoes Zion's desolate cry in Lam. 2, acknowledging that the exile had indeed been a time of God's anger at Jerusalem and the cities of Judah, when he had not shown mercy to his people. Unlike Lam. 2, the lament is answered by the Lord, with the promise of imminent reversal, which is explored in the following six intertexts.

Lamentations 2:8 and Zechariah 1:16—Stretching the Measuring Line Over Jerusalem

Many commentators detect an intertextual connection between the "measuring line" in Zech. 1:16 with Jer. 31:38-39 and/or Ezek. 40–42. However, in terms of textual parallels, by far the closest parallels are with 2 Kgs 21:13 and Lam. 2:8, read together.

```
2 Kgs 21:13   ונטיתי על־ירושלם את קו
Lam. 2:8      נטה קו
Zech. 1:16    וקוה ינטה על־ירושלם
```

By comparison, the connections with Jeremiah and Ezekiel are meagre.

```
Jer. 31:39   ויצא עוד קוה המדה
Ezek. 40:3   ופתיל־פשתים בידו וקנה המדה
```

Ezekiel 40:3 has no vocabulary in common with Zech. 1:16b, and the only word in common with Jer. 31:39 is the "measuring line" (קוה).

Presumably, commentators find an allusion to Jer. 31/Ezek. 40 because of the positive connotation of the measuring line (i.e., a "rebuilding" line), whereas in 2 Kgs 21 and Lam. 2 the metaphor works in the opposite direction (i.e., a line of judgment), and the context of Zech. 1:16 demands a positive connotation. However, perhaps this is to miss the

---

לא + with Yahweh as the subject only occurs in Isa. 9:16 (ET 9:17); 27:11, and Jer. 13:14; 21:7, where it describes Yahweh's withdrawal from his people in response to their sin. The claim of Yahweh "showing no mercy" is powerful because it inverts the normal expectation that Yahweh is the God who "shows mercy" (see, e.g., Isa. 49:15; 54:10; Ezek. 39:25). Elsewhere it is the enemies of God's people who show them "no mercy" (Jer. 6:23; 50:42). In addition, Isa. 13 promises that Yahweh would raise up the Medes to "show no mercy" to Babylon (Isa. 13:18), and he would "show mercy" (Isa. 14:1) to Jacob.

very point being made in Zech. 1. As at other points, Zechariah reverses Lam. 2. Lamentations 2:8 alludes to 2 Kgs 21:13 to make the point that the judgment promised because of Manasseh's sin had indeed happened, and Zech. 1:16 echoes the phraseology of the "negative" measuring line from both Lam. 2:8 and 2 Kgs 21:13 to stress that a great reversal is about to take place—Yahweh is about to undo the judgment and destruction of 586 BCE.[9]

Lamentations 1–2 and Zechariah 1:17—Comforting Zion and Choosing Jerusalem

It is likely that Lam. 1–2 is an (antithetical) intertext for the promise in Zech. 1:17 that Yahweh will "comfort Zion" (נחם...ציון) "and choose Jerusalem" (ובחר...בירושלם).[10] The recurring refrain of Lam. 1 is that there is *no* comforter for Zion (Lam. 1:2, 9, 17, 21—אין מנחם "There is not a comforter"; Lam. 1:16—רחק ממני מנחם "a comforter is far from me"). This theme continues in Lam. 2:13, where there are seemingly no words that can be said to comfort (נחם) Daughter Zion (בת־ציון). Furthermore, Lam. 2:7—declares—not Yahweh's "choice" of the city of Jerusalem—but its antithesis, his total "rejection" (זנח)[11] of the city (which is expressed with reference to its buildings—altar/sanctuary/walls—rather than the inhabitants). Zechariah 1:17 promises the reversal of the situation described in Lam. 1–2. Yahweh's "comfort of Zion" and "choice of Jerusalem" will be demonstrated by the restoration of the city and rebuilding of the temple (Zech. 1:16).

---

9. On the effect of the ambiguous metaphor here, see further Petersen 1984: 156–7; Love 1999: 177–8.

10. Isaiah 40–55 is also a possible intertext for the "comfort" motif. Isa. 40:1 establishes the programmatic place of words of נחם in the chapters that follow (see esp. Isa. 49:13; 51:3, 12; 52:9; 61:2; 66:13). I agree with Delkurt (2000: 82) that Zech. 1 takes up the message (and messenger) of Isa. 40ff., and thereby reactivates the Isaianic promise of comfort. The specific promise of comfort for Zion (+ נחם ציון) occurs in Isa. 51:3, but Isa. 40–55 does not provide the background for other components of the promise of Zech. 1:17 (the "choosing of Jerusalem"—ובחר עוד בירושלם), because in Isa. 40–55 the language of "choosing" (בחר) always refers to people, not to the city of Jerusalem. Only Lam. 2 provides both intertextual connotations of "comforting Zion" and "choosing Jerusalem."

11. For בחר and זנח used as antonyms, see 1 Chron. 28:1-10. See esp. the stress on Yahweh's choice (בחר) in vv. 4, 5, 6 (and v. 10) which stands in sharp contrast to the possibility of Yahweh's rejection (זנח) in v. 9. Similarly, Ps. 89 paints antithetical pictures of Yahweh's anointed using the language of "chosen" (v. 20, בחר) and "rejected" (v. 39, זנח).

Lamentations 2 and Zechariah 2:3-4 (ET 1:20-21)—Lifting Up and Throwing Down Heads and Horns

Zechariah's second vision describes four horns (קרן) that have scattered God's people so that "no-one could lift his head" (איש לא־נשא ראשו), followed by "four craftsmen" (ארבעה חרשים) who have come to terrify and throw down (ידה) those horns.

Lamentations 2 provides the conceptual background for much of this imagery. Yahweh has cut off (גדע) "every horn of Israel" (כל קרן ישראל)—Lam. 2:3), and "lifted up the horn of your foes" (הרים קרן צריך)—Lam. 2:17). He has thrown down (השליך)[12] the splendor of Israel (Lam. 2:1) and humiliated its people—"the young girls of Jerusalem bow (ירד *hiphil*) their heads to the ground" (Lam. 2:10).

Zechariah 2 both repeats and reverses Lam. 2. It repeats the imagery of the "horns" and the resultant humiliation—"bowed heads"—but also reverses the imagery of being "lifted up" and "thrown down." It will now be the nations that will be "thrown down," taking away those who have prevented God's people from lifting their head. However, Lam. 2 is not the only source of imagery in these verses. Interwoven with this imagery from Lam. 2 is imagery taken from other contexts, which results in a mixed metaphor. For example, the "craftsmen" are a contraction of the "craftsmen of destruction" (חרשי משחית) in Ezek. 21:36 (ET 21:31), perhaps nuanced by Isa. 54:16.[13]

Lamentations 2 and Zechariah 2:8-9 (ET 2:4-5)—Walls and Fire

In Zech. 2:8-9, Yahweh promises that Jerusalem will dwell in villages without walls[14] because of the abundance of his blessing. For their protection, he will be a "wall of fire surrounding them" (חומת אש סביב). Zechariah 2:9 contains a deft reversal of two metaphors in Lam. 2.

---

12. This is a different (though synonymous) word for "throw down" to the one used in Zech. 2:4. The word ידה appears in the next chapter of Lamentations (Lam. 3:53), which is the only other instance of this verb in the *piel*.

13. See Jeremias 1977: 160–1. Jeremias also has a helpful analysis of the usage of חרש on p. 160 nn. 20 and 21. Seybold (1974: 104) registers a connection to the "blacksmiths" of Isa. 54:16 as well as Ezek. 21:36. Delkurt (2000: 101) also lists these two passages as the possible source of Zechariah's imagery. See also Hanhart 1998: 102–3. For others who see a parallel between Ezek. 21:36 and Zech. 2:3 see Tollington 1993: 226; Meyers and Meyers 1987: 139.

14. פרזות ("unwalled villages") is a probable echo of Ezek. 38:11, which in that context has connotations of vulnerability. Jeremias (1977: 170) also makes this connection.

In Lam. 2, the city also has no walls (חומה), because "Yahweh determined to lay in ruins the wall of daughter Zion" (Lam. 2:8). Lamentations 2:7-9 is an extended reflection on the havoc wreaked on the walls of Jerusalem. One of the reasons for Jerusalem's destruction is that Yahweh has been a "fire" within the city—he has "burned like a flaming fire (אש) in Jacob, consuming all around (סביב)" (Lam. 2:3).

Zechariah 2:8-9 takes up these metaphors of judgment and destruction and inverts them, so that "no walls" becomes a sign of his abundant provision for them and "a wall of fire surrounding" connotes God's protection of his people.[15]

Lamentations 2:2-4 and Zechariah 2:12—The "Apple" of Yahweh's Eye

The phrase in Zech. 2:12 הנגע בכם נגע בבבת עינו ("the one touching you is striking the pupil of my eye") is unusual. The "pupil" (בבה) is a *hapax legomenon*. Its meaning would seem to be best explained by analogy with the phrase "apple of his eye" in Deut. 32:10 / Ps. 7:2 (כאישון עינו), cf. Ps. 17:8 (כאישון בת־עין). Apparently, it describes the most precious part of the eye. If this is so, then there is a possible allusion in this verse to Lam. 2:2-4. According to Lam. 2:4, Yahweh has "slain all the treasures

---

15. Lamentations 2:8-9 is not the only intertext for this imagery. Jeremias (1977: 174–6) argues that four distinct lines of tradition converge to produce this metaphor.
  1. The flaming sword guarding the Garden of Eden (Gen. 3:24)
  2. Priestly tradition: Yahweh's theophanic appearance in fire and light
  3. Zion tradition: Fire as the Yahweh's weapon for the protection of Zion (Pss. 46 and 48)
  4. The stress on Yahweh's glorious presence (כבוד) stems from Ezekiel.

While not wishing to undermine Jeremias' conclusions, one wonders why only these 4 lines of tradition where identified. Arguably, there are equally close (if not closer) thematic connections to:
  - the "pillar of fire" which provides guidance and protection (Exod. 13:21-22; 14:19-20, 24)
  - the chariots of fire that encircle Elisha for protection (2 Kgs 6:17)
  - the fire of Sinai that protected the people from drawing too near to Yahweh (Deut. 5:23-24)
  - the reversal of Lam. 2's destroyed wall and fire of judgment (as discussed above).

Instead of attempting to identify specific source text(s), the better approach is to see that all of these texts contribute to the fund of imagery in circulation in Zechariah's day, which makes his particular "wall of fire surrounding" imagery intelligible to his readers (and to us). I conclude that a diversity of imagery and tradition elements lie in the background of Zech. 2:9.

of (the) eye" (ויהרג כל מחמדי־עין). This metaphor can be understood by its parallels in Ezekiel. In Ezek. 24:16, the prophet's wife is the treasure of his eyes, symbolically representing the people's delight in the temple (Ezek. 24:21, 25). When Lam. 2:2-4 refers to Yahweh "striking" (נגע) the treasures of their eyes, it points to the dishonoring and destruction of Zion. This imagery is reversed and reapplied in Zech. 2:12—Yahweh's people are the pupil (i.e., the treasured part) of *his* eye,[16] and those who "strike" (נגע, also in Lam. 2:2) them will be plundered (Zech. 2:13).

Lamentations 2:10-11 and Zechariah 8:4-5—Elders and Children Mourning/Playing in the Streets

In Lam. 2:10-11, the elders (זקנים) of Daughter Zion sit (ישב) in lament, the young girls have their heads bowed to the ground, and children faint "in streets of the town [Jerusalem]" (ברחבות קריה). Zechariah 8:4-5 reverses this imagery—the "elders" (both men and women, זקנים וזקנות) "shall again sit" (עד ישבו) in the streets of Jerusalem (ברחבות ירושלם), and the children shall play in "the streets of the city" (ורחבות העיר). Zechariah again uses the imagery of Lam. 2 in order to reverse it, to declare the end of the conditions of exile.[17]

Observations and Conclusions

A "Sustained Allusion" to Lamentations 1–2

The foregoing analysis has established that there are eight intertextual connections between Lam. 1–2 and Zech. 1–2. Although any one of these eight connections might be explained as a mere coincidence, the cumulative effect of all eight makes it increasingly likely that there is a deliberate and sustained allusion to Lam. 1–2 in Zech. 1–2. The sustained allusion to Lam. 1–2 serves both to call to mind the devastations of exile and to provide the metaphors to explain the systematic reversal that will occur when Yahweh acts to restore his people (the "measuring line" is

---

16. Barthélemy (1963) has argued, followed by C. McCarthy (1981: 61–70), that the original reading in Zech. 2:12 was "my eye," as indicated by the logia recording a תיקון סופרים (a correction of the scribes), but that this was changed to "his eye" early in the first century CE. Fuller (1990) has re-evaluated this argument, suggesting that the תיקון סופרים on Zech. 2:12 may in fact indicate euphemism, not an emendation. Fuller (who was the editor of Qumran Scroll 4Q12ᵉ) argues further that the reading in 4Q12ᵉ on Zech. 2:12 supports the MT reading עינו (1990: 26). The majority of Greek and Latin versions support the MT reading.

17. Nurmela (1996: 197–9) registers this as a sure allusion.

used to rebuild rather than to judge, the "horns of the nations" are now the ones being cast down, Yahweh himself will be their "wall" and a fire of protection, not a fire of destruction, etc.).[18]

Having established this intertextual link between Lam. 1–2 and Zech. 1–2, it opens the door to three other possible echoes of Lam. 2 in Zechariah (which I admit are of a more speculative nature). Firstly, there may be other overtones of the reversal motif. Lamentations 2:6-9 is an extended reflection on the destruction of Jerusalem and its temple—("Destroyed his tabernacle, scorned his altar, disowned his sanctuary"…), and so it is not surprising that Zech. 1–8, which has a keen interest in the rebuilding of the temple, should take up Lam. 2 and reverse many of its metaphors. Secondly, Lam. 2:6 describes how Yahweh has "spurned king and priest in the heat of his anger." Could it be that Zechariah's focus on Joshua (priest) and the "Branch" (a messianic figure) reflects the fact that this "spurning" is being reversed by Yahweh (see esp. Zech. 6:9-15)? Thirdly, is Zechariah's own experience of "night visions" and "oracles" intended to be understood as a reversal of Lam. 2:9 ("prophets who find no vision from Yahweh") and Lam. 2:14 ("false visions" and "misleading oracles")?

A Sustained Allusion to Lamentations 1–2 Only

When the same intertextual method is applied to test for connections between the book of Zechariah and other parts of the book of Lamentations, the results are scant. Whereas the eight allusions identified above with Lam. 1–2 are "likely," because of *multiple* and *unusual* verbal and thematic connections, the rest of the book only registers *single* or *commonplace* points of connection with Zechariah, which makes them "possible" intertexts (echoes) at best. For example, the haunting question with which Lamentations ends—"Does Yahweh's exceeding wrath remain on his people forever?" (Lam. 5:22)—*may possibly* be answered by the "wrath reversal" motif of Zech. 1:2, 15. This must remain a speculative intertext, because the verb "wrath" (קצף) is the single point of verbal connection. A second example is the rhetorical question in Zech. 1:4, "Where are your fathers?," which *may possibly* be intended to invite the answer provided in Lam. 5:7—"Our fathers sinned and are no more, and we bear their punishment." This too is nothing more than a speculative intertext, because it rests on the thematic similarity of a present generation reflecting on the fate of their fathers. A third example of a speculative intertext is the "turn" (שוב) motif in Lam. 5:21—"Cause us to turn to you

---

18. For a (partially) different interpretation of the way that Zech. 1–2 reverses Lam. 2, see Love 1999: 182, 185.

and we will turn," which *may possibly* be echoed in Zech. 1:3—"Turn to me and I will turn to you."

These three examples of speculative intertextual connections are among the clearest that occur in Lam. 3–5. The stark difference in quality between these three examples and the eight examples identified above highlights the fact that the book of Zechariah is using Lam. 1–2 (and particularly Lam. 2) in a focused and particular way, and that the same pattern of sustained allusion does not occur with respect to Lam. 3–5.

Zechariah 1–2 as Yahweh's response to Daughter Zion's lament in Lamentations 1–2

Why is Lam. 1–2 singled out for this intertext treatment in Zech. 1–2? My suggestion is that Zech. 1–2 is Yahweh's intertextual response to the lament of Daughter Zion.

In Lam. 1–2, we hear the voice of Daughter Zion as a female personified speaker, a mother lamenting the loss of her children. She repeatedly cries out "See, O Yahweh,..." (1:9, 11, 20; 2:20), appealing to a God who seems not to see her anguished state. We do not hear her voice in Lam. 3–5.[19] Yahweh does not answer the lament of Daughter Zion anywhere in the book of Lamentations, which serves to underscore the desperation of her plight, leaving people to wonder whether "Yahweh's exceeding wrath will remain on his people forever." Lamentations 1–2 raises disturbing questions which are not answered by Yahweh—for a time. However, Yahweh does not remain silent forever. When the complaint of Lam. 2:6 that Yahweh has been angry at Jerusalem and the cities of Judah is echoed in Zech. 1:12, the words immediately following are "And Yahweh answered" (ויען יהוה). Moreover, he answers with "comforting words" (דברים נחמים); words that could not be found in Lam. 2:13. Zechariah 1–2 activates and inverts the images of deprivation and destruction in Lamentations to answer the challenges posed by Daughter Zion's lament in Lam. 1–2.

Patricia Tull Willey (1997: 264) argues that a similar dynamic occurs in between Lamentations and Second Isaiah, especially Isa. 50–52.

> Second Isaiah takes on the terms of Lamentations not to continue their prayers but to answer them, to dispute, reverse, and reinvent them. In its most argumentative moments it restates the discourse of lament and the lamenters' viewpoints and strenuously disputes their claims, as when they

---

19. In Lam. 3, the speaker is a man (גבר) who speaks in the masculine singular. In Lam. 4, this voice modulates from singular ("my people" in 4:6, 10) to plural from v. 17 onwards ("*our* eyes," "save *us*" etc.). The voice is consistently plural in Lam. 5.

call YHWH their destroyer or ask why YHWH has forgotten them. More often, Second Isaiah acknowledges the validity of the lament's claims and argues that what has been will no longer be: the fallen will rise from the dust, while the oppressors will sink to the ground; the weak will become strong and the hungry will be fed; the abandoned will be redeemed, and most of all, comfortless Zion will be comforted by YHWH.

Isaiah 40:1-2 announces: "Comfort, comfort my people," says your God. Speak tenderly to Jerusalem, and proclaim to her that her hard service has been completed. In Zech. 1–2, we hear Yahweh speaking tenderly to Daughter Zion, answering her anguished laments. Zechariah 1–2 affirms the assessment of Lamentations that the exile had occurred because "the Lord has done what he purposed to do" (Zech. 1:6; cf. Lam. 2:17) and had "shown no mercy/pity" because of his anger at Jerusalem and Judah (Zech. 1:12; cf. Lam. 2:6; 21), while at the same time promising an imminent reversal. No longer will there be "no one to comfort" Jerusalem (Lam. 1:16-17, 21), because "the LORD will again comfort Zion and choose Jerusalem" (Zech. 1:17). Metaphors of devastation and destruction from Lam. 2 are systematically reversed in Zechariah to become images of rebuilding and restoration. The Lord will "stretch the measuring line" to rebuild rather than to judge (Zech. 1:16; cf. Lam. 2:8), the "horns of the nations" are to be cast down (Zech. 2:1-4 MT; cf. Lam. 2:3, 17), and the Lord himself will become a protective "wall of fire" (Zech. 2:9; cf. Lam. 2:3). His people will again be the apple of his eye (Zech. 2:12; cf. Lam. 2:2-4), and it will be obvious from the elders and children in the streets that the Lord has restored people to Daughter Zion (Zech. 8:4-5; cf. Lam. 2:10-11). Zechariah uses sustained allusions to Lamentations—especially Lam. 2—to turn metaphors of devastation and destruction into images of rebuilding and restoration, and to provide Yahweh's words of comfort to the hitherto unanswered lament of Daughter Zion in Lam. 1–2.

Isaiah 40:1-2 announces: "Comfort, comfort my people," says your God. Speak tenderly to Jerusalem, and proclaim to her that her hard service has been completed. In Zech. 1–2, we hear Yahweh speaking tenderly to Daughter Zion, answering her anguished laments. Zechariah 1–2 affirms the assessment of Lamentations that the exile had occurred because "the Lord has done what he purposed to do" (Zech. 1:6; cf. Lam. 2:17) and had "shown no mercy/pity" because of his anger at Jerusalem and Judah (Zech. 1:12; cf. Lam. 2:6; 21), while at the same time promising an imminent reversal. No longer will there be "no one to comfort" Jerusalem (Lam. 1:16-17, 21), because "the LORD will again comfort Zion and choose Jerusalem" (Zech. 1:17). Metaphors of devastation and destruction from Lam. 2 are systematically re-versed in

Zechariah to become images of rebuilding and restoration. The Lord will "stretch the measuring line" to rebuild rather than to judge (Zech. 1:16; cf. Lam. 2:8), the "horns of the nations" are to be cast down (Zech. 2:1-4 MT; cf. Lam. 2:3, 17), and the Lord himself will become a protective "wall of fire surrounding" (Zech. 2:9; cf. Lam. 2:3). His people will again be the apple of his eye (Zech. 2:12; cf. Lam. 2:2-4), and it will be obvious from the elders and children in the streets that the Lord has restored people to Daughter Zion (Zech. 8:4-5; cf. Lam. 2:10-11). Zechariah uses sustained allusions to Lamentations—especially Lam. 2—to turn metaphors of devastation and destruction into images of rebuilding and restoration and to provide Yahweh's words of comfort to the hitherto unanswered lament of Daughter Zion in Lam. 1–2.

Part III

LAMENTATIONS IN DIALOGUE
WITH THE WRITINGS

Chapter 10

MODELS FOR PRAYER IN LAMENTATIONS AND PSALMS

John Goldingay

What might emerge in a conversation between the authors of Lamentations and the authors of the lament psalms—or protest psalms, as I prefer to call them? I here take up one theme from each chapter of Lamentations and set one or two psalms alongside each chapter.[1] I conclude that there is a time or a place in prayer for acknowledging one's guilt and for claiming one's commitment and a time or a place for protesting at Yahweh's anger and for laying hold of it, and that Lamentations and the Psalms model different ways of combining protest and trust, of articulating disappointment, and of expressing hopelessness. I treat both Lamentations and Psalms as texts provided for people to pray. I don't know how far they reflect personal experience or feelings on the part of their authors, but I assume that they found a place in their respective collections because they were thought useful for other people to pray.

Prayer and Guilt

Lamentations 1 grieves over the deserted state of Jerusalem and affirms that it came about

> Because Yahweh made her suffer
> on account of the great number of her rebellions. (Lam. 1:5)

> Jerusalem did wrong and did wrong;
> therefore she became taboo. (Lam. 1:8)

> The yoke of my rebellions was bound on,
> they interweave by his hand. (Lam. 1:14)

---

1. Translations are my own.

In describing people's grief, abandonment, sense of betrayal, anguish, humiliation, suffering, desolation, wretchedness, pain, exhaustion, bondage, and helplessness, the protest psalms use similar language to that of Lamentations. What they generally lack is a parallel sense that the suppliants have to accept any responsibility for what has happened to them. Cassiodorus (1990–91) identified a group of seven "Penitential Psalms" (6, 32, 38, 51, 102, 130, 143), but only Pss. 51 and 130 really qualify for that description, though there are other psalms that make acknowledgment of sin as a proper aspect of prayer, but do not focus on sin.

There is greater such focus in OT prayers outside the Psalter than inside, though the focus is more marked in Ezra 9; Neh. 9; Dan. 9 than in Lamentations.[2] Perhaps Lamentations simply shares the OT's regular assumption that the fall of Jerusalem was an act of judgment on Judah's waywardness. The Prophets actually put more emphasis on sin and judgment, though in contrast Dan. 1 simply sees the fall of Jerusalem as issuing from Yahweh's sovereignty; it is an interesting exception to the rule in light of the stress on Israel's waywardness in Dan. 9.

Within the Psalter, Ps. 44 is an example of a protest psalm that accepts no responsibility and feels no guilt, while presupposing a similar context of conquest to Lam. 1. It notes how God had blessed his people in the past, affirms present trust in him, describes how God has more recently let them be defeated, and in due course urges God to help and redeem. But before doing so, it declares,

> All this has come upon us and we haven't put you out of mind;
>   we haven't been false to your pact.
> Our mind has not turned backward;
>   our steps have not deviated from your path....
> If we'd put our God's name out of mind,
>   and spread our palms to a foreign god,
> God would search this out, wouldn't he,
>   because he knows the mind's secrets.
> Rather, it's because of you that we've been run through all day;
>   we've been thought of as sheep for slaughter. (Ps. 44:18-23[17-22])

Western spirituality traditionally emphasized the guilt of which Ps. 51, Ps. 130, and Lamentations speak, and felt embarrassed or superior in relation to Ps. 44's claims. Over the past half-century it has put more emphasis on lament or protest as a feature of relationships with God, without abandoning the inner sense of individual guilt. It's not clear why

---

2. On the links between Lamentations and these prayers, see Boda 2008: 81–101.

this development happened. It's not because people who enthuse about the protest psalms are going through persecution or other forms of attack; perhaps it's because we are coming to own the despair from which we had hidden (cf. O'Connor 2002: 4).

Many protest psalms suggest the circumstances of the monarchic period when Israel was at least a semi-independent nation with its kings, while the penitential prayers in the OT derive more from the decades after the fall of Jerusalem and from the Second Temple period. So possibly OT spirituality underwent a converse development. Yet the OT does not give the impression that Israel was more committed to Yahweh in the monarchic period, rather the opposite. Just before or soon after the fall of Jerusalem, Jer. 31:31-34 promised that the Torah would come to be inscribed into people's thinking, and in the Second Temple period people were more inclined to acknowledge Yahweh alone, to foreswear the use of divine images, to take care over their use of Yahweh's name, and to keep the Sabbath.

There doesn't seem to be evidence that Western Christians are more committed to God or are suffering more than in previous centuries, so it is a mystery why there should be such a difference between Western spirituality in these two periods, and such a difference between the spirituality of the protest psalms and that of Lamentations. The conversation between them has the potential to encourage protesters to ask whether they need to be more penitential, and to encourage penitents to ask if they are being too hard on themselves. Lamentations confronts the protest psalms with the need for penitence; the protest psalms urge Lamentations not to subject people to "worm theology."[3]

Whereas one reason why Lamentations has become a focus of study is that it points towards a way of thinking and of talking to God about the Holocaust, it is a complicated gift in this connection because of its linking suffering and sin. And whereas scholarship once tended to emphasize the link between sin and suffering in Lamentations, scholarship now tends to emphasize its secondary place.[4] We should neither dismiss or ignore the confession in Lamentations, nor claim that it explains everything (Wright 2015: 60; cf. Dobbs-Allsopp 2002: 27–33). Lamentations is "a polyphony of pain, penitence, and protest."[5] If tragedy suggests someone is "caught up in events involving suffering, events not completely of his or her own making, and yet at the same time he or she bears some responsibility for

---

3. The term comes from Isaac Watts's hymn "Alas! And Did My Savior Bleed," in which one line says, "Would he devote that sacred head for such a worm as I?"
4. See e.g., Boase 2006: 140–202.
5. Part of the subtitle of Bier 2015.

these events," so that "there is guilt," then Lamentations reflects a tragic situation, even if it also reflects the conviction that the suffering is out of proportion to the wrongdoing (Dobbs-Allsopp 1997: 35).

Prayer and Divine Anger

Lamentations 2 is especially insistent on Yahweh's anger (אף), fury (עברה), blazing (חרי), and wrath (חמה), though it mostly speaks of it in the third person rather than directly confronting Yahweh with it.

> Oh!—with his anger the Lord clouds over
>   Miss Zion....
> In his fury he tore down
>   Miss Judah's fortifications....
> He cut off every horn of Israel
>   in his angry blazing....
> He burned up against Jacob like a flaming fire
>   consuming all round....
> In Miss Zion's tent
>   he poured out his wrath like fire....
> In his angry condemnation he spurned
>   king and priest. (Lam. 2:1-6)

> My girls and my young men
>   fell by the sword.
> You killed them on your day of anger,
>   you slaughtered them, you didn't spare. (Lam. 2:21)

The first line expresses the main idea of the chapter in a nutshell:[6] notwithstanding the former close relationship between Yahweh and "daughter Zion," his grace has turned to anger.

Psalm 6 also begins with a plea regarding Yahweh's anger:

> Yahweh, don't reprove me in your anger,
>   don't discipline me with your wrath. (Ps. 6:2[1])

But the psalm lacks any indication that the suppliant might have earned Yahweh's anger. There is an overlap with the comparison between Lam. 1 and Ps. 44, though there's no reference to guilt in Lam. 2. Indeed, Lam. 2:20-22 has been seen as a "protest against divine injustice" and as an expression of "resistance to divine injustice and suffering, especially

---

    6. Cf. Labahn 2006: 243. She notes the close link of the fire image with the talk of Yahweh's anger.

the suffering of the city's little children"[7] (which is worse—rape, or watching your children suffer and die?).[8] But there's no actual reference to injustice or justice in the verses, only a protest at concrete acts—partly because Hebrew has no words equivalent to the English words justice and injustice.

Psalm 6 is one of Cassiodorus's penitential psalms; he presupposes that reference to God's wrath implies that this wrath would be a response to people's waywardness. Yet there are other psalms referring to Yahweh's anger or wrath whose context points away from this implication (Pss. 27:9; 74:1; 88:8[7]). So there is no reason to infer that Ps. 6 refers to anger or wrath that was earned.

Behind the language of wrath in Ps. 6 and in Lamentations may lie the consideration that wrath can denote the wounding nature of our experience of pain, suffering, torment, and affliction, rather than a concern with the attitude of the person who does the wounding. It's *as if* someone is behaving in wrath towards us; it may not imply the person actually has angry feelings. The psalm and the poem may then refer to Yahweh's bringing or allowing suffering of such fury that it seems like the expression of someone's anger. On the other hand, an upside to its being personal anger would be—well, that it's personal. Yahweh is not a detached sovereign or a dispassionate judge. Still less is Yahweh a principle or a theory. He is a person of like passions as we are (love, mercy, anger, hate), "yet without sin" (Heb. 4:15).

While some psalms speak of anger without linking it to waywardness, others do see Yahweh's anger, wrath, and fury as a response to wrongdoing. The close of Ps. 89 and the subsequent declarations of Ps. 90 make for particularly apposite comparison with Lamentations.

> How long, Yahweh—will you hide permanently,
>   will your wrath burn up like fire? (Ps. 89:47[46])
>
> We are finished through your anger,
>   through your wrath we've been fearful.
> You've set our wayward acts in front of you,
>   our youthful deeds in the light of your face....
> The days of our years in themselves are seventy years,
>   or with strength eighty years.
> But their drive has been oppression and trouble,
>   because it's passed by speedily and we've flown away. (Ps. 90:7-10)

---

7. Thomas 2013b: 162.
8. See O'Connor 2002: 37.

In the OT, seventy years is not a term for a lifespan but the classic period of Israel's affliction as a people. The burden of Ps. 90 corresponds quite closely to that of Lamentations—specifically, to that of Lam. 5:20-22 with its protest at the way oppression is dragging on. The notion that Yahweh is longsuffering, "long of anger" (Ps. 86:15), seems ironic in this context.

The protest psalms take up the theme of Yahweh's anger in another, quite different connection. As well as appealing against it they appeal to it (e.g., Pss. 7:7[6]; 56:8[7]; 59:14[13]; 69:25[24]; 79:6). Yahweh ought to be angry with the wrongdoing of the attackers who oppress the people who are praying these psalms, and he ought to express his anger by removing them from a position of power.

In the context of the position in the Writings that they share, then, one can imagine Lamentations saying to the Psalms, be bold to articulate for yourself the reality of Yahweh's anger and be bold in reflecting it back to Yahweh. And one can imagine the Psalms saying to Lamentations, recognize the positive significance of Yahweh's capacity for anger. Ask Yahweh to turn it onto your attackers.

Prayer, Protest, and Trust

"God is…a source of hope and pain" throughout Lamentations (Thomas 2013b: 2), but especially in ch. 3. The "man" in this chapter both expresses penitence and submission, and also issues protests and accusations.[9] In holding onto such admixtures "the book does not construct a theology of its own" (Berlin 2002: 18). It is "a dialogic text" (Boase 2006: 203–38).

Lamentations 3 first gives twenty lines to describing how the suppliant has been under attack from Yahweh; the entire protest concerns what "he" has done, though Yahweh is never named, nor is he addressed. He is portrayed as an attacker, a jailor, a bear, a lion, a shooter, a poisoner. Then there follows a startling move to an affirmation that Yahweh's commitment, compassion, and truthfulness are still realities. These declarations continue to be third-person but they now name Yahweh, four times. As the poem reaches the center point of this central chapter in the book, it makes one of the OT's most significant theological assertions:

> It is not from his heart that he humbles
>   and brings suffering to human beings. (Lam. 3:33)

The poem has asserted at some length that Yahweh does humble and bring suffering, but it now avows that such action does not come from his

---

9. Cf. Bier 2014: 146–67 (cf. Bier 2015: 105–41).

heart (לב), from his inner being. English translations mostly have Yahweh acting in this way "not willingly"; some translations have a phrase indicating that he doesn't enjoy it. The implication is that when Yahweh acts to bless, it does come from his heart. It's deliberate, it comes naturally, he likes doing it. When he acts to afflict, it comes from somewhere else within his person. It doesn't come as naturally to him, he doesn't enjoy it. "Yahweh is not a God of affliction; it is not in his nature to grieve human beings.... Afflicting is not of the essence of Yahweh" (Salters 2010: 239).

Yet the poem then complements that statement with

> Who is it who said and it happened,
>   when the Lord didn't order?
> From the mouth of the One on High
>   do not the bad things and the good things issue? (Lam. 3:37-38)

And there is good reason:

> Of what should a living person complain,
>   a man in connection with his wrongdoings? (Lam. 3:39)

One can therefore hardly complain when Yahweh makes bad things happen. Therefore, we need to examine our ways and turn back to Yahweh (Lam. 3:40).

The poem now becomes a prayer (or lays out a prayer for people to pray), reverts to describing Yahweh's destructive action, then speaks of how Yahweh has listened and responded in the past (unless vv. 55-62 are precative), and urges Yahweh to act against the suppliant's attackers.

Psalm 22 has in common with Lam. 3 that it interweaves protest and trust. It compares and contrasts with Lam. 3 in various ways.

- The two compositions are resolute in the way they insist on facing two sets of facts—both the fact of Yahweh's abandonment and hostility and the fact of Yahweh's compassion and commitment. In both, "God's people can be 'forsaken' but never Forsaken.... God is 'absent' *in the sense that* he is not acting to bless his people and protect them from their enemies."[10]
- In facing the two sets of facts, both compositions combine vehement protest and meek submission. Neither protest alone nor submission alone is adequate.

---

10. Parry 2010: 197; though I am not sure about the subsequent statement that "God is not 'absent' in any metaphysical sense."

- Both compositions testify to some resolution, though its reality is clearer in the psalm. There, resolution comes at the end, apparently because the suppliant knows Yahweh has responded to the protest and that he has made a commitment to deliver the suppliant from the attackers. In Lamentations the resolution may seem to come in the middle, but it is not sustained. Indeed, "in context... these orthodox affirmations become near accusations," or at least motivations for Yahweh to act in accordance with them (Bouzard 2014: 78).
- Both compositions thus testify to ongoing struggle. In the psalm, protest and affirmation alternate. In Lam. 3, the affirmations in vv. 22-24 are not the resolution of the issues the chapter raises; the poem returns in vv. 43-44 to protest at Yahweh's anger, abandonment, slaughter, and hiding.
- Both compositions speak in the first-person singular. Lamentations' first-person singular in some way represents the community; it wouldn't be surprising if the same is true of the psalm. "The effective blurring of corporate/individual identity...enabled both perspectives of suffering to intermingle," the individual and the larger corporate entity (Thomas 2013b: 196).
- The psalm addresses Yahweh throughout the protest part (vv. 2-22[1-21]) but moves to addressing the community for the thanksgiving/testimony part (vv. 23-32[22-31]). In Lam. 3 the movement is the reverse: it speaks about Yahweh for its first two-thirds, both in protests and in statements of faith, and it speaks to Yahweh for the last third.

It's clear why the last part of Ps. 22 addresses the community; this configuration belongs to the nature of testimony. Thanksgiving that no one hears has little point. It's less clear why Lamentations' protest and statement of faith address the community. Is it to provide the community with something that expresses what is true for the community as a whole? Is it designed for Yahweh to overhear and be affected by, as prophets speak *about* Ephraim or Judah as well as *to* Ephraim and Judah, in a way that they are meant to overhear and be affected by? Or is it really the self-expression of a suppliant who needs to say how things are, for the sake of no one else?

Conversely, does Lamentations broaden the question about the psalm's rhetoric? If the community was meant to hear the last third of the psalm, presumably it also heard the first third. Did it join in because the prayer and the statements of trust were ones it needed to utter? Or did it do so because it thereby made the prayer an intercession for the suppliant?

Does the psalm's presence in the Psalter imply that a suppliant would pray it in the company of family and friends, perhaps when offering a sacrifice? Does the suppliant pray publicly, thus so as to be heard by other people as well as by God? These possibilities help to reframe the idea of intercession. In Western culture someone who is suffering may find comfort through being able to articulate their pain, especially with the help of someone else and in their company. Many people who suffer want to tell their story and want their story to be heard. They wish "to witness to pain rather than to find meaning in it" (Linafelt 2000a: 43–4)—or to pray about it. They want God to see; they want people to see (Lam. 1:12). Lamentations articulates "a relentless search for comfort," which takes the form of "the cries across the poems for someone to 'see' the suffering of the people" (O'Connor 2002: 96).

It's partly for this reason that rhetoric is important in Lamentations. Lamentations 1 begins by talking about Zion in its suffering and about Yahweh as the one who caused it, and in due course about the wrongdoing that made him do so. It then talks as Zion in its suffering and about Yahweh as the one who caused it, and in due course about the wrongdoing that made him do so. Eventually it talks as Zion suffering to Yahweh as the one who caused it, and talks about the wrongdoing that made him do so. Lamentations 2 speaks about what Yahweh has done, then speaks about what Zion has experienced, then articulates the grief of the poet. Eventually there is one line that addresses Yahweh and appeals to Yahweh to heed (Lam. 2:20). Lamentations 3 is a testimony which for the first third speaks about Yahweh causing suffering. For nearly the next third the suppliant tells himself what he should still believe about Yahweh. For the last third it speaks to Yahweh about how he has caused suffering, acknowledges to him that he has listened, and appeals to him to put down the attackers. Lamentations 4 simply describes the city's suffering which Yahweh has brought on. Lamentations 5 begins and ends as appeal to Yahweh; the appeal frames and is motivated by description of the city's suffering.

Prayer and Disappointment

Genesis 12 lays out the original promises of God to Israel's ancestors, which cover a country to possess, a people to become, and a blessing to embody. Samuel–Kings adds two further promises, of a city and a kingly line that God chose and made a commitment to. The Psalms put more emphasis on these two additional promises, and Ps. 132 issues a plea on the basis of them:

> Yahweh swore to David in truthfulness,
>   he will not turn back from it:
> "One from the fruit of your body
>   I will put on your throne....
> Yahweh chose Zion,
>   which he wanted as a seat for himself.
> For all time this is my place to settle down,
>   where I will sit, because I wanted it....
> There I will make David's horn flourish;
>   I am setting up a lamp for my anointed one.
> Its enemies I will clothe in shame,
>   but on him his crown will sparkle." (Ps. 132:11-18)

But protest psalms note the collapse of these two promises (see Pss. 74; 79; 80), and Lam. 4 notes their failure:

> The kings of the earth didn't believe,
>   or all the world's inhabitants,
> That adversary or enemy would come
>   through Jerusalem's gates.
> The breath of our lungs, Yahweh's anointed,
>   was captured in their traps,
> The one of whom we had said, "In his shade
>   we will live among the nations." (Lam. 4:12, 20)

Lamentations 2:15, too, refers to the failure of the promise attached to Zion, and Pss. 48:3 [2] and 50:2 refer to the promise itself. The implication of Lam. 4:20b is that Judahites are invited to acknowledge, "we were mistaken to trust in the Davidic promise in the way we did. We had overestimated its significance. Maybe the implication is, we should never have treated the Davidic king as a shade who could protect us." In Jotham's parable, it is the thorn bush that speaks in terms of offering such shade (Judg. 9:15). Yahweh is the only true shade (e.g., Ps. 91:1; and contrast Isa. 30:2-3).

Both Lam. 4 and Pss. 74, 79, and 80 look to Yahweh's acting against the people who trampled Zion and dethroned the one Yahweh put at his right hand:

> Celebrate and rejoice, Miss Edom,
>   you who live in the country of Uz.
> To you, too, the chalice will pass;
>   you'll get drunk and you'll strip naked. (Lam. 4:21)

Both the psalms and Lamentations say little or nothing about Israel taking redress. They do look forward to Yahweh's doing so for Israel (cf. Deut. 32:35; Prov. 20:22). It is in this sense that Lamentations is concerned about justice (cf. Dobbs-Allsopp 1997: 35). But its giving more prominence to Israel's guilt than the psalms does generate an unresolved tension between deserve and injustice. While this tension is also present in the Prophets, it is missing from Pss. 74, 79, and 80. They make virtually no reference to Israel's deserving the trouble that has come to it. Paradoxically, however, Lam. 4 includes no actual prayer at all. It doesn't follow that it should not be read in isolation from ch. 5.[11] Rather, its distinctiveness needs to be honored.

Prayer and Hopelessness

Lamentations has no Hollywood ending. Printed HBs repeat 5:21 after 5:22 to take the edge off the work's dark closure. If Lamentations became a Hollywood script, the midpoint would have to become the end. But Lam. 5 is the community's real articulation of grief, "to which the earlier poems have been a preamble." Here the community speaks for itself, and does so in prayer, which is maybe now possible after grief has been expressed (Allen 2011: 22, 23).

> Be mindful, Yahweh, of what happened to us;
>   look, and see our reviling. (Lam. 5:1)

> Bring us back to yourself, Yahweh, so we may come back;
>   make our days new, as before.
> But you have totally rejected us,
>   you have been utterly furious with us. (Lam. 5:21-22)

Lamentations 5 "breaks the bounds even of the sanctioned complaint of the communal lament." It is an oversimplification to go on to say that "Israel does not protest here in order to move YHWH to respond, but rather because the extent of its degradation can no longer be contained.... In the daring honesty of unedited speech, Israel reclaims its dignity," so that thereby Israel is "making possible a viable future with YHWH" (Williamson 2008: 80). It is both a self-assertion and a prayer.

The same applies to Ps. 88:

---

11. As Parry (2010: 134) suggests.

> Yahweh, my God who delivers,
>   by day I have cried out, by night in front of you.
> May my plea come before you;
>   bend your ear to my resounding noise. (Ps. 88:1-2)

> Your acts of rage have passed over me,
>   your acts of terror have destroyed me.
> They are round me like water all day,
>   they've encircled me altogether.
> You've taken friend and neighbor far from me,
>   my acquaintances—darkness. (Ps. 88:16-18)

There the psalm stops. By stopping rather than finishing, it mirrors the reality that it reflects. As Lam. 5 closes with a line that we don't know how to translate,[12] the psalm closes with a line that does not construe.

"The reader is not so much engaged by the book of Lamentations as assaulted by it" (Linafelt 2000a: 2). Psalm 88 shares the distinction of being among the simultaneously most uncomfortable and most comfortable reads in the Scriptures. It does not create pain, but it does reveal pain (O'Connor 2002: 2). While Lam. 3 and Ps. 22 open up one way of relating to God in the midst of suffering (holding a tension between protest and trust), Lam. 5 and Ps. 88 open up another way. There is no indication that the first is better. Both texts are uncomfortable because we don't want to think that life might be as they describe. We prefer to say that God seems to have abandoned us than that God has abandoned us. They are comforting because life can be as they describe and God sometimes has abandoned us, and they give us the opportunity to face the fact and to talk to God about it. They acknowledge that in the midst of life we are in death. "The need to lend a voice to suffering is a condition of all truth" (Adorno 1973: 17; cf. Linafelt 2000a: 1). As is typical of the Scriptures, they do not seek to solve the theodicy problem by dealing with the theological and philosophical question. They do give voice to the reality that generates the theodicy problem and they challenge God to solve it. They engage in theodicy as "an existential struggle against the practical realities of lived experience" (Boase 2008a: 454).

Lamentations actually "is primarily concerned to engender a response from God" (Linafelt 2000a: 132), and Ps. 88 is not just designed to enable the suppliant to feel better through letting it all hang out. But in Ps. 88 and in Lamentations, God does not respond. There are one or two psalms that presuppose an answer from God (but only one or two), and "the silence

---

12. See e.g., Salters 2010: 373–4.

of God in Lamentations is inspired" in that "it shows a brilliant restraint"; for "if God were to speak, what could God say?" Actually the book of Job shows the answer, but supplying it would dissipate Lamentations' capacity to house sorrow. Lamentations "denies 'denial'" (O'Connor 2002: 85, 86). Lamentations is incomplete, like Ps. 88. A conclusion can only come with a response from God. But "until God responds, the people's lamentations go on" (Nguyen 2013: 224).

As is the case with Ps. 22 and other protest psalms, the suppliant's speaking as an "I" should not make one infer that it speaks only on behalf of an individual—like Lam. 3. And like Lam. 3, it is a prayer that can be used as an intercession and not just as a prayer for oneself. Indeed, "the *way* in which Lamentations engages politically is in *prayer*" (Parry 2011a: 80). If we don't need to pray Lamentations for ourselves, it "still calls us urgently to prayer for and with those whose lives too readily coincide with the brutish conditions that punctuate the book" (O'Connor 2002: 133).

Chapter 11

VERSE AND VOICE IN LAMENTATIONS 3 AND PSALM 119

David J. Reimer

Drawing together Ps. 119 and Lam. 3 seems almost inevitable. Yet, if anything deserves to be thought of as *sui generis* (with apologies to Jonathan Z. Smith),[1] the Long Psalm surely would qualify. It presents as an imposing literary monument, a soaring poetic structure—but it is delicately, deftly, determinedly woven together, more tapestry than tower. Its twenty-two, eight-line acrostic stanzas induce awe in some, but send others to sleep. Still, both the beguiled and the bored might agree: there's nothing else in the HB quite like it.

Except there is. It is not *sui generis*, and there is something much like it. And that is Lam. 3. At first blush, the superficial similarities suffice to bring Ps. 119 and Lam. 3 together. These two poems are the most sustained examples of acrostic poetic art in the HB. While there are other acrostic poems, these two stand out for the protraction and rigor of the form. Of those taking their starting point in the Psalms, Leslie Allen (1983: 139) writes: "Psalm 119 is an acrostic psalm.... It is the most developed instance in the OT. The closest parallel is Lamentations 3...." From those beginning with Lam. 3, Robin Salters (2011: 432) observes: "[Lamentations] 3 echoes Psalm 119 in that, of the sixty-six lines, three are devoted to א, three to ב, etc." While Pss. 111 and 112 might display a more dense form of acrostic art, Ps. 119 and Lam. 3 alone share the

---

1. Thus Hans-Joachim Kraus: in Ps. 119, "[t]he art of alphabetical organization has produced an unusual opus which in schematism and compulsion of form has no parallel in the OT." Cf. Smith 1990: 36–48. The corpus of more-or-less complete acrostic poems of the HB (thus setting aside Nah. 1:2-8) includes Pss. 9–10 (four letters missing); 25 (lacks *qoph*); 34 (lacks *waw*); 37; 111; 112; 119; 145 (lacks *nun*); Prov. 31:10-31; Lam. 1–4; and beyond the canonical HB, also Sir. 51:13-30.

multi-line acrostic approach. From a purely formal standpoint, then, this feature accounts for a minimal sense of cross-reference. Once the acrostic form is mentioned for one, it is difficult not to think of the other—even if some seem to manage that feat.[2]

This formal echo that draws together our two poems contains further elements which reinforce that impression, as well as other aspects in which they seem to pull apart. As the formal elements are explored, their common concerns come into focus. Beyond the formal, each poem contains certain puzzles about its dominant speaking "voice." Reading these poems "intertextually" both brings to the fore their shared properties, and at the same time elicits ways in which their disparate modes, moods, and concerns address each other in suggestive ways. Observing commonality draws them together, exploring difference launches a fruitful dialogue between them. What follows here, it should be understood, constitutes only an initial exploration of this readerly approach of attending to these two poems together, and what happens when one does.

Formal Echoes

Once the superficial formal similarity of the acrostic approach has been noted—that each consecutive line of a stanza, eight lines for Ps. 119 and three for Lam. 3, begins with the same letter—there is yet more to be observed about how those alphabetic "head words," or "acrostic words," are used.

There are some "false friends" to be discounted. Both poems make use of the *wāw* conjunction to begin each line of their *wāw* stanzas. In Lam. 3, the three initial words each use a *wayyiqtol* verb form, as the poet continues the catalogue of brutal treatment contributing to his being "the man [*geber*] who has seen affliction" (3:1).[3] In Ps. 119, none of the eight *wāw* conjunctions that begin the lines of this stanza are of this kind: six are prefixed to first-person cohortatives, one to a third-person jussive, and one to a negation. Similarly, both poems make almost exclusive use of the inseparable preposition *lāmed* for each of those lines—only Ps. 119:92 breaks the pattern. Yet here again, how this preposition is used differs markedly between the two poems. All three of the forms beginning Lam. 3:34-36 are infinitive constructs, but none of those in the *lāmed* stanza in Ps. 119 are of this type. In fact, none of the *lāmed* prepositions which

---

2. For clarity throughout the essay, I use "lament" and "poet" when referring to Lam. 3, but "psalm" and "psalmist" when discussing Ps. 119.

3. Translations are my own, unless otherwise indicated.

begin this stanza in the psalm are prefixed to verbs of any kind. The last stanzas of both poems, *tau*, are made up entirely (almost so, in the case of the psalm) of *yiqtol* verb forms.[4] In the lament, all three are straightforward second-person singular imperfects, "You will…," whereas in the psalm, these forms are jussives, with five of these six lines being in some sense reflexive, a form of self-reference ("my cry," "my supplication," etc.) with the sole exception referring to the hand of YHWH (119:173).

Most stanzas simply employ different strategies for their acrostic words. But there are some cases where lines share identical head words, and a few cases where the stanzas have some striking similarities, even granting the very different stanza lengths between them.

The first substantial match between acrostic words displays the disparities that can be seen when similarity at one level highlights difference at another. The second *dālet* line in each poem begins with *dərākay* "my ways."[5] Psalm 119 makes frequent use of the root *d-r-k* (14×), although only once as a verb (119:35 as a *hiphil*, where it begins the third line of the *hê* stanza). The significance of *derek* "way" for the psalm can be seen in the first stanza: it appears in 119:1 as part of a broad observation on those who walk with integrity, in 119:3 referring to "his ways," that is, the ways of YHWH, and again in 119:5 now with "my ways" in view. Five lines in the *dālet* stanza begin with *derek* (and, for good measure, it also appears in the first line of the *hê* stanza which follows, 119:33). The first of these is 119:26, "My ways I recounted, and you answered me: teach me your statutes!"[6] The "way" of fidelity in this stanza contrasts with the psalmist's anxiety at moral failure. When we turn to Lam. 3, the first impression of the *dālet* stanza might suggest some resonance with the Long Psalm, as the middle line, 3:11, shares the same acrostic word as 119:26, as noted above, and the third line begins with a verbal form of *dārak*. In the lament, the preceding stanza's closing line uses *dərākay* "my ways," thus anticipating its use in 3:11. In the lament, however, the context is the catalogue of destructive behavior the poet has experienced from his unnamed assailant, who comes to be identified as YHWH. The poet's "ways" have also fallen prey to this destruction.

---

4. There are two exceptions in the psalm: 119:174, 176 are both first-person *qatal* forms of verbs beginning with *tau*. Thus, seven of the eight lines of the psalm's final stanza begin with language focusing on the psalmist.

5. This is the second of eight lines for Ps. 119, but the second of three for Lam. 3. I will only note the differing stanza lengths again if there is particular reason for this to be registered.

6. My translations will often woodenly (and awkwardly) follow the word order of the Hebrew in order to reflect the position of the acrostic word.

The seventh stanza, *zayin*, offers something more. Memory, affliction, and hope make uneasy companions, but this is the remarkable combination that occasions the turning point in Lam. 3 away from the distressing catalogue of pain to the poet's anticipation of divine compassion. This follows immediately on what at first appears to be the final breath of the poet, expiring in 3:18, strength vanished, and along with it, hope from YHWH. This is the first explicit mention of YHWH in the poem, at once both identifying the previously unnamed assailant of the preceding verses, and at the same time serving as a trigger for memory which follows in the next three lines comprising the *zayin* stanza. Verse 19 begins with a singular imperative, *zəkor*—"Remember my affliction [*'onyî*]!"[7]— although it is difficult to be sure to whom this command is directed. It could be the hearer or reader of the poem, thus continuing the quality of soliloquy which the poem has sustained thus far. It could be directed to YHWH, just named, although this might seem too sudden a turn, given the hostility described in the preceding lines. Or the instruction could be self-directed, as the poet bids to survive the last gasp of the preceding verse. This last option has some attraction given the affirmation of the following line, that the poet does, indeed, with sorrow bear in mind (*zākôr tizkôr...napšî*) his previous afflictions. The final line of Lam. 3's *zayin* stanza asserts that in some unspecified "this" (*zō't*)—whether in spite of memory ("but" or "yet," supplied in many English versions [there is no conjunction in the Hebrew]) or as a result of it (what has just been present in memory, the poet will keep in mind)—hope is found.

The counter-intuitive combination of memory, affliction, and hope also features in the *zayin* stanza of Ps. 119. Like Lam. 3:19, it begins (119:49) with the imperative *zəkōr*, although this is clearly directed to YHWH, as is the vast majority of this psalm. It is a plea for YHWH to "remember" his word, and here for the psalmist, that word is the basis of hope. The next verse brings the use of the demonstrative *zō't*, like Lam. 3:21, now pointing to the psalmist's comfort in "my affliction" (*'onyî*). The stanza uses two more verbal forms of *zākar* (119:52, 55) and concludes with a further *zō't* (119:56), although these do not overtly correspond to the constellation of the lament. Meanwhile, the earlier resonances with the lament are pronounced, even while the atmosphere evoked by them differs. There may yet be more subtle echoes between these *zayin* stanzas than those observed here, where it is the formal correspondence which is in focus. This will be considered below.

---

7. I read with the Masoretes here (and cf. Ps. 25:6). For other grammatical possibilities, see Hillers 1972: 55; Salters 2010: 219 (and cf. Ps. 111:4; 145:7).

The opening and closing lines of the following *ḥet* stanza have inverted acrostic words—that is, the phrase *ḥasdê yhwh* ("the steadfast love of YHWH") which begins the stanza in Lam. 3:22 finds a counterpart in *ḥasdəkā yhwh* ("your steadfast love, O YHWH") in the closing line of the stanza at Ps. 119:64. And the stanza's first line in Ps. 119:57, *ḥelqî yhwh 'āmartî* ("'YHWH is my portion,' I said...") finds its counterpart in the closing line of Lam. 3:24, *ḥelqî yhwh 'āmərâ napšî* ("'YHWH is my portion,' said my soul"). Both poets stress the limitless quality of YHWH's *ḥesed*, although this is conceived temporally in the lament,[8] but spatially in the psalm. Similarly, there is resonance plus difference in having YHWH as "portion" (*ḥēleq*): in the lament, this develops the quality of hope discovered and expressed in the preceding stanza, whereas it galvanizes the psalmist to persist in fidelity.

Moving to the ninth stanza, it is difficult to judge the significance of the predominance of *ṭ-w-b* in these two poems, as fully half of the corpus of Hebrew acrostic poems make use of *ṭôb* (or a closely related form) as the acrostic word, including five lines in our psalm (119:65, 66, 68, 71, 72) and all three lines of the *ṭet* stanza in Lam. 3 (vv. 25-27).[9] Even so, there remain some clear resonances between our two poems. They both open with an affirmation of YHWH's goodness (Ps. 119:65; Lam. 3:25), stated as a general principle regarding those dependent on YHWH in the lament, but as a lived experience of divine consistency by the psalmist.[10] The second and third lines of the lament both extol patience, even in adversity (*ṭôb... l-...* "it is good for..."). The final two lines of Ps. 119 (vv. 71-72) use the same formula (*ṭôb-lî...* "it is good for me...") to claim that it was in affliction that the psalmist learned YHWH's statutes, and to praise the surpassing worth of divine law. Just as with the first line, the general principles of the lament are found in personal terms in the psalm.

"Eyes" and "tears" go together, and both feature in the *'ayin* and *pê* stanzas of our poems. Here a difference should be noted: in Ps. 119 the letters run in the expected order, *'ayin* and *pê* as stanzas XVI and XVII

---

8. Although the MT's *tāmənû* "we have [not] ceased" can be defended (e.g., Provan 1991: 93), the widely adopted reading *tāmmû* "they [i.e., the 'mercies'] have [not] ceased" (attested in a single Hebrew manuscript, supported by Peshitta and Targum) is preferable in context. Salters (2010: 225) points out Rashi's explanation of these alternatives which sees them as roughly equivalent. The MT might have arisen at an early stage through dittography, as *mem* and *nun* are graphically similar in paleo-Hebrew script.

9. The other acrostics joining them are Pss. 25:8; 32:16; 112:5; 145:9; and Lam. 4:19; but cf. also Prov. 31:18.

10. A similar note is also struck in Pss. 25:8; 145:9.

respectively. However, the sequence is reversed in Lamentations, with *pê* as stanza XVI, and *ʿayin* as XVII.[11] Be that as it may, the two *pê* stanzas contain a line which shares the fullest resonance of all those noted here.

3:48 *palgê-mayim tērad ʿênî ʿal-šeber bat-ʿammî*
<u>Streams of tears my eye sheds</u>
<u>because</u> of the destruction of the daughter of my people.

119:136 *palgê-mayim yārədû ʿênay ʿal lōʾ-šāmərû tôrāteka*
<u>Streams of tears my eyes shed</u>
<u>because</u> they do not keep your law.

There are small differences in formulation.[12] Lamentations 3:48 has a *yiqtol* form of the verb "shed" (*yārad*), uses the singular "eye," and has a nominal phrase introduced by *ʿal* in v. 48b; Ps. 119:136 has a *qatal* form of the verb, uses the plural "eyes," and a verbal clause introduced by *ʿal*.[13] Still, the first five lexemes of the two verses coincide, and this makes their completion the more noteworthy. The rivers of tears in the lament are occasioned by the destruction of the people, but the psalmist's weeping arises from observing "their" infidelity. While the lament has the actions of the "enemies" clearly in view, it is not so obvious who is intended by the psalmist's "they" in 119:136b. Often, a couple of verses in a stanza of Ps. 119 will contrast the psalmist's integrity or fidelity with the hostility of the "wicked" or "insolent" who despise God's law and those who keep it—the psalmist in particular. These are not named in this stanza, which refers rather to "human oppression" (*ʿōšeq ʾādām*, 119:134), although without any closer identification. But there is a good reason for this, when we glance at the preceding stanza in this psalm.

Both psalm and lament make use of "[my] eye(s)" as an acrostic word. Unusually for Ps. 119, attention on the "oppressors" in the *ʿayin* stanza occupies the psalmist's thoughts in the opening lines, 119:121-22, both using a form of *ʿāšaq* (thus the connection with 119:134); this theme usually comes later in the stanza, if it is present.[14] This opposition gives

---

11. The ordering in Lam. 3 is also found in Lam. 2 and 4. Salters (2011: 430 n. 14) regards the order as "not entirely rigid," citing further examples of the *pe-ʿayin* sequence.

12. The acrostic phrase, *palgê-mayim*, is not frequent in the HB, although it is found in four other settings: Ps. 1:3; Prov. 5:16; 21:1; Isa. 32:2. In each of these cases it is either a river or other free-flowing source of water. Using this figuratively of tears is restricted to Ps. 119:136 and Lam. 3:48.

13. For this use of *ʿal*, see Joüon-Muraoka 2006: 600 (= § 170h).

14. Note that *ʿāšaq* is not an acrostic word.

pause to the psalmist in 119:123: *'ênay kālû* "my eyes fail" in awaiting YHWH's salvation. As noted above, in Lam. 3 the *pê* stanza is followed by *'ayin*, and there is a strong sense of continuity between them. The weeping that concluded the preceding stanza here persists interminably (3:49, with *'ênî* as the acrostic word, cf. 3:48).[15] This persistence is pledged "until YHWH peers down from heaven and sees." So the "eye" that "ceases" in relation to YHWH's saving action in the psalm contrasts with the tenacity asserted by the poet of the lament towards YHWH's notice (3:49). These lines in the lament also mark the shift from hearing the first-person plural voice of the community, "we, us, our," in a brief but pivotal phase of the poem in 3:40-46, back to the voice of the individual which dominates the first and last parts of the lament.

While both poems express a sense of hostility experienced in their *ṣādê* stanzas, they do this with quite different choices in their language. But as the poems draw towards the end of the alphabet and their close, the *qôp* and *rêš* stanzas exhibit some notable acrostic parallels.[16] The three acrostic words of the lament's *qôp* stanza are used in five of the psalm's eight *qôp* lines, in the same sequence, and, in three of those lines, in the same linguistic form. In the lament, this stanza sees a narrative progression from the poet's calling to YHWH (*qārā'tî* "I called," 3:55), to "my voice" being heard (*qôlî šāmā'tā*, 3:56), to YHWH drawing near in response to that call (*qārabtā* "you drew near," 3:57). The same sequence is plotted in the psalm as well. Its first two lines match the acrostic word of the lament (*qārā'tî* "I call," with the second having the second-person suffix, "you," referring to YHWH, 119:145-46). The psalm stanza's fifth line coincides with the middle line of the lament stanza, as "my voice—hear!" (*qôlî šim'â*, 119:149) matches the first two words of the corresponding line of the lament.[17] And the motif with which the lament stanza closes, YHWH

---

15. The verse concludes with a difficult *hapax legomenon*, although the rendering common in modern versions reflects an ancient understanding: e.g., RSV: "My eyes will flow without ceasing, without respite..."

16. A question has long been debated regarding the temporal reference of the *qatal* (i.e., "perfect") forms in these stanzas of Lam. 3 (specifically, 3:52-61); the issue has no direct bearing on the present analysis. Still, Parry's discussion is illuminating (2010: 120–4). Once one realizes, as Parry does (p. 122), that the opposition shifts from a divine to human source between the beginning and end of the poem, and that the poet's previous experience of deliverance becomes the basis for a renewed appeal, then the issue perceived with the verb tense recedes dramatically, and there is no need to try to avoid a past-time reference in these lines.

17. The form *šim'â* is analyzed as an imperative masculine singular with a paragogic *he*; cf. Joüon-Muraoka 2006: 131–2, § 48d.

"drawing near," is found in the sixth and seventh lines of the psalm stanza, as those hostile to the psalmist "come near" (*qārəbû*, 119:150) at first, before this is trumped by YHWH being near (*qārôb*, 119:151).[18] Together, then, the *qôp* stanzas in both poems plot a cry arising out of distress, and as that voice is heard, the presence of YHWH draws near.

Speech in the *qôp* stanza gives way to sight in the *rêš* stanza. Although only two acrostic terms are shared, this last set of formal parallels in these poems provides some striking examples, including a set of shared lexemes exceeded only by Lam. 3:48 // Ps. 119:136 discussed above. Some form of the verb *rā'āh* ("to see") begins the second and third lines of the stanza in the lament, and the first, sixth, and seventh lines of the psalm. The first occasion of "seeing" in both cases contains strong resonances:

3:59a   *rā'îtā yhwh 'awwātî*
          You <u>have seen</u>, O YHWH, my oppression

119:153a   *rə'ēh 'onyî*
          <u>See</u> my affliction

This line in the lament goes on to call for "justice" (*mišpāṭ*), a term used in only one other line of this poem (3:35). In Ps. 119, the *mišpāṭîm* of YHWH occur frequently (23×)—it is one of the eight "revelation" lexemes—but only four times as a singular, one of those in the concluding line of this stanza (119:160) where "every righteous judgment" of YHWH is said to be "eternal."[19] "Sight" in the psalm oscillates between what YHWH ought to see (119:153, 159) and what the psalmist does see (119:158). YHWH ought to see the psalmist and his fidelity; the psalmist sees the "faithless" and is filled with loathing. In the lament, on the other hand, it is YHWH's vision alone which is of interest, whether it falls on the poet (3:59) or his oppressors (3:60).

But it is the other shared acrostic term that yields an even stronger resonance: *rîb* "contend, plead [a legal case]." In their respective *rêš* stanzas, it is used in the first line of the lament and the second line of the psalm:

3:58   *rabtā 'ădōnāy rîbê napšî gā'altā ḥayyāy*
              You <u>have contended</u>, O Lord, <u>my</u> [soul's] <u>case</u>
              you <u>redeem</u> my <u>life</u>.

---

18. The remaining lines of this stanza—all three of them—use a form of *q-d-m* "(be) early" as the acrostic term.

19. The others are 119:84, 120, and 132.

> 119:154 rîbâ rîbî ûgə'ālēnî lə'imrātəkā ḥayyēnî
> Contend my case and redeem me;
> according to your promise give me life.

Both lines share a doubled use of *rîb*, as both verb and noun, the verb *gā'al* "redeem," and reference to the life of the poet, as noun (*ḥayyim*) in the lament, and verb (*ḥāyâ, piel*) in the psalm. The line in the lament is cast as a set of observations, but in the psalm as carrying forward the appeal (grammatically imperative) to "look!" from the preceding verse. Still, the premise in both the lament and the psalm is that a life redeemed depends on YHWH's taking up the case of this "plaintiff." There are only two other verses in the HB that bring together *rîb* and *gā'al*, Prov. 23:11 and Jer. 50:34, which have their own connectedness through their shared assertion that "their Redeemer is strong" (*gō'ălām ḥāzāq*).[20] They also reinforce the impression of our two poetic lines, in that this language in all four cases places YHWH on the side of the oppressed against their oppressor.

The last two stanzas of these poems do not exhibit further formal similarities. In all, then, about eight of the twenty-two stanzas (roughly a third) exhibit some resonance, parallel, or "echo" between them. While their shared approach to a heightened acrostic form initially suggests a connection between them, these more specific, sustained, and in some cases striking parallels not only permit some intertextual dynamic between our two poems, but invite further reflection on this level.

Our survey so far has attended mostly to shared acrostic features, although some aspects in which they diverge have also been noted. There is more to be said about divergence between them, however, and how this too contributes to an intertextual reading of them. To this matter we now turn.

Aspects of Differentiation

There are, of course, many ways in which these poems diverge, but it is only necessary to observe a couple of them for the purposes of this exploration.

A swift reading of the two poems yields two very different impressions. In part this reflects the dynamic quality apparent in the lament, as

20. Reynolds (2010: 44) somewhat oddly offers Pss. 74:22; 106:10; and 107:2 as parallels to "plead my case; redeem me" in 119:154, although the first one lacks *g-'-l* and the latter two both lack *r-y-b*.

contrasted with the apparently static quality of the psalm. Lamentations 3 has clearly distinct movements, even if commentators differ on how to describe the poem's structure in precise terms. Roughly the first third is focused on the poet's suffering. The middle section explores possibilities of hope, arising out of YHWH's nature and expressed in appeal to the community. The final third turns overtly to prayer, as the poet addresses YHWH, in a muted sense on the community's behalf, but arising also out of personal distress in facing unidentified but human oppressors. Psalm 119 does not have this kind of narrative movement, at least not on the surface. Its most pronounced macro-structural device is found at the beginning of the *lāmed* stanza, the first three lines of which share a property found elsewhere in the Long Psalm only in the first four lines of the psalm as a whole: there is no first-person reference. Rather, in both cases there is generalized reflection, on the beatitude of the faithful (119:1-3 in particular), and on the persistence of the divine word (119:89-92). The psalm as a whole is thus divided into two equal spans of eleven stanzas each.

While the building blocks of the poems display different poetic strategies, their beginnings and endings exhibit a sort of inversion. The lament begins with a clear focus on the poetic self: "I am the man," the poet declares, putting down as a marker the first acrostic word, *ănî*, the first-person pronoun. The only other occurrence of this independent pronoun comes towards the lament's end, in 3:63b: "I am their taunt-song." The situation may have shifted, but the poet's affliction has not. Predicating self-identity in this way is also found in the psalm but sprinkled through it, the first occurrence at 119:19, *gēr 'ānōkî* ("A sojourner I am"), using the variant form of the first-person pronoun (see also 119:63, 94, 125, and 141). Together, they place the psalmist in proximity to the deity and among the faithful, although not without a hint of persecution, too (119:141, "belittled I am [*'ānōkî*], and despised").

The psalm offers a different opening strategy. Once the "thesis statement" of the first three lines is completed, the next line—still lacking a first-person form—also uses a pronoun as its acrostic word, but in this case it is *'attâ*: "You have commanded your precepts..." (119:4). The pronoun is the pivot on which the stanza turns: moving from a focus on "them" (vv. 1-3), through "you" with the independent pronoun (v. 4), to "me" (vv. 5-8).[21] As the succeeding lines unfold, the concern of the psalmist is to declare his life lived in light of the assertion in v. 4, that YHWH's precepts are to be kept to the uttermost (v. 4b). The rest of the

---

21. I owe this formulation to Oliver O'Donovan (private communication).

psalm is peppered with direct avowals of who YHWH is, portrayed as the one who "is blessed" (119:12), "is good" (119:68), "is my hiding-place and shield" (119:114), "is righteous" (119:137), "is near" (119:157).[22]

The poems, then, begin with differing personal focal points: the poet's self in the lament, but YHWH in the psalm. At their conclusion, this scenario is inverted. It was noted above that their common employment of *yiqtol* verb forms was a "false friend" in terms of convergence in their acrostic strategies. But in view of the contrast as they begin, this divergence now gains interest as they conclude. The lament closes with a flurry of direct addresses to YHWH, so named. The distribution of the Tetragrammaton through the lament is uneven. There is a cluster as the divine attributes form the basis for hope in 3:22-26. It appears again as an invitation to the community to "return" to YHWH at 3:40. From 3:50 to the end of the poem, it appears with regularity (3:50, 55, 59, 61, 64, 66), and is, in fact, the last word of the lament (in stark contrast, then, to *'ănî*, "I," which is its first word). The focus of the lament as it concludes is firmly on YHWH and what intervention might come against the poet's oppressors—envisaging that the wrath that the poet suffered in the first part of the poem might now be directed against his own assailants. By contrast, the psalm's closing jussive verbs (five out of six in this stanza) are circumlocutions for poetic self-reference. The remaining two lines (119:174 and 176) are first-person verbs, and so too is its last word (*lō' šākāḥtî*, "I do not forget," v. 176). Rather than the godward vision and confident claims for, and commitment to, fidelity to divine instruction at the psalm's inception, the psalmist ends in deep introspection in spite of the persistence of his commitment. We will return to these matters below.

The signals given by the independent pronouns remain somewhat subtle. There is a more obvious distinction between the two poems, however, and that relates to their most distinctive vocabulary. The hallmark lexeme of Lam. 3, *geber*, which plots the trajectory of the lament (3:1, 27, 35, 39), is absent from Ps. 119. On the reading suggested here, the use and distribution of first- and second-person independent pronouns suggest differences in self-identity between the two poets as inscribed in their poems. The more dramatic difference runs in the other direction. The Long Psalm's dependence on eight key "revelation" terms to provide one set of elements for the compositional matrix for the Long Psalm's development is well

---

22. The only other *'attâ* in the psalm is the subject of a verbal clause in 119:102, "you [*'attâ*] have instructed me," still with reference to YHWH. There is only a single *'attâ* in the whole of Lam. 3. It comes at 3:42, "We have transgressed and rebelled; you [*'attâ*] have not forgiven."

known.²³ But, apart from the occurrences of *mišpāṭ* in Lam. 3:35 and 59, they are otherwise absent from the lament. There is a key verb in Ps. 119 which co-occurs with these nouns: *šāmar* ("keep") which occurs 25 times, that is, on the same scale as the most frequently used of the "revelation" vocabulary (*tôrâ* also occurs 25×). It, too, is absent from Lam. 3, and the book as a whole.²⁴ Given the proximities noted at certain points in the acrostic strategy, these differences in fundamental compositional elements deserve some exploration, if not an explanation. There is one further matter to consider before we do so.

Hearing the Voices

The scholarship on both of these poems has posed the same question: who is its speaking voice? Who is the "man who has seen affliction" in Lam. 3? Who is the psalmist of the Long Psalm? These questions cannot be given sustained attention, but a brief survey of attempts to address them is suggestive for my intertextual reading.

So, who is *geber* of the lament? An early answer was, of course, Jeremiah.²⁵ Even aside from the difficulty of the rejection of Jeremiah's intercession,²⁶ scholars have not found this identification satisfactory and other suggestions have proliferated. They can be conveniently grouped as suggesting a prophetic figure of some kind, a royal figure (some Davidic king, whether specific or generic), a Job-like righteous sufferer (whether individuated or representative), or some personification of the community.²⁷ Although agreement on an identity for "the man" has proved elusive, recent discussions have begun to show some convergence in sketching the main contours of the *geber*.²⁸ In part this is achieved through

---

23. The set is comprised of the eight semantically related lexemes: *tôrâ*, *dābār*, *mišpāṭ(îm)*, *ʿēdōt*, *miṣwōt*, *piqqûdîm*, *ḥuqqîm*, and *ʾimrâ*, almost always with the second-person masculine singular suffix. These terms appear a total of 177 times in Ps. 119.

24. The only occurrences of any of these terms in Lamentations are *tôrâ* in 2:9 and *ʾimrâ* in 2:17.

25. Kugel (2017) provides a thorough account of the contribution this identification makes to Jeremiah's post-biblical persona.

26. On which, see Kugel 2017: 485–7.

27. Parry (2010: 94–5) provides a convenient and comprehensive catalogue; an earlier treatment by Saebø (1993) remains a useful survey and analysis, although his own positive suggestion of Zedekiah has not found support elsewhere. Middlemas 2006 and Bier 2014 both offer additional perspectives informing the discussion below.

28. I have in mind especially Bier 2014, Parry 2010, and Salters 2010, although others might also fit in here (e.g., Provan 1991).

perceiving a sustained voice through the poem as a whole, rather than fragmenting it into different voices. This combines with an effort to resist speculation and to attend instead to the concerns evidenced in the poem itself. Middlemas' (2006: 523–4) summary statement captures it well:

> The man of Lamentations iii is no ordinary individual who has experienced the tragedy of the fall of Jerusalem. His lament and the wisdom verses appended to it function within the book of Lamentations to provide the sanctioned response to disaster.

Unlike the poems which surround this central lament in the book, Lam. 3 takes no overt interest in the destruction of Zion. Its interest is personal, moral, and relational. Like Job and many of the psalms, this poet sees that YHWH is both "the origin and the goal of all distress," all suffering.[29] Significantly, this poet is not a representative or personification *of* the community, because the first-person plural section is rather addressed *to* the community.[30] While Westermann (1994: 192) thinks in terms of a "compiler" rather than a poet, he is right to note that the main interest in the composition is its "didactic content."

Who, then, is the psalmist of Ps. 119? The psalm lacks the degree of historical and literary situatedness that Lam. 3 possesses, and the identification of the psalmist is consequently more obscure.[31] There has been a move in recent years towards reaffirming a royal persona,[32] although this is not a claim the psalm itself makes, nor does it help with reading the poem. The self-identifications made are not of this kind. One clue many cling to comes at the beginning of the second stanza: "How shall a youth (*na'ar*) purify his way?" (119:9), understanding this to imply the persona of the psalmist—and such a persona does tally with the eager and insistent, but fragile, even vulnerable voice that is consistently found throughout the psalm. The leading characteristic of the psalmist is the commitment to divine instruction, which leads Reynolds (2010: 57–9) to identify this voice as that of an "exemplary Torah student."[33] So advanced

---

29. This wording comes from Bonhoeffer 1970: 48.
30. Noted by Parry 2010: 95.
31. Mensah (2016: 279–82) offers a concise overview and helpful critical assessment.
32. E.g., Grant 2004, Fishbane 2007, among others.
33. It might have been helpful for my interest if *geber* and *na'ar* showed some linguistic affinity, but they do not. They are only found twice in meaningful proximity. One comes with the reference to the *na'ar* in Lam. 2:21, thus in the poem preceding Lam. 3:1, so merely "canonically" connected. More suggestive is

is this "student," however, that his teachers have been left behind: the psalmist's understanding is directly rooted in the divine word.[34]

Reading Intertextually

What have we observed so far, then? The starting point for this exploration was the fundamental structural affinity between the acrostic approaches shared by Lam. 3 and Ps. 119. A number of convergences in their use of the acrostic technique were identified, further drawing together these two poems in a more significant way, and pointing towards a closer relationship between them than has usually been noted. The *zayin* and *qôp-rêš* stanzas in particular were seen to contain some striking resonances, while the five-lexeme match in Ps. 119:136 // Lam. 3:48 in the *pê* stanza is remarkable. Describing these parallels invited attention also on ways in which the two poems diverge, especially in the self-identity of their poets and the nature of their relationship with YHWH. Taking this all together provides sufficient commonality between the poems to discern potential for dialogue between them, while their differences help to focus that conversation.

Before exploring only a few of the intertextual gains found between these two poems I pause to note the work of the classicist Stephen Hinds, whose remarks on allusion and intertextuality inform my thinking in the discussion below. Working chiefly with Latin poets, Hinds (1998: 4–10) draws attention to the way in which speech and memory serve the allusive ends of his texts. His examples include the possibility, even the probability, of authorial self-consciousness in evoking an earlier poet's work. His remarks share some resonances with the project of identifying quotation and allusion within biblical studies, whether in the HB, or in the NT with reference to the OT.[35] In Hinds' wider discussion, the

---

Ps. 37:23-25, another acrostic setting, in which the *geber* who delights in YHWH's way is established and steadied by YHWH; the psalmist proceeds to recount how he was a *na'ar* and is now an elder, but has consistent experience of the stability of the righteous. If Kosmala (1975: 379) is correct to observe that in the Psalms "a man is called a *gebher* when he stands in an intimate relationship with God, trusts and fears God, and does what God requires of him," then the absence of the lexeme from Ps. 119 is all the more striking. It also potentially adds some nuance to the identification of Lam. 3:1, given the widely recognized psalmic overtones of that lament. But cf., also, the remarks below on Lam. 3:27.

34. Cf. Levenson 1987.
35. Tooman (2011: 4–21) provides an insightful orientation to the varied contributions in this broad area.

problem of authorial intentionality is faced, and with it the question of what part a reader's perceptions of allusion play in the dynamic between two (or more) texts.[36] His analysis is illuminating, even if his inclination is towards "allusion" rather than "intertextualism"; he leaves ample space for the readerly construction of meaning while not abandoning the author-poet whose contribution cannot finally be "occluded." So, with deliberate circumlocution, Hinds (1998: 49) describes the way in which "text-and-reader-oriented intertextuality" still finds a role for authors, since

> one of the most persistent ways in which both Roman and modern readers construct the meaning of a poetic text is by attempting to construct from (and for) it an intention-bearing authorial voice, a construction which they generally hope or believe (in a belief which must always be partly misguided) to be a reconstruction; and the author thus (re)constructed is one who writes towards an implied reader who will attempt such a (re)construction.

I find this a helpful framework for conceptualizing the relationship between the poets of Lam. 3 and Ps. 119 and their readers.

As the examination of formal acrostic parallels between these poems demonstrated, there are significant shared aspects which forge connections between them. At the same time, both contain curious gaps which relate in some ways to the divergence in the "voices" heard in them. Once the poems are connected, they can mutually inform the "gaps" in each other. A pointer in this direction can already be found in *Lamentations Rabbah*. In the expansive midrash on Lam. 3:19-21, while pondering v. 21, "This I call to mind and therefore I have hope," the question arises as to what "this" refers to, the memory which brings hope. A parable is recounted in the name of R. Abba bar Kahana on the authority of R. Yohanan, telling the story of a royal marriage settlement that enables a bride to sustain hope for her absent royal husband's return. This document is likened to Torah, and the moral of the story is drawn together in pointing to Ps. 119:92, "So David says, 'Unless your Torah had been my delight, I should then have perished in my affliction'" (Neusner 1989b: 265).[37] In the lament, just what was the trigger of memory that led to such hope remains opaque. In the tradition of rabbinic commentary, this gap is explained through appeal to Torah, and this finds its demonstration in the words of Ps. 119. Here, then, is one small example of a dialogue between these poems that goes far beyond this single instance.

---

36. Cf. in particular Hinds 1998: 47–51.

37. Text in Buber 1899: 132; cf. the extract anthologized by Epstein 1904, q.v. Lam. 3:21, in which the Ps. 119:92 intertext is picked out as the salient comment.

11. *Verse and Voice in Lamentations 3 and Psalm 119*

There are various ways in which the voices of these poems intertwine. Already in the analysis of formal parallels above, the convergence on the trio of memory, affliction, and hope was observed, and is implicated in the connection made in *Lamentations Rabbah*. The turn from suffering to hope in Lam. 3 seems mysterious and unmotivated (*zayin* stanza, 3:19-21). The poet, undaunted by perplexed readers, proceeds to outline the character of YHWH (3:22-24), and then in the *ṭêt-yôd* stanzas asserts the benefits that come from waiting on YHWH, even in accepting harsh treatment from the hand of God. Here, the experience of the psalmist reinforces and fills out the scenario described in the lament. Signaling this trajectory already in 119:49-50 (*zayin* stanza), the *ṭêt-yôd* stanzas provide an account of how divine affliction benefitted the psalmist in adhering to divine instruction and faithful living (119:67, 71, 75). The affirmation of the good that accrues to this posture is mutually informing:

> Good it is for a man (*geber*) that he should bear a yoke in his youth (*nə ʿûrā[y]w*). (3:27)

> Good it was for me to be afflicted so that I would learn your statutes. (119:71)

At this point, the identity of poet and psalmist are at their closest, as the "man" reflects on the training of "youth" (*nə ʿûrîm*).[38] The "salvation" (*təšûʿâ*) for which the lamenting poet waits emerges, too, in the experience of the psalmist in the first line of the *kaph* stanza:

> Good it is to wait [*yāḥîl*] quietly for YHWH's salvation. (Lam. 3:26)

> Longs for your salvation does my soul—for your word I hope [*yiḥāltî*]. (Ps. 119:81)

Repeatedly in these passages, the free-floating expectations of the lament are earthed in persistent adherence to divine instruction as celebrated in the psalm.

If this catches something of the constellation of themes relating to memory, something similar can be observed in relation to speech. While for Hinds this had mostly to do with more concrete allusion, it is also the case that speech gives rise to echoes between our two poems. This comes in its most concentrated form in the *qôp-rêš* stanzas (Lam. 3:55-60; Ps. 119:145-60), and some account of this has already been provided in the

---

38. Cf. the comments on Ps. 119:9 at n. 32, above.

analysis of their formal connections. In these stanzas both poets explicitly articulate their speech to YHWH, anticipate a just response, and recruit YHWH's active inclinations to the writer's cause. Gladson (2010: 325–31) further brings to the surface the way in which divine speech, absent for so much of the lament, in this *qôp* stanza can be heard at first faintly, then in 3:57b clearly, if briefly: "You said, 'Do not fear!'" In light of the striking resonances between the poems in these stanzas, the effusion of divine speech found in these lines of the psalm takes this word of comfort beyond an assumed cultic setting.[39] Once again, the word of YHWH in all its fullness provides security for the psalmist. If one wonders what there is for the psalmist to fear, the answer is: only YHWH himself (119:63, 74, 79, 120).[40]

In these cases, the psalm seems to be informing lament; but there are ways, too, in which the lament informs the psalm. If the psalm fills up some of the absence of content from the lament, by contrast the lament provides the explicit exhortation that is lacking in the psalm. In the lament we hear the voice of a man who has suffered, but has come to find hope in YHWH, and so appeals to the community: "Let us search and examine our ways, and return to YHWH" (3:40). In spite of an affirmation of YHWH's justice (3:34-36), the man who urges his community to follow YHWH's ways never provides any content as to what that looks like. The psalmist, on the other hand, is entirely occupied—even preoccupied—with divine instruction, and recognizes around him a community lax, at best, in its commitment to live in accordance with it. And yet, there is no exhortation: as Reynolds (2010: 80, 96) pointedly observes, to the wicked who "do not observe Torah…there is no exhortation to repent," neither does "the author…exhort the reader to obey and study Torah, instead he portrays someone [who] does so." This, however, is what the poet of the lament sets out to do: to urge those who have departed from YHWH's ways to repent of their own ways and turn to him. There is a sense of tessellation between the two poems, as the space in one is seamlessly filled by juxtaposition with the other.

Finally, there is the curiously ambivalent conclusion to the Long Psalm. How is it that the psalmist, so confident of heeding divine instruction and so committed to living in accord with it, could at last confess himself to have "wandered like a lost sheep," and plead to be sought by YHWH? Here the perspective of the poet of the lament provides one explanation,

---

39. Gladson 2010: 329 and n. 37; Parry 2010: 124. Other options are explored by Salters 2010: 269–70.

40. For an elaboration of this theme in Ps. 119, cf. Creach 1996: 70–1.

which lies beneath the surface of the psalm. The individual may come to understand YHWH's ways, to see YHWH as ultimately responsible for both grief and compassion (3:31-33). Yet, apart from solidarity with the wider community of God's people, there remains the possibility, even reality, of ongoing opposition (3:61-63). At one of the points of sustained overlap between the poems (Lam. 3:49-51; Ps. 119:136) this perspective can be discerned: through unceasing tears the poet of the lament sees the pain of the "daughters of my city" (3:51), but through tears the psalmist sees that "people do not keep your law" (119:136). There is a sense of isolation that runs through the psalm, yet with it also an impression that the psalmist is ultimately bound to those who do not share his zeal (119:63, 98-100, 139, 141).

Alan Cooper has drawn attention to the ways in which the book of Lamentations can sustain quite divergent interpretations. He illustrates the manner in which attention to ancient Near Eastern city lament informs one understanding of the book, in that its laments are a vehicle for fixing the deity's attention on the suffering of poet and people, and so elicit divine comfort. The purpose of the laments, he argues, is "to bring the god's wrath...to an end by calling his attention to the penitent's wretched state" (Cooper 2011: 14). Even if the present study travels by a very different route, this closing note of the psalmist's which seems so pathetic—as strangely inadequate, and arousing pity—strikes a similar note to Cooper's handling of Lamentations, and provides at least some framework for understanding the psalmist's curious pessimism.

Altogether, then, this begins to suggest some of the ways in which a dialogue between the two most sustained acrostics in the HB demonstrates not only a shared poetic strategy, but a meaningful intertextual relationship.

Chapter 12

DEBATING SUFFERING:
THE VOICES OF LAMENTATIONS PERSONIFIED IN JOB'S DIALOGUE

Will Kynes

Suffering is a constant undercurrent of the HB that frequently lashes at the surface, creating deep swells of emotion, towering peaks of hope, and crashing waves of complaint. Though the troughs of these breakers often descend into despair, their crests reach upward from the tumult, at least for a moment, grasping at hope. In its intense representation of this experience, the book of Lamentations claws at its readers like a drowning man, pulling them into the churning currents. The interpretation of Lam. 3, which combines the book's highest whitecap with some of its deepest troughs, reveals how readers flail to keep their heads above the surface. To bring order to this chaos, interpreters consistently organize the chapter into different "voices."

In these efforts, modern readers are following the lead of what appears to be one of the book's earliest interpreters, the author of Job. Since the book of Job likewise lurches through surging suffering, reading Job and Lamentations together has a certain "inevitability" (Aitken 2013). And yet, despite the common recognition of the "Job-like" character of Lamentations, particularly ch. 3, in commentaries (Berlin 2002: 85), surprisingly little research has attempted to weather the waves churned up by the intersection of these two books (Aitken 2013: 205). The echoes of the "voices" in Lam. 3 in the speeches of both Job and his friends amplify that chapter's dialogical reflection on suffering, and reveal how interpreters, ancient and modern, instinctively separate and personify the voices in Lam. 3, even as they struggle to hold them together. This intertextual comparison also illuminates the figure who struggles to keep his head above the turbulent waters of Lam. 3.

Intertextual Method

I will dive into this issue while putting diachronic and synchronic, or author-oriented and reader-oriented, approaches to intertextuality in dialogue, since these two approaches are inextricably intertwined.[1] From a diachronic perspective, I will argue that the striking use of the siege metaphor from Lam. 3 in Job 16 and 19 provides compelling, though admittedly not conclusive, evidence of an allusion, an "intentional implicit reference to an earlier expression" (Kynes 2012: 31), that encourages readers to compare Job's experience with that described in Lamentations. This connecting allusion invites readers into a broader synchronic comparison between the texts, which considers other potential allusions between them while reflecting on how each text illuminates the meaning of the other.

Because biblical authors rarely cited their sources, most arguments for intentional references to earlier texts must roam in the realm of probability, where some will weigh the evidence differently than others. However, the Job poet clearly demonstrates an affinity for allusion through the frequent allusions Job and his friends make to each other's speeches, often while changing both the wording and context of the original (Kynes 2012: 46–9; Lyons 2013). Further, I find some of the evidence for intertextual allusion, such as the parody of Ps. 8:5 in Job 7:17-18 or the verbatim repetition of an entire verse from Ps. 107:40 in Job 12:21, 24, to be such compelling indicators of authorial intentionality that the possibility of further allusions must be considered (see Kynes 2012: 63–7, 80–1). Even so, the implicit nature of allusions means that the possibility of shared reference to a lost common source or some other cultural influence can never be definitively denied. These texts were written in the midst of a "wide-ranging network of interconnections," but using this fact to oppose the search for allusions is a false dichotomy (*pace* Kwon 2016b: 41), since such a network would facilitate allusions, even if its complex nature may make them difficult to prove. This uncertainty, however, only limits the diachronic conclusions that may be reached. The elusiveness of authorial intent may reduce the force of the synchronic comparisons that potential allusions inspire, but it does not eliminate their interpretive value altogether.

"I am the גבר who has seen affliction" (Lamentations 3:1)

The steady flow of the acrostic form of Lam. 3 hardly matches the thematic and syntactic currents that intermingle within it. As a result,

---

1. For more on this intertextual method and its compatibility with intertextual theory, see Kynes 2012: 17–60; 2013a.

scholars consistently break the text into different sections but rarely agree on where the divisions occur. I will focus on the first two sections of the chapter, the complaints of the "man" (גבר)[2] regarding the divinely initiated violence he has suffered in vv. 1-18, and the "sapiential consolation" which responds in impersonal, abstract generalizations to his complaints in vv. 25-39, declaring divine goodness and justice and eschewing complaint (Dobbs-Allsopp 2002: 119), as well as the transitional verses immediately surrounding them.

The Voices of Lamentations 3

Though perhaps the most striking, the tension between these two sections is hardly the only one in the chapter. Magne Sæbø (1993: 300–301) notes the tensions between the unifying overarching acrostic pattern of the chapter and the "variegated tradition fragments" within it, between the "I" and the "we" (vv. 40-47) that speak, between the chapter's personal and historically situated features and its "timeless" instructions, and between the theology of Lam. 3 and that of the chapters which surround it. These factors all contribute to the common conclusion that the chapter consists of multiple "voices." Some, such as Westermann (1994: 191), externalize these voices as different individual "components" compiled from different traditions over time. Others, such as Bier (2015: 108), internalize them as an "internal dialogue" within a single speaker (similarly, Berlin 2002: 84 n. 1; Dobbs-Allsopp 2002: 105). Some argue the move to first-person plural indicates a second voice (e.g., Hillers 1972: 72), while others see the transition as an effect of the collective nature of the "I" who speaks in the chapter (Albrektson 1963: 126–8).

Proposals of different voices, either behind the text or within it, do not actually resolve any of the tensions Sæbø identifies; they simply personify them. Even when those voices are simply reflections of an inner debate, it is a debate nonetheless, in which the single speaker "reasons with himself" (Berlin 2002: 92; similarly, Provan 1991: 95; Bier 2015: 125). This leads naturally to interpretations of Lamentations as a polyphonic dialogue, in which the text's message exists only in the plurality of consciousnesses, is embodied, resists systemization, and is unfinalizable (see Bier 2015: 33–4; cf. Boase 2006: 23–34).

---

2. Commentators generally agree a gender-neutral translation obscures important connotations of the Hebrew word גבר, which consistently has a male referent (see Bier 2015: 106–7).

Who Is the גבר?

Interpreters have long attempted to personify Lam. 3 in another way, however, by identifying the person who speaks in the text, but who only refers to himself as "the man who has seen affliction" (v. 1). A number of proposals have been made. These include Jeremiah, the traditional view (see 2 Chron. 35:25), resurrected in modern scholarship in a figurative sense, as well as a series of other figures, including Jehoiachin and Zedekiah, or a former soldier or temple singer (see Bezzel 2011: 253–4). To these historical individuals have been added proposals for a number of different historical communities, such as Zion, all Israel, or the exiles (see Salters 2010: 186). Arguing that an individual can better lament and engage in private contemplation and repentance and prayer than a community, Hillers (1972: 64) considers the speaker as representative of the typical sufferer, an "everyman" who serves as a "model for the nation." Thus, even though he opposes the collective interpretation of the speaker, his reading still leans in that direction. After all, other features of the text, most notably the first-person plural, draw the community into the text even if an individual is speaking throughout (Salters 2010: 185–6). Heath Thomas (2013b: 172–3) argues that the many different speakers that have been proposed for the chapter, of which he lists fourteen, both display "the poetry's elusiveness regarding the specific identity of the speaker(s)" and "promote an open strategy for the model reader."

The openness of this text and the debate it engenders reflect the "fluid personality" in texts across the HB, in which the individual and the community flow into one another, such that communal complaints are frequently communicated in individual terms (Gordis 1974: 170–3). This phenomenon, evident in the debate over the "I" in the Psalms, reflects a basic Israelite instinct toward personifying lament (Kynes 2013c). This personification makes the sufferings of the community more concrete in the experience of a single individual, which infuses it with the authority of firsthand experience, even if the figurative experience is of a fictive persona (Berlin 2002: 84, 88). "An individual human being relating personal experiences" need not be set against the representation of the suffering of the community (*pace* Westermann 1994: 172), but may be the most effective means for doing so. Lamentations 3, then, demonstrates how this "fluid personality" flows both ways, as it takes general experience and narrows it down to an individual, but then, over the course of the chapter, "gradually broadens to include human experience more generally" (Dobbs-Allsopp 2002: 107).

When interpreters attempt to associate Lam. 3 with a particular historical individual, they are following the lead of the scribes who added the superscriptions to the Psalms or incorporated them into biblical narratives (1 Sam. 2:1-10; Isa. 38:10-20; Jer. 11:18–12:6) and thereby made them more broadly applicable by applying them to a specific individual (see Childs 1979: 521). Arguing, then, that the descriptions in Lamentations are too "concrete" for the "everyman" or representative figure interpretations (Saebø 1993: 299) misunderstands this imagery's intended rhetorical effect. Only through being concrete enough to represent real experience can it truly resonate with any other sufferer or even the community as a whole. The continuing debate over which individual or communal experience Lam. 3 represents testifies to the text's deft tiptoe along the line between generality and specificity, as its conventional and yet concrete language both enables and invites the text to be applied to a wide variety of specific situations. Dobbs-Allsopp (2002: 115), while arguing along these lines, claims the song's literary context in Lamentations provides the text with its particularity, associating it with Jerusalem's destruction. Readers who use other intertextual connections to put the text in different literary contexts, connecting it with other individuals or communities, however, demonstrate that this experience of suffering hardly exhausts its semantic potential.

"What גבר is like Job?" (Job 34:7)

Drawing on that potential, another specific figure has been associated with the גבר of Lam. 3: Job. Gordis (1974: 174) refers to the chapter as a "Job lament," and Berlin (2002: 85) finds it "perhaps more than coincidental" that Job refers to himself as a גבר in his first speech (Job 3:3).[3] Aitken (2013: 206–7) cites several instances of the association between Job and the devastation of Jerusalem in Lamentations in rabbinic interpretation, including an early midrash that considers "I am the גבר" in Lam. 3:1 a reference to Job in light of Elihu's question, "What גבר is like Job?" (34:7) (*Lam. Rab.* 3:1). The synchronic intertextual comparison the rabbis make between the two books, in which Lam. 3 is prominent, is justified by numerous lexical parallels they note between them, to which Aitken (2013: 207–8) adds several more, with Lam. 3 appearing the most frequently. These include the common experience of suffering from God's "rod" (Lam. 3:1; Job 9:34-35) and his "arrows" (Lam. 3:12-13; Job 6:4),

---

3. See, similarly, Brandscheidt (1983: 51), who notes the large role the term plays in Job, where it appears 15 times, more than any other biblical book.

and being made a "laughingstock" (Lam. 3:14; Job 12:4) and "filled with bitterness" by God (Lam. 3:15; Job 9:18). For Aitken, however, these isolated parallels do not justify a diachronic intertextual relationship between the texts, since they could simply result from the similar subject matter they share. Though he considers the recurrent parallels to Lam. 3 in Job 19 (Lévêque 1970: 1:382–6) and Job 16 (Mettinger 1993: 269–71) as possible exceptions, Aitken concludes that they too more likely result from common motifs (2013: 210; see Clines 1989: 442; cf. Hillers 1972: 63).

Connecting Allusions: Job under Siege

Lévêque, however, argues that Job is alluding to Lamentations, though, as Aitken observes (2013: 210), he simply presents a "mosaic" of lexical parallels rather than "a consistent allusion to one passage." Lévêque (1970: 384) simply lists a series of 16 isolated lexical and thematic parallels, many consisting of only one repeated word. The sheer number and precision of the parallels all grouped in a single chapter of Job, however, are sufficient to convince Lévêque that they cannot be the result of chance (382). Because parallels to all five chapters of Lamentations are found together in a single chapter of Job, he concludes Job must be the alluding text, rather than the multiple authors of Lamentations all drawing on one chapter from Job (382–3).

A closer look at Lévêque's table reveals, though, that the allusions are not as isolated as they may at first appear. One collection of parallels in Job 19:6-8 corresponds to another in Lam. 3:6-9.[4]

Job 19:6-8	Lam. 3:6-9
⁶ know then that God has put me in the wrong [עִוְּתָנִי], and closed his net around me.	⁶ he has made me sit in darkness [מַחֲשַׁכִּים] like the dead of long ago.
⁷ Even when I cry out [אֶצְעַק], "Violence!" I am not answered; I call aloud [אֲשַׁוֵּעַ], but there is no justice.	⁷ He has walled [גָּדַר] me about so that I cannot escape; he has put heavy chains on me;
⁸ He has walled up [גָּדַר] my way so that I cannot pass, and he has set darkness [חֹשֶׁךְ] upon my paths.	⁸ though I call [אֶזְעַק] and cry [אֲשַׁוֵּעַ] for help, he shuts out my prayer;
	⁹ he has blocked [גָּדַר] my ways with hewn stones, he has made my paths crooked [עִוָּה].

Figure 12.1 Job 19:6-8 and Lam. 3:6-9.

---

4. Unless otherwise noted, all translations are from the NRSV.

This extended parallel has a number of notable features. First, starting in the middle (Job 19:7; Lam. 3:8), the verb שׁוע ("cry") is combined with one of the biforms of "call" (זעק or צעק) in only two other verses in the HB (Hab. 1:2[5] and Job 35:9, both using זעק). In both Job and Lamentations, these unanswered cries are enclosed by the imagery of being surrounded. In Lamentations the verb גדר is repeated in both instances (vv. 7, 9), while Job first speaks of God "closing" (*hiphil* of נקף) him in his net (v. 6) and then repeats the verb גדר when he, like Lamentations, speaks of his "way" being walled up (v. 8), though using a different word for "way." Finally, both passages use the imagery of God making them "crooked" and putting them in "darkness," but the order of the shared terms is reversed. Job begins with a reference to being made crooked (*piel* of עוה[6]) and ends with a reference to "darkness" (חשׁך); Lamentations begins with a reference to "darkness" (מחשׁך) and ends with paths made crooked (*piel* of עוה). The passages, then, combine lexical, thematic, and structural parallels. Job does use a different form for three of the five shared words, but the Job poet makes changes like this even in allusions within the book (e.g., Job 21:17; cf. 18:5-6), so small variations like these may accord with his allusive technique rather than argue against it (see Kynes 2012: 46–9).

This indicates at least a strong correspondence between the two texts, if not an actual allusion from one to the other, but one more factor should be considered. After a potential allusion to Lam. 5:16 in v. 9 (see Kynes 2012: 73–4 n. 65), Job continues in vv. 10-12 to expand on the imagery from Lam. 3:7-9 and depict himself as a besieged city. This metaphor is "somewhat unexpected" in Job (Clines 1989: 442), but fitting in Lam. 3, where Zion's suffering stands behind the individual's agony (Provan 1991: 85). For Mettinger (1993: 272–3), this tips the balance toward affirming the Job poet's allusion to Lamentations, since, citing Michael Riffaterre, markers of an intertext are "both the problem, when seen from the text, and the solution when their other, intertextual side is revealed." When shared terminology appears in different contexts, that contextual divergence may enforce rather than militate against an intentional allusion, as both the internal coherence of the potential allusion in its new context and external coherence of its fit with its original context are considered (Kynes 2012: 52–4; *pace* Kwon 2016b: 41).

---

5. Habakkuk also cries out "violence" (סמח) as does Job. It would not be beyond the literary skill of the author of Job to combine allusions to two different passages in a single verse, since he does this with passages within the dialogues, e.g., Job 25:4; cf. Job 9:2; 15:14 (Kynes 2012: 48).

6. See *HALOT*, which suggests this verb may be a secondary form of עוה.

Reinforcing this intertextual connection, Job applies siege imagery to himself in a second passage, 16:12-13, where he again draws on language from Lam. 3.

Job 16:12-13	Lam. 3:11-13
12 I was at ease, and he broke me in two [וַיְפַרְפְּרֵנִי];	11 he led me off my way and tore me to pieces [וַיְפַשְּׁחֵנִי];
he seized me by the neck and dashed me to pieces [וַיְפַצְפְּצֵנִי];	he has made me desolate;
he set me up as his target [מַטָּרָה];	12 he bent his bow and set me as a mark [מַטָּרָא] for his arrow.
13 his archers surround me.	13 He shot into my vitals [כִּלְיוֹתָי]
He slashes open my kidneys [כִּלְיוֹתַי], and shows no mercy;	the arrows of his quiver
he pours out my gall on the ground.	

Figure 12.2 Job 16:12-13 and Lam. 3:11-13.

Both texts begin with accusing God of breaking the sufferer into pieces, though using different words, before making him into a "target,"[7] and damaging his "kidneys." The analogy of the destruction of a person with the destruction of a city again appears to be inspired by Lam. 3 (Schmid 2007: 249).

Comparing Job 19 and Lam. 3, Lévêque (1970: 385) notes how in both hope bursts forth (Lam. 3:21-24; Job 19:25) without transition from a crescendo of despair (Lam. 3:18; Job 19:10, 20). He also notes the similar move to confidence in Job 16:19-21. Job follows some of his angriest accusations against God with his highest flights of hope. The common juxtaposition of hope and despair in both texts suggests, at least, that the two emotions were not as inimical to each other as they may seem. Job testifies with Lam. 3 to "the peculiar biblical idea that hope is born out of pain" (Dobbs-Allsopp 2002: 117).

Recurrence: The Friends' Attempted Consolation

The structural parallels between Lam. 3 and Job do not end here, however, as the potential allusions to Lam. 3 in Job 16 and 19 solder the texts together and encourage readers to see where else the current running between them might flow (see Kynes 2012: 55). The whiplash between despair and hope in Lam. 3 is matched by a similarly disorienting juxtaposition of

---

7. Again, the spelling differs slightly. The word, which appears 16 times in the HB, means "guard" in every other instance, with the exception of the narrative in 1 Sam. 20:20.

impassioned complaint and reasoned instruction. Lee (2002: 180), for example, observes that the second singer she hears in Lam. 3:25-41 is "diametrically opposed" to the first, as he defends God instead of accusing him and advocates keeping silent before God's punishment, rather than complaining. Commentators commonly note the resonance between Job's friends and the "sapiential consolation" in the middle of Lam. 3, which is unified by its contrasting viewpoint, mood, and subject matter from 3:1-18 and involves "contemplation of traditional attitudes about how to cope with suffering" (Dobbs-Allsopp 2002: 119–21; cf. Gordis 1974: 139–40; Lee 2002: 174; Bouzard 2014: 77). Berlin (2002: 94) even calls these verses the "most Joblike" in the chapter.

Though the lexical connections are not as strong as the links between the chapter's opening complaints and Job's laments, this "sapiential consolation" includes sentiments remarkably similar to those of Job's friends. Nearly every idea expressed in these verses appears at some point on the lips of Job's friends, occasionally with the same words. Like the "sapiential consolation" in Lam. 3, the friends encourage Job to "seek" (דרש) God (Lam. 3:25; Job 5:8), chastise him for speaking (Lam. 3:26; Job 8:2; 11:2-3; 15:2-3; 18:2),[8] declare the blessing of divine reproof (Lam. 3:27-28; Job 5:17; 33:19-30; 36:7-15), combine the possibility of "hope" (תקוה) with the imagery of a shut "mouth" (פי) (Lam. 3:29; Job 5:16), and promise the overcoming of insults (Lam. 3:30; Job 5:21), the end of divine rejection (Lam. 3:31; Job 8:20-21[9]), and the divine compassion that follows divine affliction (Lam. 3:31-32; Job 5:18), since the just deity "does not oppress" (ענה לא), at least not willingly (Lam. 3:33; Job 37:23), though humans may be "crushed" (דכא) (Lam. 3:34; Job 4:18-19; cf. 5:4; 22:9; 34:25). Whereas Lam. 3:35-36 may use a rhetorical question to affirm that the Lord sees when the "justice" (משפט) of a גבר is perverted and his case "subverted" (עות), Bildad uses rhetorical questions to deny that God will "pervert" (עות)[10] "justice" (משפט) (Job 8:3; cf. 34:12, 17-21; 37:23-24). As Lam. 3:37-38 attributes all things, good and bad, to the "command" (צוה) of the Lord, so Elihu speaks of the rain and lightning obeying God's "command" (צוה) "whether for correction, or for his land, or for love" (Job 37:11-13).[11] Both texts consider complaint an

---

8. The prologue also advocates the silent submission of Lam. 3:26 through the initial responses of both Job (Brandscheidt 1983: 62) and the friends (Aitken 2013: 213).

9. Cf. 5:18-27 (Brandscheidt 1983: 63).

10. This verb appears 11 times in the HB, but only in Job and Lamentations in a legal context (Salters 2010: 271).

11. Job also accepts "good" and "bad" from God in the prologue (2:10) (Berlin 2002: 85).

inappropriate response to God's gifts, whether that is life (Lam. 3:39; see Provan 1991: 99) or other comforts (Job 15:11-13; cf. 34:36-37). Both advocate careful "examining" (חקר; Lam. 3:40; Job 5:27) and "return to the Lord" (ונשובה עד יהוה; Lam. 3:40; תשוב עד שדי; Job 22:23). Finally, in Lamentations, this repentance involves "lifting up" (נשא) "hearts" (לבב) and "hands" (כף) (Lam. 3:41), while for the friends, Job must prepare his "heart" (לב) and stretch out his "hands" (כף), before he can "lift up" (נשא) his face (Job 11:13, 15).[12]

This section of Lam. 3, which shares its "basic outlook" with Job's friends, also shares their "choric function" in that, like the chorus in Greek tragedy, both provide "the link to the known and familiar" and thus become "the foil against which one is to read the rest of the book" (Dobbs-Allsopp 1997: 49; 2002: 119). As Lam. 3 descends back into affliction, it, like the book of Job, derives its "power and success" from "its ability to hold and affirm conflicting and contradictory truths without eventually surrendering either" (Dobbs-Allsopp 2002: 120). The conflicting positions of Job and the friends are mirrored in the contradictions between the sentiments in the "sapiential consolation" and those expressed elsewhere in the book, as this voice even appears to allude to and dispute other voices. It appears, for example, to take the "yoke" (על) as a symbol of suffering from Lam. 1:14 to declare the benefits of divine reproof (Lam. 3:27). These "intentional" correspondences, like those in Job, "force the reader to measure and compare traditional attitudes and dispositions with the suffered reality that comprises the fabric of these poems" (Dobbs-Allsopp 2002: 121–2). Reading these conventional ideas in the midst of Lamentations forces one to ask with Berlin (2002: 94) whether the poet of Lam. 3 believes them like Job's friends or rejects them like Job.

Recognizing the intertextual interplay between Job and Lam. 3 adds a further dimension to this intratextual conflict. As in the dialogical interpretation of the Psalms in Job (see Kynes 2012: 183–7), potential allusions to the same verses from Lam. 3 by both Job and his friends make their theological debate a hermeneutical one. They also interpret and apply Lam. 3 to Job's situation in different ways. For example, while similarly endorsing the blessing of divine reproof (Job 5:17; Lam. 3:26-27), Eliphaz in 5:21 claims even more forcefully than Lam. 3:30 that the righteous need not fear insults, but Job uses three of the five Hebrew words in Lam. 3:30 in 16:10 to claim he has suffered precisely this indignity, before going on to draw on the siege imagery from Lamentations (see Brandscheidt

---

12. See Salters 2010: 250. See also the parallel to Job 22:26, which comes on the heels of the encouragement to "return to the Almighty" (v. 23) as it does in Lam. 3:40-41.

1983: 63). Similarly, when Bildad in 8:3 more emphatically denies divine perversion (עות) of justice than Lam. 3:35-36, Job in 19:6 uses the same verb to retort that God has indeed perverted justice in his case in the midst of a second allusion to the siege metaphor.

Mandolfo has observed how a didactic voice typically intrudes into psalmic laments to express traditional views. She has traced this interplay of voices both in Lam. 3 (2007b: 71), where she sees the didactic voice speaking in vv. 22-42, and in Job, where Job and the friends make the implicit dialogue in the Psalms explicit and literal (2007a: 47 n. 5, 52). In both cases, she argues the authors are engaging with generic expectations evident in psalmic laments. However, if the author of Job does indeed allude directly to a number of psalms, such that Job and the friends draw on the tensions within the psalms as weapons in their argument (Kynes 2012), then the striking contrast between the supplicant's suffering and the didactic voice's instruction in Lam. 3 could have easily inspired him to do the same thing with that text. As he has Job personify himself as the גבר in Lam. 3, the author of Job personifies the polyphonic debate in that chapter in Job's dialogue with his friends.

From a ritual perspective, Lambert (2015: 561–2) argues, the friends' "agonistic relationship" with Job actually fulfilled their prescribed role, providing "consolation," not to transform Job's subjective emotional state, but to restore him from a state of mourning to normal participation in society. In Lamentations, the "sapiential consolation" performs a similar role, as it too attempts to bring the גבר out of his mourning and into acceptable social behavior. However, like the friends, these words also fail, as "the language of wisdom is overwhelmed by the language of lament" (Berlin 2002: 95).

Holistic Interpretation: The "Missing Voice" Speaks

Further thematic and lexical resonances between Lam. 3 and Job could be explored, but the close correspondence both between Job's speeches and the chapter's first section and between Job's friends and the second section, is sufficient to highlight the polyphonic dialogue in Lam. 3. When compared to Dostoevsky's novels, which Bakhtin considered exemplary dialogic texts, the גבר of Lam. 3 is more like the internally conflicted Raskolnikov of *Crime and Punishment*, while Job and his friends embody the positions of that debate like Alyosha, Ivan, and Dimitri in *The Brothers Karamazov*. The dialogic features of Lam. 3 are accentuated by comparison with Job's dialogue, and may very well have been the result of the Job poet's appropriation and adaptation of the chapter given the connecting allusions between them, as he created a true dialogue of suffering that is even more plural, embodied, unsystemizable, and unfinalizable.

And yet, he cannot quite pull it off. Like so many readers of Lamentations, the author of Job is unable to allow this debate to remain unresolved. He inserts the divine voice that readers of Lamentations often feel is "missing" (O'Connor 2002: 83–95; cf. Provan 1991: 25). Whether or not the "orthodox confessions" in the middle of Lam. 3 are intended rhetorically to force this response (Bouzard 2014: 70, 77), their failure to console, like that of Job's friends, creates an expectation for a divine answer. God, in Job, provides the effective "consolation" that Lamentations lacks, and that Job's friends are unable to provide, which can overcome Job's ritual mourning (Lambert 2015: 563). If the intertextual comparison of the two texts uncovers "a dispute over…the inefficacy of certain types of comfort" (Aitken 2013: 215), then, by associating the consoling sentiments from Lam. 3 with Job's friends, the Job dialogue demonstrates the failure of even orthodox human speech to console some types of mourning (see Mandolfo 2007a: 62–3), with the divine verdict against the friends' consolations added for good measure (Job 42:7). Whether through its absence or its inclusion, the two texts together argue that some storms of suffering can only be stilled by a divine word, which is in keeping with theophanies in other laments, such as Pss. 18; 74; 77 (Gowan 1992: 95). Rather than undermining human speech and "quashing the dialogic" (Bier 2015: 193–4), God's speeches dignify it with a response and become its ritual consummation (see Lambert 2015: 574–5).

Canonical Reciprocation

Indeed, the author of Job does not appear to be the only biblical author to share this instinct to provide a divine response to Lam. 3. In Isa. 40–55, which shares with Job a belief that divine speech can effectively console mourning (Lambert 2015: 569), the deity declares "comfort" for Jerusalem (Isa. 40:1). As Jeremiah stands behind Lam. 3, so Lam. 3 may also stand behind Isa. 40–55, serving as one of the models for the suffering servant (Gottwald 1954: 115–16; Tull Willey 1997: 220), and an inspiration for its words of consolation for Jerusalem (see Bier 2015: 205–7). Allusions to each of these texts in Job indicate its author intertwined his work with all three.[13]

---

13. See Dell 2013a; Kynes 2013b; Seow 2013: 41–2.

Whether intentional or not, the connections between these texts inevitably draw Job into a network of texts reflecting on the destruction of Jerusalem (Lévêque 1970: 385). The reciprocal relationship created between the texts by their intertextual dialogue means, on the one hand, that Job's restoration may provide hope to the גבר and the exiled community he represents (see Lambert 2015: 569–71). However, since Job was likely written after that national restoration had occurred, Job's allusions to Lam. 3 within the dialogue could be intended to set his continuing innocent suffering against the redemption of sinful Jerusalem (see Brandscheidt 1983: 352; Mettinger 1993: 274). This makes the contrast of culpability between Job and Jerusalem not an argument against their comparison, but precisely the rhetorical reason for Job's allusions. And, finally, the dialogical nature of both texts, in which swirling accusations crash against rigid orthodoxy, endorses the canonical dialogue in which they participate. Far from silencing Job or the גבר, the divine voice who enters into this dialogue endorses Job's complaints (Job 42:7). Through its inclusion of both books, the canon does the same.

Chapter 13

ALL IS DECAY:
INTERTEXTUAL LINKS BETWEEN LAMENTATIONS 5 AND ECCLESIASTES 12:1-7

Katharine J. Dell

The edifices of the biblical city consist of a rich environment of metaphor and imagery, the materials of which biblical texts are constructed. It is in the nature of this type of language to be thick-stranded and to offer plurality of meanings. Thus the reader's imagination can play over the buildings of the biblical city, viewing them now in one light and now in another. (Mills 2003: 5)

In this paper I want to invite you to imagine, through an intertextual reading of Lam. 5 with Eccl. 12:1-7, a possible cityscape, that of Jerusalem, the city at the heart of the destruction in Lamentations and the royal abode of "the son of David, king in Jerusalem" (Eccl. 1:1).[1] However this is no longer the city of optimistic temple building (1 Kgs 5–6) and opulent grandeur (1 Kgs 7); this is a city in decline, under threat and a place of suffering. In this city all is decay.

The background of the city is clear in both books. In Lamentations the laments focus around the siege of Jerusalem at the exile, with invading armies leaving its inhabitants to starve and die. Indeed the wider "towns of Judah" are mentioned in Lam. 5:11 as places where the rape of women occurred. In Ecclesiastes, Qoheleth's "business" concerns,[2] with money and with work, are clear, indicated by the frequent use of mercantile language, and could well indicate a city setting.[3] Whilst the interpretation

---

1. All translations are from the NRSV.
2. As highlighted by Weeks 2012, in which he argued for Qoheleth's key role as a businessman.
3. For a thorough discussion of this mercantile language and of dating issues, see Grant 2000.

of 12:1-7 is much debated due to the highly metaphorical and enigmatic imagery it contains, it is clear that the context is one of houses, doors, streets, and cisterns (i.e., the familiar signposts of a town or city; cf. Lam. 2:7-12; 4:5, 14).[4] Whilst Jerusalem is not explicitly mentioned, one can argue for that city being more likely than others in this description, forming an inclusion with Eccl. 1:1, with the rise and fall of a great city.[5] As Barbour (2012: 157) writes, "The ruins of Jerusalem, carried within the collective memory of Qohelet and his readers, are here the landmark that acts as the location for recollection." I will argue here that in the intertextual echo of the themes of Lamentations that possibility is strengthened—the author, Qoheleth, at the end of the book is conveying a deliberate reminder of the disastrous siege of the same city that was at the center of Solomon's empire. This is not the only reading of 12:1-7; indeed it is rich in readings—it is simply part of the "double entendre," or indeed many "entendres" conveyed by this highly metaphorical passage.

Let us turn to consider the intertextual parallels. I hesitate to use the word "intertextual" in this case,[6] because in fact the actual textual overlap is very small. Rather what I see here is more of a genre analogy[7] in terms of the city lament and a thematic link of these texts.[8] The most I would claim here is intertextual echo, i.e. implicit, unintentional reference of one text to another. Nor am I claiming historical reminiscence *per se* on the

---

4. Some commentators have identified a house or palace here (e.g., Crenshaw 1988; Gilbert 1981). Fox 1999 uses the language of an estate or village, but others (Krüger 2004; Barbour 2012) argue for a city setting.

5. As argued by Barbour 2012: Chapter 5. She writes, "The outrage in Lamentations is that these things happened in the streets of Jerusalem: so, the vignettes of citizens fainting and dying and mourning are strung out along a repeated refrain of 'in the streets of the city', 'in the squares of the city' (2:11, 12, 19; cf. 4:1, 5, 14, 18). Three mentions of the city streets in these few verses of Ecclesiastes convey that same attachment to a material place and that same sense of the unfitness of mourning in familiar streets" (145).

6. The criteria for "intertexts" are complex. Kynes 2012 defines them as quotation (explicit, intentional reference), allusion (implicit, intentional reference), and echo (implicit, unintentional reference).

7. The more traditional method, as I pursued in Dell 1991, is to look at common genres rather than verbal textual connections. This necessitates links in form, content, and context.

8. As I asked before, in my 2014 article on "Exploring Intertextual Links Between Ecclesiastes and Genesis 1–11," "Is thematic similarity enough on its own" (4) for defining an intertext? Do we not also need linguistic connection, citation, common words, and literary characteristics as well?

part of either author (unlike Barbour[9]), although because of the relative dating of these texts it is more likely that the author of Ecclesiastes is writing well after the events of the Exile and so could have had contact with a text such as Lamentations[10] and knowledge of the exilic experience. My focus, though, is a literary and thematic one that hopes more to uncover further rich meanings in the texts, notably in the highly enigmatic Ecclesiastes text, rather than claiming any historical dependence. I am not claiming high levels of literary dependence either; rather, my intertextual stance, if it can be called that, is more in the area of thematic echo, with some interesting genre connections with the city lament.[11]

Lamentations 5 is one of two communal laments in the book, the other being in Lam. 3. Both have close resonances in psalms of lament, e.g. Pss. 44; 60; 74; 79; 80; and 85 and other city laments, e.g. Isa. 15; 16 over Moab.[12] The other laments of the book of Lamentations are less obviously communal, although they all concern the communal disaster of the siege of Jerusalem. Lamentations 5 describes homes given up to "aliens," foreign nations who have enslaved the people. Women are raped, princes are brought low, the elderly are shown no respect, the young are put to work—the normal societal rules have been broken. The dignity of the people at all levels has been crushed. The joy shown in music, dancing, and song has left the hearts of the people and sickness replaces them—sickness, grief, and desolation. The chapter ends with an affirmation of God's everlasting rule but also with the immediate accusation that God has forgotten his people and the call to God to restore. Why this rejection? Is God "angry with us beyond measure" (Lam. 5:22)? The people believe they must have sinned and feel disgraced (5:1, 16). There is even the

---

9. Barbour (2012) argues for a deliberate historical reminiscence of the fall of Jerusalem on the part of Qoheleth. Her convincing seven motifs found in Eccl. 12:1-7 that link up with city laments she sees as "the standardized way of speaking of national disaster in Second Temple Judaism" (156). Whilst I agree that the argument for such connections is strong, I see it more in literary (genre) and thematic terms than in "historic forms that were being constantly renewed in the literary expression of the later generations who received that tradition" (157).

10. The common view on the dating of Lamentations is that it dates from the Exilic period, shortly after the events described of the siege of Jerusalem in 586 BCE. See Salters 2010: 7–9 for a balanced discussion of this issue.

11. See Dell and Kynes 2013 and 2014 on differing definitions of intertextuality, as indicated by different approaches made in the various articles.

12. Barbour (2012) also mentions Jer. 9:19 (as a dirge) and Amos 5:16, both with streets and squares as spaces for mourning. She prefers the nomenclature of city lament for this description in Lamentations, however.

suggestion that their ancestors sinned and that this generation is bearing their iniquities (5:2).[13]

Certain of the sentiments of this chapter have a thematic intertextual resonance in Eccl. 12:1-7. The sudden change described in Lam. 5:15 of heartfelt joy to sickness of heart in Lam. 5:17 and of dancing being turned to mourning in Lam. 5:15 has a resonance in the "days of trouble" that inevitably come in Eccl. 12:1 and the years that "draw near" and "lack any pleasure." Of course the usual context of this sentiment in Eccl. 12:1 is thought to be that of the advance of old age.[14] This is because of the contrast in this verse between "the days of your youth" and the "days of trouble" and lack of pleasure, i.e. old age. But another suggestion, by Michael Fox (1999: 336),[15] is that the context is death and a funeral; thus, the "days of trouble" are the "old age" prelude to the "time of death and mourning" which is the main concern of 12:2-7, a prelude that forms a contrast with enjoying one's youth. It is interesting that Fox agrees with the old age interpretation for this verse, even though he diverges from it later in the passage.[16] My argument here is that the genre resonance of the city lament is also a layer of meaning in this verse and in the passage as a whole, so that the "days of trouble" could indicate the particular experience of a siege with its disaster, destruction, and decay, rather than simply being a reference to the general decline of old age or the inevitability of death.

There is also an interesting contrast between the "remember" (זכר) of Eccl. 12:1 and the "remember" (זכר) of Lam. 5:1, paralleled at the end of the lament by the accusation that God has "forgotten us" in Lam. 5:20.

---

13. This forms a contrast to the countering of the "sour grapes" proverbs by Jeremiah (31:29) and Ezekiel (18:2) at this same time of the exile.

14. Definitively proposed by Gilbert 1981.

15. Fox does indicate though that there are different ways of reading this passage—literal, symbolic, allegorical—and that the "pertaining to mourning at a funeral" suggestion is simply the literal base-line he finds the most convincing for this powerful and enigmatic poem. He picks up and adapts an old suggestion by Taylor (1874), although he argues that the passage is not strictly a dirge. Barbour (2012: 142 n. 16) makes the point following Lee 2002 that "'city-laments' are really a mixed genre of both 'lament' (appeal to the deity) and 'dirge' (commemoration or warning of the disaster)," so that strictly it is the dirge that is paralleled in the Lamentations passage, although she chooses to use the conventional language of "lament."

16. Fox (1999: 322) writes, "Old age is described here from the perspective of the adverse reaction of the old-man-to-be, the universal addressee. The funeral is described later from the perspective of the disturbed onlookers." His acknowledgement of a change of focus in this passage seems to undermine the latter interpretation, unless, of course, one takes 12:1 separately (which he also opposes).

The opposition of these two sentiments is very familiar from psalmic laments (e.g., Ps. 74). Of course the context in Ecclesiastes is remembrance of God as creator, "Remember (זכר) your creator in the days of your youth," a theme lacking in the Lamentations text, and its parallel verse lies in v. 7 with the returning of the life breath of the human being to God, a clear indication of death in that last verse: "and the breath returns to God who gave it" (12:7).[17]

In Eccl. 12:2 there is a description of a darkening sky, such as occurs before it rains: "before the sun and the light and the moon and the stars are darkened and the clouds return with the rain." There are overtones here of the prophetic "day of Yahweh" perhaps (Amos 5:18, 20 which adjoins the city lament in 5:16-17), although a this-worldly rather than other-worldly event is more likely in the context (cf. Amos 5:8). This verse is interpreted by Fox (1999) as a metaphorical darkening of the luminaries before a funeral—the light of a human life has gone out. The image of the return of the clouds after the light has gone out is a puzzle, though. Fox (1999: 337) argues that "the clouds coming *after* the rain…betokens death," a second description of death in the one verse. According to the old age reading, the verse would refer metaphorically to the preamble to death, with the dulling of the senses and gradual fading out of a life. Another alternative, I suggest, is that this verse is simply a literal reference to nature's force, as a parallel to human life. This may recall the parallel between the human circularity of life and that of the elements in Eccl. 1:5-7,[18] but this passage has many layers of possible interpretation. With the context of an intertextual reading with Lamentations in mind, a comparison is sometimes made with Lam. 3:2, 6, which describe the darkness of affliction and then the darkness of death (using חשך), the one following the other. The only physical description of darkness in Lam. 5 is of the scorching heat of famine that blackens the skin, a way of describing lack of protection from the sun and lack of water as well as food. The heat contrasts with the rain threatened by the darkening sky of Eccl. 12:2.

Ecclesiastes 12:3 is most usually read on the old age allegory model as referring to the gradual decay of the individual human body: "in the day when the guards of the house tremble, and the strong men are bent, and the women who grind cease working because they are few, and those who look through the windows see dimly." These images are seen to denote the trembling legs, the back bent over, the lack of (grinding) teeth, and the dimming of the eyesight. Fox (1999) interprets these images as referring

---

17. See Gilbert (1981: 100) on the essential link between being a created being and death, with the return of the life-spirit to its giver (as in Eccl. 12:7).

18. See Dell 2013b: Chapter 1.

to the day on which the funeral happens, when activity grinds to a halt, and to the effect that a funeral has on a place. Perhaps this indicates the "metaphorical" place where all humans inevitably grow old or die, the place we all recognize when "we see sturdy men writhing" (Fox 1999: 337). It is representative, then, for Fox (1999: 338), of all funerals: "the bell tolls for you and for everyone." However, for Fox, the images themselves belong to death rather than old age—the trembling represents the spasm of the limbs, the lack of teeth and darkening of the eyes telling of what happens at death, and the distorted body or "writhing" indicating death throes. I find this suggestion less convincing here than the old age explanation. However, in relation to my intertextual reading with Lam. 5, the emphasis falls slightly differently and away from these old age and death options. It falls rather on the range of people mentioned in the verse—the guards, the strong men, the women, and the voyeurs looking out from their windows.[19] The point is made well by Barbour, that often in city laments there is a whole range of people in different walks of life.[20] So in Lam. 5:11-14, the range includes women, virgins, princes, the elderly, young men and boys, old men and young. There is no level of society or type of person who is unaffected by these events.[21] Closer parallels with Lam. 5 in this verse include the "grinding" (טחן) of the women, which of course can be taken literally to refer to laboring at the mills,[22] a task commonly undertaken by maidservants that ceases, as compared to the young men who are compelled to grind (טחן) by their overlords (Lam. 5:13). Does this suggest a task usually done by women taken over by these young men, hence a demeaning task for them? Or is it simply a mark of the way the youngsters are being employed as workhorses? The lack of grinding in Eccl. 12:3 perhaps suggests a strange quiet in the

---

19. Fox (1999), too, notes that the women who look out from their windows may be well-to-do, paralleling the "strong" men who are also likely to be wealthy, indicating different societal groups in the verse.

20. Barbour suggests that although the well of v. 6 and the mills of v. 4 could be within a house, they are more likely in shared public spaces. Cf. Whybray's (1996) mention of doors, streets, squares, crowds, and more as marks of an urban setting, as part of his argument for an urban setting for Prov. 1–9. Cf. Dell 2016.

21. Barbour (2012: 149) writes, "In Eccles. 12:3, the merismus of ages and social classes—from guards to patricians, from mill women to ladies of leisure—is a trope that city-lament uses to register catastrophe at every level."

22. Barbour (2012) draws attention to an interesting comparison with Jer. 25:10, a city lament where the silencing of mills and snuffing out of life are paralleled in the context of silenced agriculture as the land is predicted to come to ruin. See p. 148 for other examples of silence in everyday tasks as a sign of city lament.

city as the darkness falls and the "day of trouble" approaches. The other parallel is the dimness of the eyes in Lam. 5:17, which accompanies the sickness of heart felt by the people. This is usually a sign of grief (cf. Job 17:7). However, the interpretation of grief barely fits Eccl. 12:3, where the dimness refers to those who look through windows. This might remind us of the image of the woman (Woman Wisdom) at the window in Proverbs, looking out with confidence on all she surveys (Prov. 7:6).[23] Here the contrast is a lack of viewing society, perhaps because the streets are empty of people and "society" has disappeared.[24] Fox makes the point that the lookers are ladies (fem. pl.) who grow dark (וחשכו) in the sense of becoming gloomy. Fox (1999: 324) compares (with וחשכו) עינינו "our eyes grew dark" in Lam. 5:17, which he rightly interprets as "become despondent—blind with grief, so to speak." So he sees Eccl. 12:3 here as belonging to the context of emotional darkness and links this with the bowing and writhing of the men earlier in the verse. He writes, "Within the literal level of the events described the sentence means the women of the locale are in grief" (325). I would add that it is not just about the relative loss of eyesight, but about loss of joy, as in Lam. 5:15. On the old age model it is a verse about individual ageing and decline in the functions of the body. On the city lament model, however, this verse is more about the cessation of normal activity, with people no longer doing their assigned tasks, and the desolation of the city as a whole.

Ecclesiastes 12:4 goes on to describe the doors on the street being shut: "when the doors on the street are shut, and the sound of the grinding is low, and one rises up at the sound of a bird, and all the daughters of song are brought low." This fits well with the interpretation of a city at rest or in decline. Other interpretations of this image are more forced—is this a reference to lack of sexual activity in the elderly or the door finally closing on a life? Does it refer to the doors closed and mill quiet "because the owner of the estate has died" (Fox 1999: 325)? Or might doors stand for market gates or city gates (Barbour 2012: 144), closed for a siege? We are back to the low sound of grinding suggesting inactivity, and we encounter the idea of early rising. Lack of grinding could refer to an individual's gradual incapacity to do these tasks, and early rising does fit well with

---

23. Barbour (2012: 145) suggests that the female observers "echo the motif of the woman at the window that is a stock figure of female metropolitan hauteur and predatory sexuality."

24. Barbour (2012: 145) inverses the image so as to make it refer to the view into a house from the street—the lights go out in a house with no more lamp oil and so the women at the windows are darkened. This seems unnecessarily complicated in my view.

the way that the elderly experience an inability to sleep and are known for their erratic sleeping habits. But it could indicate a situation of grief where people are unable to sleep or indeed a situation of siege in which rest is difficult to find. The "daughters of song" that are "brought low" is an enigmatic image—it may simply refer to the lack of joyful song in the environment, whether it be about old age, funerals, or the decay of a city. Fox suggests that these are singing female (probably professional) mourners bent low in a posture of lamentation. If the reference is to old age, it may be simply telling us that the voice can no longer produce a pleasant singing tone. Barbour (2012: 145) has a suggestion that the rare verb שחח "brought low" "sounds a note characteristic of the humbling of proud cities and citizens especially in the book of Isaiah" (cf. Isa. 2:9, 11, 17; 5:15). Barbour notes that the reference here is clearly to the cessation of singing.[25] She ingeniously interprets the "sound of a bird" in relation not to early rising but to the desertion of the city and the birds of prey, as found in oracles over hostile nations such as Isa. 13:21 and Jer. 50:39. If we compare with Lam. 5:14 and 5:18, the young men have left their music in the city siege, indicating the loss of joy (5:15), and that proud mountain, at the center of Jerusalem, Mount Zion, is now a place of desolation, left to the jackals (5:18). This parallels the idea of a quiet, empty, deserted city (cf. Lam. 1:1) and hints at Solomon's proud city, Jerusalem, now a place of decay.

Ecclesiastes 12:5 again fairly easily refers to old age: "when one is afraid of heights, and terrors are in the road; the almond tree blossoms, the grasshopper drags itself along and desire fails; because all must go to their eternal home, and the mourners will go about the streets." The elderly experience a fear of heights and imagine "terrors" when they are not there, suggesting a lack of confidence about going out and an irrational sense of fear that often develops at that stage of life. The almond tree goes white when it blossoms, a natural parallel to the whitening of the hair of older people. The grasshopper dragging its leg could refer to limping, and the lack of desire to the waning of sexual desire. The end of all this is death, an inevitable fate for all of us. Here the old age and funeral interpretations start to coincide. Fox (1999) interprets this verse as a reference to God on high, feared by the bending mourners, the references to nature being about rebirth rendered cheerless in the context.[26] Barbour (2012:

---

25. Barbour also cites city laments elsewhere in the Bible that predict desertion for Jerusalem (e.g., Isa. 32:14; Jer. 13:27).

26. Fox (1999: 337–8) writes, "The mourning women bend low. People fear what is above their heads, an anxiety whose unnamed source may be God. All about

146) suggests that those who fear and imagine terrors in the road in Eccl. 12:5 are travelers, who no longer dare to pass through the city as in other biblical city laments (cf. the city lament in Jer. 6:25). We might compare with Lam. 1:4 where no one travels to Zion for the festivals any longer. However, when we compare with Lam. 5:15 the emphasis falls more heavily on the mourners at the end of the verse. In Lam. 5:15 the dancing has turned to mourning. In Eccl. 12:5 the only people left in the streets are the mourners of death, albeit individual or communal, both levels of interpretation being possible.

In Eccl. 12:6 we have perhaps the most enigmatic verse of the passage: "before the silver cord is snapped, and the golden bowl is broken, and the pitcher is broken at the fountain, and the wheel broken at the cistern." Exactly what is meant by the snapping of the silver cord, and the breaking of the golden bowl is very open. On the "old age" argument it refers to the decline of the body, but why a silver cord and a golden bowl has not been satisfactorily explained, in my view. Fox (1999: 331) sees the cord as an image of the suddenness of death—"the snapping of the cord is the instant when a person's connection to life is ruptured," but why a silver one? The golden bowl holds liquid such as lamp oil (cf. Zech. 4:2). Both images for me suggest riches and the demise of such riches. Could we tentatively make a link with the bringing low of princes in Lam. 5:12? The golden bowl is broken just as riches and grandeur come to naught. The broken pitcher for water and the wheel broken at the cistern are easier to comprehend—these are everyday activities of getting hold of water. The cessation of such activity might suggest decline or death. The whole verse then may refer to the end of human life—the functions of the body are broken or snapped, but it is clearly a highly metaphorical set of images. In comparison to Lam. 5:14 the more general reference is to the destruction of the main meeting places. The city gate no longer has its elders in communal oversight who judge and rule the inhabitants of the city. Indeed the elderly are no longer respected (Lam. 5:12). In Eccl. 12:6 the wheel is broken at the cistern or well, a place of meeting, largely by the women of the town going to fetch water by bringing it up from the cistern and filling their pitchers. As Barbour (2012: 150) writes, "Qohelet has a snapped silver cord, a crushed golden bowl, a broken pitcher, and a smashed wheel, and while the mechanics of what happens to each

them too, as they walk along the way, lurk unnamed terrors. There will be rebirth, the annual budding, growing and blooming of nature. But this is without cheer, because it mocks the finality of our end." I find his interpretation of this verse (12:5) particularly forced.

object may be obscure, the final image of a heap of fragments is clear and typical."[27] Fortunes have been reversed.[28] Again, the busy life of the city has fallen away and into decay.

The final verse of Eccl. 12:1-7 returns us to v. 1 and to the thought of the creation of human beings: "and the dust returns to the earth as it was, and the breath returns to God who gave it." On the old age or death models[29] the meaning is clear, that the body returns to the earth as dust (recalling Gen. 2–3) and the life-breath returns to God. This signifies the end of life, just as, on the city lament scheme, the last note is seemingly of despair, as the ravaging jackals are the last inhabitants of a once noble city. The only hope left for Lam. 5 is that God has not totally forsaken his people and their abode (Lam. 5:19-22). For Ecclesiastes there is no hope—the decay of the individual human body or the communal human lot is inevitable. So too, on the city lament model, the city that was once bursting with life and vitality in its youth, is now declining and dying.

This level of reading the Ecclesiastes text, then, inspired by an intertextual thematic and genre-orientated comparison with Lamentations, is another readerly angle for understanding this passage. There are clear thematic links between the two passages, and the genre of city lament certainly sheds fresh light on the Ecclesiastes passage. It inspires a more collective or communal reading rather than a strictly individualistic one. I find that suggestions for "one" meaning of this passage, or for uniting the disparate verses, have some strange contortions and so this approach helps to solve such problems. As Mills suggested in the quotation at the start of this paper—plurality of meanings means that the imagination can "play over the buildings of the biblical city." The darkening sky and threatening rain of this passage cast a shadow on this biblical city that was once so light; its joyful heart is gone, its youth has aged, its activity declined, its demeanor has become one of mourning, and all is decay.

---

27. Barbour (2012) argues that the advantage of a "city lament" parallel for the whole passage is that it gets around the need to propose a shift at v. 6 away from a funeral scene (as Fox does) towards the vessels being ciphers for something else. She writes, "All these things, from v. 2 to v. 6, are things we might see in a ruined city as the poet's eye ranges around, exactly like the eye of the Lamentations poet resting on spoiled finery" (151).

28. See discussion by Barbour (2012: 149–50) of the feature of "Kontrastmotiv" in Lamentations and Eccl. 12:1-7 and her discussion of how the destruction of vessels features in scenes of urban collapse in the biblical city lament tradition.

29. Fox (1999: 332) sees this as the climax of the whole passages with its "harsh description of death," but it can of course be seen as the death that is the inevitable result of the difficulties of old age.

Chapter 14

CONSPICUOUS FEMALES AND AN INCONSPICUOUS GOD: THE DISTINCTIVE CHARACTERIZATION OF WOMEN AND GOD IN THE *MEGILLOTH**

Brittany N. Melton

Introduction: Distinctive Features of the Megilloth

In the concluding chapter of *The Compilational History of the Megilloth*, Timothy J. Stone recognizes God's inconspicuous role in the *Megilloth* when he says: "God is not mentioned in the Song or Esther; in Ecclesiastes, God is in heaven and you are on earth. With the tragedy of Zion's downfall poured out before God in Lamentations, he still does not appear; in Ruth God gives bread and a baby, but on the whole remains behind the scenes" (2013: 205). However, Stone diminishes the significance of this theme when he says, "Another common theme, more abstract and therefore less compelling, is the absence of God" (2013: 205). Instead, he notes the shared motif "of a prominent female character set in relationship to a male character" in all the *Megilloth* except Ecclesiastes (Stone 2013: 205 n. 114).[1] The coexistence of and possible correlation between these two distinctive and significant features—conspicuous females and an inconspicuous God—in the collection of the *Megilloth* provide interesting grounds for a broadly defined intertextual, and more specifically *dialogic*, reading of these texts.[2]

---

* An earlier version of this chapter was presented at the 2016 meeting of the Textual Strategies of the Writings session of the Evangelical Theological Society conference in San Antonio, Texas. For this revised edition I am most grateful to my graduate student workers, Emma Riley and Dylan Watson.

1. Here Stone cites this observation in Sailhamer 1995: 214 n. 28.

2. See the introduction to this volume for more on intertextuality as the way texts work to express cultural perspectives as opposed to its narrower methodological use in biblical studies.

I have elsewhere made the case that the absence of God in the *Megilloth* is, contra Stone, a significant and illuminating theme for the collection (Melton 2018). While it is necessary to summarize those findings here, for the purpose of this essay I intend to explore primarily if and/or how the theme of divine absence interfaces with the prominent role of females in the *Megilloth*. In doing so I will further Stone's observation about the role of females (whether they be female characters or voices) in Esther, Ruth, Song of Songs, and Lamentations by discerning the shared characteristics of this feature, which include: (1) expressing vulnerability, (2) taking initiative and bold risks, and (3) a protesting, antithetic voice. The conspicuous females of the *Megilloth* are vocal and take bold action, in contrast to the inconspicuous God who is completely silent and is only possibly operative through hidden action. Thus, at the same time that this collection foregrounds females it also seems to background God.

The emphasis on human initiative in each of these books has been noted, sometimes in conjunction with the observation that divine action is only possibly implied behind the scenes (Fullerton-Strollo 2016). However, this essay takes a fresh approach by examining how Lamentations, Ruth, Esther, and Song of Songs portray the dynamic between conspicuous females alongside an inconspicuous God in order to explore how this interface might be illuminating.

Methodology: Hearing the "Heteroglossia"

In her work *Countertraditions in the Bible* (1992), Ilana Pardes attempts to recover past antithetical voices (especially female voices) in biblical texts. By placing these voices in dialogue with one another she highlights their antithetical features. Pardes' commitment to hearing past voices gives particular attention to skeptical and controversial voices.[3] This emphasis on recovering subversive voices, which derives from Mikhail M. Bakhtin's attention to *heteroglossia* (i.e., "social diversity of speech types"),[4] will be utilized in the present study for the purpose of highlighting

---

3. Pardes 1992: 4, cited in Green 2000: 152. Similar to Pardes, Carleen Mandolfo (with particular reference to 2007b), "participates in this wider interest by focusing on the theological implications of the dialogue of biblical characters that offers a contrary perspective to the mainstream biblical tradition. Furthermore, her approach speaks to a biblical theology that values contrary perspectives about the human relationship to the Divine and the Divine to the human person" (Middlemas 2012: 51–2).

4. An example of Bakhtin's use of this term is provided in his essay "Discourse in the Novel" in Holquist 1981: 263. See also Vice 1997: Chapter 1, esp. 18–25.

the unconventional features of the *Megilloth* regarding the place of God and females within the canon of the Hebrew Bible. In like manner to Pardes, the method employed for this study is "compatible" with Bakhtinian thought rather than "dependent" upon him, in the sense that it aims "to illustrate how one can find antithetical...voices by paying attention to underexamined fragments on the margins of biblical historiography...[which] entails a reversal of canonical hierarchies" (Pardes 1992: 11). The *Megilloth* are antithetical to canonical texts where God is clearly present and females typically only play a supportive role, and as such are often marginalized or ignored. In other words, these texts offer a counterbalance to the dominant voice of the canon.[5] By demonstrating "sensitivity to the *heteroglossic*" (Green 2000: 156) this essay employs a Bakhtinian approach, since dialogic theology seeks to recover these texts, and in so doing "mirror[s] the text and allow[s] dissenting voices into the conversation" (Middlemas 2012: 40).

Especially in light of their juxtaposition[6] in the Hebrew canonical ordering, these books read alongside one another probe the reader to ask questions such as: Why has God receded into the background? and Why are women foregrounded? Accordingly, two key questions will drive the intertextual investigation which follows: (1) How are the women presented in these texts, and (2) How is God presented in these texts? Listening to heteroglot voices enables intertextual connections to be drawn that highlight the expression of a collective female experience, one which expresses vulnerability and isolation, necessarily takes initiative and bold risks, and speaks with a protesting, antitheodic voice. After exploring these female characteristics in each book, a summary of the experience (or lack thereof) of the divine in the *Megilloth* will further clarify the distinctive perspective of this collection. Once these shared features have been established and examined, the impact of this intertextual relationship will be explored.

Examining the Shared Characteristics of
Conspicuous Females in the Megilloth

Many scholars have noted the prominent role that females play in Ruth, Esther, and Song of Songs (e.g., Brenner 1989, 1999). The significance of female personae within the book of Lamentations has also been

---

5. See my fuller treatment of this methodology likened to a table conversation in Melton 2018: 54–6.

6. Newsom (1996: 299–300) explains, "they become dialogic, each casting the shadow of its own idea on the other, each being illuminated by the other."

acknowledged.[7] Through a brief examination of each book it will become apparent that these females share several characteristics; namely, they play a prominent role, take initiative and bold, at times even provocative, action, and speak daringly. These similarities, along with more detailed intertextual connections, support the claim that the *Megilloth* share the distinctive canonical feature of conspicuous females.

The book of Esther derives its name from its protagonist, Esther. She is a Jewish "orphan" living in the Persian Diaspora (2:7). In the opening scenes we discover, in contrast to the former queen, Vashti, that Esther has been gaining favor in the eyes of many including King Ahasuerus (2:9, 15, 17). It is important to note that Vashti fell out of the king's favor due to her defiance, and accordingly his stance is that women should be subdued (1:20). After becoming queen Esther takes greater and greater risks in order to plead for the life of her people before the king. Her bold action is accompanied by daring speech, which is emphasized through Mordecai's words in 4:14—"For if you keep silent at this time, relief and deliverance will rise for the Jews from another place, but you and your father's house will perish. And who knows whether you have not come to the kingdom for such a time as this?"[8] Rather than keeping silent, Esther devises a plan to appeal before the king. Her plan involves appearing before the king three times (5:1; 7:1; 8:3), even though each time her life hangs on the whims of his displeasure (2:16). The second time she appears before him, once she has gained the king's favor and he is eager to grant her request, Esther boldly voices her petition directly in front of her opponent, Haman (7:3-4). She continues to convince the king to act on behalf of her people in 8:5 and 9:13. By the end of the story Esther is portrayed as having the authority and power to rule, as she "set(s) Mordecai over the house of Haman" (8:2, 7), creates royal decrees (9:13-14), and institutes the *Purim* celebration (9:29-32). These elements evidence the characteristics of the prominent role Esther plays in the book.

Although the book of Ruth is named after only one woman, it has two female protagonists, Ruth and Naomi.[9] Through their initiative, schemes, and speech, the plot progresses toward resolution. Ruth and

---

7. This is especially the case following Lanahan 1974. More recently, Rah (2015: 59) calls attention to its "dominant feminine voice."

8. The ESV has been used throughout this chapter.

9. While I am greatly indebted to Phyllis Trible's abundance of insights on the women in Ruth (1978: Chapter 6), I am not here contrasting male and female or relating these designations to the image of God (as she does). Rather, I am simply highlighting the predominant role of females in Ruth (as well as Esther, Songs, and Lamentations), which starkly contrasts with the more backgrounded role of women in

Naomi are, furthermore, surrounded by a larger cast of women, including the foil female to Ruth, Orpah, the female workers in Boaz's field, and the Bethlehem townswomen. In light of the acknowledged importance of dialogue in the narrative, it is of note that "the first and last characters to speak in the story are women" (Hawk 2015: 27). Moreover, female speech and women's discourse is a prominent feature of the book of Ruth (Rashkow 1993). In the opening scene all three characters present are widowed women: Naomi and her two daughters-in-law, Ruth and Orpah. Their destitute state is made apparent, and Naomi assigns blame to God (1:13). She, again, voices her complaint about God's treatment of her to the townswomen when they arrive in Bethlehem (1:20-21). Upon arriving in Bethlehem Ruth almost immediately makes a plan to secure nutritional provision for herself and Naomi and sets out to glean (2:2-3). She works tirelessly (2:7) and recognizes the opportunity to procure even more sustenance through gaining the favor of the field owner, Boaz (2:10-17). After she returns from the field and reveals to Naomi that she gleaned in Boaz's field, Naomi recognizes the opportunity to pursue a more secure future, since Boaz is a close relative of hers. She strategically plans for Ruth to suggest to Boaz that he become a more permanent source of their provision by instructing Ruth to go to the threshing floor and lay at the feet of Boaz at night (3:1-4).[10] Ruth carries out this risky plan under the guise under the cover of darkness, and even boldly requests for Boaz to fulfill his earlier prayer (in 2:12) for God to provide for her, saying, "...Spread your wings over your servant, for you are a redeemer" (3:9). After Boaz redeems Naomi and determines to take Ruth as his wife, the townspeople pray that Ruth would be like the matriarchs of Israel, specifically naming Rachel, Leah, and Tamar (4:11-12). These elements evidence the predominant role of women in the book of Ruth and confirm shared characteristics with the role of Esther.

J. Cheryl Exum (2005: 25) and Garrett Galvin (2016: 133) both claim Song of Songs is "unique" within the canon for its "attention" toward and characterization of the woman and its relaying of the female

---

the remaining books of the Hebrew Bible. Trible (1978: 166) claims that these women "risk bold decisions and shocking acts to work out their own salvation in the midst of the alien, the hostile, and the unknown."

10. Avnery (2016: 65) calls attention to the provocative nature of this scene: "The atmosphere of Ruth 3—the suggestive location in the dead of night, kneeling by a man's feet in the darkness, and the washing and anointing of the female body with intimate intentions—seems to fit in with the erotic sensual revelry of the Persian palace—especially considering that Ruth approaches Boaz when 'he had eaten and drunk, and his heart was merry' (3:7)."

perspective. Athalya Brenner (1989: 90) asserts the "predominance of the female" in Songs, noting specifically the supportive role of the Daughters of Jerusalem chorus (2:7; 3:5; 5:8-9; 6:1, 9; 8:4). However, the female protagonist's experience is not without "limitations" (Galvin 2016: 128–9), as the Shulamite woman in searching for her lover must risk the brutality of the watchmen (3:3; 5:7). In these two scenes, she takes initiative by leaving the security of her house to search alone in the city streets for her beloved. The woman boldly proclaims her affection and desire for her beloved, both directly to him and to the Daughters of Jerusalem in extended speeches (e.g., 2:3–3:11; 5:2-8, 10-16; 7:10–8:7). Davis even regards the character of her speech as the most bold and self-confident in all of scripture.[11] Along with the voices of the Daughters of Jerusalem, female speech predominates over the only other voice (that of the male lover).[12] The gynocentric stance of Songs is also recognized in the seven references to "mother" (1:6; 3:4, 11; 6:9; 8:1, 2, 5), especially in the two occurrences of the rare designation, בית אם "mother's house" (3:4; 8:2).[13] These elements evidence the conspicuousness of females in Song of Songs and confirm shared characteristics with females in Esther and Ruth, particularly concerning female speech.

In Lamentations, rather than female characterization, we find a predominance of female voice and imagery. The first two chapters especially focus on the literary personae of Daughter Zion (1:1), a female metaphor for the destroyed city and people of Jerusalem cast as widow, mother, etc.[14] In Lam. 1 and 2 Daughter Zion voices her pain using vivid imagery in the stance of protest and lament, and we are told over and again that she is lonely and has no one to comfort her (1:1, 2, 9, 21). Moreover, her affliction has come at the hand of God, who has become "like an enemy" (1:5, 12-15; 2:1-9, 20, 22; 4:11; here 2:5). God is ultimately behind her distress, dejection, and devastation. Aside from Daughter Zion,

11. Davis 2001: 70.
12. To Brenner-Idan's (2015: 49) calculation, female speech accounts for more than 53 percent of the book.
13. An observation of Meyers 1993a.
14. Mandolfo (2007b: 58) states: "the poet of Lamentations draws part of his rhetorical impact from the maintenance of the female metaphor for Israel. In this way, the poet provides his audience with a recognizable voice for their pain. Repeating the shameful figuration of Israel as female might seem an odd choice if the goal is *comfort*, but in light of the treatment this figure receives at the hand of YHWH in the prophetic texts, granting this voice subjectivity makes a powerful and corrective theological statement."

Lamentations utilizes the language of "mothers" (e.g., 5:3), "daughters" (e.g., 3:48, 51; 4:3, 6, 21, 22), and "women" (e.g., 5:11) frequently throughout to express extreme vulnerability (e.g., 2:11-12, 20; 4:10). More broadly the genre of lament was associated with women in ancient Israel (Gruber and Yona 2016: 72). Each of these elements evidences the conspicuousness of females in Lamentations and demonstrates the accordance of its characteristics with the other females of the *Megilloth*.

The prominent role of females in Esther, Ruth, Songs, and Lamentations starkly contrasts with the amount of attention afforded females in the other books of the Hebrew Bible. Beyond the larger parallels of these prominent, vocal females who take initiative exist several specific intertextual elements that bind the connection between them. The rare designation בית אם, "mother's house," in Song 3:4 and 8:2 only appears in two other places in the Hebrew Bible, in Ruth 1:8 and in the story of Rebekah in Genesis. This is significant in light of the contrast with the high frequency of the designation בית אב, "father's house," in the Hebrew Bible (Trible 1978: 169; Meyers 1993a: 212; 1993b). I have elsewhere argued for the intertextual connection between the widow Naomi's antitheodic complaints in Ruth and those of Daughter Zion who is likened to a "widow" in Lam. 1 and 2 (Melton 2018: 83–102). The "Daughters of Jerusalem/Zion" in Songs call to mind "Daughter Zion" of Lamentations, both female voices representing a female perspective (Galvin 2016). Lastly, the "gaining/finding of favor" in Esther and Ruth forms an intertextual link regarding the means of accomplishing the goals of Ruth and Esther.[15] These intertextual resonances[16] further bond the *Megilloth* and support the claim that therein females are conspicuous.

Summarizing the Shared Characteristics of the Inconspicuous God of the Megilloth[17]

The degree to which God is considered to be inconspicuous in each of the *Megilloth* is debated.[18] However, that God is significantly less conspicuous in the collection, when compared with its wider context in the Hebrew Bible, is undeniable. A brief overview will be sufficient for

---

15. See Melton 2018: 154–8.
16. For my use of this term see Melton 2014: 130–2.
17. For a detailed discussion of divine presence and absence in the *Megilloth* see Melton 2018.
18. See a summary in ibid.: 20–38.

confirming their shared characteristics of divine silence, a lack of divine appearance, and a lack of explicit divine action,[19] thus confirming God's backgrounded role.

Among this collection are the only two books of the Hebrew Bible which do not speak explicitly of God, Song of Songs and Esther, as both of these books display divine literary absence. Though at times directly addressing God, Lamentations is composed solely of the laments of God's people, to which no divine response is given therein. The book of Ruth speaks often of God, but it is impossible to tease out divine action from human initiative; thus, God is only possibly at work behind the scenes through human agents. When Qoheleth speaks of God in Ecclesiastes, God is portrayed as transcendent and his ways are indiscernible. At no point in these five books is divine speech directly or indirectly reported. Therefore, God remains inconspicuous in this collection.

Exploring the Correlation between Conspicuous Females and an Inconspicuous God

Examining the characteristics of these two seemingly unrelated, distinctive features of the *Megilloth* reveals an inverse correlation between them: While females feature in the foreground, God is found only in the background of these books.[20] Women take bold action, whereas God's action is hidden. Whereas females are unconventionally vocal in these books, God is completely silent throughout the collection. Although these features and the correlation between them have not been examined before now, two previous suggestions have been made pertaining to the perspective of these books which might shed light on this distinctive combination. James L. Crenshaw (2009: 1), in his foreword to Jerry A. Gladson's book, *The Five Exotic Scrolls of the Hebrew Bible*, attributes the distinct vantage point of the *Megilloth* to their viewing "reality from below." In a similar vein, Garrett Galvin claims they all exhibit horizontal theology. He asserts, "[t]heological reflection on the books of the *Megilloth* posits literature that privileges human actors who have to try to understand human suffering and see its connection to God" (2016: 138). Recognizing a common vantage point or theological perspective

---

19. With the exception of the narrator's report of divine action related to famine and birth, in accordance with the wider ancient Near Eastern worldview, in the frame of Ruth (1:6; 4:13). See Linafelt 1999: 28.

20. Saxegaard (2010) makes this observation about the book of Ruth.

among the *Megilloth* aids a better understanding of these books. However, it does not explain fully why their characterization of God and females are similar to one another and distinct from the rest of the canon.

If we step back from the individual characteristics of how women are portrayed in these texts and simply ask why women are uncharacteristically foregrounded in these books, it seems a diachronic explanation suffices and leads to further insight. If the *Megilloth* were composed, or even increasingly consulted as sacred texts, following the Babylonian exile, then it makes sense that Judah's exilic experience leads them to resonate more readily with the experience of women in an ancient context. By this I mean, Judah's experience leading up to, during, and post-exile left a general sense of vulnerability, disempowerment, and obscurity about how God was working in the world and on their behalf and how they should act in accordance with this. This experience mirrors the plight of women in ancient Israelite society, who were more vulnerable, less empowered to act, and forced to navigate the world on the basis of a system that was determined by patriarchal structures. Is there any traction to this line of thinking which could lead to further insight, if we consider Judah's experience to resonate with female characters in these stories and embodied in female voices in these texts? If a people feel vulnerable, disempowered, and uncertain of God's action on their behalf, then might the ideal texts for communicating and understanding this experience strongly feature women? Does Israel's experience of foreign powers lead them to resonate with how the female characters in these texts respond to their situation? Despite expressing vulnerability and isolation, they act boldly, taking initiative and risks. Did these texts function for the post-exilic community as empowering "underdog" stories? Did they find hope in the triumph of God's purposes through the least likely members of society: the orphaned, the widowed, the childless, the foreigner (be she Shulamite, Moabite, or Jewish under or in the midst of foreign rule)? I conclude that there is a possible correlation between the foregrounding of females and the backgrounding of God in the *Megilloth*, if these four books embody in their final forms Judah's experience of subjugation and uncertainty about God's action on their behalf. Jewish readings of these texts often emphasize their message of human initiative in the midst of unclear divine action.[21] While there is certainly more human initiative taken in these texts than overt divine action, what else could explain the prioritization of female characters and voices at this time?

---

21. E.g., Friedman 1995: 58.

It is certainly not profitable to follow Wayne Grudem's line of argument, that women must act when there are no real men around, which he takes to explain the leadership role of Deborah in Judges.[22] Setting aside blatant prejudice, Boaz and Mordecai are presented as pious and capable men; so the prominent roles of Ruth and Esther cannot be deemed necessary simply due to a lack of eligible men. It is also the case that the male lover in Song of Songs and the male voice of the גבר in Lam. 3 are complemented rather than replaced by female voices. Meyers (1993b: 207–8) takes a different approach regarding Song of Songs, arguing that women feature prominently when the setting is a domestic domain. Even if the prominence of female voice in Lamentations can be explained by the existence of women as professional mourners in ancient Near Eastern society,[23] this still leaves unexplained the role of Esther in a court setting. It appears that no sufficient explanation for the prominence of females in these books has been offered.

On the other hand, suggestions for why God appears absent in this collection are insufficient as well if they simply follow Fretheim's decreasing trajectory of divine involvement, whether this is asserted on a literary or chronological basis or some confused notion of the two.[24] It is, however, worthwhile to note a diachronic factor, which is that God was spoken of less directly during the Second Temple period.[25] Perhaps by considering this literary observation in conjunction with an increase in texts which feature prominent females, an explanation for *why* these features arose can be ascertained. This is especially pertinent in light of the fact that these two features bear out in later Second Temple texts, namely Judith and Susanna;[26] though certainly this observation calls for further research and pushes beyond the bounds of the current essay.

---

22. Grudem suggests, "Something is abnormal, something is wrong—there are no men to function as judge! This impression is confirmed when we read of Barak's timidity and the rebuke he receives as well as the loss of glory he could have received" (2012: 134)

23. Although Daughter Zion is better understood as a political trope which offers a sharp contrast.

24. See my critique in Melton 2018: esp. 15–18, 183–6.

25. Gladson (2010: 330–1) notes, "Lamentations shares this reticence to give voice to Yhwh with the *Khamesh Megilloth* of which it is a part. [I]n part this may be due to prevailing, post-exilic *Zeitgeist* in which these books reached their final form, when there was in Second Temple Judaism an ever-increasing reluctance to speak directly of God."

26. These features are less characteristic of Tobit, where Sara plays more of a supporting role to Tobias, and God is frequently referred to directly as θεὸς (e.g.,

At the same time, this burgeoning of prominent females toward the end of the Hebrew canon is not a new phenomenon as much as it is a past trope with a fresh situation. Female voice has always been the vehicle through which the community could voice its appeal for God to vindicate the lowly and have mercy (e.g., Hannah's song in 1 Sam. 2:1-10), and we see this continue beyond these texts when we get to Judith's song (16:1-17) and the Magnificat (Lk. 1:46-55). Therefore, it is reasonable to assert that the use of female voice and characters in the *Megilloth* serves to empower a disempowered community under foreign oppression as they seek to understand the hidden ways of God on their behalf.

Conclusion

A dialogic reading of the collection of the *Megilloth* unearths an unconventional collection within the Hebrew Bible that distinctly foregrounds females and backgrounds God. The relationship between these features cannot be explained simply on the basis of their inverse relationship as Grudem and others might suggest. Instead, the presence of these two features is better accounted for by considering the collection's early reception and the audiences' resonance with these features. If we consider the place of women in ancient Israelite society to be a microcosm of the people of Israel's experiences in the ancient Near Eastern world during the seventh and sixth centuries, then it is possible to imagine how the post-exilic community would read these books and more readily identify with female characters who are expressing vulnerability and isolation, having to take initiative on their own behalf, and finding ways to navigate in society as the marginalized, especially compared with other moments in their history. At times when God's involvement is not as obvious, perhaps female characters and female voice are employed to embody Israel's experience as a vulnerable and marginalized people who are forced to take initiative and speak boldly in faith.

1:12) and κύριος (e.g., 2:2) and acts by giving grace and favor (1:13) and is said to hear prayers (3:16). The book does, however, ascribe a much greater weight to human action than divine, uses the angel Raphael as a divine mediator (esp. 3:7; chs. 5 and 6), and it at times avoids direct mention of God (e.g., using instead the designation "most High" [1:4] and "Holy One" [12:15]).

Part IV

LAMENTATIONS IN DIALOGUE BEYOND THE
HEBREW BIBLE

Chapter 15

LAMENTATIONS AT QUMRAN

Gideon R. Kotzé

With little fear of exaggeration, it can be claimed that the Dead Sea scrolls, especially the manuscripts discovered in the eleven caves near Khirbet Qumran, have had a great impact on almost all areas of the critical study of the HB writings, from composition to canon.[1] Two areas where these manuscript finds from sites in the Judean Desert have contributed to research on Lamentations are the textual history of the five poems in this collection and the reception of their wordings in early Jewish writings of the Second Temple period.[2]

The four manuscripts from Qumran, 3QLam, 4QLam, 5QLam[a], and 5QLam[b], are the oldest available copies of Lamentations, dating between the first centuries before and after the Common Era, and represent parts, ranging from large chunks of text to single letters, of all five of the poems. Although these fragmentary Lamentations manuscripts are not as well

---

1. The large and small variations in length and content exhibited by the manuscripts of authoritative scriptures from Qumran imply that the wordings of these writings were still creatively developed and adapted when copies were made in the time between the third century BCE and the first century CE. The evidence provided by the Qumran manuscripts suggests that a generally recognized standard text of authoritative scriptures and a closed canon (in the sense of an agreed upon list of writings that are considered to be authoritative for beliefs and behavior) did not exist during the Second Temple period. Regarding the nature and characteristics of authoritative literary writings, some of which were later included in the HB corpus, and the developmental growth of these texts, see Ulrich 2015: 1–27. On the manuscripts of HB writings from Qumran and their significance for text-critical research, see, for example, Würthwein and Fischer 2014: 59–72; Tov 2012: 94–110; Hendel 2010: 281–302; Van der Kooij 2002: 167–77.

2. See, for example, Brooke 2006: 287–319; Henze 2005; Fishbane 2004: 339–77; Davies 2003: 144–66.

preserved as those of, for example, the Isaiah manuscripts, or as numerous as the Psalms and Deuteronomy manuscripts, and their variants are, arguably, not as sensational and spectacular as those in the manuscripts of some other HB writings, such as Samuel and Jeremiah, they nevertheless preserve readings that are important for text-critical examinations and interpretations of the poems' content. 4QLam is, undoubtedly, the prize find among the four manuscripts. Three of its fragments preserve the wordings of Lam. 1:1-18 and a small fourth fragment contains a portion of Lam. 2:5 (Cross 2000: 229–37). The wordings of these verses in 4QLam display a number of important differences when compared to their counterparts in manuscripts of the Masoretic text (MT) and the ancient translations, the Septuagint, Peshitta, Vulgate, and Western and Yemenite versions of the Targum (Kotzé 2013: 26–9, 177). Some of these variants can be taken to be more original than those in the other textual representatives, while others are scribal errors. Some of the most interesting variant readings are those that exemplify how ancient scribes changed details in the wordings of passages when they made new copies of Lamentations. In certain of these cases, the changes in the wording markedly affect the content communicated by the passages.[3] This is also true of the few variant readings that are not orthographical or morphological in the wordings of Lam. 4 and 5 represented by 5QLam[a] (Kotzé 2013: 31–3, 178).[4] The Qumran manuscripts, therefore, provide evidence of ways in which scribes interpreted Lamentations by shaping the wordings and content of the poems during the process of textual transmission.

In addition to the manuscripts of Lamentations, the Qumran sectarian movement owned writings whose wordings show striking similarities to words and phrases in the five poems. This raises the possibility that there are textual connections between Lamentations and the writings, that the latter deliberately made use of formulations or phrases in passages from the former, and that the content of the earlier text influenced the content of the later text. The textual connections between HB writings and other Second Temple literature are relevant to the study of the later texts' composition and their rhetoric.[5] Those textual connections that can be categorized as

---

3. See, for example, the readings of Lam. 1:7, 11, and 13 in 4QLam and the comments on these verses in Kotzé 2013: 41–52, 63–70, 81–6.

4. The small fragments of 3QLam present only single words from Lam. 1:10-12 and 3:53-62, while 5QLam[b] contains words of 4:17-20. For the readings in these manuscripts, see Kotzé 2013: 22–3, 34, 121–4.

5. The textual connections are sometimes referred to as "intertextual" relations in biblical scholarship, but this can create confusion in view of the use of the concept of intertextuality in poststructuralist literary studies. See, in this regard, the discussions

quotations are also important sources of data regarding the early textual history of HB writings, especially in cases where the quotations preserve wordings that differ in details from those of other textual representatives.[6] Furthermore, the textual connections provide valuable evidence of how authoritative scriptures were interpreted during the Second Temple period. The Qumran scrolls (the writings that can be attributed to the Qumran movement, as well as the non-sectarian literature) exhibit a variety of different forms of textual interpretation. These include, for example, interpretations of legal material, commentaries on prophetic literature (such as the *pesharim*), retellings of scriptural narratives, the use of scriptural passages as examples to influence behavior, and the incorporation of the language of passages from existing authoritative compositions in the formulation of new content (Brooke 2005: 134). Examples of the last category of textual interpretation are found in the wordings of two Qumran scrolls, 4Q179 and 4Q501, which share some words and phrases with passages from Lamentations.[7] These two manuscripts (somewhat infelicitously dubbed "Apocryphal Lamentations" A and B by scholars) are important witnesses to the reception of Lamentations within early Judaism.[8]

of, e.g., Zevit 2017: 12–15; Meek 2014: 280–91; Barton 2013: 1–16; Carr 2012: 505–35. Nevertheless, it is defensible to speak of correspondences between texts as forms of intertextuality, if it is clear that intertextuality serves as "a category in which to discuss the relationship of texts and ideas to other texts and ideas" (C. B. Hays 2008: 24). This relationship includes allusion (C. B. Hays 2008: 26). Intertextuality is something different when it is used as a designation for a theory of texts and meaning, or as a reference to a reading method where readers, who are unconcerned with historical links between texts and authorial intent, make connections between many texts, irrespective of their dates and provenance.

6. Cf. Lange and Weigold 2011: 15; Van der Kooij 2006: 581.

7. Lange and Weigold (2011: 185–6, 374–5) identify other Qumran scrolls that may contain textual connections with Lamentations, but this chapter will only focus on the two "Apocryphal Lamentations," 4Q179 and 4Q501.

8. Regarding the presence of these two scrolls among the writings kept by the Qumran movement and the possibility that the sectarians composed them, Horgan (1973: 223) notes that there is nothing in 4Q179 that would link it with the sectarians: "There is neither reference to specific tenets of the Essene sect, nor is there mention of persons or events prominent in the history of Qumran." Davila (2000: 178) maintains that 4Q501 also contains "nothing explicitly sectarian" and suggests that "the most likely possibility is that the sectarians adopted this communal lament because they found elements of it appropriate for their own situation." See also the comments of Berlin 2003: 15–17.

4Q179 comprises five fragments, two large and three small ones. The two large fragments contain parts of three columns (two on fragment 1 and one on fragment 2), whereas the other three fragments preserve only parts or single letters of individual words. The manuscript can be dated before the Herodian period (ca. 50–25 BCE), based on its semi-formal script (Webster 2002: 403; Strugnell 1970: 250). Scholars differ in opinion on whether the manuscript presents one composition or a collection of short poems, the question of genre, as well as the possible historical setting of the destruction of the temple and the desolation of Jerusalem, its surrounding settlements, and the land that are lamented in the surviving wording of 4Q179.[9] The fragmentary nature of the manuscript and the incomplete wording make the task of interpreting the text quite taxing, and scholars have suggested differing reconstructions to fill in the gaps.[10] There is, nevertheless, agreement among interpreters of the manuscript that its wording was heavily influenced by passages from Lamentations and prophetic writings. With regard to the words and phrases in 4Q179 that resemble those in passages from Lamentations, scholars describe these similarities in wording as "quotations," "allusions," and "citations," and discuss the various ways the words drawn from Lamentations were expanded, adapted, and combined with words from other writings to create the composition's/collection's unique content. Not all these descriptions are equally convincing, in my opinion, but it can be reasonably argued that the following formulations in 4Q179 *might* have connections to the wordings of cola in Lam. 1 and 4:

4Q179		Lam.
I ii 4	ובת עמי אכזריה[	4:3
I ii 7	אשפותות	4:5
I ii 9	המסלאי֯ם [	4:2
I ii 10	ה֯אמונים עלי תול[ע	4:5
II 4	[בדד העיר[...]ו֯[...]לים	1:1
II 9	בכו֯ תבכה ֯יר[...]ו על לחיה על בניה	1:2

Figure 15.1 4Q179 and Lamentations 1 and 4.

9. See the discussions of Körting 2017: 143–52; Berlin 2003: 2, 8–12; Høgenhaven 2002: 118; Pabst 1978: 137–9; Horgan 1973: 222–4.

10. Cf. the transcriptions and translations of 4Q179 in Bernstein 2014: 414–17; Høgenhaven 2002: 113–16; García Martínez and Tigchelaar 1997: 368–71; Horgan 1973: 225–7; Allegro 1968: 75–7 (with the corrections suggested by Strugnell 1970: 250–52); and the translations of Wise, Abegg, and Cook 2005: 268–9; Vermes 2004: 327–8; García Martínez 1996: 401–2.

Given that the wordings of the sentences are incomplete, none of the expressions can be clearly identified as an explicit or implicit quotation. While quotations refer to verbal parallels,[11] an allusion can be defined as the borrowing by one literary work of identifiable material from a recognizable existing writing whereby the understanding of the receptor text is affected by elements of the source text's content.[12] Given the broken wording of the sentences, the ideas and themes they communicate are only partially decipherable. Therefore, it cannot be claimed that the words and phrases that 4Q179 have in common with Lam. 1 and 4 were undoubtedly used with the aim of alluding to the content of the Lamentations passages.

Turning to 4Q501, this composition is preserved in only one small manuscript of which the top, bottom, and left margins are intact, but the right side of the scroll is damaged.[13] The single surviving column of the text consists of nine unruled lines of writing with the orthography and morphology of the words characterized by *plene* spellings and lengthened

---

11. According to Lange and Weigold (2011: 26, 27), an implicit quotation is "any uninterrupted verbal parallel of at least four words which does not alter the quoted text but is not introduced by a quotation formula or otherwise explicitly identified," whereas an explicit quotation is, in their opinion, "any verbal parallel of at least two words which is explicitly identified by a quotation formula or other means." Fitzmyer (1997: 6) notes that explicit quotations of the HB in the Qumran literature "are introduced by special formulae and are cited to bolster up or illustrate an argument, to serve as a *point de départ* in a discussion or to act as a sort of proof-text."

12. Cf. Sommer's discussion of allusions (1998: 10–12). On this definition, a correspondence between texts can be regarded as an allusion when readers modify their interpretation of the receptor text in light of their understanding of the source text. Cf. Kelly 2017: 28–9. In other words, readers detect an allusion when they recognize passages in one or more texts that are potentially determinative for the interpretation of the wording of another text. They then go on to make sense of the latter on the basis of how they understand the former. The allusion may be described as "intentional" when readers are of the opinion that the semantic connection they perceive between texts was purposefully made by the persons who were responsible for the formulation of the receptor text's wording. Kelly (2017: 33–5) warns that shared language is not a sufficient criterion to identify an allusion, given the existence of non-referential shared language. This means that verbal correspondence does not necessarily imply that the meaning of one text is directly dependent on, or referencing, the content of the other text. If an investigation indicates that the content of the source text is not determinative for the interpretation of the receptor text, the correspondence need not be defined as an allusion.

13. A seam on the left margin of the scroll implies that this sheet was joined to another one.

forms of pronominal suffixes.[14] The handwriting is identified as Herodian (second half of the first century BCE) (Webster 2002: 406; Baillet 1982: 79). The text seems to be a type of literary prayer addressed by first-person plural speakers to God.[15] The damage to the right side of the manuscript causes gaps in the wording, and this means that not all the sentences are completely preserved. The lacunae create difficulties in ascertaining the structure and colometry of the composition. Nevertheless, the available wording of the column exhibits a recognizable pattern in which pleas to the deity in the form of directives to refrain from certain actions or to perform particular deeds (cf. lines 1, 2-3, 5, 7 and 8) are alternated with complaints about what a third party of people has (not) done or what has happened to the speakers (expressed with *qatal* and *wayyiqtol* verbs; cf. lines 4, 6 and 9). The complaints deal especially with how the "lying" and "slanderous tongue" of their opponents distress and enrage the speakers.[16] The speakers and their opponents are members of God's people (lines 2 and 4), but whereas the speakers claim that the scoundrels have not "put you in front of them" (line 9), they plead with God to remember them as the abandoned, deserted, and spurred ones of the covenant people (lines 2-3). They further describe themselves as "wanderers" and "wounded" without someone to return or tend to them (line 3).[17] With these literary images, the speakers create the impression that they have to fend for themselves against their opponents. They call on the deity to accept their portrayal of themselves and their reconstruction of events as a ploy to elicit divine vengeance and punishment upon their opponents (lines 7-8). These petitions and complaints in 4Q501 display language that

---

14. On the dimensions of the scroll, the scribal corrections, and orthographical and morphological features of the text, see Tov 2004: 85, 101, 191, 198, 343.

15. Although the deity is not explicitly mentioned in the available wording, the references to "your people" (עמכה; lines 2 and 4), "your inheritance" (נחלתכה; line 2), "your covenant" (בריתכה; line 2), "your glory" (פארתכה; line 5), "your commandments" (מצוותיכה; line 7), "your strength" (כוחכה; line 8), and the sentence "they did not put you in front of them" (לוא שמוכה לנגדמה; line 9), which calls to mind Ps. 54:5, point to God as the addressee in 4Q501.

16. The image in line 4 of scoundrels who have surrounded the speakers with their false speech describes distress in terms of an experience of being constrained or encompassed. On this imagery, see P. D. King 2012: 167–73, especially in connection with Ps. 109:2-3, which contains a similar image to the one in 4Q501 line 4.

17. In line 9, the speakers claim that their opponents lord it over the needy and the poor. Given the incomplete nature of the text, it is not clear whether "needy" and "poor" are used as self-designations or whether this sentence lodges a new complaint about the opponents' mistreatment of the less fortunate.

is characteristic of laments, and some of the phrases in the scroll are reminiscent of passages in Lam. 5:

4Q501		Lam.
1	אל תתן לזרים נחלתנו ויגיענו לבני נכר	5:2
5	הביטה וראה חרפת בני	5:1
6	עורנו וזלעופות אחזונו מלפני לשון גדופיהם]	5:10

Figure 15.2 4Q501 and Lamentations 5.

Seeing as a number of scholarly investigations have been devoted to the textual connections between 4Q179 and Lam. 1 and 4, but not as many to those between 4Q501 and Lam. 5, this chapter, in what follows, focuses on the latter. The proposed textual connections between 4Q501 and Lam. 5 are not quotations and, therefore, the chapter briefly examines whether the words in the Qumran scroll that are similar to phrases from Lamentations can be adequately described as allusions.

Possible Textual Connections between 4Q501 and Lamentations 5

Lamentations 5:2 in 4Q501 Line 1

The first possible connection between 4Q501 and Lam. 5 is found in line 1: אל תתן לזרים נחלתנו ויגיענו לבני נכר ("do not give our inheritance to strangers and our property to foreigners").[18] The negative directive in this bicolon is structured chiastically (a b c c′ b′). The opening verbal phrase is not repeated in the second colon, but the prepositional phrase לזרים in the first colon corresponds to לבני נכר in the second one, while the noun phrase נחלתנו has יגיענו as its counterpart in the second colon. This bicolon shares the phrases לזרים and נחלתנו with the wording of Lam. 5:2, and the status construct phrase בני נכר in 4Q501 is similar to the plural noun נכרים in the MT version.[19] Lamentations 5:2 records the speakers' complaint to YHWH about their disgrace and powerlessness in the form of an image of societal role reversals whereby strangers and foreigners have been made the owners of the landed property belonging to the speakers. In other words, "outsiders" have been given the position of "insiders" in relation to the speaking community's real estate, while the "insiders" have been

---

18. English translations are my own.

19. MT: נחלתנו נהפכה לזרים בתינו לנכרים ("our inheritance has been turned over to strangers, our houses to foreigners"). Unfortunately, only very little text of Lam. 5:2 has survived in 5QLamᵃ: ם בתינו לנוֹכריᵃ*ם[(Milik 1962: 177).

"alienated" from their own. This type of *mundus inversus* imagery that describes outsiders becoming insiders and vice versa is familiar from other ancient Near Eastern texts, and the first line of 4Q501 also makes use of such an image. The bicolon in the Qumran scroll portrays God in the role of a sovereign landowner who has the right and power to reallocate land and property to whom he wishes. This image of the divine landholder is used to express the plea that the deity not turn the world of the speakers upside down by treating them (insiders) as though they are not members of his covenantal people (outsiders). From this perspective, the *mundus inversus* image in 4Q501 line 1 communicates the speakers' fear of being ostracized by God. Given that, in lines 2–3 of the composition's extant wording, the speakers maintain that they are, in fact, members of God's people, inheritance, and covenant, albeit "abandoned," "deserted," and "spurned" members, the image of a topsy-turvy world in 4Q501 line 1 directs the speakers' appeal to their divine covenant partner not to punish them in the style of treaty curses by relegating them to the position of outsiders. On this interpretation, it would appear that the wordings of 4Q501 line 1 and Lam. 5:2 employ similar literary images, but they do so in different types of utterances addressed to the deity, a negative directive and a complaint, to achieve different rhetorical purposes. In the complaint section of Lam. 5, the *mundus inversus* image in v. 2 is part of an imaginative description of disgrace and powerlessness placed in the mouth of first-person plural speakers, whereas the negative directive in 4Q501 presents the speakers' attempt to avoid being ostracized by God. Although the similarities between the first line of 4Q501 and Lam. 5:2 do not preclude the possibility that the later composition borrowed individual words from the earlier writing to formulate its world-turned-upside-down image, the differences between their respective bicola suggest that the wording of the scroll from Qumran is not an allusion to the content of Lam. 5:2.

Lamentations 5:1 in 4Q501 Line 5

The second instance where 4Q501 has words in common with Lam. 5 is in line 5: הביטה וראה חרפת בני ("look and see the reviling of the sons of…"). The set of imperatives הביטה וראה and the direct object, חרפה, agree with the two directives and their complement in Lam. 5:1.[20] From

---

20. MT: זכר יהוה מה היה לנו הביט וראה את חרפתנו ("Remember, O YHWH, what happened to us. Look and see our disgrace"); 5QLam\[a\]: זכ]ור [ ] מֹה [ ] לֹנוֹ הביטה [ ] את חרפותי]נו ("Remem[ber] what [ ] to us. Look [ ] [our] disgraces"). Although the

the perspective of the observable structure of 4Q501's extant wording, it is noteworthy that the statements in lines 4-5 are flanked by sentences that formulate the speakers' pleas to God with the same imperatives as the ones appearing in the two cola of Lam. 5:1: זכור (lines 1-2 and 2-3) and הביטה וראה (line 5). These considerations, coupled with the rarity of the combination of the two verbs of perception נבט and ראה with חרפה as their complement, leave little doubt that 4Q501 borrowed the words from Lam. 5:1. This borrowing, however, does not imply that the words in the Qumran scroll necessarily allude to the content of the earlier composition. In the opening bicolon of Lam. 5, the speakers invoke the name of YHWH and plead with him to remember "what has happened" to them and to mark their disgrace well. In other words, in the first colon of the verse, the speakers attempt to bring the deity into contact with the particular picture of past events that they present in the complaint section of this communal lament (vv. 2-18). The outstanding feature of the speakers' construction of the past is the disgrace they suffer and, in the second colon of Lam. 5:1, they appeal to YHWH to perceive this. While, in this bicolon, the suffix of חרפתנו / חרפותי[נו refers to the speakers in the lament, in 4Q501 it is not clear who the referents of בני in the phrase חרפת בני are, because the *nomen rectum* of בני was written on a piece of the manuscript that has, unfortunately, not survived. The frustratingly incomplete nature of the manuscript also causes doubt about the sense of the polysemous noun חרפה in the context of the line. If בני refers to the speakers, חרפה would most likely mean "disgrace," as in Lam. 5:1. If, however, the opponents of the speakers are the referents of בני, חרפה would probably have the sense of "reviling, taunt." In this regard, it is suggestive that the opponents' lying and slanderous tongues are mentioned in close proximity to חרפה. The lacunae in the manuscript rule out any certainty in the interpretation of the lines, but it is possible that the speakers in 4Q501 plead with God to heed the opponents' insulting verbal abuse (line 5) in the immediate context of their complaints about the distressing and enraging effects of the opponents' false and damaging speech on them (lines 4 and 6). It, therefore, cannot be confidently claimed that the words which 4Q501 have in common with Lam. 5:1 allude to the content of this passage.

wording of Lam. 5:1 is not completely preserved in 5QLam^a, the manuscript does exhibit two small differences when compared to the *kethib* version of the MT (as represented by Codex Leningradensis): the lengthened form of the imperative הביטה, which agrees with the *qere* reading and those in other MT manuscripts, and the plural form of חרפותי[נו. See Kotzé 2013: 149–51.

Lamentations 5:10 in 4Q501 line 6

Finally, line 6 of 4Q501, עורנו וזלעופות אחזונו מלפני לשון גדופיהם] ("[o]ur skin and burning rage seized us because of their slanderous tongue"), contains two words that have equivalents in Lam. 5:10: עורנו and זלעופות.[21] Berlin sees in this line a conflation of words from Lam. 5:10 and Ps. 119:53.[22] In her opinion, the line

> recontextualizes the Lamentations verse in terms of the Psalm 119 verse. "We are physically devastated," says the poem, "like the Jerusalemites in Lamentations, not by famine but by the wicked people who have abandoned the Torah." The poet clarifies the nature of their wickedness by adding the explanatory words מלפני לשון גדופיהמה [sic], "from before their insolent tongue." Insolent words are the cause of the harm. The poet's problem comes not from famine but from Jewish opponents. (Berlin 2003: 14)

The main problem with the suggestion that the wording of 4Q501 line 6 contains such an allusion to Lam. 5:10 is the gap in the text before the word עורנו. The sentence of which עורנו is a part is incomplete and, therefore, the syntactic function of this noun phrase is unknown.[23] The relationship between this, incompletely preserved, sentence and the following one can also not be established with certainty. Furthermore, the sense of the first colon of Lam. 5:10 is difficult to determine. According to the speakers in the lament, the "rages of hunger" cause their skin to be comparable to an oven. This is a curious image that likens famished bodies, suffering the effects of hunger, to a particular type of clay oven used for baking bread, a staple in ancient Near Eastern peoples' diet.[24] The verb נכמרו furnishes

---

21. The Hebrew wording of this bicolon in 5QLam[a] reads as follows: עור[נ]וּ כֹתנור נכמרו מֹ[פ]ני זלפות רֹעב ("o[ur] skins have become shriveled like an oven, be[cau]se of the rages of hunger"). The MT is almost identical: עורנו כתנור נכמרו מפני זלעפות רעב. Regarding the difficulty involving the disagreement in number between עורנו and נכמרו in this version of the MT, as well as the variant readings עור[נ]וּ and זלפות in 5QLam[a], see Kotzé 2013: 160–1, 165–6.

22. MT Ps. 119:53: זלעפה אחזתני מרשעים עזבי תורתך ("rage has seized me because of the wicked, who abandon your law").

23. Reconstructions of the sentence's wording that insert the verb נכמר with עורנו as its subject on the basis of Lam. 5:10 are, of course, completely conjectural. For such reconstructions, see the transcriptions of the text by Baillet 2014: 698; 1982: 79 and García Martínez and Tigchelaar 1998: 994, as well as the different translations of Vermes 2004: 328; Davila 2000: 179; and García Martínez 1996: 403.

24. See Borowski (2003: 66), P. J. King and Stager (2001: 67), and Shafer-Elliott (2013: 119–25) for ethnographical and ethnoarchaeological comments on the *tannur* and other types of clay-baking ovens.

the *tertium comparationis*, but its meaning in the context of the colon is disputed. The ancient translations differ in their renderings of Lam. 5:10a and the manuscripts of the Septuagint and Peshitta translations even transmit double translations of the Hebrew verb.[25] Some scholars are of the opinion that the verb in the Hebrew text indicates discolouration as the point of comparison between an oven and skin (Deist 2000: 195; Hillers 1992: 158), while others think that the comparison pertains to emitted heat (Frevel 2017: 338; Westermann 1994: 209; Kraus 1983: 89). A third group of scholars argues that נכמרו in this colon expresses the sense "shriveled" and, therefore, that the skin of the speakers is said to be wrinkled or cracked like the wall of a *tannur* (Driver 1950: 143; Renkema 1998: 607–8; cf. also Salters 2010: 355; House 2004: 454; Berges 2002: 271; Rudolph 1962: 258). Koenen (2015: 398), however, suggests that the skin is not shriveled, but sunk in like a collapsed oven. In view of the fact that the sentence of 4Q501 in which עורנו appears is not completely preserved, the unclear semantic relationship between the two sentences that feature the words that are similar to ones in Lam. 5:10, and the uncertain sense of this verse's first colon, it is difficult to maintain that there is an allusion to the content of Lam. 5:10 in the wording of the Qumran scroll.

Concluding Remarks

Variant readings in the Qumran manuscripts of Lamentations and the wordings of 4Q179 and 4Q501, where the two "Apocryphal Lamentations" from Qumran possibly exhibit textual connections with passages from their "canonical" counterpart, are potential sources of knowledge about early Jewish scribes' reception of the poems' content. With regard to 4Q179 and 4Q501, the gaps in the wordings due to the fragmentary nature of the Qumran manuscripts cause much uncertainty in the interpretation of the evidence for textual connections with Lamentations. Nevertheless, this chapter briefly discussed the three instances where the surviving wording of 4Q501 shows similarities to words and phrases in Lam. 5 and attempted to determine whether these perceived textual connections could be regarded as allusions. The discussion indicated that the scribe who put the text of 4Q501 into writing probably used words and imagery from Lam. 5 to formulate the content of sentences in lines 1 and 5. The scribe seems to have penned the wordings in such a way that the content of the source text is not determinative for what these sentences communicate.

25. For discussions of these readings in the ancient translations, see Kotzé 2012b: 284–9.

Therefore, according to the definition adopted in this chapter, none of the instances where 4Q501 shares words and imagery with Lam. 5 can conclusively be characterized as an allusion. This determination concerning the textual connections between 4Q501 and Lam. 5 is relevant for further research into the composition and rhetoric of the Qumran text, as well as for surveys of biblical interpretation in the literature from Qumran. For Lamentations studies, it provides a small, but significant glimpse into the reception of the fifth poem's wording during the later Second Temple Period.

Chapter 16

From Anonymity to Biography: Jeremiah as a Character Memorizing the Past in the Septuagint Version of Lamentations

Antje Labahn

It is widely accepted that Lamentations in its Hebrew form generally contains communal laments over the fate of Jerusalem and its inhabitants caused by the destructive exilic events in Judah in the sixth century BCE.[1] The poems reflect the disastrous experiences caused by these events and interpret them according to contextually well-known motifs and ideas. The laments are communicated anonymously; they neither present nor reveal a particular author, nor are they ascribed to a certain place of origin. Of course, they are transparent to a potential background of an historical situation, one which is likely to have provoked remarkable words about the exilic defeat. Yet the book itself does not mention anyone in particular being responsible for the composition of the poems of collective mourning. It seems that anonymity serves as an important marker for understanding the laments and what they want to communicate.[2]

---

1. Reference is made to the issue in general in Uehlinger 2013: 614. He describes it as "Versuche, die Katastrophe zu begreifen." I thus refer to the oldest parts of the book whose origin was initiated by the exilic events, as emphasized by the majority of research; cf., e.g., Kraus 1960: 13f.; Renkema 1998: 45f., 56f. Such a statement does not, of course, exclude later redactional modifications or additions; cf., e.g., Berges 2002: 52, 65–72; Berges 2000: 1–20, esp. 3f.; Berlin 2002: 1; Uehlinger 2013: 619f.; Frevel 2017.

2. According to Gerstenberger (2001: 474f.), such a mode is central for the character of "communal worship" (475) of the poems which he anticipates in Lamentations, reading the laments as products of "a social group of rather educated people" (474).

The laments present themselves as undetermined, widely open for various interpretations and identifications in particular. Due to such an openness in communication, the laments may be read, heard, or performed by anyone who regards these songs of grief as an adequate expression of his or her own fate. Regardless of the details of the cultural mode of reception, the laments offer words, motifs, ideas, metaphors, and pictures of how to interpret the massive catastrophe, analogous in perception to the one that had happened in Judah, and particularly in Jerusalem, deemed the exilic catastrophe. The laments serve as modes of interpretation of loss and destruction. Therein, they preserve a polyvalent openness to join in (parts of) the multiple ways of expressing grief and, finally, coming through it.[3] Such an openness provides multiple possibilities for sharing interpretation and reception of the laments with their various reflections, regardless of the time and place of reception.

One famous interpretation came with the Greek translation of Lamentations, which offers its own reception. It does so by creating intertextual links to other writings. The Septuagint versions of Lamentations (hereafter LamLXX) offer modes of reception and interpretation that may, with good reason, be called an intertextual reading. Reception and interpretation in LamLXX work extensively through intertextuality.[4] When using the term "intertextuality" here, I use it as re-reading of previous texts with a reuse of motifs and ideas. Reception and interpretation work through intertextual links to established views and acquainted beliefs or well-known writings. The present study presents modes of interpretation and reception in LamLXX, which in their use hint at intertextual relations to various biblical (Hebrew as well as Greek) writings read from a translator's (and thus scribal interpreter's) point of view.

Due to the limited space available here, only a few aspects of such relations by way of reception and interpretation will be offered. It will become clear that LamLXX provides a distinct reception of particular aspects in order to present a new interpretation of the laments and also of its newly introduced main figure: the prophet Jeremiah. Through identifying Jeremiah with the former anonymous speaker of Lamentations, LamLXX creates intertextual links to the portrait of Jeremiah as it is presented in the prophetic writing of Jeremiah. In the horizon of that characterization of the prophet Jeremiah, the subscribed author of LamLXX receives a new function, while sharing the fate of the prophet and the people as well.

---

3. Cf. Labahn 2002.
4. On intertextuality as a methodological feature in Lamentations, cf. Labahn 2003 (including the discussion of method; see, e.g., Allen 2000).

Such a reading is a somewhat new endeavor in research since the question of the intertextual relations between the Hebrew *Vorlage* and its Greek translation has not yet been addressed in detail. Furthermore, LamLXX has not yet amassed a large corpus of research output,[5] although Lamentations has seen "an unprecedented increase in scholarly interest" in the last decades.[6] In addition, the (partly still ongoing) translation projects of the LXX focus predominantly on translation techniques,[7] giving less attention to variations due to theologically or culturally motivated new concepts and interpretations in the LXX.[8] Against such a desideratum, this essay intends to shed new light on the mode of interpretation of history through the figure of Jeremiah as presented in LamLXX in a new role. In LamLXX, the character of Jeremiah becomes responsible for interpreting history. This is achieved by altering the previously anonymous individual into his own role, one of coping with the past through remembering.

Reception and Interpretation

Writings that are not fully determined provide the potential to initiate various readings. In general, multiple ways of reception are conceivable— not only contemporary readings, but also and even more so receptions after a distant span of time. While most of the ancient readings are unknown, one prominent reception is preserved: the Greek version of Lamentations transmitted by the LXX.[9] In its reception, it presents a characteristic interpretation deserving of attention.

5. For negative evidence see, e.g., the report of Thomas 2013a.
6. Thomas (2013a: 8) calls that recent period a "fertile era." Astonishingly enough, LamLXX does not participate in that flourishing stream of research to a great deal.
7. See, e.g., Albrektson 1963; Gottlieb 1978; further, Ueberschaer contributed two articles (2012; 2016) on LamLXX to the Wuppertal translation project focusing on translation technique. On the translation project itself, see Maier and Hirsch-Luipold (2011), as well as their annotated translation (2009). Finally, Kotzé published a number of articles on LamLXX (2009a; 2009b; 2011a; 2011b; 2012a; 2012b; 2012c; 2014; 2015), looking for text-critical intentions as well as pointing to some intended changes (see also Kotzé 2020).
8. With the exception of research done recently be Youngblood; see his short essay (2011). See also Youngblood's dissertation (2004); Labahn 2005.
9. With the Greek version of Lamentations I refer to the version of Codex Vaticanus which represents the most remarkable recension of Lamentations communicating its own message; cf. Ziegler 1976: 41f., 125–27; Tov 1997: 116; Labahn 2005: 150–52. According to Tov (1997), Vaticanus represents the oldest version in an original form that did not undergo later revisions and assimilations to the Hebrew text like the Hexapla version or the Lucian recension.

The LXX interprets Lamentations inasmuch as it presents a distinctive author of the once anonymous laments. LamLXX inserts a new heading over the entire book, ascribing the poems to the prophet Jeremiah[10] (additionally it creates a homonymous subscription Θρῆνοι Ἰερεμίου following after 5:22).

The new heading preceding 1:1 reads:[11]

| Θρῆνοι Ἰερεμίου. | Lamentations of Jeremiah. |
| Καὶ ἐγένετο μετὰ τὸ αἰχμαλωτισθῆναι τὸν Ἰσραήλ, καὶ Ἰερουσαλὴμ ἐρημωθῆναι, ἐκάθισεν Ἰερεμίας κλαίων, καὶ ἐθρήνησεν τὸν θρῆνον τοῦτο ἐπὶ Ἰερουσαλὴμ καὶ εἶπε. | And then it happened, after Israel was made captive and Jerusalem was made desert, Jeremiah sat down, cried and mourned that lament over Jerusalem; and he said. |

Jeremiah appears twice in the new heading: once in a genitive expressing the author in the initial ascription (Θρῆνοι Ἰερεμίου),[12] and a second time as an acting character crying over the fate of Judah and Jerusalem and expressing it (Ἰερεμίας κλαίων…καὶ εἶπε). In both occurrences Jeremiah is made the author of the subsequent words of the five poems contained in the writing LamLXX.

Additionally, the portrait of the prophet is elaborated. The heading creates a new situation with Jeremiah present in Jerusalem during the exile, looking out over the destruction of the city and the temple, and with that the misery of the people. Furthermore, LamLXX lets the prophet react with the strong emotion of grief, in that he is crying over the fate of Judah and Jerusalem. What Jeremiah experiences while sitting there provokes reactions: first a reaction of grief (κλαίων), and afterwards a reaction of coping with their fate while creating and transmitting words of interpretation (καὶ εἶπε).

Overall, LamLXX establishes Jeremiah as a figure with the potential to create the subsequent laments, namely, LamLXX 1–5. Jeremiah is regarded as a character able to interpret history and to articulate its meaning in poetic laments. Such a strategy requires a character who was known for these abilities. When LamLXX puts Jeremiah in such a position it takes up and develops various ideas found in the growing book of Jeremiah.

---

10. According to Youngblood (2011: 66), the "prologue," which he calls the new heading, serves as a hermeneutical guide by allocating LamLXX into the scribal Jeremiah tradition.

11. Translation my own.

12. The phrase Θρῆνοι Ἰερεμίου is only present in those Greek manuscripts that depend on the reading of Codex Vaticanus (on the character see above n. 9).

In that respect, it offers an intertextual reception of the prophet. With such a conception, LamLXX presents itself as an intertextual play with modified interpretations about and receptions of Jeremiah. These aspects will now be analyzed in detail. Together, they present a new way of interpreting history through the innovatively developed figure of Jeremiah with his strong biographically elaborated abilities.

Jeremiah as the Author of Lamentations

The newly added heading in LamLXX creates the idea of Jeremiah as the author of the subsequent laments, and thus the entire writing, that is, Lamentations. When LamLXX makes Jeremiah the author of the laments it intertextually enters into an idea found elsewhere in Chronicles:

> Then Jeremiah chanted a lament...behold, they are also written in the Lamentations (2 Chron. 35:25 NAU; LXX: καὶ ἐθρήνησεν Ἰερεμίας καὶ ἰδοὺ γέγραπται ἐπὶ τῶν θρήνων).

2 Chronicles 35:25 mentions Jeremiah composing a lament over the death of King Josiah. The concept of Jeremiah as a composer of laments is then broadened to include more than just the dirge over Josiah. In particular, LamLXX 1:1 interprets the "laments" mentioned in 2 Chron. 35:25 as laments in general, including the book of Lamentations.[13] Through such a reception of Jeremiah,[14] a new aspect, elsewhere present in writings associated with Jeremiah, enters into the prophetic picture in LamLXX.

While in the book of Jeremiah Baruch takes the office of scribe for Jeremiah,[15] LamLXX develops its own picture of Jeremiah designated as the author of Lamentations.[16] Furthermore, the notion of Jeremiah speaking these words may build an intertextual link to Jer. 36:32, where additional words of the prophet are mentioned. Whereas those words were not designated in the book of Jeremiah, the heading of LamLXX fills that gap.[17]

---

13. Cf. Maier and Hirsch-Luipold 2011: 2827; Berges 2002: 31.
14. Cf. further hints of prophet Jeremiah in 2 Chron. 36:12, 21f. and the interpretation of history through his voice/words. Regardless, the mode of reception may be discussed; see Jonker 2012.
15. Cf. JerLXX 43:4, 10, 27, 32; 51:31; Bar. 1:3.
16. In LXX Jeremiah does not only appear as the author of the prophetic book itself and Lamentations, but also of the Epistle of Jeremiah and Baruch.
17. See Uehlinger, 2013: 615.

As we can see, LamLXX takes up an idea from Chronicles and makes Jeremiah the author of its poems. In doing so, it fills a gap in the Hebrew text, with its previously anonymous laments. In order to fill this gap, it was neither the book of the prophet nor any other writing associated with Jeremiah that was recalled in LamLXX; rather, an idea from a divergent background was utilized. Therefore, an intertextual link with an additional writing, namely, Chronicles, was made. The particular mode of reception is hard to capture, but I think it was no accident that in both writings Jeremiah was presented as an author of laments open for an analogous situation of loss and destruction.

Hence, I assume various vivid traditions about Jeremiah, including a number of pictures concerning an overall polyvalent prophetic character. The idea that Jeremiah was the author of Lamentations belongs to such biographic traditions about the prophet. Most of them emerged in a later period and ascribe more and more influence and authority to him. The idea was present and ripe for intertextual reception. In LamLXX, such a reception works as an intertextual link widening the portrait of Jeremiah. In that way, LamLXX partook in the polyvalent vivid traditions and molded a further aspect of Jeremiah into its own presentation of the prophet.

Jeremiah Acting in Jerusalem during Exilic Times

LamLXX's heading creates a new situation that is historically feasible. Although not explicitly stated, the language strongly visualizes Jeremiah sitting on one of the surrounding hills of Jerusalem, looking upon the ruins beneath him. The heading takes up the motif of Judah as an "empty land,"[18] presenting the land and its capital city in such a state of ruin that no one was able to live there anymore. The sense of deflation and depression was the consequence of extensive deportation of Jerusalem's and Judah's inhabitants, which resulted in the creation of a "desert land" (see the heading: Ἰερουσαλὴμ ἐρημωθῆναι) where wild animals take the place of former inhabitants (cf. also LamLXX 5:18). The heading lets Jeremiah envisage such a mysterious scene while also creating an intertextual link to such a conceptual mind map of exilic Judah and Jerusalem.

---

18. References like 2 Chron. 36:20f. and the seven decades of vacancy/Sabbath in Judah expressed in Jer. 25:11f.; 29:10 and Zech. 1:12 produced such a myth; but it is far from historically reliable. Therefore, the idea of an "empty land" reveals itself as a myth, cf., e.g., Barstad 1996; Scott 1997; Grabbe 1998.

The portrait of Jeremiah acting in Jerusalem during exilic times disregards those notions within the book of Jeremiah that transport him to Egypt. According to the book of Jeremiah (43:5-7; 44:1ff.; 46:13f.), the prophet belongs to the group deported from Judah to Egypt. Henceforth, legend has it that Egypt was the place where Jeremiah was actively admonishing people (see Jer. 44[51]).[19] In the book of Jeremiah, Egypt is the place where the biographic notes and the active phase of the prophet come to their end.

In contrast, LamLXX establishes Jeremiah as a figure present in Jerusalem giving advice to people, yet through hearing and/or reading the Greek Lamentations, which Jeremiah is responsible for as an interpreter of history (see below). Such a perception of Jeremiah acting in Jerusalem can be built intertextually on the "letter to the exiles" found in Jer. 29(36):1ff. This letter says that Jeremiah is writing to officials in Babylon (v. 1), giving advice on how to behave in order to enable the possibilities of future life. The role of Jeremiah there is to communicate God's will to the people:[20]

> [1] Now these are the words of the letter which Jeremiah the prophet sent from Jerusalem to the rest of the elders of the exile, the priests, the prophets and all the people whom Nebuchadnezzar had taken into exile from Jerusalem to Babylon… [4] "Thus says the Lord of hosts, the God of Israel, to all the exiles whom I have sent into exile from Jerusalem to Babylon…" (Jer. 29:1, 4 NAU)

The new heading in LamLXX ascribes an analogues role to Jeremiah. Although there is no particular addressee mentioned, the idea behind the introduction is to let Jeremiah articulate how to overcome distress. Jeremiah is acting as a character with authority and abilities. His role is to communicate[21] the interpretation of history as well as of God's will to the people. Of course, the letter in Jer. 29(36) contains more positive elements on how to act and keep on living than the subsequent verses in LamLXX do. The point to be stressed here is the comparable role and

---

19. Jeremiah 44 presents a multilayered retrospective from the Persian period, collecting various motifs with social critique and addressing people in Egypt in a later period after Jeremiah; see, e.g., Carroll 1986: 728–43.

20. This is not a statement about the nature of the letter nor of its various redactional stages (cf., e.g., Carroll 1986: 555–63). I simply refer to the entire letter in its shape from the period when LXX translation was done.

21. On a communicative task see also Gitay (2008: 210), who regards that task as "conceptualising the world view of family and social crisis" in Lamentations' poetry.

even the common acting place of the prophet, namely Jerusalem. Such a model was present in the book of Jeremiah and was ripe for reception in LamLXX. Such a reception comes about through a certain intertextual link to a particular passage of the book of Jeremiah and its portrait of the prophet's role.

The Suffering Prophet

Another intertextual link to the book of Jeremiah occurs with the idea of Jeremiah as a suffering prophet. Already the Hebrew text—and also the LXX version—presents the prophet as a character struggling with his life (Jer. 15:10; 20:9, 14-18; see also 11:19) and with his office (Jer. 15:15; 20:7-9; see further 11:19-21). The most prominent examples for such a characterization are found in the so-called confessions of Jeremiah.[22] There, the reader meets an emotional prophet who is angry about what he is experiencing in life. In a self-reflective way he is at odds with multiple circumstances in life, cursing the day of his birth (Jer. 15:10; 20:14-17), quarrelling with hostile contemporaries (Jer. 11:19-21; 15:15; 17:15; 18:18-20, 22f.; 20:10), and finally even accusing God (Jer. 12:1; 20:7). In these passages, the prophet appears as a character abounding with negative emotions. Jeremiah is suffering, and in that suffering life and ministry are linked with one another. Jeremiah is neglected as a person and also as a prophet whose office it was to admonish people.

When LamLXX presents Jeremiah as a lamenting, hence suffering, individual it adopts such a notion of the prophet,[23] creating an intertextual play with the suffering character in the book of Jeremiah.[24] Moreover, the new situation in LamLXX, with Jeremiah crying (κλαίων) over the fate of Judah, presents itself as an extension of the prophet's former suffering. The picture of the prophet sitting in distress occurs prominently in JerLXX 15:17: καταμόνας ἐκαθήμην, ὅτι πικρίας ἐνεπλήσθην ("I sat alone because bitterness filled me up"). Although the term "crying" is not used in the book of Jeremiah, the idea is similar, due to the overall "bitter" (πικρίας) situation which additionally leaves Jeremiah sitting alone.

---

22. The portrait of the prophet in the book of Jeremiah is consistent, regardless of if the confessions represent Jeremiah's voice (see, e.g., Hubmann 1978; 2013) or if they, at least in parts, belong to a later stage(s) of the prophetic book which interpret Jeremiah's life and office from a perspective of refutation (cf., e.g., Bezzel 2007; Pohlmann, 1978).

23. Similarly, Youngblood (2011: 67) reads an allusion to Jer. 20:9 in LamLXX 1:13.

24. Cf., in general, my previous article: Labahn 2005: 147–83.

The term κλαίων itself is already present in Lam. 1:15 when Zion is lamenting over her fate of being abandoned (ἐπὶ τούτοις ἐγὼ κλαίω).[25] In Lamentations, Zion is personified, reckoned predominantly as a city[26] and, by this, as female character accompanying Jeremiah. The metaphor "daughter of Zion" (Lam. 1:6; 2:1, 4, 8, 10, 13; 4:22; cf. also 4:2, "sons of Zion"), prominent in Lamentations, addresses her inhabitants who share the fate of the city, and, yet, suffer the challenging of the once invulnerable and indestructible mountain of God.[27] In LamLXX, Jeremiah now steps into the former role of Zion, even taking over the function of lamenting women.

Regarding these analogies as modes of reception, "crying" in the heading of LamLXX implies a polyvalent meaning. At first sight, it represents an essential element within a process of grief,[28] while fulfilling the purpose of condensing past experiences into one scream.[29] At a second glance, crying can also be read as an expression of negative emotion.[30] Such an interpretation links the negative emotions with the negative judgment, thereby taking the harmful situation of loss and destruction seriously. The parallel term in the heading, καὶ ἐθρήνησεν ("mourning"), supports such an interpretation.

An analogous procedure, compared to the suffering prophet, is used in the heading of LamLXX. Although the experience of suffering was changed (from personal life and ministry in the book of Jeremiah to communal fate in Lamentations), the structure remains the same. Against evil fate, Jeremiah reacts with harsh emotions. He is separated from the people suffering against Judah's fate.[31] Moreover, he puts these emotions into words recognizable through reading.

---

25. Cf. Berges (2002: 117), who summarizes the desolate abandonment: "So beklagt Zion...die Ferne...des Schutzgottes, der ihr die Lebenskraft zurückgeben könnte."

26. Cf. Wischnowski 2001; Berges 2002: 52–64.

27. On the motif "daughter of Zion," cf. Labahn 2003 (further references there).

28. Crying essentially belongs to the process of grief as one of its elements; cf. Archer 1999: 74f.; Labahn 2002: 516f., 519f.; Rüsen 2001: 66f.

29. Characteristically, Lamentations often uses the one word scream אֵיכָה / πῶς ("alas") at the beginning of laments: Lam. 1:1; 2:1; 4:1f.

30. Such a negative emotion also plays a role within the process of grief, where it belongs to the second step when strong emotions come to terms with grieving; cf. Kast 1987: 61–78; Archer 1999: 70–2, 92f.

31. See also my previous article Labahn 2005, which focuses on the peculiar characterization of Jeremiah in LamLXX, especially on the variations by metaphors which highlight LXX's intention in intensifying Jeremiah's suffering.

Interpretation of History through the Prophet

The new LamLXX heading makes Jeremiah the author of the subsequent laments. Thereby, he is also reckoned as a voice giving words of interpretation,[32] in particular the interpretation of history through the laments (ἐθρήνησε τὸν θρῆνον τοῦτον; cf. also LamLXX 3:1; see below). Jeremiah is presented as a lamenting character; the subject of his laments touches on the loss and destruction of Jerusalem and Judah resulting from the exilic catastrophe. Therein, LamLXX presents its own interpretation of history in providing reasons and explanations for what happened, including God's actions. Finally, such interpretation is turned into Jeremiah's words.

Thereby, another point of intertextual reception comes from interpreting history. In the book of Jeremiah, the prophet is often presented as someone who interprets history. Of course, these elements do not go back to the prophet himself, but originate from later Deuteronomistic redaction(s).[33] Hence it follows that the exilic catastrophe needs to be judged as God's punishment of the people for not respecting God's will.

The prophet is integrated into that conception as someone who is communicating God's will to the people, by preaching, giving warnings and admonishing people on how to behave and react. The most prominent examples are the presentation of Jeremiah's "call" in Jer. 1 (esp. vv. 9, 16ff.) and his office as speaking to the people in the name of God (cf. Jer. 7:1-15; 23:9ff.; 26:1ff.) shaped according to the more general characterization of the role of a prophet in Deut. 18. The Deuteronomistic redaction(s) of the book of Jeremiah present(s) the prophet as such a figure alongside the Deuteronomistic characterization of a prophet. Such a presentation of the prophet's role is embedded in the Deuteronomistic concept of interpreting history, and furthermore interpreting Jeremiah's prophetic role anew. The concept of success and failure in history explains spending life in peace and wealth as a result of obedience to the divine will, whereas disregard for God's commandments will lead to loss and destruction, which are interpreted as punishment brought on by divine anger.[34]

---

32. Each process of putting anything into words implies an approach of interpretation, see, in general, e.g., Searle 1995; Häfner 2006: 67–96.

33. See, e.g., the two prominent groundbreaking monographs by Thiel (1973, 1981). His model in general is accepted by scholars and was developed further into various redactions in exilic or post-exilic times; see, e.g., Albertz 2001: 231–60; Hardmeier 1998, 2013.

34. Cf. my previous article on God acting with punishment against his people and its representatives: Labahn 2006.

When such a conception of interpreting history is reused in LamLXX, Jeremiah is incorporated into it with a communicative aim. He fulfills his task by interpreting history and communicating that worldview to the people, hence accusing the people of disregarding God's will and holding them responsible for the resulting loss.

Once LamLXX presents Jeremiah as a character interpreting history, it articulates an extension of such a concept, since the reference to the Deuteronomistic conception of history is still strong, even though LamLXX integrates it into its own theological markers and presents it in its own terminology with additional motifs of various traditions. The new heading introduced the idea that fate was brought upon by God, reading αἰχμαλωτισθῆναι τὸν Ἰσραήλ as a *passivum divinum*, that is, it was God (cf. explicitly Lam. 2:17, 21) who destroyed Judah/Jerusalem and put his people into exile, because of their sins (cf., e.g., Lam. 1:5, 8, 14, 18, 20, 22; 2:14; 3:42; 4:6, 22; 5:7, 16)[35] in not respecting his will (Lam. 1:18, 20, 22); he punished the people with the wrath of his anger (cf. Lam. 1:13; 2:1-6, 21f.; 3:43; 4:11, 16).[36] As seen, the subsequent laments allude to this idea a couple of times and create an intertextual link to the Deuteronomistic concept of interpreting history. When LamLXX puts these words in the voice of Jeremiah it makes him an interpreter of history according to the Deuteronomistic model of history itself and the prophetic role, although the full range of Deuteronomistic elements is not completely present in LamLXX.[37] Of course, further motifs amplify the entire conception of interpreting history in LamLXX. Regardless, the heading of LamLXX makes Jeremiah the main, authoritative character in interpreting history. That both modes of the interpretation of history—Deuteronomistic theology and LamLXX—focus on the exilic catastrophe may be due to coincidence. But more likely, it seems to me that there was a need for LamLXX to reevaluate current conceptions of worldview and history after they had been questioned to a great extent by the exilic

---

35. Cf. on various Greek and Hebrew terms for expressing "sin," Kotzé 2008: 83–86. According to Boase (2008a: 457–63), sin belongs to a concept of "retributive theodicy" in Lamentations, because sin of the people as a cause is linked with God's action as a punishing reply to sin.

36. Cf. especially Lam. 2:22; 5:22; see also Lam. 1:12; 2:3, 14, 21f.; 3:43; 4:16, 22; 5:19f. (LXX uses two different Greek terms, either θυμός or ὀργή; see the list given by Kotzé 2009b: 86–8). On the Deuteronomistic concept of God's anger/wrath also present in Lamentations, see, e.g., Brandscheit 1983: 210–31; Berges 2005: 34–40; Labahn 2020: 351–53.

37. See, with regard to the Hebrew version, the overall estimation of Longman 2008: 339 (but see with divergent assumption of influence p. 341).

events of loss and destruction. Therefore, the intertextual reception of presenting history is less strict (especially in terms of the reception of typical Deuteronomistic terminology), rather creatively developing new insights with extended potential to finally overcome distress.

LamLXX gives its own statement about loss and getting over it (cf. Lam. 3:22-26,[38] 31-33; 4:22). Jeremiah plays an important role in the conception of history as a figure remembering the fate of the city and merging time (3:19-21, see below). The role of Jeremiah in overcoming distress is strengthened in LamLXX, especially because God's strong actions therein are less extensively communicated.[39] With such a strategy Jeremiah leaves the exilic catastrophe in the past and opens a new way of life for the future. The role of the prophet includes communicating the interpretation of history to the people, even beyond time and place.

The Reception of Jeremiah's Portrait in LamLXX

To summarize, the new LamLXX heading turns Jeremiah into a figure responsible for interpreting history by writing the subsequent laments. In various intertextually available traditions the prophet was known for such abilities, in responsibly and authoritatively acting like this. Such a portrait of the prophet, which was even increased through various modes of reception, is taken up. Yet, LamLXX adds another aspect by inserting Jeremiah into a prominent position. By way of reception, LamLXX generates its own view on how to present the fate of loss and destruction and how to overcome it and to enable a brighter future. Jeremiah plays a crucial role in this process according to LamLXX. He is made responsible for reflecting on history and therein coping with the past.

The former collective mourning had a strong appeal in the past, involving many of the people of Judah. In switching from collective mourning to individually authored poems, LamLXX suggests various ideas linked with the figure of Jeremiah and the potential ascribed to him within a process of interpretation and reception, which is intertextually

---

38. LamLXX 3:22-24 are missing in the bulk of Greek manuscripts depending on Codex Vaticanus. Discussion continues if the gap is due to a matter of *homoioteleuton* or if there was Greek text which was lost in transaction. Ziegler (1976: 482f.) offers text with comments in annotations only later made available through reconstruction. Although strong Hebrew words about hope brought up by God's merciful actions in future are absent, still expressions of hope open space for life in future times; although they are shaped differently according to the overall intention of the Greek version of Lamentations.

39. Cf. the previous note on the gap in 3:22-24, which consequently means that God's mercy in overcoming distress is less accentuated in LamLXX.

transmitted. Such prophetic potentials are used to elaborate a new role for Jeremiah, with its central function in overcoming distress. As will be shown, the approach which helps overcoming the past is a peculiar remembering of a single character.

The Memorizing Individual

Jeremiah is particularly positioned at the center of the laments. In Lam. 3:1f., he is again presented as the suffering individual[40] who is getting over the past. Some verses later, partly against its Hebrew *Vorlage*, Lam. 3:19-21 establishes Jeremiah as a figure remembering fate and merging time. We need to examine these verses in more detail to appreciate fully how LamLXX overcomes the past while ascribing a central role to Jeremiah.

I am the Man—Jeremiah

While Lam. 1–2 and 4–5 present communal laments, Lam. 3 is the only individual lament.[41] This is immediately clear, as Lam. 3:1 begins with a male "I" speaking (in LXX as well as in MT). But whereas in the Hebrew *Vorlage* the character remains anonymous,[42] LamLXX with its new heading makes Jeremiah this individual.[43]

1	Ἐγω ἀνὴρ ὁ βλέπων πτωχείαν ἐν ῥάβδῳ θυμοῦ αὐτοῦ ·	I am the man who sees poverty under the rod of his [= God's] anger.
2	ἐπ' ἐμέ παρέλαβέ με καὶ ἀπήγαγεν εἰς σκότος καὶ οὐ φῶς,	Me he took and led into darkness and no light,
3	πλὴν ἐν ἐμοὶ ἐπέστρεψεν χεῖρα αὐτοῦ ὅλην τὴν ἡμέραν.	even against me he turned his hand the whole day long.[44]

40. Concerning Jeremiah's suffering in LamLXX 3:1-21, see in more detail Labahn 2005.
41. This may mean that Lam. 3 "turns away from 'the outside' towards 'the inside'" of a lamenting view of an inhabitant of the city in ruins, as Renkema (1998: 344) describes the difference.
42. On various identifications proposed in discussion cf. the presentations by Renkema (1998: 348–52) and Berlin (2002: 84).
43. Cf. Youngblood 2011: 67. His general observation deserves a more sophisticated reading, as will subsequently follow, which serves to even amplify Youngblood's thesis in integrating LamLXX into Second Temple Jewish writings with their own impetus.
44. Translation of LamLXX 3:1-3 my own.

Lamentations 3:1-3 recall the initial heading, going back to its tone as well as to its qualification of Jeremiah. Jeremiah is again presented as a suffering individual. According to the Deuteronomistic interpretation of history and alongside the heading, the events which destroyed and impoverished land and people, that is, the exilic events, are ascribed to God's anger (θυμοῦ αὐτοῦ), yet interpreting these events as an outcome of a divine reaction responsible for what happened. The prophet himself is now the one suffering punishment, which is interpreted as brought upon by God himself (v. 2: παρέλαβέ με καὶ ἀπήγαγεν; v. 3: πλὴν ἐν ἐμοὶ ἐπέστρεψε χεῖρα αὐτοῦ). Whereas, according to Deuteronomistic theology, the people or their leaders are taken as objects of God's anger (cf., e.g., also Jer. 18:20, 23), here it is the prophet himself. When the lament continues with motifs of darkness and lack of light (v. 2; cf. 3:6), Jeremiah's suffering, as described in his confessions, is recalled,[45] though new motifs compared to the confessions appear. Such receptions present further intertextual interplays.

Therefore, Lam. 3:1ff. presents itself as a continuation, yet also an elaboration, of LamLXX's heading. The former anonymous man has now become Jeremiah. If it holds true that the Hebrew term "man" (גבר) implies an impression of a strong individual with a close relationship to God,[46] LamLXX draws on such an idea when it inserts Jeremiah. In doing so, LamLXX ascribes that qualification upon the prophetic character, now not only established with nearness to God, as was known from the prophetic portrait through the book of Jeremiah, but also with power. This becomes an important element in the new portrait of the prophet, because power is needed to create a new perspective for the future—though such a perspective will also arise later on in the chapter.

As a result of the LamLXX heading, which is recalled in 3:1ff., the subsequent verses speak about Jeremiah. LamLXX composes another chapter in Jeremiah's confessions; on one hand, it maintains the main idea

45. The idea of Jeremiah sitting in a pit (Jer. 18:22) was transformed into the motif of darkness, yet including its deadly function. Furthermore, elements from Deut. 28:28 using darkness as expression of exile may be recalled, like Berlin (2002: 86) proposes.

46. For such interpretation see Renkema 1998: 351. Although Berges (2002: 184f.) agrees with Renkema in that respect, he also establishes a quite different interpretation of the גבר when he identifies the figure with "die reflexive Seite der Frau Zion, der leidenden und auf JHWH hoffenden Vorbildgestalt für die Gemeinde der Frommen" (2002: 182f., quote 183) in post-exilic Judah. Another proposal was raised by Brandscheit (1988: 82), when she assumes that the Hebrew term גבר implies an aspect of "ein Mensch...der Gottesfurcht besitzt, auf Gott vertraut."

of the former prophetic portrait of the suffering prophet[47] and on the other hand it includes new aspects with enlarged potentials of Jeremiah.

Memories in Soul

Lamentations 3:19 continues to recall the LamLXX heading when pointing to the suffering prophet, though it takes the suffering of Jeremiah one step further. In Lam. 3:19-21 Jeremiah's role is switched from passive suffering to a mode of more or less actively coping with the past:

19	ἐμνήσθην ἀπὸ πτωχείας μου καὶ ἐκ διωγμοῦ,	I remembered from my poverty and out of persecution,
20	πικρία καὶ χολῆ μου μνησθήσεται καὶ καταδολεσχήσει ἐπ' ἐμὲ ἡ ψυχή μου·	bitterness and my gal will be remembered, and my soul will meditate with myself;
21	ταύτην τάξω εἰς τὴν καρδίαν μου, διὰ τοῦτο ὑπομενῶ.	this I will devote to my heart, therefore I will endure.[48]

Although in the majority of verses LamLXX is more or less close to its Hebrew *Vorlage*,[49] Lam. 3:19-21 presents a number of characteristic variations. These variations are not centered on terminology;[50] rather, they can be found in syntactic details, especially in vv. 19 and 20,[51] developing a new interpretation of the lament.

In v. 19, one of the main differences comes with the verb, which is now first person singular, "I remembered," as a word of Jeremiah, instead of an imperative appeal to God as in the Hebrew version. Further, the LXX inserts two prepositions, ἀπό and ἐκ, into its Hebrew *Vorlage*. In the Hebrew, the substantives "poverty" and "persecution" appear as objects of the appeal to God, alongside the subsequent objects πικρία καὶ χολῆ, thus

---

47. LamLXX 3:1ff. presents Jeremiah as chained and almost poisoned, as a victim of lethal fortune. LamLXX 3:15 especially implies Jeremiah is as grieving individual who has to carry the guilt of his people in his body and soul, for his entire life. This idea will be treated in more detail in my nascent commentary on LamLXX.

48. Translation and edition of LamLXX 3:19-21 my own.

49. Cf. Kotzé 2009b: 78–88; Youngblood 2011: 65; Maier and Hirsch-Luipold 2011: 2829f.; Koenen 2013: 31–43.

50. This holds true in general, although LXX renders some Hebrew idioms in LamLXX 3:19-21 in an unfamiliar way, as shown by Pietersma 1995: 197. The estimation of Pietersma underscores the arguments presented in this essay.

51. More than that, in most codices LXX deletes the following three Hebrew verses (Lam. 3:22-24). The Lucian version, as well as some other manuscripts (e.g., Ambrosius), offers a Greek textual version, but they are later additions and present various recensions; cf. the apparatus with Ziegler 1976: 79–92.

reading: "Remember my affliction and my wandering, the wormwood and bitterness" (NAU). The LXX splits the sentence and begins a new saying with πικρία καὶ χολῇ, turning them from objects into subjects. The new subjects fit with the subsequent passive verb form and therein they mention that which is recalled, namely, the bitter and humiliating experience of the exilic events (cf. Lam. 1:3, 5, 7, 8, 9, 12; 2:5; 3:32-34; 5:11, with the frequently used favorite term ταπείνωσις; Lam. 3:15, 19: πικρία).

In v. 20, the strategy continues and turns the statement of the suffering individual[52] into a self-reflection of the prophet. Of course, such an interpretation depends on the notion of the verb καταδολεσχήσει and on the reading of ἐπ' ἐμέ. The main meaning of καταδολεσχέω is "to meditate, to chatter."[53] Here, it represents a more intense meaning compared to the already intense double use of "to remember" (זכר) in Hebrew.[54] More than that, καταδολεσχήσει points to a continuing process of reflection which is running again and again. The site of this process is identified afterwards, with the mentioning of the "heart"; as such, the soul (ψυχή) is installed. Whereas in the Hebrew the heart is seen as the center of thoughts and emotions,[55] in the LXX the soul is used instead. Such an alteration corresponds with Hellenistic anthropology.[56]

---

52. Longman (2008: 368) interprets the reading of "my soul is downcast within me" in Hebrew as an expression of "depression."

53. Cf. Lust, Eynikel, and Hauspie 2003: 312. The editors qualify such a notion of καταδολεσχήσει in Lam. 3:20 as neologism (since it is a *hapax legomenon* in LXX analogies in reading are lacking). According to Muraoka (2009: 370), the term means "to chatter" in the mode like the verb ἀδολεσχέω means "to meditate, ponder (…to talk to oneself)" similarly to διαλογίζομαι (2009: 11). Muraoka points to various parallels in the Psalter.

54. In general, LXX uses μιμνήσκομαι to translate Hebrew זכר (cf. Lust, Eynikel, Hauspie 2003: 404). According to Berges (2002: 196), the Hebrew notion of זכר in v. 20a already implies a way of self-reflection, but in a depressive mode, as if the suffering individual is thrown back to his/her own thoughts throughout so that he/she finally will have to face "Auflösung seiner Persönlichkeit." Renkema (1998: 381) interprets the text similarly when he translates: "My soul is abundantly aware of it and it pities me" (1998: 332). See also Uehlinger 2013: 617f. A methodologically varied assessment has recently been presented by Bier 2014: 146–67. Divergent from such a fashion, LamLXX favors a different mode of reflection with a more positive view of future days when past defeat will finally have been overcome (see below).

55. Cf. Wolff 1984: 105f.; Schroer and Staubli 1998: 46–56, 75–9; Janowski 2009: 170–3; Janowski and Liss 2009.

56. Overall, such an alternation is common in LXX; cf. also 1 Chron. 15:29; 2 Chron. 31:21; 35:19; see Labahn and Sänger 2011: 1042.

The key terms in 3:19-21 are "remembering" (ἐμνήσθην), "heart" (καρδία), and "soul" (ψυχή).[57] The terms point to a reflective mode for the individual's way of coping with the past. Even more than that, v. 20b emphasizes that reflective mode while subsequently using the verb καταδολεσχήσει. In my opinion, the second verb is to be read in a self-reflective way: "my soul will meditate with myself." Since such a notion is not inherent in the Hebrew version, LamLXX highlights the way in which it enables the prophet to cope with the past.

Twice the verb "to remember" occurs, with Jeremiah as the subject. It is not one single act which enables one to get over the disaster; rather, it is a longer process indicated by the self-reflective mode. Such a process of remembering forms the mode of coping with the past, illuminating an ordinary process of grieving and finally overcoming it. LamLXX regards the prophet as one to fulfill such a role, not only on behalf of himself but also on behalf of the people. Although he is a single character, he takes on the entire burden of the destructive events when he meditates on the defeat in his soul. LamLXX interprets the role of Jeremiah as a character who overcomes the fate of the nation through his involvement in the process of remembering.

Remembering as a Model of Coping with the Past

When speaking of such a process, LamLXX makes use of the strong term, "to remember." It does not come as a surprise that the mode of remembering is recognized as essential to the process of grief. Nowadays, models of remembering to the extent of remembering have become the predominant approach for coping with the past. We may think in terms of the repetitive realization of the past and its commemoration (more precise in German: "Vergegenwärtigung"[58]).

Memories go back to the past and recall experiences of an individual through his/her specific mode of reception. Such an individual mode of reception represents a particular interpretation shaped due to its individual perception. Each memory collects a vast array of experiences, desirable as well as undesirable, and links these elements with their representation in the mind while screening and evaluating them.[59] Such a process interprets

---

57. According to Berlin (2002: 92), such motives are common in individual laments like they were present, e.g., in Psalms (77:7f.) and Job (7:11; 10:1). However, their use in LamLXX is more specific.

58. Cf. Rüsen 1994, 214f.: "'Geschichte' meint deutend vergegenwärtigte Vergangenheit"; similarly Y. Gitay 2008: 212: "to perpetuate the trauma of the people."

59. On this function of brain within the process cf., e.g., MacCormac (1988: 149–75) with regard to models generated by cognitive sociology.

elements of the past and creates its own conception of what the past was like. Memorizing starts to become one of the core features in the process reckoned as a basic instrument that displays the past for present desires.

When LamLXX inserts Jeremiah into such a position he is assigned the role of one coping with the past in order to gain new potential possibilities for future life, not only for himself but even more for the people. LamLXX introduces Jeremiah as the one remembering historical experiences and thereby giving words to them, hence interpreting history. LamLXX links such a process of coping with the past to the prophet Jeremiah, whose role is enlarged so as to include a new way of managing the past when remembering past disastrous experiences. Memorizing takes the role of responsibility for executing the shift from past to future. According to LamLXX, such a process of remembering will be most possible when a single character fulfills the role, such as Jeremiah.

LamLXX uses a term that has become famous in contemporary research in the last couple of decades—"remembering." Initiated by Jan Assmann (2007), cultural science elaborated theories of remembering. Of course, the complex model cannot be presented here in detail, but it is worth noting that there is a central core in these models that shows powerful analogies between Jeremiah's role in remembering and Assmann's approach to remembering. Both have in common the mode of repetition as a way of producing connective structures. Through repetition, formerly known elements become recognizable due to a chain which links them in the brain of a recipient. In the process of repetition certain structures come up, arranging events into clusters and producing a system of order with certain provisions.[60] Such a system of clusters of order presents itself as a mode of interpreting the world. It does so especially when world order becomes written in scripture, since scripture creates connective structures which work as interpretative memory.[61] However, while Assmann works with cultural memory taking the role within a dynamic cultural process of remembering society,[62] in LamLXX it is Jeremiah's unique role as one especially qualified individual capable of structuring and interpreting the past by way of remembering.

---

60. Cf. Assmann 2007: 17: "Die vergegenwärtigte Erinnerung vollzieht sich in der Deutung der Überlieferung."

61. Due to Assmann (2007: 18) that holds true because "ihre Bindekräfte heißen nicht Nachahmung und Bewahrung, sondern Auslegung und Erinnerung."

62. Cf. Assmann 2007: 19ff.

Through the interpretation of the prophet's words of remembering, LamLXX presents its own interpretation of the past. The past events are characterized as evil and bitter, deadly and humiliating experiences. Regardless of the theological modifications in the details, all the poems in Lamentations share the same tone; hence LamLXX represents Jeremiah's voice, including his prophetic interpretation of the past experienced with his body and soul.

When LamLXX lets Jeremiah take on the role of remembering, the character does so from a retrospective position. In the initial scene of the laments, Jeremiah is looking back on desolation and loss. Even more so, in his memory, time is amalgamating when present merges with past. The assumed present time represents LXX's point of view and is far beyond the prophet's own time. Yet still the process of coping with the past is going on according to LamLXX. History has not yet been completely overcome, but the past is still present in the memory of the people, who are represented by Jeremiah's memories in LamLXX.

In the process of remembering, LamLXX presents its own interpretation of history dominated by intertextual reception. LamLXX establishes a strong character to take on the role of coping with the past through his memories that, of course, represent memories of the people, as well as the writers and translators of LamLXX. Reflections of the past in interpretation from a later point of view are bound together in memories. These memories do not represent hard historical facts, but rather reflections of experiences of loss and defeat. Even after so much time has passed, such reflections are still so poignant that LamLXX interprets them as a vivid picture of the past. Even a couple of generations later, the historical defeat is still present in memory.[63]

Therefore, according to the conception of LamLXX, Jeremiah's meditative reflections are needed in order to get over these experiences and to develop a new perspective on history and the present. Jeremiah, as a strong character who is close to God, someone capable of suffering and also able to interpret history, is offered as character well suited to fulfill that task.

---

63. Cf. Uehlinger (2013: 615, 624), who points to the consequences of the "collective historical drama" in memory which is still present generations later; Lamentations give words to these. See also Boase (2008a: 449f.), who is reading Lamentations as a writing "to construct meaning" in order to "encompass…distress, …a loss of coherence and the collapse of the very traditions which helped to form community identity…within this existential crisis."

In the process of remembering, time is amalgamated; the past is merged especially with the present in memory. Furthermore, the process also serves a future purpose when LamLXX lets Jeremiah speak about his potentials of enduring lifetime (cf. the use of future tense in 3:21: ὑπομενῶ).[64] The future aspects are not that strong in LamLXX, yet the few glimpses there open space for the future. Theological aspects point to the future. The coming of a brighter future depends on God's grace, which will decide if and when that future arrives. The theological interpretation of LamLXX lets God act and is still waiting for more to come. Hope in God's prospective actions is still a matter with ample potential to be realized in the future.

When LamLXX 3:32 announces God's mercy (ἔλεος), which will appear over against humble experiences (ὁ ταπεινώσας) because of his characteristic of being "good" (3:25: ἀγαθὸς κύριος), it expresses hope that God will act according to his merciful benevolence again in favor of his people, who at that time remain humiliated individuals. Chief among these is Jeremiah. In that process, Jeremiah gets an extraordinary role, since he becomes the one appealing to God to listen to his prayer (3:56: φωνήν μου ἤκουσας μὴ κρύψῃς τὰ ὦτά σου εἰς τὴν δέησίν μου; cf. also vv. 50, 55, 57) and finally to come close for help (3:57: εἰς τὴν βοήθειάν μου ἤγγισας) and to do justice (3:58: ἐδίκασας, κύριε, τὰς δίκας) to the suffering soul of the prophet (τῆς ψυχῆς μου) and at the end redeem his life (3:58: ἐλυτρώσω τὴν ζωήν μου). Because Jeremiah was known as the one having close access to God, he bears such potential and therein fulfills the role of a kind of mediator with God. Consequently, Jeremiah's appeal to God to reestablish his benevolence will not only touch his own reversal of suffering but will also be valid for the people.

Memories as Interpretations and Reflections of History

Telling history is, of course, neither a (more or less objective) report nor a summary of past events; rather, it is predominantly an interpretation of the past. Any statement about the past is a result of a cognitive process which evaluates data and characterizes the people involved, which creates links and order between events, which elaborates reasons and provides judgments. A cognitive process draws lines and structures procedures, yet therein providing significant interpretations of the past.[65]

---

64. The verb implies an aspect of "to wait for...something beneficial"; cf. Muraoka's (2009: 704) notion of Lam. 3:21.

65. Cf. J. Rüsen 1994: 214–16; see also Straub 1998.

In that regard, history is an elaborated construction of the past due to certain ideas shaped by their specific ideological, sociological, cultural, and religious imprint. These general remarks hold true for history writing as well as for memories about the past, regardless of whether they are merely present in the mind(s) or finally become literate in writing(s). Presenting history is the result of mental operations in memories generating interpretations of the past with relevance for contemporary times.[66]

LamLXX links both, history writing as well as memories about the past, when it implies memories of the past and constructs a historical picture with them. LamLXX presents its own model of history about the past period of distress which is illusively described in the laments, as far as they present a picture of desolate circumstances of life and what they tragically mean to the people involved. The mode of history writing in LamLXX is created through verbalizing strong emotions about loss and disaster. LamLXX uses the model of memories to present history in a specific manner according to its interpretation of past, which, for sure, is an interpretation from a much later point of view, but not less emotional. Remembering and interpretation of the past work as a cognitive process that includes aspects of repetition, reorganization, and redefinition.

However, there is one major distinction. When LamLXX verbalized experiences it characterized these as experiences of the prophet Jeremiah. Jeremiah is not along in experiencing distress, since he shared experiences with the majority of his people. Yet LamLXX articulates its picture of the past as Jeremiah's memories. LamLXX does so by inserting Jeremiah as a dominant character interpreting history and communicating LamLXX's view to its readers. Compared to its Hebrew *Vorlage*, this is a new model of presenting the past—LamLXX's interpretation is presented as Jeremiah's memories. By doing so, history writing in LamLXX establishes itself as the mind of the assumed strong and yet suffering prophet in whose authority interpretation of the past is organized.

LamLXX assumes a need to reevaluate previous interpretations in such a way that the mode of remembering now contains possibilities for coping with distress and creating ways for a new future. Since collective memories ultimately failed to wipe out distress, single memories of an assumed capable strong individual are installed instead. Remembering the past means structuring the past into clusters which open up new ways to finally get over trauma. History, therefore, is presented as Jeremiah's memories including potential possibilities of coping with the past, merging time, and opening up future life.

66. Cf. Rüsen 1994: 214f.; 2003: 110–15.

*The Character of Jeremiah in LamLXX as a Model for
an Extraordinary Individual*

As demonstrated, in LamLXX Jeremiah becomes a character with an important role in interpreting history and communicating the enduring value of history to people. Compared to its Hebrew *Vorlage*, LamLXX presents Jeremiah in a modified role as a character capable of overcoming distress and opening new ways for the future life of the people. In such a new role, LamLXX creates the figure of Jeremiah alongside contemporary presentations of extraordinary individuals.

In the Second Temple period, particular figures became famous for what they had done, even more for what their role in society was assumed to be like. As Ulrich Berges puts it:

> Dabei wurden bekannte Persönlichkeiten der Geschichte Israels literarisch so ausgestaltet, dass an ihnen, ihrem Leben und Leiden theologische Fragen und Probleme sichtbar und gelöst wurden. (Berges 2002: 183)

This holds true for varying modifications of the portrait of Jeremiah in the prophetic book itself.[67] LamLXX continues that mode of reception in reestablishing the prophet and in redefining his role anew. Developing a model to cope with the past, Jeremiah takes on the role of representative of the people by remembering the past and realizing interpretation of the past.

In such a process, past and present time tend to become interchangeable. By way of repetition, past and present time share common features in experiencing distress. Past and present modes share clusters of interpretation. Therein, time is amalgamated especially in verbalized and literalized memories which link past and contemporary evaluations of events and people involved and the way they were and still are recognized.

Through repetition, reception, and interpretation in remembering new images of the past, present, and future emerge in LamLXX. Admittedly, future potentials are nascent. They are not strongly present in the laments, but hope in God is strong—that God will one day bring a brighter future. God's powerful hero, the prophet Jeremiah, is deemed as one who saw these potentials a long time ago. LamLXX installs Jeremiah as a figure in whom time is merging. Good fortune did not come to everyone, not even to the prophet himself who experienced extended suffering. But the

---

67. Alongside supplementary elaborations of Jeremiah's portrait in further writings associated with Jeremiah in LXX, like Baruch and the Epistle of Jeremiah. These cannot be demonstrated here.

prophet did not give up hope in God, maintaining (or reestablishing) an effective connection to God full of hope.

According to LamLXX an extraordinary individual was necessary to create a shift. A new evaluation of the past was needed which could be encapsulated by a single mind, that is, in the memory of Jeremiah—in fact, the condensed "memory" of the construction of history through LamLXX. The (partly) new picture of the past was retrospectively attributed to the figure of Jeremiah, whom LamLXX installs as an authoritative figure because expectation was there that his communication would be recognized. LamLXX does not need many words to generate a new portrait of history. It is enough to insert a strong individual and to let his memories give new interpretations of the past, while merging past with present, even future, in order to finally overcome distress.

Chapter 17

"Let us test and examine our ways, and return to the Lord": Josephus' Interpretations of Lamentations

Honora Howell Chapman

> The five extant canonical Sumerian city laments attest to the enduring allure of the "city" and all that "civilization" has to offer.... This haunting image of the city, abandoned to her fate by her patron god, appears not only in the Bible (e.g., Isaiah, Jeremiah, Lamentations, Ezekiel, even Revelation 18), but also in the extra-biblical literature (e.g., 4Q179, from the caves at Qumran)—as well as, *mutatis mutandis*, in the literature of the ancient Mediterranean, specifically, ancient Greece. (Jacobs 2016: 30–31)

In discussing the world's oldest recorded lamentations, John Jacobs constructs a cultural bridge from Sumer to Israel to Greece in a recently edited volume, *The Fall of Cities in the Mediterranean: Commemoration in Literature, Folk-Song, and Liturgy*, yet despite the biblical references here, Jerusalem does not receive a dedicated chapter. Considering the biblical underpinnings of civilization in the Mediterranean basin over the past two millennia and the centrality of Jerusalem as a holy city in the collective consciousness of Jews, Christians, and Muslims, this oversight is especially surprising. We can fill this lacuna, however, with an examination of a piece of extra-biblical literature that unlike the Dead Sea Scrolls actually did have a very wide audience through the centuries: Josephus' *Jewish War* (*J.W.*). Reading key portions of this historical text in light of Lamentations provides us with a richer understanding of biblical reception and interpretation in late antiquity and beyond.

No other contemporary eyewitness accounts of the Jewish War (66–73 CE) survive, not even Tacitus' account of the siege of Jerusalem in his *Histories* from a generation later. Therefore, we can read Josephus' Atticized Greek text in order to see how he shapes the fall of Jerusalem in 70 CE in light of the biblical background, including the book of Lamentations, as well as with an eye to the reality of Roman hegemony and the expectations of his readers, who were both Jewish and not. The horrible scenes that Josephus describes for his pagan and Jewish audience, however, had an unintended and hideous afterlife in later Christian hermeneutics as divine vengeance for the Jews supposedly killing Jesus (e.g., Eusebius, *History of the Church* 3.5-7), and they were read as commentary on Lamentations as well. On the other hand, Jews each year still commemorate the terrible synchronicity of the destructions of both the first and second Jerusalem temples with a fast on *Tisha B'Av* (in July or August) with readings from Lamentations. This chapter will address briefly Josephus' self-presentation and then specific episodes from *J.W.* that echo themes inspired by Lamentations; to support this intertextual approach, we have finally the testimony of late antique Christian authors.

Josephus as a Messenger

In *J.W.* 3, Josephus recounts that after being captured at Jotapata in the summer of 67 CE he had an audience with the Roman commander Vespasian in which the Jewish prisoner of war predicts that the general will become emperor, as will his son, Titus. He opens his speech, reported in direct discourse, with reference to *himself*, not really the commander: "You, Vespasian, think that you have taken Josephus as only a captive, but I have come as a messenger (ἄγγελος) to you of greater things" (*J.W.* 3.400). In Greek tragedy, as his readers were well aware, the messenger tells the characters and audience in detail what has already happened off stage. Here, however, Josephus becomes a Hebrew ἄγγελος who forecasts what is going to happen according to God's will; in fact, he identifies himself twice as a messenger from God (*J.W.* 3.400, 402).[1]

With his ability to predict the future through the application of knowledge gained through his previous dreams (*J.W.* 3.351-53), Josephus is playing a latter-day Joseph and/or Daniel. Shaye Cohen (1982a: 369) has observed that "although Josephus does not call himself a prophet

---

1. At about the same time that Josephus composed *War*, the Gospel of Matthew (11:9) has Jesus ask the crowd about whether they have gone to see a prophet when they followed John the Baptist out into the desert; to describe John, Jesus quotes Exod. 23:20 on the *angelos* of God who will lead the Israelites into Canaan. Both Josephus and Matthew are working within the Jewish mindset but writing in Greek for Hellenized audiences.

(*prophetes*) or ascribe to himself the power of *prophetia*, these terms being restricted to figures of the biblical period, he does see himself as the minister (*diakonos*; cf. *J.W.* 4.626) and messenger (*angelos*) of God who understands and makes known God's will."[2] Josephus' Jewish audience surely was expected to understand the biblical significance of his self-definition. In the larger scheme, however, through the very act of composing his *J.W.*, Josephus in a certain sense also plays the traditional role of the messenger in Greek tragedy by recounting the horrors of the war in vivid detail for his audience in order to evoke pity and catharsis—and to stimulate respect for the surviving Jewish people (including himself). We, therefore, need to read Josephus' history in light of the varying cultural backgrounds of the audience with whom he was trying to communicate.

The sector of his audience that was acquainted with Jewish culture and literature (i.e., Hellenized Jews) was expected to appreciate the biblical subtext of his portrayal of the fall of Jerusalem. For instance, Josephus as a character in the text delivers a speech at the walls of Jerusalem to the besieged Jews inside (*J.W.* 5.362-419), providing an account of Jewish history that celebrates pious Jewish pacifism in the face of the enemy, while drawing a direct parallel between himself and Jeremiah (*J.W.* 5.392-93). David Daube (1980) has shown that Josephus retrofits a number of biblical personalities (Jeremiah, Joseph, Daniel) and events (the interview of Esther with Ahasuerus) with aspects of his own life, thereby creating a recognizable typology;[3] in the same way, we can see that Josephus applies biblical events to the contemporary siege of Jerusalem in his speech at *J.W.* 5.376-419. Here he clearly sets up a typology that identifies himself with Jeremiah, the Romans with the Assyrians, and the Jews with their ancestors who were attacked by both the Assyrians and the Babylonians. He refers to this connection between Jeremiah and the first-century destruction of Jerusalem in his later *magnum opus*, the *Jewish Antiquities*, when he claims, "This prophet proclaimed in advance the terrible things that awaited the city; he also left behind writings about its capture in our own time and the destruction of Babylon" (*Ant.* 10.79);

---

2. See also Lindner (1972), Gray (1993: 37), Gnuse (1996: 139–42); none of these scholars dilates fully on the range of meanings of *angelos*.

3. Daube (1980: 26 n. 72) disproves the idea that Josephus does not use typology, as advanced by L. Goppelt (1966: 47), "Josephus, since offering no eschatological discussions, cannot be expected to practice typology." On typology and the recasting of biblical events and characters in Josephus, also see Cohen 1982b; 1987: 208; Momigliano 1987: 118.

in his commentary on this passage, Paul Spilsbury (Begg and Spilsbury 2005: 231 and n. 337) interprets these "writings" to be "likely...the Book of Jeremiah and the Book of Lamentations (which LXX Lam. 1:1 and *b. Bat.* 15a attribute to the prophet explicitly)."

Lamentations, therefore, provided the historian with at least some inspiration for shaping and interpreting the events he chose to disclose, even if he did not utilize Lamentations' full array of poetic imagery (such as the jackals and ostriches; cf. Lam. 4:3). For instance, his Jewish readers would have known Lam. 1:10:[4]

> Enemies have stretched out their hands
>   over all her precious things;
> she has even seen the nations
>   invade her sanctuary,
> those whom you forbade
>   to enter your congregation.

Josephus, then, could make the complete destruction of this sanctuary all the more poignant and tragic by lovingly describing it in detail *before* it is violated, pillaged, and burned by the Romans in Book 6. In *J.W.* 5, the Temple appears as the crowning glory in his explanation of the city's topography and monumental defenses, setting the stage for the climax of the entire narrative, the Temple's destruction in Book 6. In his extensive description (*J.W.* 5.184-237), Josephus conducts his readers on a tour that leads from the outermost court of the entire complex to the inside of the Temple itself. He also outlines its contents, some of its purity restrictions, and the garb of its priests, including the high priest. In this expansive digression on the Temple, Josephus clearly determines both to impress his audience and to preserve an intelligibly organized and detailed memory of a place whose permanent loss would perhaps be unfathomable for him, but which he knows has happened before (Lam. 2:6-7). After all, back in *J.W.* 5.19, he has described rebels impiously murdering all sorts of people sacrificing at the Temple, and then launches into an aside lamenting the city's pollution, but then suggests, "You would be able to become better again, if you propitiate the God who has destroyed you." Aware of the constraints of genre and that he therefore cannot further indulge in lamentation as an historian (cf. *J.W.* 1.11-12), he rededicates himself in *J.W.* 5.20 to writing a history of this factional strife.

---

4. The NRSV translation has been used throughout.

A Mother's Cannibalism

How then could such a beautiful sanctuary end up torched and the city destroyed? Despite repeated efforts to get the Jews to surrender, the rebels, who are fighting in factions against each other, refuse to entertain the offers of the Romans, and famine deepens in the city, reminiscent of the famine that the prophet Jeremiah describes during Nebuzaradan's siege of Jerusalem, the previous great disaster to strike the city: "On the ninth day of the fourth month the famine became so severe in the city that there was no food for the people of the land" (Jer. 52:6). Famine is also plaintively represented in Lam. 2:19-20:

> Lift your hands to him
>   for the lives of your children,
> who faint for hunger
>   at the head of every street.
> Look, O LORD, and consider!
>   To whom have you done this?
> Should women eat their offspring,
>   the children they have borne?
> Should priest and prophet be killed
>   in the sanctuary of the Lord?

Horribly, these events of maternal cannibalism and slaughter in the Temple play out again in Josephus' narrative of the siege of Jerusalem.

Josephus introduces the story of a famished mother eating her baby with a rather lengthy prologue:

> But why should I tell about their shamelessness in eating inanimate food because of the famine? For I am about to reveal a deed of such a kind that has never been recorded by Greeks or barbarians,[5] awful to tell and unbelievable to hear. For my part, so that I did not seem to my future audience to be telling tales, I would gladly have left out this misfortune, if I had not had countless witnesses among my own contemporaries. Above all, I would be paying cold respect to my country if I lied in my story of the things it has suffered. (*J.W.* 6.199-200)

There are several issues to address in this introduction to the cannibalism episode: its supposed uniqueness in both the Greek and Jewish worlds, its emotional impact, its credibility with respect to his future

---

5. Josephus has referred to Jews as "barbarians" previously (e.g., *War* 1.3); Michel and Bauernfeind (Band II, 2, 1969: 169 n. 80) observe that Paul uses this term at Rom. 1:14.

audience, his insistence upon the use of eyewitnesses, and, finally, his desire not to be considered a traitor to his country but to present accurately through his historical account the sufferings of his own people. One can argue that this prologue, in fact, is a reflection of and counterpart to his much broader presentation of his historiographical aims in the introduction to *J.W.* (1.1-30).

In this prologue to the cannibalism, Josephus first tantalizes his audience by claiming that he will reveal a deed unparalleled in Greek or Jewish history. The few modern scholars who have examined this passage assume that Josephus has made a slip, is ignorant, or is lying, but none provides satisfactory explanation for his motives in doing any of the above. Henry St. John Thackeray (1928: 434) notes, "Josephus strangely ignores the parallel incident at the siege of Samaria, recorded in 2 Kings vi.28f." Thackeray seems to assume that Josephus knew the Hebrew story and chose not to include it. One can, however, argue that Josephus' omission is not "strange" but actually essential to his historiographical goals.

Seth Schwartz (1990: 43 n. 79) acknowledges Thackeray's opinion, but he instead proposes that since Josephus does not mention the mothers' cannibalism in Samaria, the Jewish historian, therefore, did not even *know* this story in 2 Kings when he was composing the *J.W.* I find this hard to believe, considering Josephus' education and status as a Jewish priest. Furthermore, Schwartz does not provide adequate additional evidence to prove his contention of Josephus' "ignorance of the historical books and Jeremiah." I think we can assume that Josephus was at least aware of the story in 2 Kings but chose not to allude to it directly. Considering his use of biblical typology in *J.W.* 5 (376-419) in his own reported speech, we should consider him a Jewish priest who was at least acquainted with his own scriptures (Daniel Schwartz 2016).

Jonathan Price presents a different view: "Josephus' claim that cannibalism had never happened before is *deliberately misleading*" (1992: 155–6, emphasis mine). Price, following Thackeray, recognizes that Josephus chose to omit reference to the biblical material. Thackeray in his note relates this incident in *J.W.* to the warnings of God's retribution for Israel's violation of the commandments in Deut. 28:57 and Bar. 2:2. Price augments these biblical citations with others, including rabbinic parallels; furthermore, he speculates, "Josephus may also have known of the many incidents [of cannibalism] outside the Jewish tradition," and Price (1992: 156 n. 124) cites examples from several Greek historians and even Petronius' *Satyricon*.

None of these modern scholars, however, has drawn a comparison between Josephus' claim here of the incomparable nature of Mary's cannibalism and the historian's larger claim at the very beginning of *J.W.*

that this war between the Romans and the Jews was the greatest of all ever waged (*J.W.* 1.1). In this, he is harking back to Thucydides' (1.1) claim that the Peloponnesian War surpassed all previous wars. Great wars require great climaxes. In his story of the mother's cannibalism, Josephus is laying out an extraordinary explanation for why the cataclysmic destruction occurs in Jerusalem. It, therefore, would only have deflated the grandeur and supposed uniqueness of his material at this point to refer to the Samaritan cannibalism in 2 Kings.

As happened before in the Hebrew scriptures, including Lamentations, a starving woman (named Μαρία in Josephus' account) resorts to killing and eating her own baby. When Josephus introduces her, he gives her name and a patronymic (πατρὸς Ἐλεαζάρου), names her village (Βηθεζουβᾶ), provides an etymology for the village's name ("house of Hyssop"), and then provides a key detail: she is "eminent because of her birth and wealth" and came to Jerusalem as a refugee. By focusing on her prestige and wealth in the midst of famine, Josephus may be signaling an intertextual nod to Lam. 4:

> Those who once feasted on delicacies
>   perish in the streets;
> those who were brought up in purple
>   embrace ash heaps. (Lam. 4:5)[6]

After delivering a tragic soliloquy, slaying the baby, and roasting and eating half of it, Maria even offers the remaining half of the baby as food for the rebels when they smell it roasting and threaten her (*J.W.* 6.208-11).[7] Notice, however, that her baby has been cooked differently than those in Lam. 4:10:

> The hands of compassionate women
>   have boiled their own children;
> they became their food
>   in the destruction of my people.

Whether or not Josephus changed the cooking method (from boiling to roasting) in order to reflect what actually happened during the siege of 70,

---

6. The reference to Sodom in the next verse, Lam. 4:6, also inspires intertextual play in *War* 4.412-13 and 5.562; Chapman (2020) explores the Jewish use of Sodom to explain urban disasters in the 70s CE.

7. Chapman (1998) analyzes this passage also in light of intertextuality with Greek tragedy and historiography; for the awful afterlife of this tale, see Chapman 2000 and 2007; Mason 2016a: 116–21.

there is no doubt that a first-century Jewish reader would have recalled Lamentations, especially since the text would have had an especially profound currency and impact among Jews right after the destruction of the city in 70. When word of the cannibalism spreads, the Roman commander Titus vows that he will "bury this abomination of infant-cannibalism beneath the ruins of their country" (*J.W.* 6.217), thus creating a catalyst for the Temple's destruction, which was caused directly by the rebels' strife against one another. As Paul Joyce and Diana Lipton (2013: 98) observe, "Reading the biblical book in light of Josephus highlights both the striking absence of references to such internal conflicts in Lamentations and its unswerving insistence on collective guilt as opposed to the guilt of a particular faction."

In shaping the acts of maternal cannibalism during the sieges of Jerusalem, both Lamentations and *J.W.* display ring composition, a device that poets such as Homer found quite useful for drawing attention to a dramatic point at the center of the ring. With their references to this horrifying act of cannibalism, Lam. 2 and 4 balance each other out in ring composition around the longer centerpiece, Lam. 3, with its inspiration for Josephus as an historian: "Let us test and examine our ways, and return to the LORD" (Lam. 3:40). Conversely, the structure of *J.W.* 6 revolves around this cannibalism scene, as Steve Mason (2016b: 22) explains, "The nearly precise halfway point of Book 6's 12,462 words comes at the dramatic conclusion of Maria's cannibalism, itself the climax of increasingly desperate famine and brutality, with Titus' resolve to bury the city (6.219 ending 6,202 words)." Thus Josephus inverts the structure of Lamentations, making the cannibalism the highlighted center of *J.W.* 6 and a catalyst for the most tragic event of all.

The Destruction of the Temple

The stage has been set for the Temple's destruction. Titus plans an assault to take hold of the sanctuary being used as a stronghold, but according to the historian, God has long since condemned it to fire (cf. Lam. 2:3). Even the date of the event in *J.W.* 6.250, the 10th (not the rabbinic 9th) of *Lous/Av*, aligns perfectly with the destruction of the first Temple in Jer. 52:12 (Thackeray 1928: 448–9). Josephus again blames the Jewish rebels for the Temple's destruction: "But the flames got their start and their cause from their own countrymen" (*J.W.* 6.251), yet the historian does record that a Roman soldier, "urged by some supernatural impulse" (Leoni 2007: 40), threw a flaming torch through a golden door of one of the Temple's chambers. Josephus shifts back and forth between levels of responsibility, from the Jews to God to the Romans, and now adds "supernatural impulse" (which will return as an explanation for the mass suicide at Masada in *J.W.* 7.348). The Jews rush to save the burning building, and "pay no heed to preservation of living anymore," since their reason for living is disappearing before their very eyes (*J.W.* 6.253). Josephus quickly presents Titus' reaction: when word came, "he leapt up as he was and went to the Temple to confine the fire" (*J.W.* 6.254). He is too late, but he does get to "see the inner sanctum of the Temple and its contents" (*J.W.* 6.260), thus desecrating the sanctuary, as had Pompey the Great (*J.W.* 1.152). Titus pleads with his soldiers to put out the fire, but for a variety of reasons given they do not, and "the Temple thus was set on fire against Caesar's will" (*J.W.* 6.266).

Josephus then pauses from his narrative to provide an obituary for the Temple, commenting how one might mourn the loss of such an extraordinary work. Josephus indicates here that he understands the general expectation of consolation in Greek and Roman social practice: adding "consolation" (*J.W.* 6. 267: παραμυθίαν) to his obituary implies or expects that the reader is one of the bereaved. This recalls the introduction to *J.W.* (1.11-12), which asks pardon for his own emotion and provides a mini-obituary for Jerusalem and his long-suffering people. Josephus does not wish to be just a good historian but also would like to show the emotional restraint of "a Roman gentleman," as one scholar puts it with respect to Plutarch (Hope 2007: 205), a rough contemporary of Josephus. Laments were a scriptural genre for Jews, but Josephus chose the Graeco-Roman historiographical route.

Josephus dates (by years, months, and days) the destruction of the second Temple during the second year of the reign of Vespasian both from the point of its first foundation by King Solomon and its second with Haggai in the second year that Cyrus ruled as king. These calculations of dates offer a greater truth: the Temple may have been destroyed once before, but in a matter of years it was rebuilt again, according to the Hebrew scriptures. He may very well be suggesting here indirectly that the cycle could begin anew. In the meantime, in *J.W.* 7, Josephus explains that the Temple's most precious objects, after surviving the fire and being obtained by the Romans, were carried in the triumphal procession at Rome (*J.W.* 7.148-49), as was depicted a decade later on the Arch of Titus; he then jumps several years in time in his narrative and specifies that Vespasian dedicated the golden items from the Jerusalem Temple at a new Temple of Peace, and ordered purple hangings and a Torah from the Temple to be placed in his palace (*J.W.* 7.161-62; Chapman 2009). Josephus and fellow Jews at Rome must have thought, "Enemies have," indeed, "stretched out their hands over all her precious things" (Lam. 1:10). Yet Josephus emphasizes Roman respect for the Jews' precious objects.

The Afterlife of Josephus

Josephus wrote three other works at Rome besides his *J.W.*, and this corpus was saved thanks to later Christian readers who interpreted, copied, transmitted, and translated his works. Sadly, as with the scriptures, passages from *J.W.* became touchstones for anti-Jewish polemic, even when the Church Fathers understood the intertextual relationship with Lamentations. Sabrina Inolowcki (2016: 360–2) explains the origin of this approach:

> Origen regarded the whole Book of Lamentations as referring to the devastation of 70 C.E....[and] was first to use Josephus's *Jewish War* for anti-Jewish purposes. Indeed, he employed this work to support his theology of punishment. For him, there was a direct connection between the destruction of Jerusalem and the Jewish rejection of Jesus: the Jews were punished by God for their behavior towards the Christ, and this punishment is recorded in detail and confirmed by the Jew Josephus.... Other Josephan passages were alluded to by Origen, notably the *teknophagia* of Mary...[that] was to become iconic for the description of Jewish suffering in Christian anti-Jewish rhetoric.

Other Christian Fathers also read Josephus' description of the destruction of Jerusalem as fulfillment of Jesus' predictions in the Gospels, yet they saw literary resonances beyond the biblical: both Basil and John Chrysostom understood this scene of a mother's cannibalism as a piece of a dramatic tragedy playing out the punishment of the Jews for the crucifixion of Jesus (Schreckenberg 1987: 324 n. 25), since as astute readers they understood the literary nature of the presentation, while at the same time insisting upon its "truth" as support for their arguments, just as Josephus did. The tragic irony, however, is that Josephus created his account of the rebellion in order to exonerate the majority of his people of responsibility for it, yet Christians later used it to condemn *all* of the Jews, a truly lamentable afterlife for Josephus' *J.W.*

Chapter 18

JESUS AND JERUSALEM: CHRISTOLOGICAL INTERPRETATION OF LAMENTATIONS IN THE CHURCH

Robin A. Parry

It was the conviction of the early followers of Jesus that all of the Jewish Scriptures speak of him (Lk. 24:25-27). This conviction is born out in much of the NT's use of the OT and in many of the texts in the early church.[1] In the first part of this essay I consider some sample christological interpretations of Lamentations from church history.[2] Then, in the second part, I offer some reflections on the legitimacy and potential of christological readings. I propose that while such interpretations do not give us the "intentions" of the original author they can be hermeneutically responsible, theologically fruitful, and spiritually enriching.

Case Studies in Historical Christological Readings of Lamentations

Christological Readings of Lamentations in the New Testament

Lamentations does not feature strongly in the NT documents. Indeed, there are no direct quotations from the book at all, although there are some possible allusions, most of which are not directly christological.[3] To

---

1. For instance, Irenaeus' second-century work *On the Demonstration of the Apostolic Preaching*, which outlines basic Christian teaching, seeks to ground all Christian teachings about Jesus in the Jewish Scriptures, which are now seen afresh in the light of his story.
2. In this essay, when I write of the christological interpretation of a text, I simply mean that the text is being interpreted as speaking of Christ in some sense.
3. In addition to those mentioned in the main text, possibly Lam. 1:15 in Rev. 14:20 and 19:15; Lam. 3:15 in Acts 8:23; Lam. 3:45 in 1 Cor. 4:13.

explore a very early christological reflection we must turn to Matthew's Gospel.[4]

During Jesus' seven woes on the teachers of the law and the Pharisees, Jesus says that they reject and kill those God sent to warn them ("some of them you will kill and crucify"), and for this their generation will face dire consequences: "so that upon you may come *all the righteous blood* shed on land, from the blood of righteous Abel to the blood of Zechariah son of Barachiah, whom you murdered between the sanctuary and the altar" (Mt. 23:35).[5] More specifically, the city and its temple will be left desolate (23:37-39; 24). The expression "righteous blood" only occurs in LXX Joel 3:19, Jn 1:14, and Lam. 4:13, and of these only the Lamentations text links the shedding of the righteous blood with the destruction of the temple in the way Matthew does. LXX Lam. 4:13 explains the fall of Jerusalem as follows:

> Because of the sins of her prophets,
>   the injustices of her priests
> Who poured out the blood of the righteous
>   in her [i.e., Jerusalem's] midst.[6]

The Gospel of Matthew presents Jesus as denunciating the religious leaders in Jerusalem in his day via the language of Lamentations—they resist and kill the righteous. Now, this is not christological as such, except that Matthew's Jesus clearly sees himself as the righteous victim *par excellence* (note his reference to how they *crucify* some of the righteous), whose execution precipitates the destruction of the city. This link becomes clear in the passion narrative, when Pilate's wife urges him to have nothing to do with that "righteous man" (27:19) and Pilate declares, "I am innocent of the blood of this righteous one" (27:24),[7] at which the people cry, "His blood be upon us and upon our children" (27:25). So the shedding of the innocent blood of the righteous man Jesus is the climax of the shedding of righteous blood, and the fall of Jerusalem is, in Matthew's view, the result.

During the crucifixion scene itself, Matthew draws from Lamentations again: he writes, "Those who passed by derided him, shaking their heads and saying, 'You who would destroy the temple and build it in three

---

4. Cf. Lam. 2:15 in Mk 15:29-30. On Lamentations in Matthew see especially Moffitt 2006.
5. NRSV, slightly modified. All non-Lamentations quotations are from the NRSV.
6. All translations of Lamentations are my own.
7. For a defense of this reading of 27:24 see Moffitt 2006: 317–19.

days, save yourself! If you are the Son of God, come down from the cross'" (27:39-40). This verse appears to incorporate the language of Lam. 2:15:

> They clapped their hands against you,
>   all those who passed by.
> They whistled and shook their heads, because of
>   Daughter Jerusalem.
> "Is this the city of which they said, 'Perfection of beauty,
>   the joy of all the earth'?"

This verse speaks about Lady Jerusalem, the personified city, as she sits in utter devastation, mocked by those passing by. Like exilic Jerusalem, Jesus, too, has been destroyed by a pagan occupying force, publicly humiliated, and ridiculed by onlookers.

Another connection between Lamentations and the Gospel of Matthew appears in reference to the destruction and rebuilding of the temple. There is an accusation made against Jesus in his trial (26:61), though Matthew provides no clue as to its basis in Jesus' teaching. The Gospel of John, however, records Jesus as saying to his opponents, "Destroy this temple, and I will raise it again in three days" (Jn 2:19), and it seems possible that a distorted version of this comment lay behind the accusation at Jesus' trial as reported by Matthew. John tells us that Jesus was actually speaking about the temple of his own body, which would be destroyed and raised (Jn 2:21-22). Now, Lam. 1–2 speak of the destruction of the temple and the consequent cessation of cultic festivals (1:4, 10; 2:1, 6-7). Indeed, the mocking of Jerusalem for losing its status as the perfection of beauty and the joy of the earth surely relates to Jerusalem as the cultic center in which YHWH dwelled amongst his people. Perhaps Matthew's destruction-of-the-temple motif in 27:40 was triggered in part by the allusion to Lamentations. In which case, the irony is that it is not Jesus who destroys the temple, as the mockers claim, but rather that Jesus is the temple that is destroyed, and by destroying him they bring about the destruction of the city and its temple.

What is interesting is that Matthew's second allusion directly associates the fate of Jesus with the fate of the city of Jerusalem in Lamentations. We shall return to this.

Christological Readings of Lamentations in the Church Fathers

The church fathers do not make a great deal of Lamentations, and most of the Christian readings of Lamentations in both the patristic and the medieval periods have more of an ecclesiological and spiritual-formation focus than a christological one. Nevertheless, certain passages are picked up and given a christological interpretation. Two stand out in particular: Lam. 3:30, 53 and 4:20.

Christ in 3:30, 53
The first is 3:28-30, which advises the sufferer as follows:

> Let him sit alone and be silent
> for he [i.e., God] lifted [it] upon him.
> He should give his mouth to the dust,
> perhaps there is hope.
> He should give his cheek to his smiter,
> he should eat his fill of scorn.

Here the language of giving one's cheek to the smiter prompted Irenaeus (130–202 CE) to read the text alongside Isaiah's oracle about the suffering servant (52:12–53:5) and the servant's own words in an earlier passage: "I gave my back to the blows and my cheeks to the blows and I did not turn my face away from the shame of the spittle" (Isa. 50:6). Lamentations 3:30, read intertextually alongside such passages and the Gospels, was understood as a prophecy from Jeremiah of the yet-to-come sufferings of the Messiah, Jesus.[8] This interpretation was aided by the LXX, which translates the passage not as advice regarding what the suffering man *should* do, but as a description of what the man *will* do: "He will offer to the striker his cheek; he will be sated with insults." So understood it is more amenable to a prophetic reading.

Augustine (354–430 CE) interpreted Lam. 3:30 alongside Jesus' command in the Sermon on the Mount to "turn the other cheek" (Mt. 5:38-39).[9] Jeremiah and Jesus, said Augustine, were making the same point. But while reading the text in light of Jesus' teaching, Augustine did not think it was about Jesus as such, except insofar as Jesus exemplified such teaching in his own life, which, of course, he did. (And so Augustine's interpretation complements Irenaeus'.) Augustine's reading of 3:25-39 as teaching on spiritual formation for saints was more typical of the tradition than Irenaeus' christological interpretation.

There is precedent for other, perhaps more satisfying messianic readings of the chapter. In 3:53 the persecuted man complains, "They destroyed my life in the cistern, and they placed a stone over me." Lamentations speaks here of a metaphorical pit of death for the man, a pit from which

---

8. Irenaeus, *Demonstrations of the Apostolic Preaching* 68.
9. Augustine, *Reply to Faustus the Manichaean*, Book 19.28, *NPNF¹* 4, 250.

God subsequently delivered him.[10] In the fourth century we find Cyril of Jerusalem (313–386 CE) and Rufinus (ca. 345–ca. 410 CE) both interpreting this as a reference to Christ's burial in a tomb with a stone across the doorway.[11] We shall return to defend this proposal later.

The Captured Messiah in 4:20

The main focus of christological reading of Lamentations is 4:20.[12] Here is a translation of the Hebrew and the LXX:

Hebrew

[The] breath of our nostrils, YHWH's Anointed (*meshiah*),
    was captured in their pits—
[He of] whom we said, "In his shade,
    we will live among the nations."

LXX

The breath/spirit (*pneuma*) of our face, the Lord's Anointed (*christos kuriou*) [or, with most Gk mss, *christos kyrios*, the Lord Christ]
Was taken in their corruptions/snares.
Concerning him we said, "In his shade
we will live among the nations."

Lamentations is speaking of the capture of the king of Judah—most likely Zedekiah, although ancient Jewish and Christian traditions normally saw it as a reference to Josiah, the righteous king killed by the Egyptians (2 Kgs 23:29; 2 Chron. 35:20-27)—as he flees the besieged city. The reference to the king as YHWH's Anointed (Messiah/Christ) unsurprisingly caught the attention of Christian readers and indicated a deeper meaning in the text.[13] Indeed, most LXX mss read both nouns as nominative, thus not "the Lord's Christ" but "Lord Christ," which would inevitably draw

---

10. I argue in my Two Horizons *Lamentations* commentary (2010) that this traditional understanding of ch. 3 can be defended against some modern dissenters, who see no experience of deliverance for the man.

11. Rufinus, *A Commentary on the Apostles Creed* 27, *NPNF*² 3, 553; Cyril, *Lecture 13*, *NPNF*² 7, 91.

12. The discussion that follows is based upon Parry 2010: 188–90. See also Thomas 2011: 113–19.

13. Aphrahat (ca. 280–ca. 345) was unusual in resisting the christological reading of Lam. 4:20. He was adamant that it referred to Israel's king only and *not* to Jesus. His reasoning is that Lam. 5:16 refers back to 4:20 with the image of the crown falling

Christian eyes. Jerome's (347–420 CE) Latin Vulgate followed suit and read *Christus Dominus*, "the Lord Christ," making christological interpretation almost inevitable in the West.

First, the passage was taken to suggest an intimate association of some sort between Jesus Christ and "S/spirit." Tertullian (160–220 CE) saw an identification between Christ and the Spirit of the Creator: "The person of our Spirit, Christ the Lord."[14] Cyril of Jerusalem explains that it is Christ's spiritual *nature* that comes out in Lam. 4:20. The Father is spirit (Jn 4:24), *the Son is spirit* (Lam. 4:20), and the Spirit is spirit.[15] This spiritual nature of Christ is applied to the Eucharist by Ambrose (340–397 CE): in the sacrament we partake in the body of Christ; not bodily food but *spiritual food* for "the body of Christ is the body of the divine Spirit." He quotes Lam. 4:20 to support this.[16]

Second, 4:20 was linked to Christ's *death*. Augustine took the verse to briefly show "that Christ is our Lord and that he suffered for us."[17] It was employed by Rufinus as part of an apologetic argument used in dialogue with Jews to show that the Christ was to suffer: "You hear how the prophet says that Christ the Lord was taken, and for us, that is, for our sins, delivered to corruption. Under whose shadow, since the people of the Jews have continued in unbelief, he says the gentiles lie, because we live not in Israel, but among the gentiles."[18] The linking of Lam. 4:20 with the death of Jesus and a polemic against Judaism can also be seen in Cyril's *Catechetical Lectures*. There he contrasts the (spiritual) Jerusalem

from the head of the people. But, objects Aphrahat, "Christ has not fallen, because he rose again the third day" (*Select Demonstrations* 9, *NPNF²* 13, 355).

Perhaps the strangest christological appropriation of Lam. 4:20 is that of Justin Martyr (100–165). Seeing signs of the cross hidden throughout creation by God, Justin draws attention to the human form. He sees the nose extending from the forehead as having the form of a cross. Through this sign of the cross life-breath is drawn as the prophet said, "The breath before our face is the Lord Christ" (*The First Apology of Justin* 55, *ANCL* 11, 55). Understandably Justin's reading of the text did not initiate a fruitful tradition of reception.

14. *Against Marcion*, Book III, *ANCL* 7, 129.

15. *Catechetical Lectures* 34, *NPNC²* 7, 132. The same argument is in Ambrose (*Of the Holy Spirit*, Bk I.105, *NPNF²* 10, 107) and Gregory of Nyssa (ca. 335–ca. 395) (*Against Eunomius*, Bk 11.14, *NPNF²* 5, 128). Interestingly Basil (ca. 329–379) sees Lam. 4:20 as a reference to the *Spirit* as "the anointed of the Lord" rather than to Jesus (*On the Spirit* 19.48, *NPNF²* 8, 30).

16. *On the Mysteries* 58, *NPNF²* 10, 325.

17. *The City of God* 33, *NPNF¹* 2, 379.

18. *A Commentary on the Apostles Creed* 19, *NPNF²* 3, 551.

that now is (Gal. 4:25) with the (earthly) Jerusalem that was. The Jerusalem-that-*is* worships Christ but the Jerusalem-that-*was* crucified him. Thus, Jeremiah lamented the destruction of earthly Jerusalem. "Christ the Lord was taken in their corruptions." As a result, citing 4:20b, "the grace of life is no longer to dwell in Israel, but among the gentiles."[19]

Lamentations 4:20 unsurprisingly continued to be associated with Jesus' death through the Middle Ages, as we can see, for instance, in Aquinas' (1225–74 CE) commentary on the verse: "Or it [i.e., 4:20] can even be referred to Christ. As the prophet Isaiah foretold: 'But he was wounded for our transgressions, he was bruised for our iniquities' (Isa. 53:5)."[20]

What should we make of such appropriations of the text? The anti-Judaic overtones are unhelpful and theologically misplaced. More positive Christian attitudes towards Jews who do not believe in Jesus are found in Rom. 11. But what of the christological interpretation? Interestingly, even a contemporary critical scholar like Gerstenberger (2001: 499) sees the Messiah in this verse as a *future* deliverer. While I think that Gerstenberger is mistaken in this, the connection with Jesus is not unjustified. Indeed, a christological re-reading of the passage opens up interesting new ways of construing it. The capture of the king in 4:20 is the climax of the woes in the chapter: he who embodied the whole nation representatively has fallen to the foe. Immediately after this we have the unexpected oracle of salvation (4:21-22) with no hint in the text as to how one could move from the lowest pit to the highest point of hope in the book. What precipitates that shift? The reader is left to fill in the gap.

On a christological interpretation, the move from v. 20 to v. 21 makes perfect sense. The loss of the king of Israel to the pagan foe in 4:20 is simultaneously the climax of the exilic woes *and the means by which those woes come to an end*. That is not what the poet had in mind, but a Christian reader looking back with the advantage of hindsight can make such connections. This introduces an interesting new theological perspective into Lam. 4 not contained within the text, but one that can frame the Christian reading of the text. The violence of the enemy is engraved on the subjugated and broken body of the Messiah, and yet in the act of being overcome by evil the evil is itself overcome by nonviolence. A subversive, cruciform element is introduced in the reception of the text.

---

19. *Catechetical Lectures* 7, *NPNC*² 7, 84.
20. Aquinas, *Commentary on Lamentations*; trans. F. F. Reilly.

Tenebrae: A Medieval Christological Use of Lamentations

The most interesting medieval contribution to christological interpretation of Lamentations comes not in a commentary or a sermon, but in a piece of liturgy.[21] This was Tenebrae, originally the Divine Office of Matins on Maundy Thursday, Good Friday, and Holy Saturday in the Western church. During Tenebrae, which functioned as a kind of funeral service commemorating the death of Jesus, the church was in darkness,[22] lit only by candles. There were readings from Scripture, and as each text was finished one of the candles would be extinguished until only a single candle was left alight. The number of candles and the number and order of the readings varied from region to region until the Council of Trent (1545–63 CE) standardized it. However, what is striking is the prominent place that Lamentations always played at Tenebrae. Indeed, it became customary from at least the twelfth century to set the Lamentations readings to music, and there were many very striking arrangements, especially from the Renaissance period. Readings from across the book were employed (1:1-5, 6-9, 10-14; 2:8-11, 12-15; 3:1-9, 22-30; 4:1-6; 5:1-11) and juxtaposed with readings from various psalms (focused on the suffering of the righteous individual [Pss. 69, 70, 71, 73?, 26], the suffering of Zion [Pss. 74, 76, 53, 87?, 14, 53, 87], God's saving the suffering one [Pss. 71, 73, 75, 37, 4, 23], and God's being in control [Pss. 68, 93, 29]), passages from Hebrews and 1 Corinthians, and readings from Augustine. The Lamentations texts are resituated in the context of these psalmic themes, which do point to a "resurrection" hope beyond the despair manifest in the book of Lamentations itself, but most importantly are located in a liturgical context that is very overtly all about the sufferings and death of Jesus.

No interpretative comments are offered as to how the Lamentations passages relate to Jesus. Nevertheless, the association was not random. It seems to me that the use of psalms about a suffering and vindicated Davidic king opens up the hermeneutic. The second psalm used is Ps. 69, in which the righteous Davidic Messiah suffers, cries out to God, and looks forward not simply to his salvation, but to that of Zion and Judah as well—the logic being that the king represents the people, and his story

---

21. For a detailed exploration of the hermeneutics of Tenebrae see Parry 2011b. See also Cameron-Mowat 2011; Joyce and Lipton 2013: 41-3, 47-9.

22. Matins took place before dawn, though the service was brought forward to early evening of the previous day (Wednesday, Thursday, Friday) from perhaps as early as the thirteenth century. Nowadays, when Tenebrae is celebrated, it is usually conflated into a single service.

of suffering and vindication mirrors their own. The story of the suffering Messiah parallels the story of his suffering people. And this, I suggest, is how Lamentations was being framed in the service. The passages were seen to concern the suffering of the people of Zion—which in the Middle Ages would have been understood typologically to refer to the church—but these communal sufferings are the very sufferings that the Davidic King (understood here as Jesus) came to participate in and redeem his people from. The parallel of his affliction and their affliction comes out in the very first Nocturne of the first service. There Ps. 69 is read, in which the Messiah prays, "I looked for pity, but there was none, and for comforters, but I found none" (v. 20). Then, in the very same Nocturne, we have Lamentations readings in which Zion, like David, has none to comfort her in her suffering (1:2, 9). In this way the sufferings of David are brought alongside Zion, and the sufferings of Jesus alongside the church. The Messiah shares in the sufferings of his people. The difference, also brought out in the first Nocturn, is that unlike David/Jesus, Zion/the church is not a righteous sufferer (Lam. 1:5, 8, 14). This difference provides scope for the Tenebrae service to invite the congregation to reflect on their own sins and repent. Thus, each Lamentations reading is followed by an exhortation from Hos. 14:1, *Jerusalem convertere ad Dominum Deum tuum* ("Jerusalem, return to the Lord your God"). In sum, through Lamentations, the congregation is invited to see itself as the beloved yet sinful and afflicted people of God, awaiting their salvation as they look to their Messiah, who shared in their afflictions, and who also looked ahead to his coming vindication. This is a fascinating, well-balanced blend of christological and ecclesiological readings of Lamentations.

Proposals for New Christological Interpretations

Christological readings are not unidirectional, but open up an ongoing dialogue between the OT and the NT texts. As such, Lamentations is seen in light of Christ and Christ is seen in light of Lamentations. The reflective back-and-forth dialogue can generate ever-fresh insights into both.

The Valiant Man and Jesus

The links between the man in ch. 3 and Jesus are more than superficial. At a structural level their stories parallel each other:

> First, the connection between his suffering and Jerusalem's suffering is much like the link between Jesus' death and [that of] the holy city. The man embodies the divine judgment on Jerusalem in his own story. Jesus'

crucifixion at the hands of the Romans embodies the eschatological judgment of Jerusalem.

The man is metaphorically thrown into the pit of death and God delivers him from that pit. The connection with Jesus' *literal* death and resurrection is clear....

The current status of the man vis-à-vis his enemies is not unlike that of Jesus. On the one hand, he has been redeemed from the pit. On the other hand, his opponents are still out there and their full defeat is yet to come. This is close to the New Testament understanding of Christ as raised by God from the dead and reigning, but currently not all his enemies are under his feet. The final defeat of death and sin lies in the future (1 Cor. 15:24-28).

The redemption of the man from his pit is presented as a sign of hope that God will do the same for the population at large. His past redemption is a sign of their coming redemption. So too Christ's resurrection from the dead is presented as the firstfruits of a general resurrection of those who belong to him, a sign of the future of the people of God (1 Cor. 15:12-22). What God did for the man he will do for Israel; what God did for Christ he will do for the church. (Parry 2010: 185–6)[23]

We can summarize these parallels as follows:

Valiant Man	Christ
Embodies the suffering of Jerusalem	Embodies the suffering of Jerusalem (and humanity)
In the pit (metaphorical death)	In the grave (real death)
Redeemed from the pit	Raised from the dead
His redemption is a sign of hope for the Israel	His redemption is a sign of hope for Israel (and the world)
His enemies still plot against him	His enemies still fight against him
Final defeat of his enemies is future	Final defeat of his enemies is future

Figure 18.1 The Valiant Man and Jesus.

So Rufinas' identification of the man in the pit with Christ in the tomb is not ad hoc, but has a certain theo-logic underpinning it. We can see Lam. 3 afresh in the light of Christ.

---

23. Note that these parallels depend upon the exegesis of the text defended in the commentary. Some of the exegetical moves made are open to alternative construals.

This connection also allows us to reverse the hermeneutical flow. In other words, not only can we see Lam. 3 through Christ, but we can see Jesus in a new perspective through the lens of Lam. 3. For instance, we might ask what our understanding of Jesus' cry of dereliction—"My God! My God! Why have you forsaken me?"—would look like if filtered through the fierce protest of the valiant man in 3:1-18. This is the protest of a man who feels not only abandoned by God ("even though I cry out and plead, He shut out my prayer"), but actively targeted and attacked by God. The relentless barrage of dark and painful poetic images, wave after wave of them, drives home just how desperately God-forsaken the man feels. Might this be a fruitful theological resource for reflection on the cross? And might his subsequent turn towards hope in God's loving kindness (3:21-24) help Christians in their theological reflections on Jesus' prayer, "Father, into your hands I commit my spirit"? Let me stress that I am not suggesting that we use Lam. 3 to make historical claims about what Jesus actually prayed or what Mark had in mind when he wrote his Gospel. Most likely neither Jesus nor Mark had our poem in mind. Rather, my suggestion is that the play of texts can potentially generate theological and existential insight into the meaning of Jesus' sufferings and death.

The Narrator and Jesus

Jewish and Christian traditions saw Jeremiah as the author of Lamentations,[24] and while virtually no modern critical scholars take this approach, there is a case for saying that the narrator is deliberately presented as a Jeremiah-like figure.[25] Now in the Christian tradition Jeremiah was often seen as a type of Christ,[26] and one could argue that this suggests the possibility of seeing the narrator as a Christ-like figure in some respects.

One might think in particular of his Jeremiah-like empathetic sorrows over the sufferings of Zion in 2:11, 13:[27]

---

24. A tradition found in LXX, Syriac, Targum, and the Vulgate and almost unanimously affirmed in church and synagogue until the eighteenth century.
25. See Lee 2002.
26. Numerous parallels between Jeremiah and Jesus were drawn (e.g., both were prophets who wept over Jerusalem and became considered enemies of the state for their messages of doom against the temple; both were consequently opposed and persecuted by their own people).
27. Nancy Lee identifies the language in Lam. 2:11ff. as containing numerous links to passages in the book of Jeremiah, deliberately intended to identify the narrator as Jeremiah (2002: 147–8).

> My eyes were worn out from tears,
>   My stomach churned,
> My liver bile was poured out on the ground,
>   because of the destruction of the daughter of my people;
> When a child and a suckling baby grow weak
>   in the town squares....
>
> What can I testify to you? What can I liken to you
>   Daughter Jerusalem?
> What can I compare to you so that I can comfort you
>   Maiden Daughter Zion?
> For as vast as the sea is your destruction.
>   Who can heal you?

Consider this alongside Jesus' lament over Jerusalem's coming destruction.

> As he approached Jerusalem and saw the city, he wept over it and said, "If you, even you, had only known on this day what would bring you peace—but now it is hidden from your eyes. The days will come upon you when your enemies will build an embankment against you and encircle you and hem you in on every side. They will dash you to the ground, you and the children within your walls. They will not leave one stone on another, because you did not recognize the time of God's coming to you." (Lk. 19:41-44)

Here Jesus, like the narrator of Lamentations, weeps over the terrible fate of the city of Jerusalem at the hands of an invading pagan army (cf. Lk. 23:27-31). Notice that both Jesus and the Jeremiah-like narrator address Jerusalem as a traumatized mother whose children suffer. Also, both the narrator (Lam. 2:14) and Jesus (Lk. 19:41) see the city as having stumbled blindly into this fate, unaware of the consequences their sins would have.

Might we be able to "fill out" and enrich our theological understanding of Jesus' lament over Jerusalem through reflection on the narrator's lament? Luke has a bare "he wept over [the city]," while Lamentations is far more visceral and may authorize us to imagine Jesus' own lament as similarly gut wrenching. (Not in the service of history, but of spirituality.)

And to reverse the flow, may we not see Jesus weeping over Jerusalem in Lamentations? Indeed, in orthodox Christian theological terms, the subject of the suffering of Jesus is the divine *Logos* suffering in his humanity: *unus ex Trinitate carne passus est* ("one of the Trinity suffered in the flesh"). So may we not also hear the echo of the weeping of the *Logos*, the weeping of God, in the narrator of Lamentations? This approach moves God from the position of being silent and distant into that of traumatized observer.

Jerusalem and Jesus

The association of Jesus, in his Messianic representative capacity, and the sufferings of Zion on display in the Tenebrae liturgy is very suggestive and taps into deep subterranean theological streams in Scripture. In my commentary I develop the notion of Christ's death and resurrection as a microcosm of Israel's exile and restoration, and thus of Lamentations as Israel's Holy Saturday lament—caught between exile and hoped-for-restoration, between death and resurrection. This approach sees Matthew's allusion to the humiliation of Zion (Lam. 2:15) in his depiction of Jesus' crucifixion as more than a superficial allusion; instead, it is the tip of a hermeneutical iceberg.

Here we may note various parallels between Jesus and Lady Zion (the personification of Jerusalem in Lam. 1 and 2):

> Like Jerusalem, tears were upon his cheeks as he prayed alone in the garden. Like Jerusalem, he knew betrayal by his "friends" who left him to suffer alone. Like Jerusalem Jesus was beaten, stripped naked, publicly humiliated, and afflicted. Like Jerusalem, he was reduced from a high and noble status to dust. Like Jerusalem, he bore the divine curse for covenant disobedience. Like Jerusalem, he was violently attacked by a pagan occupying force. Like Jerusalem, he felt abandoned by YHWH in the face of these pagan military oppressors. Like Jerusalem, he was mocked and despised by those who looked on at his destruction. (Parry 2010: 182)

In Christian theological terms, God-in-Christ is not simply seen in the traumatized narrator as he looks on, but *right inside the sufferings of Jerusalem herself*: God experiencing our God-forsakenness. Lamentations, in which God's presence and voice seem so distant, can look very different when read in this way.

And what if we turn this around and see Jesus in light of the sufferings of Lady Zion? For instance, the focus in Lam. 1 on the public shaming of Zion could alert us to the important role of social shaming in the crucifixion, or the metaphor of Zion's rape in Lam. 1:10 may open us up to seeing the passion of the Christ in terms of that potent metaphor (being crucified naked was a form of sexual violence), or even considering the possibility that Jesus was himself raped prior to his crucifixion.[28] This

---

28. A historical possibility defended by Tombs 2016.

avenue might bring out all sorts of new and disturbing readings of the Gospels.

Christological readings of Lamentations could explore down further rabbit holes,[29] but I hope that enough has been said to indicate the imaginative possibilities opened up by reading Lamentations intertextually with NT texts concerning Jesus.

---

29. E.g., if Lamentations speaks from within Israel's equivalent of Holy Saturday then might Lamentations have something to contribute to Christian reflection on the doctrine of Christ's descent into hades? Or if Christ and his body, the *ekklēsia*, are the temple of God (Jn 2:19-21; 1 Cor. 3:16-17; 2 Cor. 6:16; Eph. 2:21) then might the destruction of the temple motif in Lamentations be connected with the death of Christ and the death of Christ connected with the loss of the temple, with all the cosmic symbolism involved?

Chapter 19

The Rabbis Talk Back Through the Prophets: Intertextuality, Lamentations, and Divine Mourning

Heath A. Thomas

Introduction

Jewish literature readily displays the phenomenon of intertextuality, especially in midrashim over biblical books. Midrashim are explanatory works of biblical texts comprised by the Sages in the first six hundred years of the Christian era. Because they comment upon or paraphrase books from the HB, midrashim therefore are "openly and radically intertextual" (Boyarin 1987).[1] Susan Handelman goes so far to say the midrashim, like the rest of Jewish literature, comprise "a world of 'intertextuality'" (1982: 78).[2]

The phenomenon of intertextuality conserves and destabilizes tradition simultaneously. On the one hand, links between earlier and later texts renew literary tradition for each new generation, thereby regenerating and perpetuating tradition.[3] On the other hand, each new use of earlier texts disrupts previous convention, destabilizing tradition while providing new ways of conceiving of it. This intertextual double movement is an essential characteristic of the midrashim, even "its *raison d'être*," as Boyarin avers (1987: 541, italics his). *Lamentations Rabbah* (hereafter *Lam. Rab.*) provides a window to witness the double-movement of intertextuality in its reading of the biblical book of Lamentations (hereafter Lam.).

1. See his more extensive work: Boyarin 1990.
2. For discussion and dispute of Handelman's portrayal, see Neusner 1987.
3. "A quoting Jew places contemporary experiences into the framework of a particular tradition, and in so doing perpetuates and expands that tradition" (Marmur 2014: 13–14).

This essay assesses how intertextuality in *Lam. Rab.* disrupts previous tradition (namely the silence and distance of God and the sinfulness of the Daughter of Zion in Lamentations) while simultaneously preserving and advancing Jewish tradition (affording a new way of envisioning the relationship between God and God's people through divine pathos in mourning). In so doing, I expand Alan Mintz's (1996: 57–62) description of divine empathy in *Lam. Rab.* by assessing an underexplored aspect of divine pathos in the work: God as a bereaved mourner. Instead of undermining Jewish tradition, intertextuality in *Lam. Rab.* enables a new relational horizon between God and God's people while representing that relationship in fresh ways via divine mourning.

Specifically, I explore the intertextuality at work in *Lam. Rab.* I. I, § I, which is a rabbinic reflection on Lam. 1:1. The midrash innovates in its presentation of the pathos of God and emphasizes his proximity to his people through the unusual presentation of God as a bereaved mourner. *Lam. Rab.* I. I, § I depicts a God who is present for his people in mourning, even in the face of defilement, suffering, and sin, and God's presence in the mourning rite with them is justified by the prophetic word.

Lamentations Rabbah I. I, § I

R. Nahman reported that Samuel said in the name of R. Joshua b. Levi: The Holy One, blessed be He, summoned the ministering angels and said to them: "If a human king had a son who died and mourns for him, what is it customary for him to do?" They replied, "He hangs sackcloth over his door." He said to them, "I will do likewise." That is what is written, *I clothe the heavens with blackness, and I make sackcloth their covering* (Isa. L, 3). "What does a human king do [when mourning]?" They replied, "He extinguishes the lamps." He said to them, "I will do likewise"; as it is said, *The sun and the moon are become black, and the stars withdraw their shining* (Joel IV, 15). "What does a human king do?" They replied, "He overturns his couch." He said to them, "I will do likewise"; as it is stated, *Till thrones were cast down, and One that was ancient of days did sit* (Dan. VII, 9)—if it is possible to say so, they were overturned. "What does a human king do?" They replied, "He walks barefoot." He said to them, "I will do likewise"; as it is stated, *The Lord, in the whirlwind and in the storm is His way, and the clouds are the dust of His feet* (Nahum I, 3). "What does a human king do?" They replied, "He rends his purple robes." He said to them, "I will do likewise"; as it is written, *The Lord hath done that which He devised* (bizza' emrato), *He hath performed his word* (Lam. II, 17). (R. Jacob of Kefar-Hanan explained: what means "*bizza' emrato*"? He rent His purple). "What does a human king do?" They replied, "He sits in silence." He said to them, "I will do likewise"; as it is stated, *He sitteth alone and keepeth silence* (*ib.* III, 28). "What does a human king do when mourning?" They replied, "He sits and weeps." He said to them, "I will do likewise"; as it is written, *And in that day did the Lord, the God of hosts, call to weeping, and to lamentation, and to baldness* (Isa. XXII, 12). ["What does a mortal king do?" "He sits solitary." "So I will do likewise." Hence it is written, *How sitteth solitary* (Lam. I, 1)].[4]

This section fits within the larger framework of *Lam. Rab.*, which is comprised of two major recensions. Recension A likely circulated in North Africa and Spain (some version of it circulated in Yemen); Recension B disseminated in Italy, Provence, northern France, and Germany. Recension B is the earlier version and emerged in Babylonia after the Arab conquest prior to its circulation around Europe. Recension A arose in Byzantium, later than Recension B and in different circumstances.[5] Similarities between Recensions A and B, however, indicate an Ur-text of *Lam. Rab.*, which emerged in Palestine by the fifth century CE prior to the growth of the two recensions and their dissemination.[6]

This Ur-text likely contained the two-part midrash (indicated in both recensions) one finds today, comprised of: (1) the thirty-six introductory proems (*petihot*) and (2) a running verse-by-verse commentary (*parashiyyot*) (Alexander 2007: 52–3). The proems introduce the theological messages of Lam., and the *parashiyyot* are selective commentaries on portions of the biblical text. Alexander believes the proems were likely read in an oral context of the Beit Knesset (synagogue) in Palestine and the running commentary likely in the Beit Midrash. Even if they emerged in different life-settings, as Alexander (2010: 183–204, esp. 191–2) surmises, these two portions were combined in Palestine (perhaps in Galilee) into what is now *Lam. Rab.* and then this was transmitted to Babylon and beyond.

Key to understanding the overall logic of *Lam. Rab.* is its presentation of Israel's covenantal relationship with God, who judged his people because of their sin. Neusner summarizes the "single message" of *Lam. Rab.*: "Israel suffers because of sin, God will respond to Israel's

---

4. For ease of reading, English translations of *Lam. Rab.* are from Cohen 1983: 67–8. The last line in this reading (in brackets in the pericope above) represents the better, alternative conclusion to this section, although not present in all extant texts of the midrash. This last line is preferred by Cohen 1983: 68 n. 2, and Neusner 1989a: 110.

5. Mandel 2000: 74–106. See also his more extended analysis in Mandel 1997.

6. See Mandel 2000: 74–106; Strack and Stemberger 1996: 286.

atonement, on the one side, and loyalty to the covenant in the Torah, on the other" (Neusner 1994: 511). Alan Mintz rightly critiques Neusner's view; in short, the midrash is more complex than Neusner would have it, and Cohen's earlier analysis (1982) bears out Mintz's critique.

Although *Lam. Rab.* vindicates God for punishing Israel because of their sin, Mintz (1996: 49–83) draws out two other threads present in the work beyond sin and punishment: the empathy of God and the suffering of the victims of destruction, both of which provide a way forward with God. The pathos of God in *Lam. Rab.* especially demands more reflection because of the myriad of ways God is anthropomorphized in the work.

As indicated above, I expand upon Mintz's description of divine empathy in *Lam. Rab.* by investigating God as a bereaved mourner in the work. Two types of divine mourning emerge in the midrash: mourning over the punishment of his people and mourning over bereavement. Both are important; but here more emphasis will be laid on the latter. Mintz and others have investigated the former presentation of divine mourning in *Lam. Rab.* Proem 24.[7] There, God mourns over his people's sin. However, none that I have encountered execute an in-depth analysis of God as a bereaved mourner in the *parashiyyot*, especially *Lam. Rab.* I. I, § I, which in its own way touches on the concept of divine mourning as well.

Lam. Rab. I. I, § I is almost identical to *Lam. Rab.* III, 28-30 § 9, and they build upon the same rabbinic story. The differences between the two are:

1. The passages from Lam. they elucidate (Lam. 1:1 and Lam. 3:28, respectively).
2. *Lam. Rab.* III, 28-30 § 9 is shorter in length than *Lam. Rab.* I. I, § I.
3. The object of the comparison in the two texts is God and the Daughter of Zion (Lam. 1:1 // *Lam. Rab.* I. I, § I) and God and the *geber*/ "the strongman" (Lam. 3:28 // *Lam. Rab.* III, 28-30 § 9).

Despite these differences, both texts present God as a human king, justifying his mourning through prophetic proof-texts. Both texts are "Scripture-stories," simple narratives that proceed through dialogue between speakers, with Jewish Scripture giving rationale for the main points of speakers or action (Neusner 2003: 22). Neusner (2003: 22)

---

7. For specific explorations of *Lam. Rab.* (esp. Proem 24), see Cohen 1982; Mintz 1996: 57–62; Stern 1992: esp. 160–1; Kraemer 1995: 140–6; Linafelt 1998: 106; Kühn 1978: 160–2; Last Stone 1996; Mandolfo 2007: 102. Jacob Neusner (2003: 22) only mentions *Lam. Rab.* I. I, § I. Mintz (1996: 60) mentions *Lam. Rab.* I. I, § I, but then focuses upon Proem 24.

recognizes *Lam. Rab.* I. I, § I in his study, but prefers to exclude it from his documentary exploration of the midrash. Mintz (1996: 60) does not treat it in full, glancing over *Lam. Rab.* I. I, § I and focusing upon *Lam. Rab.* Proem 24.

However, this essay draws attention to *Lam. Rab.* I. I, § I and its presentation of divine mourning and how that emphasis opens a fresh perspective on Israel and their God. Figuring God as a bereaved mourner remains significant theologically and ritually. The intertextual web created between Lam., *Lam. Rab.*, and the prophets provides the rabbis with a resource to humanize God and to transform God's position toward his people from distant judge to present mourner, suffering with the people from the inside, as it were.

Lam. Rab. I. I, § I sits within a larger complex of engagements with the phrase, "how solitary sits," which derives from Lam. 1:1, which reads: "How lonely sits the city once full of people / She has become like a widow. Great among the nations / Princess among the provinces, she has become a slave laborer."[8] In its originating context, Lamentations personifies the city as a woman in mourning, naming her "Daughter of Zion" (*bat-siyyon*) in Lam. 1:6.[9] The "Daughter of Zion" is bereaved of her husband ("like a widow") and her children ("once full of people"), and her honor is gone ("Great among the nations, princess among the provinces, she has become a slave laborer"). She sits alone, mourning her dead and her situation. The reversal motif, so common in Lamentations, enables the reader to see Zion's reversal from glory to shame, life to death, honor to dishonor.[10]

---

8. All translation is the author's unless otherwise noted. The rabbis provide five different meanings of the phrase, "how lonely sits the city" from Lam. 1:1 other than the section isolated above. In their exploration, the phrase "how lonely sits the city" testifies to God's pain over Israel's sin, reveals the prophet Jeremiah's sorrow over the city's disgrace, indicates Israel's sin (from a numerological understanding of the letters in the word *'ekah*), reveals Israel's exile-garments (linking the Hebrew word *bedad* to the Aramaic word *bedadin*), and exposes an open reproof for sin. See Cohen 1983: 66–9.

9. Scholars debate the meaning of *bat-siyyon*. The title may be linked to a city goddess ("daughter") associated with a geographical place ("Zion"), a genitive of relation translated as a term of endearment ("Dear Zion" or "Daughter Zion"), or as a traditional construct chain that associates a metaphorical term for a collective people ("daughter") with the place that those people live ("of Zion"). For discussion see Thomas 2013: 106–8. Here, we translate *bat-siyyon* as "Daughter of Zion" and use "Zion" interchangeably.

10. Thomas 2013: 97–100.

Zion's reversal not only draws attention to her suffering, it also intensifies God's silence in the book of Lamentations, as Melton recently demonstrates.[11] God causes her suffering but remains aloof to Zion's pleas. In Lamentations, a variety of images of God appear, providing fecundity and complexity to divine presentation therein. Despite the variety of images, Zion persistently cries out to God for help and response. But her persistent prayer is met with shuddering silence.[12]

Divine Mourning

By contrast, in *Lam. Rab.* I. I, § I, the rabbis enable God to talk back to the Daughter of Zion. Though silent in Lam., here God speaks about his experience of mourning. The basic logic of the passage is clear:

God // Human King
Israel and Zion // Son
God Mourns // Human King Mourns

That the Sages humanize God, as they do here, fits with a common feature in the amoraic (200–600 CE) and post-amoraic periods (post-600 CE). In this period, the Sages tended to humanize the divine anthropomorphically and anthropopathically. And although the HB presents similar features, amoraic and post-amoriac "rabbinic literature expands the anthropomorphic and anthropopathic field by having God assume humanlike roles and features never before entertained by biblical authors" (Weiss 2017: 149–60). For the rabbis, "Only the human image, in all its fallibility and mortality, could provide the rabbis with a model sufficiently complex to serve as the basis for their own attempts to imagine God's personality, so as to convey their own feelings about Him and His treatment of Israel" (Stern and Mirsky 1990: 48).

But *Lam. Rab.* I. I, § I stands out in the way the Sages depict God as a bereaved mourner in a double correlation: Human King // God // Zion. Their imagination correlates God and Israel, who in Lam. is represented by the personified Daughter of Zion. In the rabbis' reckoning, God sits as a human king in mourning over his "son" who has died. God becomes the one who sits lonely, whereas in Lam. the base-text refers to the Daughter of Zion (God's city and people). The correlation between God and Zion happens through the vehicle of the human king in mourning.

---

11. Melton 2018: 58–135, 164–78.
12. See Thomas 2013: 242–8. For Zion's prayers in Lamentations, see Thomas 2008: 137–47.

Through this double correlation, God becomes present to his people in *Lam. Rab.* Rather than a distant God, aloof from the mourning of the people in Lam., the rabbinic vision opens a new horizon from which the community can view their relationship to the divine. Note the figure, below:

Human King in *Lam. Rab*	God in *Lam. Rab.*	Personified Zion in Lam.
(a) Hanging sackcloth	(a) Hanging sackcloth	(a) Elders in Sackcloth (2:10)
(b) Extinguishing lamps	(b) Extinguishing lamps	(b) —
(c) Turning over the couch	(c) Turning over the couch	(c) Sits on the ground (1:1-2)
(d) Walking barefoot	(d) Walking barefoot	(d) —
(e) Rending purple robe	(e) Rending purple robe	(e) Nakedness (1:7)
(f) Silence	(f) Silence	(f) Silence of Elders (2:10)
(g) Weeping	(g) Weeping	(g) Weeping (1:2)
(h) Sitting alone	(h) Sitting alone	(h) Sitting alone (1:1)

Figure 19.1 Correlating God and Zion.

Intertextuality between mourning practices in Lam. and *Lam. Rab.* connects Zion's and God's shared experience in mourning, as the figure above implies. In so doing, the rabbis draw God close to Zion's experience of loss and death. As she is bereaved of her children and husband, God now is bereaved of his son, Israel. God answers Zion's cries for help and comfort in Lam. by positioning him as a mourner in the midrash. Neusner (1989a: 111) states, "The systematic application to God of various human rites of mourning is accomplished by appeal to appropriate prooftexts; the effect is to have God the subject of the sense, 'how lonely sits…'."

This move recasts the deity between the base-text and the rabbinic commentary. Whereas in Lam. he is aloof, unresponsive to Zion's pleas, in *Lam. Rab.* God literally *sits in her place*. God sits alone in *Lam. Rab.* as does Zion in Lam. In this spatial relocation, the Sages bring God from the heavens to earth in Jerusalem, where Zion sits in her suffering as described in Lam. Whereas God is silent in Lam., God now speaks to Zion's cries in *Lam. Rab.* By presenting God as a bereaved mourner, the Sages provide God's people with a different valence by which they can engage and understand their relationship with their God: he is immanent in suffering and responsive to it. The experience of God, then, is one of comfort rather than punishment.

Intertextual links within Lam. reinforce the transformation of divine punishment to divine comfort through mourning. The rabbis explain Lam. 1:1 with Lam. 2:17 (*The Lord hath done that which He devised, He hath performed his word*) and Lam. 3:28 (*He sitteth alone and keepeth silence*). The first statement transforms God's action of punishment in Lam. to an act of mourning in *Lam. Rab.* Lamentations 2:17 indicates God's action or his *'emrah* ("word") in punishment against his people, but the rabbis re-read the verse not as an action of punishment but as an indicator of divine mourning. Lamentations 3:28 is a command for penitent silence for the "man" who sits under the wrath of God. The "man" in its originating context is God's people. But in *Lam. Rab.* I. I, § I, the Sages refashion Lam. 3:28 from an affirmation of penitent silence in the face of divine punishment to a rationale for divine silence in mourning. Both texts share the concept of isolation ("sitting alone"), which God, the man, and Zion enact as they experience bereavement.

Divine mourning over death stands out in *Lam. Rab.* I. I, § I because of its ritual significance. Several types of mourning emerge in the biblical and rabbinic literature: mourning over death, mourning over calamity, and mourning over sin, among others (Olyan 2004). In the HB and in rabbinic Judaism, despite the range of time and diversity of literature, mourning over the dead presents a stable ritual dynamic.[13] Mourners over death remove themselves from normal life and associate themselves with death through ritual actions: rending one's garments, upending one's house and couch, sitting on the ground, weeping on the ground, going barefoot, or throwing dust and ash on oneself, sitting outside the camp, etc. These actions are not expressive of emotion, at least not most significantly. Rather, they are indicative of ritual dynamics and a symbolic world. Ritual actions symbolically associate mourners with the realm of the dead and death—outside the normal order of life.[14] Those enacting mourning rituals are understood as "diminished," "desacralized," and "depersonalized" persons, existing at the threshold between the world of the dead and the world of the living.[15]

Mourning over death impacts how the bereaved relate ritually to the divine. Because these mourners associate with death through ritual action, they are separated from normal relationship with God, especially through worship practices. Emanuel Feldman describes why:

---

13. For ancient Near Eastern mourning and mourning practices presented in the HB, see Anderson 1991: 59–97. For rabbinic Judaism, see Kraemer 2000. For rabbinic practices, see also Feldman 1977: 91–107.

14. This may be one of the reasons why mourners sit on the ground, tear clothes, and throw dust or ashes on their bodies. See, for instance, Anderson 1991: 97.

15. Feldman 1997: 91–9.

> The livingness of God is His fundamental and primary characteristic. Death, as the opposite of life, is the ultimate opposite of God. God is the Lord of life, and while He rules death *and* life, He consciously withdraws from death and separates Himself from it. Death thus represents the absence of a potential relationship with God. (Feldman 1997: 29)

Mourning over death creates a ritual gulf in the relationship between God and the worshipper. Only when a mourner traverses ritually from the realm of death to symbolic new life does the mourner ritually span the divide. The traverse into joy culminates in effective comfort as well as rituals of rejoicing and celebration (such as feasting and drinking and worship) (Olyan 2004: 13–19; Anderson 1991: 49–50). After enacting these festal rituals, one then can enter the normal order of life once again.

Divine mourning over death in *Lam. Rab.* I. I, § I mirrors Zion's mourning in Lam. 1:1.[16] In *Lam. Rab.* I. I, § I, the focus lay on divine mourning over bereavement as in the base text, which is ritually significant. When the rabbis present God as the bereaved mourner, they place God at the threshold of defilement: God implicates himself with death, which stands as the ultimate opposition to God, as Feldman avers. In their imagination, the Sages perceive that God's relationship with his people is no longer threatened by death and the defilement that ensues from bereavement. Rather, God sits *among* the ritually defiled. Zion's solitary experience in Lam. now becomes an experience of divine solidarity in *Lam. Rab.* Ritually, in the normal order of things, God would be far from the mourner. But because God becomes a mourner in the rabbinic vision, the deity can come close to Zion's ritual defilement.

The radicality of the rabbinic presentation of divine mourning over death becomes clearer when compared against another presentation of divine mourning in the midrash, specifically *Lam. Rab.* Proem 24. There, God is a mourner, who mourns over Israel's sin and calamity.[17] The proem affirms the sins of his people and God mourns over their state.[18] God asks

---

16. Zion clearly mourns over death: Zion has been bereaved ("like a widow," Lam. 1:1) and she embodies the varied actions of mourning. She sits on the ground (Lam. 1:1), alone (Lam. 1:1), groaning (Lam. 1:8, 21), and bereft of comfort (Lam. 1:2, 9, 16, 17, 21). Others in Zion are associated with mourning as well: elders in sackcloth (Lam. 2.10), elders in silence (Lam. 2.10). For the full presentation of Zion as a mourner, see Pham 1999: 48–147. Pham (1999: 61) goes so far as to argue that in Lam. 1–2, personified Jerusalem "sits alone and weeps…. The mourner needs a comforter. But Jerusalem has no one to comfort her."

17. For general explorations of God as a mourner in rabbinic literature, Kühn 1978 remains the most comprehensive resource.

18. See the discussion of Cohen 1982: 26–8.

what more he could have done for his people. But because of sin and their lack of repentance, God indicates he could not prevent their devastation. The result is divine mourning over their calamity (Stern 1992: 160). At this moment, God begins to ruminate upon punishment over the people's sin. God considers his inability to care effectively for the people. The proem reaches its climax when God compares his mourning to that of a king who is newly bereaved of his son: "and the Holy One, blessed be He, lamented saying, 'Woe to the King Who succeeded in His youth but failed in His old age!'"[19] The rabbis present God as walking faithfully with his people in earlier days in their covenant relationship ("the King Who succeeded in His youth"), but in advanced age, God failed them because they disobeyed divine decree and were exiled ("but failed in His old age"). This failure does not diminish Israel's sin but draws attention to God's powerlessness to prevent it.

Proem 24 and *Lam. Rab.* I. I., § I offer different visions of divine action and, thereby, different visions of relationship with the divine. In Proem 24, God observes his people's plight and mourns over their sin and calamity, but does nothing to prevent it. In our pericope, as a divine mourner over death, God *becomes* the bereaved and mourns in the very place of Zion: he sits on the ground in her place. He associates with death and defilement, as it were, from the inside. Through this correlation, the rabbis bring God closer to the defilement of the people than previously envisioned.

By presenting God as a bereaved and defiled mourner, the Sages open a way forward for future relationship with God. God's people could be close to the divine even in their exiled and templeless state. God was not removed from his templeless and sinful people but present with them. God suffers in and amongst, even *as* his defiled people. Although death "represents the absence of a potential relationship with God," intertextuality between Lam. and *Lam. Rab.* facilitates communion between God and his people in which he comes near to them as a mourner rather than as judge (Feldman 1977: 29). This is not the only way God appears in *Lam. Rab.*, but "God as a bereaved mourner" provides one vision of a possible future between God and Israel.

Intertextuality with the Prophets

In the midrash, each act of mourning is accompanied by God's voice ("I will do likewise") and a prophetic proof text ("as it is written", etc.). This intertextual interchange enables the Sages to affirm divine commitment

---

19. *Lam. Rab.* Proem 24 in Cohen 1983: 43.

to mourning over bereavement, softening the defiling nature of God's association with death. On the face of it, the prophetic texts drawn into the intertextual web of *Lam. Rab.* I. I, § I seem ill-suited to the logic of the pericope. After all, in their originating contexts these prophecies do not relate to divine mourning in any way:

Isa. 50:3:	God's cosmic power to judge or redeem Israel
Joel 4:15:	God judges all nations in the "valley of decision"
Dan. 7:9:	The Ancient of Days sits to enact judgment on the nations
Nah. 1:3:	God will by no means clear the guilty, which is God's people
Isa. 22:12:	God calls for mourning for the sin of God's people

These texts often speak of divine potency or divine punishment for sin. And in other places in *Lam. Rab.* the rabbis reinforce the prophetic ideology of sin and punishment in their use of prophetic intertexts, as both Mintz (1996) and Mandolfo (2007: 124) affirm. But in our pericope, prophetic intertexts function differently. Instead of justifying divine punishment because of Israel's sin, the Sages propose divine mourning over death to be sanctioned by God's prophetic word:

Isa. 50:3:	God robes himself in sackcloth
Joel 4:15:	God extinguishes lamps
Dan. 7:9:	God turns over the couch and sits upon the ground
Nah. 1:3:	God walks barefoot and takes off his sandals
Isa. 22:12:	God calls for mourning over his bereaved son

The Sages transform sin and judgment in these prophetic texts to leverage them as evidence for divine mourning over death.[20] On the one hand, such semantic transformation is not unusual in the midrashim. "One of the most characteristic features of midrash is the way in which, as a reading practice, it violates the context of the texts being interpreted and cited" (Boyarin 1987: 542). Violation may be too harsh a description of the hermeneutics at play, because the semantic reconfiguration of prophetic speech does not constitute an abuse of originating context as much as a continuation of the prophetic word for God's people. "In constant interchange with Scripture, [the Sages] found ways of delivering their own message, in their own idiom, and in diverse ways. Verses of Scripture therefore served not merely to prove but to instruct.... Scripture served as

---

20. P. D. Miller 1982 is a classic work that exposes sin and punishment in the prophets according to literary and rhetorical style as well as theological outlook.

a kind of syntax, limiting the arrangement of words but making possible an infinity of statements" (Neusner 1989b: 175). The Sages employ prophetic texts to instruct the people of God that divine mourning was sanctioned by the divine word in *Lam. Rab.* I. I, § I. His proximity with his people enabled a new way of envisioning his relationship with them.

Intertextuality at work between the prophets in *Lam. Rab.* tempers the radicality of God's association with the realm of the dead in mourning. God's presence in the realm of the dead with his people accords with the instruction of God through the prophets from ages past: "as it is written." As it relates to Lam., the rabbis "talk back" to Zion's cries and God's word of judgment in the prophets by using those same prophets to open a horizon of understanding in which God sits with his people in mourning. Traditional prophetic ideology is covenantal: God punishes his covenant people because of their sin. Through intertextuality with the prophets, the rabbis disrupt the prophetic and biblical tradition which envisions God as distant (Lam.) or mourning over Israel's sin (*Lam. Rab.*). In our *parashah*, God's power and proximity is revealed through divine mourning over the death of his beloved son, justified by the divine prophetic word.

Conclusion

Viewed from Boyarin's model of "disruption" and "regeneration" identified at the outset of this essay, the intertexts between Lam., *Lam. Rab.*, and the prophetic material generate a fresh way of envisioning the relationship between God and Israel even while perpetuating that covenantal tradition. Intertextual linkage between Lam. and *Lam. Rab.* enables a fresh perspective on the God presented in Lam. His "word" of Lam. 2:17 is no longer one of (only) judgment in *Lam. Rab.* Rather, it is a word that proclaims the mourning of God, present in suffering and even identifying with the defiled mourner, who sits alone (Lam. 3:28). In this way, tradition is simultaneously disrupted and regenerated for a new day, using Boyarin's language. Further, the rabbis' association of the divine with the realm of death and defilement, as radical as it is, at once draws God close to his people in comfort and finds its rationale in prophetic tradition: the rabbis envision divine mourning over death of God's "son" as fitting to the ancient prophetic word given from ages past. As such, the Sages soften the radical presentation of God in the realm of death by intertextually linking this action to earlier tradition. The rabbis "talk back" to the cries and tears of Lam. by rendering God in the place of his suffering people, the Daughter of Zion. Intertextuality with Jewish texts and tradition resources the conversation, providing the grammar and syntax so that the covenantal relationship between God and his people might be envisioned from a different perspective: God mourns with his people—not from a distance—but in their place, alongside them. God is now spatially and ritually implicated in their suffering.

Chapter 20

READING LAMENTATIONS AFTER THE *SHOAH*: A MANDATE TO QUESTION

Hemchand Gossai

Preface

A few years ago I had the distinct privilege of meeting and visiting with AR,[1] one of the characters depicted in the movie *Schindler's List*. He was invited to deliver a lecture at my college, and he and I had a wide-ranging conversation during the forty-five minute drive from the airport. Among the many indelible moments in that brief journey was his statement, "I no longer believe in God." There was no "why" or "why not" from me. For AR it was a matter of self-determination, self-dependency, and his inability to reconcile the *Shoah* and God's silence and inactivity in that genocide. For AR, the decision was not a theoretical or abstract issue; it was born out of a lived experience, one which for him and many others was a defining moment in wondering about the role and presence of God (see Braitherman 2011).

The Mandate to Question

The biblical portrayal of God makes it clear that God is neither monolithic nor one-dimensional. God is not only the God of love, or of mercy, or of judgment, or of war, or of peace, or of violence, etc. Lamentations exemplifies this multidimensional quality and, in all its painful reflection and questioning, is included in the canon; and as inheritors of the canon, the option *not* to question God, *not* to complain, *not* to be fearful for what is and what might be, must be dispensed with. Some have argued that God must not be questioned: "In principle, God's activity on man's behalf is

---

1. I am using the initials of the person out of respect for his identity.

always good, although in actual cases it sometimes occurs in contradiction to human conceptions and wishes" (Krašovec 1992: 232). This interpretation of the text limits itself entirely by an ideology that seeks to protect God as one who is only a God of mercy, love, and redemption. This position not only justifies God's actions, both in the Exile and the *Shoah*, but also seeks to silence the voice of those who suffer. In Lam. 3:1-33, the writer seemingly suggests that God has abundant mercy and indeed would never willingly inflict pain and violence. Complaints to, and about God, might complicate the particular trajectory that would suit one's theological perspective, but the issue is not to choose one divine quality over against the other. When we first encounter God in Lamentations, the context is not one of a historical relationship or one of comfort and deliverance, but one of God who sets out intentionally to bring about suffering. In Houck-Loomis's words: "The community left in the rubble is forced to reconcile with the destruction of their world, and the dissolution of their worldview. They are left psychologically as well as physically vulnerable" (2012: 705).

While the name YHWH is mentioned thirty times in Lamentations, and thus the name of God is very much present, God is conspicuously absent in any active and meaningful way.[2] What we must also acknowledge is that Lamentations itself disavows any association with easy and self-justifying answers to theodicy questions. Instead, the text compels readers who explore the narrative of the Exile and God's role in the suffering to do so without the compulsion to justify or rush to conclusions. Such embedded meaning is foundational for the manner in which we reflect on the role of God and the *Shoah*. Walter Brueggemann (1995: 107), reflecting on the marginalization of lament in faith traditions, suggests:

> ...if justice questions are improper questions at the throne...they soon appear to be improper questions in public places, in schools, in hospitals, with the government, and eventually even in the courts. Justice questions disappear into civility and docility.[3]

He makes the case for the essential role of lament in all aspects of life, arguing that courage to lament is a justice issue. For many, irrespective of context, frequently lamenting by necessity may have to be in the public

---

2. See also Melton 2018.
3. What we have in Lam. 5:20-22 departs from the manner in which the conventional lament ends. Instead of a hopeful note of return and restoration, the text ends on a note of devastating uncertainty and fear born out of a sense of abandonment and rejection, perhaps even of public humiliation, as Williamson (2008: 72) suggests.

eye, and so the more acceptable "civil" behavior that veils legitimate pain, abandonment, grief, despair, and broken-heartedness, is instead on display. The psychological effect is immeasurable.

"Trauma can lead to transformation, but it could also lead to absolute disintegration if we are left to our own persecutory fears and anxiety" (Seidler 2011: 706). The reality is that the trauma that one experiences is not likely to leave one untouched, and the idea that in time there will be deliverance, or reappearance, or a presence will not absolve God of the present reality. As Brian McCarthy has noted, the existential persistence of these experiences has to be reckoned with by scholars.

> After the Holocaust only scholars who are blinded by theological prejudice, or who have become pure technicians who put aside their conscience and ethical sensibilities when they work professionally, can pass over such passages with indifference. (B. R. McCarthy 2000: 618)

Williamson (2008: 71) has observed that in v. 33, the Hebrew word translated "willingly" is מלבו, that is, "from his heart." Given this, one wonders if God does not indeed bring about the Exile from the heart of God, and if so, what is the source of this punishment and violence? And if this is not from the heart of God, then is God being "forced" or is God arbitrary or capricious? Moreover, if God does not afflict willingly, then why does God not listen to the prayers and pleadings of the exiles and the prisoners in concentration camps? Why does God not act? Middlemas (2004: 94) suggests that "[t]he on-going, relentless tragedy experienced by the community in Jerusalem suggests that Yahweh has acted capriciously, with the punishment meted out far outweighing the crime." Yet, it is God who is responsible for, and precipitates the punishment and suffering, and then disappears and leaves the people to submerge under the weight of violence and suffering. Karl Plank's ideas on Ps. 137 suggest the manner in which Lamentations might be read and interpreted intertextually.

> ...intertextuality invites the interpreter to take seriously...a poem whose language is an icon of the experience it would convey; to see in the contrapuntal deixis the reality of exile. The point is not that one must read [Lamentations]...in this intertextual way, but that it is worthwhile to do so; that it opens the texts to new horizons of interpretation that take seriously the connection between displacement and deixis, exile and language. (2008: 186)

The challenge before us as readers and interpreters is not only to have a memory of the Exile and the *Shoah*, important and critical as that is, but to understand the ongoing suffering and violence in our world, and wonder about the silence and the apparent absence of God. "What happened at Auschwitz is inconceivable.... For many who live after Auschwitz, however, it is God, not genocide, that is inconceivable" (Rubenstein and Roth 2003: 290). The language of God crushing "virgin daughter Judah underfoot as in a winepress" not only speaks to an image of violence that is beyond imagination, but to particular evidence of a life cut short without the experience of a future of promise. This is the God that many would find inconceivable; perhaps this is the God that AR found inconceivable. "Lamentations gives us language to scream and cry and confess our disappointment in God and disappointment in ourselves, and our anger at God's silence," observes Houck-Loomis (2012: 707).

Invariably suffering brings with it a catalog of questions, many of which are likely to be unanswerable, but questions that nonetheless must be asked. Moreover, many of the questions that are being posed today have inter-generational, inter-textual, and inter-relational connections that must be reckoned with and inform each other. The questions and cries in Lamentations have a direct line to the *Shoah*, and the silence of God is striking and palpable, particularly since the *Shoah* was an act of human evil. In a graphic and searing moment in *Night*, Elie Wiesel recalls:

> The three necks were placed at the same moment within the nooses
> "Long live liberty!" cried the two adults.
> But the child was silent
> "Where is God? Where is He?" Someone behind me asked.
> ...For more than an hour he [the boy] stayed there, struggling between life and death, dying in slow agony under our eyes....
> Behind me, I heard the same man asking:
> "Where is God now?"
> And I heard a voice within me answer him:
> "Where is He? Here He is—He is hanging here on this gallows."
> (Wiesel 1960: 76)

There is nothing within Lamentations that begins to address the issue as to the extent of this suffering; when will the voice of the exiles or victims of the *Shoah* be heard, or what happens in the future when these questions, though asked repeatedly and persistently, remain unanswered?

> By boldly and publicly stating that YHWH has acted against it with excessive violence and anger, Israel asserts its voice, its selfhood, regardless of the consequences. In the daring honesty of unedited speech, Israel reclaims its dignity, making possible a viable future with YHWH. (Williamson 2008: 80)

Lamentations establishes a platform for the voice of grief to be heard; the voice of heart-rending complaints and indictments to be heard. Why should the people not ask questions, particularly if the emphasis on the relationship with God is to ensure that one prays, listens, and acts? Must the sufferer remain silent because God is silent?

> Linguistically,…Lamentations cannot be described as silence about God. The issue is however not literary. It is theological. God remains silent or refrains from actions towards those who have suffered *in extremis* at the hand of the Babylonian invaders. (Gladson 2010: 322)

Those who suffer must have the freedom to grieve privately and mourn publicly, and the process must have the breadth to include questioning and anger. Thus, the sufferer must have the courage to question God while sustaining faith in this very God, so as not to experience a quality of guilt that could collapse one into a state of debilitating paralysis. Profound belief in God in particular generates the greatest sense of discord, and perhaps for a while might feel like tearing asunder a relationship. Lamentations, like the *Shoah*, expresses life and death experiences; and in the midst of these experiences, it is often very difficult to reflect objectively on the role of God. It is abundantly clear that the existential question regarding God and suffering is a lived and contextualized issue, and not simply an abstract theological debate in Lamentations or the *Shoah*.

Taken literally, the Hebrew of Lam. 2:18a reads "their heart cried," צָעַק לִבָּם אֶל־אֲדֹנָי, and serves as a reminder that the suffering and despair of the exiles come from their hearts, hidden from the world but known to God. These tears will continue, and the belief is that God might still respond. For the audience then, and now, the idea of crying from the heart, or "heartbroken," is acutely understood with a sense that what comes from the heart comes from the core of who one is, stripped of all pretense, and only God ultimately knows. The exploration of this theme is predicated on the suffering of the exiles in Babylon and God's punishment, together with its influence on the *Shoah*. What cannot be lost in the reading and interpretation is that the suffering in the Exile was brought about by God's action and a promise that says, "I will return, and I will bring you home," and then the total silence and seeming impotence that ensues. Can the representation of divine speech ever regain plausibility?

The final three verses of Lamentations establish the framework for the exploration of the critical questions after the *Shoah*.

> Why have you forgotten us completely?
> Why have you forsaken us these many days?
> Restore us to yourself, O, Lord that we may be restored;
> renew our days as of old—
> Unless you have utterly rejected us,
> And are angry with us beyond measure? (Lam. 5:20-22)[4]

And the final line surely begs the question: "Are you?" And there is silence. While there is some disagreement as to the proper or right punctuation of 5:22, given the question in 5:20 and the hope in 5:21, the essence of 5:22 is most effectively captured with a question. Lamentations ends with a devastating sense of loss and despair; yet, indeed, if v. 22 ends with a question, as I would argue, then it is an invitation to struggle with the question and its implications. It seems that the grief and pain, fear and devastation are such that the people do not, and perhaps cannot, know why God is silent.

> Lamentations, like the Holocaust, fundamentally challenges any theological paradigm; therefore answering Daughter Zion with a theology that ignores suffering fails to recognize her pain and her request. (K. M. Wilson 2012: 100)

If God has ceased to function as a moral agent, then what? The end of Lamentations invites the reader to reflect, and to journey to a place of faithful courage to question, and step away from the long-established norm that questioning God is a sign of weakness of faith. As Houck-Loomis (2012: 706) suggests, "The refusal to end this book with any answer, any resolution, gives us the permission to join the psychological struggle." Readers must wonder whether questions, existential and otherwise, must be asked for the sake of questions themselves.

One of the natural human impulses in facing suffering and injustice is to seek resolution, reconciliation, and answers. Yet, there is often forced resolution before the truth of one's suffering is given voice, and this occurs frequently under the guise of "moving on" or not "dwelling on the past."

> The problem, however, is that human suffering often challenges our view of how God and the world ought to work and allowing suffering to speak therefore threatens to perpetuate an uncomfortable disorientation of one's life. The impulse then is to speak over human suffering...[and] this impulse is especially tempting when reading a text, for it is easy to ignore the suffering portrayed either by distancing oneself from the horror or ignoring it altogether. (K. M. Wilson 2012: 94)

---

4. English translations throughout this chapter are from the NRSV.

As each person or community brings their own experience to Lamentations, it provides a platform to explore and enter into these questions without the impulse or expectation to generate immediate answers. Moreover, Lam. 5:22 reminds us clearly and poignantly that Lamentations is not about form and convention, where for example praise typically culminates the litany of laments, veiling questions about God's silence and absence. To have such praise as part of the Exile and the *Shoah* would seem to be artificial and misplaced. In the midst of devastating suffering, praise is also absent. There is no word from God and there is no answer given to the many cries uttered to God. If God is silent in Lamentations, when will God speak again, and what are the circumstances under which the time is right and proper for God to speak? In a post-*Shoah* world, what would be the circumstances under which God would speak and act?

Memory and Witness of I and We

Lamentations opens with the image of Jerusalem as widow. Alone, bereft of a husband, bereft of God, Jerusalem sits alone and weeps into the night (1:1-2), such is the extraordinary beginning of the litany of laments. In the depth of her aloneness, weakness, and abandonment, punctuated by the silence and absence of God, she weeps, and cannot be comforted or consoled because there is no one to do either. The brutality of the language, for example, in 3:43, "you have wrapped yourself in anger and pursued us, slaying without pity," makes it difficult to imagine that God was not intentional in this violent punishment. In Lam. 1:1a, "how lonely sits the city," one hearkens to Gen. 2:17, where for the first time in the Bible an aspect of creation is pronounced as "not good," namely the aloneness of the man. This moment of divine reflection is the foundation for the importance of community, for companionship, and the recognition that aloneness, whether imposed or by inheritance, is not good, and has the prospects of being punitive and discordant. So the city, once filled with the noise of people, now sits lonely and abandoned; yet Jerusalem personified speaks as a singular voice and is now pictured as a ravaged, raped woman, who tells her story. We cannot be surprised that the level of suffering and violence experienced by the exiles, and by the Jews in the *Shoah*, would lead to an unraveling of trust, and that the traditions that once might have been foundational have collapsed. The God who acknowledged that aloneness was "not good" and set about creating companionship now has abandoned the people. The brutal indicting language of Lam. 4 and 5 only intensifies this description.

The emphasis in Lamentations on the suffering of women and children strikes a particular chord, as these two groups are the most vulnerable; here one sees the striking parallel with the *Shoah*, where women and children become the most instantly disposable. Berlin (2002: 76) states without ambiguity, "God who slaughters his people is no less a cannibal than the mothers who eat their children." Lamentations 2:20 and 4:10 have the most graphic and heart-stopping cannibalistic description, "Should women eat their new born infants?" and "mothers boil their own children." Not only is there the horror of the language, but the depth of despair, suffering, and the violence inflicted. Such is the suffering that these thoughts would enter the consciousness of the mothers.

> We know that the children are likely to die before their mothers. It is difficult to read about intense famine (Lam 1.11; 2.12), the rape of women (1.12), the removal of people from their homes (1.3), personal belongings taken away (1.10), and the people fainting in the streets (2.11,19, 21) while the perpetrators of the sufferings cheer and mock (1.7; 2.15) without thinking of the Holocaust. (K. M. Wilson 2012: 96)

In personifying Jerusalem as "daughter Zion," Lamentations transforms the focus from the general to the particular and sharpens the manner in which we are led to think about the violence and abandonment. The particularity of a woman being raped and ravished, abused and betrayed both by friends, and particularly by God, intensifies a sense of shared despair.

When one is able to "put a face" on the tragedy, identification with the heart is sharpened, and we are reminded that once upon a time, there was community, family, friends, God. Now, there is aloneness with the vestiges of what once was. Here memory is wrought with pain, and the despair runs even deeper. Alan Mintz (1982: 2) has observed:

> It is by individuals that pain and humiliation are experienced even if they are inflicted on a group for group reasons, and it is only by virtue of the knowledge born of our individual experience of these states that we are susceptible of being moved to pity or anger.

In abandonment and despair, it is the individual who emerges as central and it is to the individual to which we gravitate, it is the individual who sharpens the definition of the violence. Yet, in the midst of the aloneness, of "I", it is important to have a "we." In the words of Mintz (1982: 14–15), "The pursuit, torture, and the entombment suffered by the speaker at the beginning of the poem are *his own*. He has truly become a personification, an 'I' through whose singleness the pathos of the 'we' become luminous." This is also a moment of moral clarity.

Most exiles and prisoners believed in their relationship with God, and thus in their complaints, there is an insistent factor that they must be heard. There are two points to note in this regard. First, when a tragedy is so large that one struggles for the right words to capture the magnitude, it might very well lead one to abandon the quest to articulate the pain. If this is taken to the logical conclusion, then it could lead to silence, and that ironically would reflect a sense of abandonment. Second, in the midst of a communal tragedy, be it a natural disaster, an act of terrorism, enslavement, or famine, etc., given the magnitude, one is well advised to focus on an individual, on one person whose narrative and face comes to represent the whole, and in so doing shapes the breadth and depth of communal tragedy. Invariably when an individual faces tragedy, friends and family, and perhaps even the wider public, are moved in part because one is able to focus on the particular, and in so doing the individual's story becomes our story.

The memory of such moments cannot be taught simply as a historical reminiscence, but rather as an invitation to make these moments and questions pertinent and indispensable for every generation. In so doing, we ensure that it is not simply a matter of knowing the dates or the circumstances, but rather the investment in the lives of those who suffer and thus having their stories live on through us. And while we must use our voice, we must ensure that our voice does not in any way submerge the voice of the sufferers.

It is commonplace today to hear the well-trodden statements, "let's not dwell on the past" or "it is time to move on." What is often neglected in these statements is the fact that looking to the future is not exclusive of ensuring that the memory of the past is kept alive.

The stories and the experiences must be told and heard with empathy and with heart, and not be met with instant and "textbook" answers. The memory of the *Shoah* victims cannot be a momentary reminder, that God has abandoned or has been silent only in one particular time and place, but rather placing the entire relationship with God in focus—the past, present, and future. I have suggested elsewhere (2014: 166) the potential for psychological trauma when the remembering and the memory are kept deeply hidden and locked away.

Homecoming

Is it possible to imagine the triumphant return of Zion's children without betraying the memory of the one million children who did not return from Nazi death camps (Linafelt 1998: 284)? While it is the case that some of the exiles did return to Jerusalem, one must ask legitimately as to whether the exiles could have returned home again. What is it that the people were returning to, and what constitutes "home" for the exiles? Even as the exiles could no longer go "home," the survivors of the *Shoah* could no longer go home as there was no home, literally and figuratively. And, significantly, one must wonder whether God will ever return "home" to the people? There is a heartfelt longing for God to return. Not only is God's absence striking, but there is a distinct sense of loss, with little prospect of returning.

Could "there" for an exile or prisoner become what his or her "here" was in a life taken away? In the case of the Shoah, there is not only an imprisonment, but can truly live *there* when *there* is the captor's home? Can one be forced to sing in a fabricated "here" not only for the captors, but also sing songs in tribute to God, the silent God, the God who sent them into exile? Under these circumstances can that place ever become "here"? Even if it were possible to go home again, unlikely as that was, as we have seen from the *Shoah* there was no home. One may certainly point to the construction of the Second Temple and the rebuilding of the city and the reinstituting of the religious laws, or nations who opened their doors to *Shoah* survivors, but as important and even momentous as these were, the construction of meaning and trust is a much more intense and difficult process. Yet, such construction of meaning and trust are foundational.

For example, one thinks of Theresienstadt concentration camp that was often publicized as a "model" Nazi camp, aiming to shroud what it truly was, as others were, namely, a death camp. The Nazis sought to generate a cultural image, a quasi-cultural environment including music and art for the world to see; but such cannot be forced, not when the heart is not vested. "Song of home" cannot be transposed into a place of violence and death. How could the people in concentration camps possibly sing songs or play music? Yet, on occasion, they did. For some, such as the pianist Alice Hertz-Sommer who performed over a hundred concerts, playing music was a matter of survival. But not everyone survived, and for some, perhaps many, such as AR, God did not survive either. The irony is that God did not die at Auschwitz or Dachau, because for that to have happened, God would have had to be present. Perhaps in the face of life and death choices, the will to sing might be possible if only to survive, to hope beyond the reality of death and violence, and the horror of being tossed into ovens. Perhaps then, the question as to whether one can sing the Lord's song in a foreign land might not always be negative.

Finally, one cannot fully understand the many and various mysteries that surround us, yet it should not be the case that in the face of suffering, the principal explication is a justification of God, a dispensing of silence and absence in view of a hope outlined for the future. Always there is a place and moment for hope beyond the present, and the only way this might be embraced is to ensure that the reality of the present and the past are attended to.

The inscription, "You are my Witnesses" at the entrance of the National Holocaust Memorial Museum in Washington, DC, serves as a reminder of this vested responsibility. To witness is not necessarily to have been there, and to have survived, though of course, that experience is incomparable, but it is to take the memory inherited or narrated to us, painful as it is, and become one with it. Abraham Heschel's (1962: 204) reflection on prophetic justice has a particular resonance in this regard. He suggests that justice is required of everyone, and "cannot be fulfilled vicariously." Memory and its significance cannot be vicarious, and thus must be lived out personally to ensure the experience of the suffering is not lost.

Bibliography

Adorno, Theodor W. 1973. *Negative Dialectics*. New York: Seabury.
Aitken, James K. 2013. "The Inevitability of Reading Job Through Lamentations." Pages 204–15 in Dell and Kynes 2013.
Albertz, Rainer. 2001. *Die Exilszeit. 6. Jahrhundert v.Chr*. BE 7. Stuttgart: Kohlhammer.
Albrektson, Bertil. 1963. *Studies in the Text and Theology of the Book of Lamentations: with a Critical Edition of the Peshitta Text*. STL 21. Lund: Gleerup.
Albrektson, Bertil. 2010. "The Background and Origin of the Theology of Lamentations (1963)." Pages 9–34 in *Text, Translation, Theology: Selected Essays on the Hebrew Bible*. Edited by B. Albrektson. London: Routledge.
Alexander, Philip S. 2007. *The Targum of Lamentations: Translated, with a Critical Introduction, Apparatus, and Notes*. Vol. 17B of *The Aramaic Bible*. Edited by Kevin Cathcart, Michael Maher, and Martin McNamara. Collegeville, MN: Liturgical Press.
Alexander, Philip S. 2010. "Rabbinic Paratexts: The Case of *Midrash Lamentations Rabbah*." Pages 183–203 in *Paratextual Literature in Ancient Near Eastern and Ancient Mediterranean Culture and its Reflections in Medieval Literature*. Edited by Philip S. Alexander, Armin Lange, and Renate J. Pillinger. Leiden: Brill.
Alkier, Stefan. 2009. "Intertextuality and the Semiotics of Biblical Texts." Pages 3–21 in *Reading the Bible Intertextually*. Edited by Richard B. Hays, Stefan Alkier, Leroy A. Huizenga. Waco, TX: Baylor University Press.
Allegro, John. M. 1968. "Lamentations." Pages 75–7 in *Qumrân Cave 4 I (4Q158–4Q186)*. DJD 5. Oxford: Clarendon.
Allen, Graham. 2000. *Intertextuality: The New Critical Idiom*. London: Routledge.
Allen, Leslie C. 1983. *Psalms 101–150*. WBC 21. Waco: Word Books.
Allen, Leslie C. 2011. *A Liturgy of Grief*. Grand Rapids: Baker Academic.
Anderson, A. A. 1972. *Psalms (73–150)*. NCB. London: Marshall, Morgan & Scott.
Anderson, Gary A. 1991. *A Time to Mourn, a Time to Dance: The Expression of Grief and Joy in Israelite Religion*. University Park, PA: Pennsylvania State University Press.
Archer, John. 1999. *The Nature of Grief. The Evolution and Psychology of Reactions to Loss*. London: Routledge.
Assmann, Jan. 2006. *Religion and Cultural Memory*. Translated by R. Livingstone. Stanford: Stanford University Press.
Assmann, Jan. 2007. *Das kulturelle Gedächtnis: Schrift, Erinnerung und politische Identität in frühen Hochkulturen*. 6th ed. München: Beck.
Avnery, Orit. 2016. "Ruth and Esther: A Journey through Gender, Ethnicity and Identity." Pages 43–71 in Embry 2016.
Baillet, Maurice. 1982. "501. Lamentation." Pages 79–80 in *Qumrân Grotte 4 III (4Q482-4Q520)*. DJD 7. Oxford: Clarendon.

Baillet, Maurice. 2014. "4Q501 (4QApocryphal Lamentations B)." Pages 696–9 in *The Dead Sea Scrolls Reader*. 2nd ed. Vol. 2. Edited by D. W. Parry and E. Tov. Leiden: Brill.

Bakhtin, Mikhail M. 1981. "Discourse in the Novel." Pages 259–422 in *The Dialogic Imagination: Four Essays*. Edited by Michael Holquist. Translated by Caryl Emerson and Michael Holquist. Austin: University of Texas Press.

Bakhtin, Mikhail M. 1984. *Problems of Dostoevsky's Poetics*. Edited and translated by Caryl Emerson. THL 8. Minneapolis: University of Minnesota Press.

Bakhtin, Mikhail M. 1986. "Toward a Methodology for the Human Sciences." Pages 159–72 in *Speech Genres and Other Late Essays*. Edited by Caryl Emerson and Michael Holquist. Austin, TX: University of Texas Press.

Balentine, Samuel E. 2002. *Leviticus*. IBC. Louisville: John Knox.

Balentine, Samuel E. 2018. *Wisdom Literature*. CBS. Nashville: Abingdon Press.

Barbour, Jennie. 2012. *The Story of Israel in the Book of Qohelet: Ecclesiastes as Cultural Memory*. Oxford: Oxford University Press.

Barstad, Hans M. 1996. *The Myth of the Empty Land: A Study in the History and Archaeology of Judah during the "Exilic" Period*. SOSup 28. Oslo: Scandinavian University Press.

Barthélemy, Dominique. 1963. "Les Tiqqune sopherim et la critique textuelle de L'Ancien Testament." Pages 285–304 in *Congress of the International Organization for the Study of the Old Testament; Congress Volume: Bonn, 1962*. Edited by George W. Anderson. VTSup 9. Leiden: Brill.

Barton, John. 2013. "Déjà Lu: Intertextuality, Method or Theory?" Pages 1–16 in Dell and Kynes 2013.

Beal, Timothy K. 1992. "Ideology and Intertextuality: Surplus of Meaning and Controlling the Means of Production." Pages 27–39 in *Reading Between Texts: Intertextuality and the Hebrew Bible*. Edited by Danna Nolan Fewell. Louisville: Westminster John Knox.

Begg, Christopher T., and Paul Spilsbury. 2005. Flavius Josephus: Translation and Commentary, Volume 5: Judean Antiquities, Books 8-10. Leiden: Brill.

Berges, Ulrich. 2000. "'Ich bin der Mann, der Elend sah' (Klgl 3,1): Zionstheologie als Weg aus der Krise." *BZ* 44:1–20.

Berges, Ulrich. 2002. *Klagelieder*. HThKAT. Freiburg im Breisgau: Herder.

Berges, Ulrich. 2005. "The Violence of God in the Book of Lamentations." Pages 21–44 in *One Text, a Thousand Methods: Studies in memory of Sjef van Tilborg*. Edited by Chatelion Counet and Ulrich Berges. BibInt 71. Leiden: Brill.

Berges, Ulrich. 2012. *Klagelieder*. 2nd ed. HThKAT. Freiburg im Breisgau: Herder.

Berlin, Adele. 2002. *Lamentations: A Commentary*. OTL. Louisville: Westminster John Knox.

Berlin, Adele. 2003. "Qumran Laments and the Study of Lament Literature." Pages 1–17 in *Liturgical Perspectives: Prayer and Poetry in Light of the Dead Sea Scrolls*. Edited by E. Chazon. STDJ 48. Leiden: Brill.

Bernstein, M. J. 2014. "4Q179 (4QapocrLam A)." Pages 414–17 in *The Dead Sea Scrolls Reader*. 2nd ed. Vol. 2. Edited by D. W. Parry and E. Tov. Leiden: Brill.

Bezzel, Hannes. 2007. *Die Konfessionen Jeremias: Eine redaktionsgeschichtliche Studie*. BZAW 378. Berlin: de Gruyter.

Bezzel, Hannes. 2011. "'Man of Constant Sorrow'—Rereading Jeremiah in Lamentations 3." Pages 253–65 in *Jeremiah (Dis)Placed: New Directions in Writing/Reading Jeremiah*. Edited by A. R. Pete Diamond and Louis Stulman. LHBOTS 529. London: T&T Clark.

Bier, Miriam J. 2014. "'We have Sinned and Rebelled; You have Not Forgiven': The Dialogic Interaction between Authoritative and Internally Persuasive Discourse in Lamentations 3." *BibInt* 22: 146–67.

Bier, Miriam J. 2015. *"Perhaps There is Hope": Reading Lamentations as a Polyphony of Pain, Penitence, and Protest*. LHBOTS 603. New York: Bloomsbury T&T Clark.

Blocher, Henri. 2002. "Glorious Zion, our Mother: Readings in Isaiah (Conspectus, or Abridged)." *EuroJTh* 11: 5–14.

Boase, Elizabeth. 2006. *The Fulfilment of Doom? The Dialogic Interaction between the Book of Lamentations and the Pre-exilic/Early Exilic Prophetic Literature*. LHBOTS 437. New York: T&T Clark.

Boase, Elizabeth. 2008a. "Constructing Meaning in the Face of Suffering: Theodicy in Lamentations." *VT* 58: 449–68.

Boase, Elizabeth. 2008b. "The Characterization of God in Lamentations." *ABR* 56:32–44.

Boase, Elizabeth. 2016. "Fragmented Voices: Collective Identity and Traumatization in Lamentations." Pages 49–66 in *Bible Through the Lens of Trauma*. Edited by Elizabeth Boase and Christopher G. Frechette. SemeiaSt 86. Atlanta: SBL Press.

Boda, Mark J. 2008. "The Priceless Gain of Penitence." Pages 81–101 in Lee and Mandolfo 2008.

Boda, Mark J., Carol J. Dempsey, and LeAnn Snow Flesher, eds. 2012. *Daughter Zion: Her Portrait, Her Response*. Atlanta: SBL Press.

Bonhoeffer, Dietrich. 1970. *Psalms: The Prayer Book of the Bible*. Translated by James H. Burtness. Minneapolis: Augsburg.

Borowski, Oded. 2003. *Daily Life in Biblical Times*. Atlanta: SBL Press.

Bosworth, David A. 2013. "Daughter Zion and Weeping in Lamentations 1–2." *JSOT* 38.2: 217–37.

Botterweck, G. Johannes, and Helmer Ringgren, eds. 1974–2006. *Theological Dictionary of the Old Testament*. Translated by John T. Willis et al. 8 vols. Grand Rapids: Eerdmans.

Bouzard, Walter C. 2014. "Boxed by the Orthodox: The Function of Lamentations 3:22-39 in the Message of the Book." Pages 68–82 in Flesher, Dempsey, and Boda 2014.

Boyarin, Daniel. 1987. "Old Wine in New Bottles: Intertextuality and Midrash." *PT* 8.3-4: 539–56.

Boyarin, Daniel. 1990. *Intertextuality and the Reading of Midrash*. Bloomington, IN: Indiana University Press.

Brady, Christian M. M. 2001. "Vindicating God: The Intent of the Targum Lamentations." *JAB* 3: 27–40.

Brady, Christian M. M. 2003. *The Rabbinic Targum of Lamentations: Vindicating God*. SAIS 3. Leiden: Brill.

Brady, Christian M. M. "Targum Lamentations." http://targum.info/meg/tglam.htm.

Braitherman, Zachary. 2011. "Lamentations in Modern Jewish Thought." Pages 92–7 in Parry and Thomas 2011.

Brandscheidt, Renate. 1983. *Gotteszorn und Menschenleid: Die Gerichtsklage des leidenden Gerechten in Klgl 3*. TThSt 41. Trier: Paulinus-Verlag.

Brandscheidt, Renate. 1988. *Das Buch der Klagelieder erläutert*. GS 10. Düsseldorf: Patmos.

Brenner, Athalya. 1989. *The Song of Songs*. OTG. Sheffield: Sheffield Academic.

Brenner, Athalya. 1999. *Ruth and Esther: A Feminist Companion to the Bible*. Sheffield: Sheffield Academic.

Brenner-Idan, Athalya. 2015. *The Israelite Woman: Social Role and Literary Type in Biblical Narrative*. 2nd ed. London: Bloomsbury.
Briggs, Richard S. 2018. *Theological Hermeneutics and the Book of Numbers as Christian Scripture*. RTS. Notre Dame: University of Notre Dame Press.
Britten, Benjamin. 1946. *Rape of Lucretia*. An opera in two acts. Libretto by Ronald Duncan. Based on the play "Le vol de Lucrèce."
Brooke, George J. 2005. "Thematic Commentaries on Prophetic Scriptures." Pages 134–57 in *Biblical Interpretation at Qumran*. Edited by M. Henze. Grand Rapids: Eerdmans.
Brooke, George J. 2006. "Biblical Interpretation at Qumran." Pages 287–319 in *Scripture and the Scrolls*. Edited by J. H. Charlesworth. Vol. 1 of *The Bible and the Dead Sea Scrolls*. Edited by J. H. Charlesworth. Waco, TX: Baylor University Press.
Brueggemann, Walter. 1986. "The Costly Loss of Lament." *JSOT* 36: 57–71.
Brueggemann, Walter. 1995. *The Psalms and the Life of Faith*. Minneapolis, MN. Augsburg Fortress.
Brueggemann, Walter. 2008. "Lament as Wake-Up Call (Class Analysis and Historical Possibility)." Pages 221–36 in Lee and Mandolfo 2008.
Buber, Salomon, ed. 1899. *Midrash Eikah Rabbah* (Hebrew). Vilna: Romm.
Cameron-Mowat, Andrew. 2011. "Lamentations and Christian Worship." Pages 139–41 in Parry and Thomas 2011.
Carr, David M. 2012. "The Many Uses of Intertextuality in Biblical Studies: Actual and Potential." Pages 505–35 in *Congress Volume: Helsinki 2010*. Edited by M. Nissinen. VTSup 148. Leiden: Brill.
Carroll, Robert P. 1986. *Jeremiah: A Commentary*. OTL. Philadelphia: Westminster.
Cassiodorus. 1990–1991. *Explanations of the Psalms*. Translated by P. G. Walsh. 3 vols. New York: Paulist.
Chapman, Honora Howell. 1998. "Spectacle and Theater in Josephus's *Bellum Judaicum*." PhD diss., Stanford University.
Chapman, Honora Howell. 2000. "A *Myth for the World*: Early Christian Reception of Infanticide and Cannibalism in Josephus, *Bellum Judaicum* 6.199-219." Pages 359–78 in *Society of Biblical Literature 2000 Seminar Papers*. Atlanta: SBL Press.
Chapman, Honora Howell. 2007. "Josephus and the Cannibalism of Mary (*BJ* 6.199-219)." Pages 419–26 in *A Companion to Greek and Roman Historiography*. Edited by John Marincola. Malden, MA: Blackwell.
Chapman, Honora Howell. 2009. "What Josephus Sees: The Temple of Peace and the Jerusalem Temple as Spectacle in Text and Art." *Phoenix* 63: 107–30.
Chapman, Honora Howell. 2020. "Josephus' Memory of Jerusalem." Pages 181–200 in *Urban Disasters and the Roman Imagination*. Edited by Virginia Closs and Elizabeth Keitel. Berlin/Boston: De Gruyter.
Childs, Brevard. 1979. *Introduction to the Old Testament as Scripture*. Philadelphia: Fortress.
Claassens, L. Juliana M. 2010. "Calling the Keeners: The Image of the Wailing Woman as Symbol of Survival in a Traumatized World." *JFSR* 26.1: 63–77.
Clines, David J. A. 1989. *Job 1–20*. WBC 17. Nashville: Thomas Nelson.
Cohen, A. 1983. "Lamentations," Pages 1–245 in *Midrash Rabbah: Deuteronomy, Lamentations*. The Midrash: Volume VII. London: Soncino.
Cohen, Shaye J. D. 1982a. "Josephus, Jeremiah, and Polybius." *HistTh* 21: 366–81.
Cohen, Shaye J. D. 1982b. "The Destruction: From Scripture to Midrash." *Proof* 2: 18–39.
Cohen, Shaye J. D. 1983. "Jacob Neusner, Mishnah, and Counter-Rabbinics: A Review Essay." *Conservative Judaism* 37.1: 48–63.

Cohen, Shaye J. D. 1987. *From the Maccabees to the Mishnah*. Philadelphia: Westminster.
Cooper, Alan. 2001. "The Message of Lamentations." *JANES* 28: 1–18.
Creach, Jerome F. D. 1996. *Yahweh as Refuge and the Editing of the Hebrew Psalter*. JSOTSup 217. Sheffield: Sheffield Academic.
Crenshaw, James L. 1988. *Ecclesiastes: A Commentary*. OTL. London: SCM.
Crenshaw, James L. 2005. *Defending God: Biblical Responses to the Problem of Evil*. Oxford: Oxford University Press.
Crenshaw, James L. 2009. Forward to *The Five Exotic Scrolls of the Hebrew Bible*, by Jerry A. Gladson. Lewiston, NY: Mellen.
Cross, Frank. M. 2000. "4QLam." Pages 229–37 in *Qumran Cave 4 XI: Psalms to Chronicles*. Edited by E. Ulrich, F. M. Cross, J. A. Fitzmyer, P. W. Flint, S. Metso, C. M. Murphy, C. Niccum, P. W. Skehan, E. Tov and J. Trebolle Barrera. DJD 16. Oxford: Clarendon.
Daube, David. 1980. "Typology in Josephus." *JJS* 31: 18–36.
Davies, Philip. R. 2003. "Biblical Interpretation in the Dead Sea Scrolls." Pages 144–66 in *A History of Biblical Interpretation*. Vol. 1 of *The Ancient Period*. Edited by A. J. Hauser and D. F. Watson. Grand Rapids: Eerdmans.
Davila, James. R. 2000. *Liturgical Works*. ECDSS 6. Grand Rapids: Eerdmans.
Davis, Dale Ralph. 1982. "Rebellion, Presence, and Covenant: A Study in Exodus 32–34." *WTJ* 44: 71–87.
Davis, Ellen F. 2001. *Getting Involved with God: Rediscovering the Old Testament*. Lanham, MD: Rowman & Littlefield.
Day, Peggy L. 2000. "Adulterous Jerusalem's Imagined Demise: Death of a Metaphor in Ezekiel XVI." *VT* 50.3: 285–309.
Deist, Ferdinand. E. 2000. *The Material Culture of the Bible: An Introduction*. Sheffield: Sheffield Academic.
D'Elia, Una Roman. 2015. *Raphael's Ostrich*. University Park: Pennsylvania State University Press.
Delkurt, Holger. 2000. *Sacharjas Nachtgesichte: Zur Aufnahme und Abwandlung prophetischer Traditionen*. BZAW 302. Berlin: de Gruyter.
Dell, Katharine J. 1991. *The Book of Job as Sceptical Literature*. Berlin: de Gruyter.
Dell, Katharine J. 2013a. "'Cursed be the day I was born!': Job and Jeremiah Revisited." Pages 106–17 in Dell and Kynes 2013.
Dell, Katharine J. 2013b. *Interpreting Ecclesiastes: Readers Old and New*. Grand Rapids: Eerdmans.
Dell, Katharine J. 2014. "Exploring Intertextual Links Between Ecclesiastes and Genesis 1–11." Pages 3–14 in Dell and Kynes 2014.
Dell, Katharine J. 2016. "Wisdom and Folly in the City: Exploring urban contexts in the book of Proverbs." *SJT* 69: 389–401.
Dell, Katharine, and Will Kynes, eds. 2013. *Reading Job Intertextually*. LHBOTS 574. New York: Bloomsbury.
Dell, Katharine, and Will Kynes. 2014. *Reading Ecclesiastes Intertextually*. LHBOTS 587. London: Bloomsbury T&T Clark.
Dell, Katharine, and Will Kynes. 2018. *Reading Proverbs Intertextually*. LHBOTS 629. London: Bloomsbury T&T Clark.
Derrida, Jacques. 1997 [orig. 1967]. *Of Grammatology*. Translated by Gayatri Spivak. Baltimore: John Hopkins University Press.

Dobbs-Allsopp, F. W. 1997. "Tragedy, Tradition, and Theology in the Book of Lamentations." *JSOT* 74: 29–60.
Dobbs-Allsopp, F. W. 1998. "Linguistic Evidence for the Date of Lamentations." *JANES* 26: 1–36.
Dobbs-Allsopp, F. W. 2002. *Lamentations*. IBC. Louisville: Westminster John Knox.
Dobbs-Allsopp, F. W. 2009. "Acrostic." *EBR* 1: 281–90.
Dobbs-Allsopp, F. W. 2015. *On Biblical Poetry*. Oxford: Oxford University Press.
Draisma, Sipke, ed. 1989. *Intertextuality in Biblical Writings: Essays in Honour of Bas Van Iersel*. Kampen: Kok.
Driver, Godfrey. R. 1950. "Hebrew Notes on 'Song of Songs' and 'Lamentations.'" Pages 134–46 in *Festschrift Alfred Bertholet zum 80. Geburtstag*. Edited by W. Baumgartner, O. Eissfeldt, K. Elliger and L. Rost. Tübingen: Mohr Siebeck.
Durham, John I. 1987. *Exodus*. WBC 3. Waco, TX: Word.
Embry, Brad, ed. 2016. Various Essays in *Megilloth Studies: The Shape of Contemporary Scholarship*. HBM 78. Sheffield: Sheffield Phoenix.
Enns, Peter. 2000. *Exodus*. NIVAC. Grand Rapids: Zondervan.
Epstein, Baruch. 1904. *Torah Temimah: Sefer Devarim* (Hebrew). Vilna: Romm.
Evans, Paul S. 2009. *A Source-Critical and Rhetorical Study of 2 Kings 18–19*. VTSup 125. Leiden: Brill.
Exum, J. Cheryl. 2005. *Song of Songs*. OTL. Louisville: Westminster John Knox.
Feinstein, Eve L. 2014. *Sexual Pollution in the Hebrew Bible*. Oxford: Oxford University Press.
Feldman, Emanuel. 1977. *Biblical and Post-Biblical Defilement and Mourning: Law as Theology*. LJLE. New York: Ktav.
Felman, Shoshana, and Dori Laub, M.D. 1992. *Testimony: Crises of Witnessing in Literature, Psychoanalysis and History*. New York: Routledge.
Fishbane, Michael. 1985. *Biblical Interpretation in Ancient Israel*. Oxford: Clarendon.
Fishbane, Michael. 2000. "Types of Biblical Intertextuality." Pages in 39–44 in *Congress Volume: Oslo 1998*. Edited by Andre Lemaire and Magne Saebø. VTSup 80. Leiden: Brill.
Fishbane, Michael. 2004. "Use, Authority and Interpretation of Mikra at Qumran." Pages 339–77 in *Mikra: Text, Translation, Reading and Interpretation of the Hebrew Bible in Ancient Judaism and Early Christianity*. Edited by M. J. Mulder and H. Sysling. Peabody, MA: Hendrickson.
Fishbane, Michael. 2007. "Spiritual Transformations of Torah in Biblical and Rabbinic Tradition." *JSRI* 6.18: 6–15.
Fitzmyer, Joseph A. 1997. "The Use of Explicit Old Testament Quotations in Qumran Literature and in the New Testament." Pages 3–58 in *Essays on the Semitic Background of the New Testament*. Vol. 1 of *The Semitic Background of the New Testament*. Grand Rapids: Eerdmans.
Flesher, Leann Snow, Carol J. Dempsey, and Mark J. Boda, eds. 2014. *Why? ... How Long? Studies on Voice(s) of Lamentation Rooted in Biblical Hebrew Poetry*. LHBOTS 552. New York: Bloomsbury T&T Clark.
Fox, Michael V. 1999. *A Time to Tear Down and a Time to Build Up: A Rereading of Ecclesiastes*. Grand Rapids: Eerdmans.
Frechette, Christopher G., and Elizabeth Boase. 2016. "Defining 'Trauma' as a Useful Lens for Biblical Interpretation." Pages 1–23 in *Bible through the Lens of Trauma*. Edited by E. Boase and C. G. Frechette. Atlanta: SBL.

Frevel, Christian. 2013. "The Book of Numbers—Formation, Composition, and Interpretation of a Late Part of the Torah. Some Introductory Remarks." Pages 1–37 in *Torah and the Book of Numbers*. Edited by Christian Frevel, Thomas Pola, and Aaron Schart. FAT II 62. Tübingen: Mohr Siebeck.

Frevel, Christian. 2017. *Die Klagelieder*. NSKAT 20.1. Stuttgart: Katholisches Bibelwerk.

Friedman, Richard Elliott. 1995, 1997. *The Disappearance of God: A Divine Mystery*. San Francisco: Harper; Boston: Little, Brown.

Fuller, Russell. 1990. "Early Emendations of the Scribes: The Tiqqun Sopherim in Zechariah 2:12." Pages 21–8 in *Of Scribes and Scrolls: Studies on the Hebrew Bible, Intertestamental Judaism, and Christian Origins, Presented to John Strugnell on the Occasion of his Sixtieth Birthday*. Edited by Harold W. Attridge, John J. Collins, and Thomas H. Tobin. Lanham, MD: University Press of America.

Fullerton Stollo, Megan. 2016. "Initiative and Agency: Towards a Theology of the Megilloth." Pages 150–60 in Embry 2016.

Galvin, Garrett. 2016. "Horizontal Theology in the *Megilloth*." Pages 125–40 in Embry 2016.

Gane, Roy. 2005. *Cult and Character: Purification Offerings, Day of Atonement, and Theodicy*. Winona Lake, IN: Eisenbrauns.

Garber, Jr., David G. 2014. "'I went in bitterness': Theological Implications of a Trauma Theory Reading of Ezekiel." *R&E* 111: 346–57.

Garber, Jr., David G. 2015. "Trauma Theory and Biblical Studies." *CurBR* 14:24–44.

García Martínez, Florentino. 1996. *The Dead Sea Scrolls Translated: The Qumran Texts in English*. 2nd ed. Leiden: Brill; Grand Rapids: Eerdmans.

García Martínez, Florentino, and Eibert J. C. Tigchelaar. 1997–1998. *The Dead Sea Scrolls Study Edition*. 2 vols. Leiden: Brill.

Garrett, Duane A., and Paul R. House. 2004. *Song of Songs/Lamentations*. WBC 23B. Nashville: Thomas Nelson.

Gerstenberger, Erhard. 2001. *Psalms, Part 2 and Lamentations*. FOTL. Grand Rapids: Eerdmans.

Gilbert, Maurice. 1981. "La description de la vieillesse en Qohelet XII 1-7 est-elle allégorique?" *VT* 32: 96–109.

Gitay, Yehoshua. 2008. "The Poetics of Exile and Suffering: Memory and Perceptions: A Cognitive-Linguistics Study of Lamentations." Pages 203–12 in *Exile and Suffering. A Selection of Papers read at the 50th Anniversary Meeting of the Old Testament Society of South Africa OTWSA/OTSSA Pretoria August 2007*. Edited by Bob Becking and Dirk Human. OTS 50. Leiden: Brill.

Gladson, Jerry A. 2009. *The Five Exotic Scrolls of the Hebrew Bible (The Scroll of The Song of Songs, The Scroll of Ruth, The Scroll of Lamentations, The Scroll of Ecclesiastes, The Scroll of Esther): The Prominence, Literary Structure, and Liturgical Significance of the* Megilloth. Lewiston, NY: Mellen.

Gladson, Jerry A. 2010. "Postmodernism and the Deus Absconditus in Lamentations 3." *Bib* 91.3: 321–34.

Gnuse, Robert Karl. 1996. *Dreams and Dream Reports in the Writings of Josephus: A Traditio-historical Analysis*. Leiden: Brill.

Goldingay, John. 2006–2008. *Psalms*. 3 vols. Grand Rapids: Baker Academic.

Goppelt, Leonhard. 1966. *Typos: die typologische Deutung des Alten Testaments im Neuen; Anhang: Apoklyptik und Typologie bei Paulus*. BFCT 2.43. Darmstadt: Wissenschaftliche Buchgesellschaft.

Gordis, Robert. 1974. *The Song of Songs and Lamentations*. 2nd ed. New York: Ktav.

Gossai, Hemchand. 2014. *The Hebrew Prophets After the Shoah: A Mandate for Change*. Eugene, OR: Wipf & Stock.
Gottlieb, Hans. 1978. *A Study on the Text of Lamentations*. ActJut. Åarhus: Åarhus University Press.
Gottlieb, Hans. 1987. Das Kultische Leiden des Königs. Zu den Klageliedern 3,1. *SJOT* 1: 121–6.
Gottwald, Norman K. 1954. *Studies in the Book of Lamentations*. SBT 14. London: SCM.
Gottwald, Norman K. 1962. *Studies in the Book of Lamentations*. SBT 14. 2nd ed. London: SCM.
Gowan, Donald E. 1992. "Reading Job as a 'Wisdom Script.'" *JSOT* 17: 85–95.
Grabbe, Lester L., ed. 1998. *Leading Captivity Captive: 'The Exile' as History and Ideology*. JSOTSup 278. Sheffield: Sheffield Academic.
Grant, Cecil A. 2000. "'Chasing after the Wind?': An Examination of the Social and Historical Background of the Book of Ecclesiastes." PhD diss., University of Cambridge.
Grant, Jamie A. 2004. *The King as Exemplar: The Function of Deuteronomy's Kingship Law in the Shaping of the Book of Psalms*. AcBib 17. Atlanta: Society of Biblical Literature.
Gray, Rebecca. 1993. *Prophetic Figures in Late Second Temple Jewish Palestine: The Evidence from Josephus*. New York: Oxford University Press.
Green, Barbara. 2000. *Mikhail Bakhtin and Biblical Scholarship: An Introduction*. Atlanta: Society of Biblical Literature.
Greenberg, Moshe. 1983. *Ezekiel, 1–20*. AB 22. Garden City, NY: Double Day.
Greenstein, Edward L. 2004. "The Wrath at God in the Book of Lamentations." Pages 29–42 in *The Problem of Evil and its Symbols in Jewish and Christian Tradition*. Edited by Henning Graf Reventlow and Yair Hoffman. New York: T&T Clark.
Gruber, Mayer I., and Shamir Yona. 2016. "A Male Speaker's Obsessions with the Feminine: The Strange Case of Lamentations 3." Pages 72–9 in Embry 2016.
Grudem, Wayne. 2012. *Evangelical Feminism and Biblical Truth: An Analysis of More Than 100 Disputed Questions*. Wheaton: Crossway.
Häfner, Gerd. 2006. "Konstruktion und Referenz: Impulse aus der neueren geschichtstheoretischen Diskussion." Pages 67–96 in *Historiographie und fiktionales Erzählen. Zur Konstruktion in Geschichtstheorie und Exegese*. Edited by Knut Backhaus and Gerd Häfner. BThSt 86. Neukirchen-Vluyn: Neukirchener Verlag.
Halpern, Baruch, and André Lemaire. 2010. "The Composition of Kings." Pages 123–53 in *The Book of Kings: Sources, Composition, Historiography and Reception*. Edited by B. Halpern and A. Lemaire. VTSup 129. Leiden: Brill.
Handelman, Susan A. 1982. *The Slayers of Moses: The Emergence of Rabbinic Interpretation in Modern Literary Theory*. Albany, NY: State University of New York Press.
Hanhart, Robert. 1998. *Sacharja*. BKAT 14.7. Neukirchen-Vluyn: Neukirchener Verlag.
Hardmeier, Christof. 1998. "Zeitverständnis und Geschichtssinn in der Hebräischen Bibel: Geschichtstheologie und Gegenwartserhellung bei Jeremia." Pages 308–42 in *Die Vielfalt der Kulturen*. Edited by J. Rüsen, M. Gottlob and A. Mittag. EGI 4. Frankfurt: Suhrkamp.
Hardmeier, Christof. 2013. *Geschichtsdivinatorik in der vorexilischen Schriftprophetie: Studien zu den Primärschriften in Jesaja, Zefanja und Jeremia*. Zurich: TVZ.
Harris, Beau, and Carleen Mandolfo. 2013. "The Silent God in Lamentations." *Int* 67: 133–43.
Hawk, L. Daniel. 2015. *Ruth*. ApOTC 7B. Nottingham: Apollos.

Hays, Christopher B. 2008. "Echoes of the Ancient Near East? Intertextuality and the Comparative Study of the Old Testament." Pages 20–43 in *The Word Leaps the Gap: Essays on Scripture and Theology in Honor of Richard B. Hays*. Edited by J. R. Wagner, C. K. Rowe and A. K. Grieb. Grand Rapids: Eerdmans.

Hays, Richard B. 1989. *Echoes of Scripture in the Letters of Paul*. New Haven: Yale University Press.

Hays, Richard B., Stefan Alkier, and Leroy Andrew Huizenga. 2009. *Reading the Bible Intertextually*. Waco, TX: Baylor University Press.

Heffelfinger, Katie M. 2011. *I Am Large, I Contain Multitudes: Lyric Cohesion and Conflict in Second Isaiah*. Leiden: Brill.

Hendel, Ronald S. 2010. "Assessing the Text-Critical Theories of the Hebrew Bible after Qumran." Pages 281–302 in *The Oxford Handbook of the Dead Sea Scrolls*. Edited by T. H. Lim and J. J. Collins. Oxford: Oxford University Press.

Henze, Matthias, ed. 2005. *Biblical Interpretation at Qumran*. Grand Rapids: Eerdmans.

Herman, Judith. 1997. *Trauma and Recovery: The Aftermath of Violence—From Domestic Abuse to Political Terror*. New York: Basic Books.

Heschel, Abraham. 1962. *The Prophets*. Vol. 1. New York: Harper & Row.

Hillers, Delbert R. 1972. *Lamentations: Introduction, Translation, and Notes*. AB 7A. Garden City, NY: Doubleday.

Hillers, Delbert R. 1992. *Lamentations: Introduction, Translation, and Notes*. AB 7A. 2nd ed. New York: Doubleday.

Hinds, Stephen. 1998. *Allusion and Intertext: Dynamics of Appropriation in Roman Poetry*. Cambridge: Cambridge University Press.

Høgenhaven, Jesper. 2002. "Biblical Quotations and Allusions in 4QApocryphal Lamentations (4Q179)." Pages 113–20 in *The Bible as Book: The Hebrew Bible and the Judaean Desert Discoveries*. Edited by E. D. Herbert and E. Tov. London: British Library.

Holladay, William. 1986. *Jeremiah 1: A Commentary on the Book of the Prophet Jeremiah Chapters 1–25*. Hermeneia. Philadelphia: Fortress.

Holquist, Michael, ed. 1981. *The Dialogic Imagination: Four Essays*. Translated by Caryl Emerson and Michael Holquist. Austin: University of Texas Press.

Hope, Valerie M. 2007. *Death in Ancient Rome: A Source Book*. London: Routledge.

Horgan, Maurya P. 1973. "A Lament over Jerusalem ("4Q179")." *JSS* 18: 222–34.

Houck-Loomis, Tiffany. 2012. "Good God ?!? Lamentations as a Model for Mourning and Loss of the Good God." *JR&H* 51.3: 701–8.

House, Paul R. 2004. *Lamentations*. WBC 23B. Nashville: Thomas Nelson.

Houtman, Cornelis. 2000. *Exodus*. HCOT 3. Translated by Sierd Woudstra. Leuven: Peeters.

Hubmann, Franz D. 1978. *Untersuchungen zu den Konfessionen Jer 11,18–12,6 und 15,10–21*. fzb 30. Würzburg: Echter Verlag.

Hubmann, Franz D. 2013. *Prophetie an der Grenze: Studien zum Jeremiabuch und zum Corpus Propheticum*. SBAB 57. Stuttgart: Katholisches Bibelwerk.

Inolowcki, Sabrina. 2016. "Josephus and Patristic Literature." Pages 356–67 in *A Companion to Josephus*. Edited by Honora Chapman and Zuleika Rodgers. Malden, MA: Wiley & Sons.

Irenaeus. 1920. *The Demonstration of the Apostolic Preaching*. Translation and introduction by J. Armitage Robinson. London: SPCK.

Jacobs, John. 2016. "The City Lament Genre in the Ancient Near East." Pages 13–35 in *The Fall of Cities in the Mediterranean: Commemoration in Literature, Folk-Song, and Liturgy*. Edited by Mary R. Bachvarova, Dorota M. Dutsch, and Ann Suter. Cambridge: Cambridge University Press.

Janoff-Bulman, Ronnie. 1992. *Shattered Assumptions: Towards a New Psychology of Trauma*. New York: Free Press.

Janowski, Bernd. 2009. *Konfliktgespräche mit Gott: Eine Anthropologie der Psalmen*. 3rd ed. Neukirchen-Vluyn: Neukirchener Verlag.

Janowski, Bernd, and Kathrin Liss, eds. 2009. *Der Mensch im alten Israel: Neue Forschungen zur alttestamentlichen Anthropologie*. HBS 59. Freiburg im Breisgau: Herder.

Janzen, David. 2008. "An Ambiguous Ending: Dynastic Punishment in Kings and the Fate of the Davidides in 2 Kings 25.27-30." *JSOT* 33: 39–58.

Janzen, David. 2012. *The Violent Gift: Trauma's Subversion of the Deuteronomistic History's Narrative*. New York: Bloomsbury.

Jeremias, Christian. 1977. *Die Nachtgesichte des Sacharja: Untersuchungen zu ihrer Stellung im Zusammenhang der Visionsberichte im Alten Testament und zu ihrem Bildmaterial*. FRLANT 117. Gottingen: Vandenhoeck & Ruprecht.

Jonker, Louis C. 2012. "The Jeremianic Connection: Chronicles and the Reception of Lamentations as Two Modes of Interacting with the Jeremianic Tradition?" *Scriptura* 110: 176–89.

Josephus. 1926–1965. Translated by Henry St. J. Thackeray et al. 10 vols. LCL. Cambridge: Harvard University Press.

Josephus, Flavius, Otto Michel, and Otto Bauernfeind. 1959–1969. *Der jüdische Krieg*. Munich: Kosel.

Joüon, Paul, and T. Muraoka. 2006. *A Grammar of Biblical Hebrew*. Rev. ed. SubBi 27. Rome: Pontifical Institute Press.

Joyce, Paul M. 1993. "Lamentations and the Grief Process: A Psychological Reading." *BibInt* 1.3: 304–20.

Joyce, Paul M., and Diana Lipton. 2013. Lamentations Through the Centuries. WBBC. Malden, MA: Wiley-Blackwell.

Kaiser, Barbara Bakke. 1987. "Poet as 'Female Impersonator': The Image of Daughter Zion as Speaker in Biblical Poems of Suffering." *JR* 67: 164–82.

Kartveit, Magnar. 2013. "Rejoice, Dear Zion! Hebrew Construct Phrases with 'Daughter' and 'Virgin' as Nomen Regens." BZAW 447. Berlin: de Gruyter.

Kast, Verena. 1987. *Trauern. Phasen und Chancen des psychologischen Prozesses*. 8th ed. Stuttgart: Kreuz Verlag.

Kauffman, Jeffrey. 2002. Introduction to *Loss of the Assumptive World: A Theory of Traumatic Loss*. Edited by J. Kauffman. New York: Brunner-Routledge.

Kellner, Menachem. 2014. "And Yet, the Texts Remain. The Problem of the Command to Destroy the Canaanites." Pages 153–79 in *The Gift of the Land and the Fate of the Canaanites in Jewish Thought*. Edited by Katell Berthelot, Joseph E. David, and Marc Hirshman. New York: Oxford University Press.

Kelly, Jospeh R. 2017. "Identifying Literary Allusions: Theory and the Criterion of Shared Language." Pages 22–40 in *Subtle Citation, Allusion, and Translation in the Hebrew Bible*. Edited by Z. Zevit. Sheffield: Equinox.

King, Philip D. 2012. *Surrounded by Bitterness: Image Schemas and Metaphors for Conceptualizing Distress in Classical Hebrew*. Eugene, OR: Pickwick.

King, Philip J., and Lawrence E. Stager 2001. *Life in Biblical Israel*. Louisville: Westminster John Knox.

Klawans, Jonathan. 2002. *Impurity and Sin in Ancient Judaism*. Oxford: Oxford University Press.

Knoppers, Gary. 2010. "Theories of the Redaction(s) of Kings." Pages 69–88 in *The Book of Kings. Sources, Composition, Historiography and Reception*. Edited by B. Halpern and A. Lemaire. VTSup 129. Leiden: Brill.

Koenen, Klaus. 2013. *Die Klagelieder Jeremias: Eine Rezeptionsgeschichte*. BThSt 143. Neukirchen-Vluyn: Neukirchener Verlag.

Koenen, Klaus. 2015. *Klagelieder (Threni)*. BKAT 20. Neukirchen-Vluyn: Neukirchener Verlag.

Körting, Corinna. 2017. "Lamentations: Time and Setting." Pages 137–52 in *Functions of Psalms and Prayers in the Late Second Temple Period*. Edited by M. S. Pajunen and J. Penner. BZAW 486. Berlin: de Gruyter.

Kosmala, Hans. 1973. "גבר." Pages 1:901–19 in *ThWAT*.

Kosmala, Hans. 1975. "גבר." Pages 2:367–82 in *TDOT*.

Kotzé, Gideon R. 2009a. "The Greek and Hebrew Texts of Lamentations 1:4-6. Establishing the Differences in Content Between the Textual Witnesses by Means of a Text-Critical Analysis." *APB* 20: 275–92.

Kotzé, Gideon R. 2009b. "The Greek Translation of Lamentations: Towards a More Nuanced View of Its 'Literal' Character." Pages 77–95 in *Septuagint and Reception. Essays prepared for the Association for the Study of the Septuagint in South Africa*. Edited by J. Cook. VTSup 127. Leiden: Brill.

Kotzé, Gideon R. 2011a. "A Text-Critical Analysis of Lamentations 1:7 in 4QLam and the Masoretic Text." *OTE* 24: 590–611.

Kotzé, Gideon R. 2011b. "LXX Lamentations 4:7 and 4:14. Reflections on the Greek Renderings of the Difficult Hebrew Wordings of These Verses." *JSem* 20: 250–70.

Kotzé, Gideon R. 2012a. "Lamentations 1:8a in the Wordings of the Masoretic Text and 4QLam." *Scriptura* 110: 190–207.

Kotzé, Gideon R. 2012b. "Two Difficult Passages in the Hebrew Texts of Lamentations 5: Text-Critical Analysis of the Greek Translations." Pages 275–95 in *Text-Critical and Hermeneutical Studies in the Septuagint*. Edited by J. Cook and H.-J. Stipp. VTSup 157. Leiden: Brill.

Kotzé, Gideon R. 2013. *The Qumran Manuscripts of Lamentations: A Text-Critical Study*. SSN 61. Leiden: Brill.

Kotzé, Gideon R. 2014. "Text-Critical and Interpretive Comments on Differences Between the Greek and Hebrew Wording of Lamentations 5." Pages 444–66 in *Die Septuaginta—Text, Wirkung, Rezeption. 4. Internationale Fachtagung veranstaltet von Septuaginta Deutsch (LXX.D), Wuppertal 19.–22. Juli 2012*. Edited by Wolfgang Kraus and Siegfried Kreuzer. WUNT 325. Tübingen: Mohr Siebeck.

Kotzé, Gideon R. 2015. "Comments on the Expression of Hope in LXX Lamentations 5:19–22." *OTE* 28: 121–53.

Kotzé, Gideon R. 2020. *Images and Ideas of Debated Readings in the Book of Lamentations*. Orientalische Religionen in der Antike 38. Tübingen: Mohr Siebeck.

Kraemer, David. 1995. *Responses to Suffering in Classical Rabbinic Literature*. Oxford: Oxford University Press.

Kraemer, David. 2000. *The Meanings of Death in Rabbinic Judaism*. London: Routledge.

Krašovec, Jože. 1992. "The Source of Hope in the Book of Lamentations." *VT* 42.2: 223–33.

Kraus, Hans-Joachim. 1960. *Klagelieder (Threni)*. 2nd ed. BKAT 20. Neukirchen-Vluyn: Neukirchener Verlag.
Kraus, Hans-Joachim. 1983. *Klagelieder (Threni)*. 4th ed. BKAT 20. Neukirchen-Vluyn: Neukirchener Verlag.
Kraus, Hans-Joachim. 1989. *Psalms 60–150: A Commentary*. Minneapolis: Augsburg Fortress.
Kristeva, Julia. 1980. *Desire and Language: A Semiotic Approach to Literature and Art*. Edited by Leon S. Roudiez. Translated by Thomas Gora, Alice Jardine, and Leon S. Roudiez. Oxford: Blackwell. Translation of *Séméiotikè: recherches pour une sémanalyse*. Paris: Seuil, 1969.
Kristeva, Julia. 1982. *Powers of Horror: An Essay on Abjection*. Translated by Leon S. Roudiez. New York: Columbia University Press.
Kristeva, Julia. 1986. "Revolution in Poetic Language." Pages 89–136 in *The Kristeva Reader*. Edited by Toril Moi. Oxford: Blackwell.
Kristeva, Julia. 1989. "The Bounded Text." Pages 989–1005 in *The Critical Tradition: Classic Texts and Contemporary Trends*. Edited by David H. Richter. Boston: Bedford Books.
Krüger, Thomas. 2004. *Qoheleth: A Commentary*. Hermeneia. Minneapolis: Fortress.
Kugel, James. 2017. "'I am the Man': The Afterlife of a Biblical Verse in Second Temple Times." Pages 470–95 in *Jeremiah's Scriptures: Production, Reception, Interaction, and Transformation*. Edited by Hindy Najman and Konrad Schmid. JSJSup 173. Leiden: Brill.
Kühn, Peter. 1978. *Gottes Trauer und Klage in der rabbinischen Überlieferung (Talmud und Midrasch)*. AGJU 13. Leiden: Brill.
Kwon, JiSeong James. 2016a. *Scribal Culture and Intertextuality: Literary and Historical Relationships between Job and Deutero-Isaiah*. FAT 2.85. Tübingen: Mohr Siebeck.
Kwon, JiSeong James. 2016b. "Shared Ideas in Job and Deutero-Isaiah." *ZAW* 129: 39–53.
Kynes, Will. 2012. *My Psalm Has Turned into Weeping: Job's Dialogue with the Psalms*. BZAW 437. Berlin: de Gruyter.
Kynes, Will. 2013a. "Intertextuality: Method and Theory in Job and Psalm 119." Pages 201–13 in *Biblical Interpretation and Method: Essays in Honour of Professor John Barton*. Edited by Katharine J. Dell, and Paul M. Joyce. Oxford: Oxford University Press.
Kynes, Will. 2013b. "Job and Isaiah 40–55: Intertextualities in Dialogue." Pages 94–105 in Dell and Kynes 2013.
Kynes, Will. 2013c. "Lament Personified: Job in the Bedeutungsnetz of Psalm 22." Pages 34–48 in *Spiritual Complaint*. Edited by Miriam J. Bier, and Tim Bulkeley. Eugene, OR: Wipf & Stock.
Labahn, Antje. 2002. "Trauern als Bewältigung der Vergangenheit zur Gestaltung der Zukunft. Bemerkungen zur anthropologischen Theologie der Klagelieder." *VT* 52: 513–27.
Labahn, Antje. 2003. "Metaphor and Intertextuality. 'Daughter of Zion' as a Test Case." *SJOT* 17:49–67.
Labahn, Antje. 2005. "Bitterkeit und Asche—das Leiden Jeremias am Schicksal Jerusalems. Metaphern und Metaphernvariationen in Thr 3,1–21 LXX." Pages 147–83 in *Metaphor in the Hebrew Bible*. Edited by Pierre Van Hecke. BETL 187. Leuven: Peeters.
Labahn, Antje. 2006. "Fire from Above. Metaphors and Images of God's Actions in Lamentations 2.1-9." *JSOT* 31: 239–56.

Labahn, Antje. 2020. "God as a Gleaning Cook: A Conceptual Metaphor of Exodus in LamentationsLXX 2:20f." Pages 347–362 in *Network of Metaphors in the Hebrew Bible*. Edited by Danilo Verde and Antje Labahn. BETL 309. Leuven: Peeters.

Labahn, Antje, and Dieter Sänger. 2011. "Paraleipomenon I und II. Die Bücher der Chronik. Einleitung." Pages 1038–47 in *Septuaginta Deutsch. Erläuterungen und Kommentare zum griechischen Alten Testament, Band I Genesis bis Makkabäer*. Edited by Martin Karrer and Wolfgang Kraus. Stuttgart: Deutsche Bibelgesellschaft.

Lam, Joseph. 2016. *Patterns of Sin in the Hebrew Bible: Metaphor, Culture, and the Making of a Religious Concept*. Oxford: Oxford University Press.

Lambert, David A. 2015. "The Book of Job in Ritual Perspective." *JBL* 134: 557–75.

Lambert, David A. 2016. *How Repentance Became Biblical: Judaism, Christianity, and the Interpretation of Scripture*. Oxford: Oxford University Press.

Lanahan, William F. 1974. "The Speaking Voice in the Book of Lamentations." *JBL* 93: 41–9.

Lange, Armin, and Matthias Weigold, eds. 2011. *Biblical Quotations and Allusions in Second Temple Jewish Literature*. JAJSup 5. Göttingen: Vandenhoeck & Ruprecht.

Last Stone, Suzanne. 1996. "Justice, Mercy and Gender in Rabbinic Thought." *CSLL* 8.1: 139–77.

Lee, Nancy C. 2002. *The Singers of Lamentations: Cities under Siege, from Ur to Jerusalem to Sarajevo*. BibInt 60. Leiden: Brill.

Lee, Nancy C., and Carleen Mandolfo, eds. 2008. *Lamentations in Ancient and Contemporary Cultural Contexts*. SBLSymS. Atlanta: SBL Press.

Leoni, Tommaso. 2007. "'Against Caesar's wishes': Flavius Josephus as a Source for the Burning of the Temple." *JJS* 58: 39–51.

Levenson, Jon D. 1987. "The Sources of Torah: Psalm 119 and the Modes of Revelation in Second Temple Judaism." Pages 559–74 in *Ancient Israelite Religion: Essays in Honor of Frank Moore Cross*. Edited by Patrick D. Miller, Jr., Paul D. Hanson, and S. Dean McBride. Philadelphia: Fortress.

Levenson, Jon D. 1993. *The Hebrew Bible, the Old Testament, and Historical Criticism*. Louisville: Westminster John Knox.

Lévêque, Jean. 1970. *Job et son Dieu: essai d'exégèse et de théologie biblique*. 2 vols. EBib. Paris: Gabalda.

Levine, Baruch A. 2000. *Numbers 21–36: A New Translation with Introduction and Commentary*. AB 4B. New York: Doubleday.

Linafelt, Tod. 1995. "Surviving Lamentations" *HBT* 17:45–61.

Linafelt, Tod. 1998. "The Impossibility of Mourning: Lamentations After the Holocaust." Pages 279–89 in *God in the Fray: A Tribute to Walter Brueggemann*. Edited by Tod Linafelt and Timothy K. Beal. Minneapolis: Fortress.

Linafelt, Tod. 1999. "Ruth." Pages xiii–90 in *Ruth and Esther*. BO. Collegeville, MN: Liturgical Press.

Linafelt, Tod. 2000a. *Surviving Lamentations: Catastrophe, Lament, and Protest in the Afterlife of a Biblical Book*. Chicago: University of Chicago Press.

Linafelt, Tod. 2000b. "Zion's Cause: The Presentation of Pain in the Book of Lamentations." Pages 267–79 in *Strange Fire: Reading the Bible after the Holocaust*. Edited by Tod Linafelt. Washington Square: New York University Press.

Linafelt, Tod. 2001. "The Refusal of a Conclusion in the Book of Lamentations." *JBL* 120.2: 340–3.

Lindner, Helgo. 1972. *Die Geschichtsauffassung des Flavius Josephus im Bellum Judaicum: gleichzeitig ein Beitrag zur Quellenfrage*. Leiden: Brill.

Longman, Tremper, III. 2008. *Jeremiah, Lamentations*. NIBCOT. Peabody, MA: Hendrickson.
Louth, Andrew. 2003 [orig. 1991]. *The Wilderness of God*. London: DLT.
Love, Mark C. 1999. *The Evasive Text: Zechariah 1-8 and the Frustrated Reader*. Sheffield: Sheffield Academic.
Lundbom, Jack R. 2013. *Deuteronomy: A Commentary*. Grand Rapids: Eerdmans.
Lust, Johann, Erik Eynikel, and Katrin Hauspie. 2003. *Greek-English Lexicon of the Septuagint*. Rev. ed. Stuttgart: Deutsche Bibelgesellschaft.
Lyons, Michael A. 2013. "'I also could talk as you do' (Job 16:4): The Function of Intratextual Quotation and Allusion in Job." Pages 169–77 in Dell and Kynes 2013.
MacCormac, E. R. 1988. "Religiöse Metaphern: Linguistischer Ausdruck kognitiver Prozesse." Pages 149–75 in *Erinnern um Neues zu sagen: Die Bedeutung der Metapher für die religiöse Sprache*. Edited by J.-P. van Noppen. Frankfurt am Main: Athenäum.
Maier, Christl M. 2008a. "Body Space as Public Space: Jerusalem's Wounded Body in Lamentations." Pages 119–38 in *Constructions of Space II: The Biblical City and Other Imagined Spaces*. Edited by J. L. Berquist and C. V. Camp. LHBOTS 490. New York: T&T Clark.
Maier, Christl M. 2008b. *Daughter Zion, Mother Zion: Gender, Space and the Sacred in Ancient Israel*. Minneapolis: Fortress.
Maier, Christl M., and Rainer Hirsch-Luipold. 2009. "Threnoi. Die Klagelieder." Pages 1349–58 in *Septuaginta Deutsch: Das griechische Alte Testament in deutscher Übersetzung*. Edited by Wolfgang Kraus and Martin Karrer. Stuttgart: Deutsche Bibelgesellschaft.
Maier, Christl M., and Rainer Hirsch-Luipold. 2011. "Threnoi. Threni seu Lamentationes / Die Klagelieder." Pages 2827–41 in *Septuaginta Deutsch: Erläuterungen und Kommentare zum griechischen Alten Testament, Vol. 2: Psalmen bis Daniel*. Edited by Martin Karrer and Wolfgang Kraus. Stuttgart: Deutsche Bibelgesellschaft.
Mandel, Paul. 1997. *Midrash Lamentations Rabbati: Prolegomenon, and a Critical Edition to the Third Parasha*. 2 vols. PhD diss., Hebrew University Jerusalem.
Mandel, Paul. 2000. "Between Byzantium and Islam: The Transmission of a Jewish Book in the Byzantine and Early Islamic Periods." Pages 74–106 in *Transmitting Jewish Traditions: Orality, Textuality, and Cultural Diffusion*. Edited by Yaakov Elman and Israel Gershoni. New Haven: Yale University Press.
Mandolfo, Carleen R. 2007a. "A Generic Renegade: A Dialogic Reading of Job and Lament Psalms." Pages 45–63 in *Diachronic and Synchronic: Reading the Psalms in Real Time*. Edited by Joel S. Burnett, W. H. Bellinger, and W. Dennis Tucker. New York: T&T Clark.
Mandolfo, Carleen R. 2007b. *Daughter Zion Talks Back to the Prophets: A Dialogic Theology of the Book of Lamentations*. Atlanta: SBL Press.
Marmur, Michael. 2014. "Why Jews Quote." *Oral Tradition* 29.1: 5–46.
Mason, Steve. 2016a. *A History of the Jewish War, A.D. 66–74*. Cambridge: Cambridge University Press.
Mason, Steve. 2016b. "Josephus's *Judean War*." Pages 11–35 in *A Companion to Josephus*. Edited by Honora Howell Chapman and Zuleika Rodgers. Malden, MA: Wiley & Sons.
McCarthy, Brian Rice. 2000. "Brueggemann and Hanson on God in the Hebrew Scriptures." *JAAR* 68.3: 615–20.
McCarthy, Carmel. 1981. *The Tiqqune Sopherim and Other Theological Corrections in the Masoretic Text of the Old Testament*. OBO 36. Göttingen: Vandenhoeck & Ruprecht.
McDaniel, Thomas F. 1968. "Philological Studies in Lamentations." *Bib* 49:27–53

McKenzie, John L. 1968. *Second Isaiah*. AB 20. Garden City, NY: Doubleday.

Meek, Russell L. 2014. "Intertextuality, Inner-Biblical Exegesis, and Inner-Biblical Allusion: The Ethics of a Methodology." *Bib* 95.1: 280–91.

Melton, Brittany N. 2014. "Solomon, Wisdom, and Love: Intertextual Resonance Between Ecclesiastes and Song of Songs. Pages 130–41 in Dell and Kynes 2014.

Melton, Brittany N. 2018. *Where is God in the Megilloth? A Dialogue on the Ambiguity of Divine Presence and Absence*. OTS. Leiden: Brill.

Mensah, Michael Kodzo. 2016. *I Turned Back My Feet to Your Decrees (Psalm 119,59): Torah in the Fifth Book of the Psalter*. ÖBS 45. New York: Peter Lang.

Mettinger, Tryggve N. D. 1993. "Intertextuality: Allusion and Vertical Context Systems in Some Job Passages." Pages 257–80 in *Of Prophets' Visions and the Wisdom of Sages*. JSOTSup 162. Edited by Heather A. McKay and David J. A. Clines. Sheffield: JSOT Press.

Meyers, Carol. 1993a. "Gender Imagery in the Song of Songs." Pages 197–212 in *A Feminist Companion to The Song of Songs*. Edited by Athalya Brenner. Sheffield: JSOT Press.

Meyers, Carol. 1993b. "Returning Home: Ruth 1.8 and the Gendering of the Book of Ruth." Pages 85–114 in *A Feminist Companion to Ruth*. Edited by Athalya Brenner. Sheffield: Sheffield Academic Press.

Meyers, Carol L., and Eric M. Meyers. 1987. *Haggai, Zechariah 1-8: A New Translation with Introduction and Commentary*. AB 25B. Garden City, NY: Doubleday.

Middlemas, Jill A. 2004. "The Violent Storm in Lamentations." *JSOT* 29.1: 81–97.

Middlemas, Jill A. 2006. "Did Second Isaiah write Lamentations III?" *VT* 56: 505–25.

Middlemas, Jill A. 2012. "Speaking of Speaking: The Form of Zion's Suffering in Lamentations." Pages 51–2 in *Daughter Zion: Her Portrait, Her Response*. Edited by Mark Boda, Carol Dempsey, and LeAnn Snow Flesher. AIL 13. Atlanta: Society of Biblical Literature.

Milgrom, Jacob. 1990. *Numbers*. JPS. Philadelphia: Jewish Publication Society.

Milgrom, Jacob. 1991. *Leviticus 1–16. A New Translation with Introduction and Commentary*. AB 3. New York: Doubleday.

Milgrom, Jacob. 2000. *Leviticus 17–22. A New Translation with Introduction and Commentary*. AB 3A. New York: Doubleday.

Milik, J. T. 1962. "Lamentations (Premier Exemplaire)." Pages 174–7 in *Les "Petites Grottes" de Qumran: Exploration de la Falaise, Les Grottes 2Q, 3Q, 5Q, 6Q, 7Q à 10Q, Le Rouleau de Cuivre*. Edited by M. Baillet, J. T. Milik, and R. de Vaux. 2 vols. DJD 3. Oxford: Clarendon.

Miller, Charles W. 2001. "Reading Voices: Personification, Dialogism and the Reader of Lamentations 1." *BibInt* 9: 393–408.

Miller, Patrick D. 1982. *Sin and Judgment in the Prophets: A Stylistic and Theological Analysis*. Atlanta: Scholars Press.

Mills, Mary E. 2003. *Reading Ecclesiastes: A Literary and Cultural Exegesis*. Aldershot: Ashgate.

Mintz, Alan. 1982. "The Rhetoric of Lamentations and the Representation of Catastrophe." *Proof* 2.1: 1–17.

Mintz, Alan. 1984. *Ḥurban: Responses to Catastrophe in Hebrew Literature*. New York: Columbia University Press.

Mintz, Alan. 1996. *Hurban: Responses to Catastrophe in Hebrew Literature*. Syracuse, NY: Syracuse University Press.

Moberly, R. W. L. 2002. "How May We Speak of God? A Consideration of the Nature of Biblical Theology." *TynBul* 53.2: 177–202.
Moffitt, David. 2006. "Righteous Bloodshed, Matthew's Passion Narrative, and the Temple's Destruction: Lamentations as a Matthean Intertext." *JBL* 125: 299–320.
Momigliano, Arnaldo. 1987. *On Pagans, Jews, and Christians*. Middletown, CN: Wesleyan University Press.
Moor, Johannes C. de. 1998. *Intertextuality in Ugarit and Israel: Papers Read at the Tenth Joint Meeting of the Society for Old Testament Study and Het Oudtestamentisch Werkgezelschap in Nederland and België, Held at Oxford, 1997*. OtSt 40. Leiden: Brill.
Moore, Stephen D., and Yvonne Sherwood. 2011. *The Invention of the Biblical Scholar: A Critical Manifesto*. Minneapolis: Fortress.
Muilenburg, James. 1956. "Chapters 40–66: Introduction." Pages 5:381–773 in *IB*.
Muraoka, Takamitsu. 2009. *A Greek-English Lexicon of the Septuagint*. Leuven: Peeters.
Najman, Hindy. 2006. "Towards a Study of the Uses of the Concept of Wilderness in Ancient Judaism." *DSD* 13.1: 99–113.
Nelson, Richard D. 2002. *Deuteronomy*. Louisville: Westminster John Knox.
Neusner, Jacob. 1987. *Canon and Connection: Intertextuality in Judaism*. StJ. Lanham: University Press of America.
Neusner, Jacob. 1989a. *Lamentations Rabbah*. Vol. 1 of *The Midrash Compilations of the Sixth and Seventh Centuries: An Introduction to the Rhetorical, Logical, and Topical Program*. BJS 187. Atlanta: Scholars Press.
Neusner, Jacob. 1989b. *Lamentations Rabbah: An Analytical Translation*. BJS 193. Atlanta: Scholars Press.
Neusner, Jacob. 1994. *Introduction to Rabbinic Literature*. ABRL. New York: Doubleday.
Neusner, Jacob. 2003. *Rabbinic Narrative: A Documentary Perspective*. Vol. 3. BRLJ 16. Leiden: Brill.
Neusner, Jacob. 2007. *Isaiah in Talmud and Midrash: A Source Book Part B The Later Midrash-Compilations and the Bavli*. Lanham, MD: University Press of America.
Newsom, Carol. 1996. "Bakhtin, the Bible, and Dialogic Truth." *JR* 76: 290–306.
Nguyen, Kim Lan. 2013. *Chorus in the Dark*. Sheffield: Sheffield Phoenix.
Nicholson, Ernest. 2014. *Deuteronomy and the Judean Diaspora*. Oxford: Oxford University Press.
Nurmela, Risto. 1996. *Prophets in Dialogue: Inner-Biblical Allusions in Zechariah 1–8 and 9–14*. Åbo: Åbo Akademis.
O'Connor, Kathleen M. 1992. "Lamentations." Pages 178–82 in *WBC*.
O'Connor, Kathleen M. 2001. "The Book of Lamentations." Pages 1011–72 in *NIB*.
O'Connor, Kathleen M. 2002. *Lamentations and the Tears of the World*. Maryknoll, NY: Orbis Books.
O'Connor, Kathleen M. 2011. *Jeremiah: Pain and Promise*. Minneapolis: Fortress.
Olley, John W. 1999. "'Trust in the Lord': Hezekiah, Kings and Isaiah." *TynBul* 50: 59–77.
Olyan, Saul M. 2004. *Biblical Mourning: Ritual and Social Dimensions*. Oxford: Oxford University Press.
Owens, Pamela Jean. 1990. "Personification and Suffering in Lamentations 3." *ASB* 105.2: 75–90.
Pabst, H. 1978. "Eine Sammlung von Klagen in den Qumranfunden (4Q *179*)." Pages 137–49 in *Qumrân: Sa Piété, sa Théologie et son Milieu*. Edited by M. Delcor. BETL 46. Leuven: Leuven University Press.
Pardes, Ilana. 1992. *Countertraditions in the Bible: A Feminist Approach*. Cambridge: Harvard University Press.

Parry, Robin A. 2010. *Lamentations*. THOTC. Grand Rapids: Eerdmans.
Parry, Robin A. 2011a. "Lamentations and the Poetic Politics of Prayer." *TynBul* 62: 65–87.
Parry, Robin A. 2011b. "Wrestling with Lamentations in Christian Worship." Pages 175–97 in Parry and Thomas 2011.
Parry, Robin A., and Heath A. Thomas, eds. 2011. *Great Is Thy Faithfulness? Reading Lamentations as Sacred Scripture*. Eugene, OR: Pickwick.
Paschen, Wilfried. 1970. *Rein und Unrein: Untersuchung zur biblischen Wortgeschichte*. Munich: Kosel.
Petersen, David L. 1984. *Haggai and Zechariah 1–8: A Commentary*. OTL. London: Westminster.
Petitjean, Albert. 1969. *Les Oracles du Proto-Zacharie: Un programme de restauration pour la communauté juive après l'exil*. Paris: Gabalda; Leuven: Éditions Imprimerie Orientaliste.
Pham, Xuan Huong Thi. 1999. *Mourning in the Ancient Near East and the Hebrew Bible*. JSOTSup 302. Sheffield: Sheffield Academic Press.
Philip, Tarja S. 2006. *Menstruation and Childbirth in the Bible: Fertility and Impurity*. New York: Peter Lang.
Pietersma, Albert. 1995. "The Acrostic Poems of Lamentations in Greek Translation." Pages 183–201 in *VIII Congress of the International Organization for Septuagint and Cognate Studies Paris 1992*. Edited by Leonard Greenspoon and Olivier Munnich. SCS 41. Atlanta: SBL Press.
Plank, Karl A. 2008. "By the Waters of a Death Camp: An Intertextual Reading of Psalm 137." *L&T* 22.2: 180–94.
Pohlmann, Karl-Friedrich. 1978. *Studien zum Jeremiabuch*. FRLANT 118. Göttingen: Vandenhoeck & Ruprecht.
Porteous, Norman. 1961. "Jerusalem-Zion: The Growth of a Symbol." Pages 235–52 in *Verbannung und Heimkehr. Beiträge zur Geschichte und Theologie Israels im 6. und 5. Jahrhundert v. Chr. (FS Rudolph)*. Edited by A. Kuschke. Tübingen: Mohr Siebeck.
Price, Jonathan J. 1992. *Jerusalem Under Siege: The Collapse of the Jewish State, 66–70 C.E.* Leiden: Brill.
Provan, Iain W. 1991. *Lamentations*. NCB. Grand Rapids: Eerdmans.
Rah, Soong-Chan. 2015. *Prophetic Lament: A Call for Justice in Troubled Times*. Downers Grove, IL: InterVarsity Press.
Rainer, Albertz. 2003. *Israel in Exile: The History and Literature of the Sixth Century B.C.E.* Atlanta: SBL Press.
Rashkow, Ilona. 1993. "Ruth: The Discourse of Power and the Power of Discourse." Pages 26–41 in *A Feminist Companion to Ruth*. Edited by Athalya Brenner. Sheffield: Sheffield Academic.
Reimer, David J. 1993. "Good Grief? A Psychological Reading of Lamentations." *ZAW* 114: 542–59.
Renkema, Johan. 1998. *Lamentations*. HCOT. Leuven: Peeters.
Reynolds, Kent Aaron. 2010. *Torah As Teacher: The Exemplary Torah Student in Psalm 119*. VTSup 137. Leiden: Brill.
Ricoeur, Paul. 2000. *The Rule of Metaphor: Multi-disciplinary Studies of the Creation of Meaning in Language*. Translated by Robert Czerny. Buffalo: University of Toronto Press.
Roberts, Kathryn L. 2003. "Between Text & Sermon: Isa 49:14–18." *Int* 57: 58–60.

Rubenstein, Richard L., and John K. Roth. 2003. *Approaches to Auschwitz: The Holocaust and its Legacy*. Louisville: Westminster John Knox.

Rudolph, Wilhelm. 1962. *Das Buch Ruth, Das Hohe Lied, Die Klagelieder*. KAT 17. Gütersloh: Mohn.

Rüsen, Jörn. 1994. "Was ist Geschichtskultur? Überlegungen zu einer neuen Art, über Geschichte nachzudenken." Pages 211–34 in Rüsen, *Historische Orientierung: Über die Arbeit des Geschichtsbewußtseins, sich in der Zeit zurechtzufinden*. Köln: Böhlau.

Rüsen, Jörn. 2001. "Historisch trauern—Skizze einer Zumutung." Pages 63–84 in *Trauer und Geschichte*. Edited by B. Liebsch and J. Rüsen. BG 22. Köln: Böhlau.

Rüsen, Jörn. 2003. *Kann gestern besser werden? Zum Bedenken von Geschichte*. Berlin: Kulturverlag Kadmos.

Saebø, Magne. 1993. "Who is 'The Man' in Lamentations 3? A Fresh Approach to the Interpretation of the Book of Lamentations." Pages 294–306 in *Understanding Poets and Prophets: Essays in Honour of George Wishart Anderson*. JSOTSup 152. Edited by A. Graeme Auld. Sheffield: Sheffield Academic.

Sailhamer, John H. 1995. *Introduction to the Old Testament Theology: A Canonical Approach*. Grand Rapids: Zondervan.

Salters, Robert B. 2010. *Lamentations: A Critical and Exegetical Commentary*. ICC 45. London: T&T Clark.

Salters, Robert B. 2011. "Acrostics and Lamentations." Pages 425–40 in *On Stone and Scroll: Essays in Honour of Graham Ivor Davies*. Edited by James K. Aitken, Katharine J. Dell, and Brian A. Mastin. BZAW 420. Berlin: de Gruyter.

Sanders, James A. 2005. *Torah and Canon*. Philadelphia: Fortress, 1972. Repr. 2nd ed. Eugene, OR: Cascade.

Sarna, Nahum M. 1986. *Exploring Exodus: The Heritage of Biblical Israel*. New York: Schocken.

Saxegaard, Kristin Moen. 2010. *Character Complexity in the Book of Ruth*. FAT II 47. Tübingen: Mohr Siebeck.

Schipper, J. 2010. "Hezekiah, Manasseh, and Dynastic or Transgenerational Punishment." Pages 81–105, 189–94 in *Soundings in Kings: Perspectives and Methods in Contemporary Scholarship*. Edited by M. Leuchter and K. P. Adam. Minneapolis: Fortress Press.

Schmid, Konrad. 2007. "Innerbiblische Schriftdiskussion im Hiobbuch." Pages 241–61 in *Das Buch Hiob und seine Interpretationen: Beiträge zum Hiob-Symposium auf dem Monte Verità vom 14.–19. August 2005*. ATANT 88. Edited by Thomas Krüger et al. Zurich: TVZ.

Schreckenberg, Heinz. 1987. "The Works of Josephus and the Early Christian Church." Translated by H. Regensteiner. Pages 315–24 in *Josephus, Judaism, and Christianity*. Edited by Louis H. Feldman and Gōhei Hata. Detroit: Wayne State University Press.

Schroer, Silvia, and Thomas Staubli. 1998. *Körpersymbolik der Bibel*. Darmstadt: Wissenschaftliche Buchgesellschaft.

Schwartz, Daniel. 2016. "Many Sources but a Single Author: Josephus's Jewish Antiquities." Pages 36–58 in *A Companion to Josephus*. Edited by Honora Howell Chapman and Zuleika Rodgers. Malden, MA: Wiley & Sons.

Schwartz, Seth. 1990. *Josephus and Judaean Politics*. Leiden: Brill.

Scott, James M., ed. 1997. *Exile: Old Testament, Jewish and Christian Conceptions*. JSJSup 56. Leiden: Brill.

Searle, John R. 1995. *The Construction of Social Reality*. New York: Free Press.

Seidler, Victor Jeleniewski. 2011. "'Their Hearts Melted and Became as Water.' Lamentations: Ethics After Auschwitz." *EuroJ* 44.2: 91–105.
Seitz, Christopher R. 2001. "The Book of Isaiah 40–66." Pages 6:307–552 in *NIB*.
Seow, C.-L. 2013. *Job 1–21: Interpretation and Commentary*. Illuminations. Grand Rapids: Eerdmans.
Seybold, Klaus. 1974. "Die Bildmotive in den Visionen des Propheten Sacharja." Pages 92–110 in *Studies on Prophecy: A Collection of Twelve Papers*. Edited by G. W. Anderson et al. VTSup 26. Leiden: Brill.
Seybold, Klaus. 1977. *Die aaronitische Segen: Studien zu Numeri 6.22-27*. Neukirchen-Vluyn: Neukirchener Verlag.
Shafer-Elliott, Cynthia. 2013. *Food in Ancient Judah: Domestic Cooking in the Time of the Hebrew Bible*. Sheffield: Equinox.
Sharp, Carolyn J., ed. 2011. *Disruptive Grace: Reflections on God, Scripture and the Church*. Minneapolis: Fortress.
Shields, Mary E. 1998. "Body Rhetoric and Gender Characterization in Ezekiel 16." *JFSR* 14.1: 5–18.
Smith, Jonathan Z. 1990. *Drudgery Divine: On the Comparison of Early Christianities and the Religions of Late Antiquity*. London: School of Oriental and African Studies.
Smith-Christopher, David L. 2002. *A Biblical Theology of Exile*. OBT. Minneapolis: Fortress.
Smith Landsman, Irene. 2002. "Crises of Meaning in Trauma and Loss." Pages 13–30 in *Loss of the Assumptive World: A Theory of Traumatic Loss*. Edited by J. Kauffman. New York: Brunner-Routledge.
Sommer, Benjamin D. 1998. *A Prophet Reads Scripture: Allusion in Isaiah 40–66*. Stanford, CA: Stanford University Press.
Stead, Michael R. 2008. "Sustained Allusion in Zechariah 1–2." Pages 144–70 in *Tradition in Transition: Haggai and Zechariah 1–8 in the Trajectory of Hebrew Theology*. Edited by Mark J. Boda and Michael H. Floyd. LHBOTS 475. London: T&T Clark.
Stead, Michael R. 2009. *The Intertextuality of Zechariah 1–8*. New York: T&T Clark.
Stern, David. 1992. "Imitatio Hominis: Anthropomorphism and the Character(s) of God in Rabbinic Literature." *Proof* 12: 151–74.
Stern, David, and Mark J. Mirsky, eds. 1990. *Rabbinic Fantasies: Imaginative Narratives from Classical Hebrew Literature*. New Haven: Yale University Press.
Stevens, Wallace. 1982a. "The Plain Sense of Things." Pages 502–3 in *Wallace Stevens: The Collected Poems*. New York: Random House.
Stevens, Wallace. 1982b. 'The Snow Man." Page 10 in *Wallace Stevens: The Collected Poems*. New York: Random House.
Stevens, Wallace. 2009. "The Course of a Particular." Accessed 16 January 2017. https:www.bestamericanpoetry.com/the_best_american_poetry_/2009/01/the-course-of-a.html.
Stiebert, Johanna. 2003. "Human Suffering and Divine Abuse of Power in Lamentations: Reflections on Forgiveness in the Context of South Africa's Truth and Reconciliation Process." *Pacifica* 16: 195–215.
Stone, Timothy J. 2013. *The Compilational History of the Megilloth: Canon, Contoured Intertextuality and Meaning in the Writings*. FAT II 59. Tübingen: Mohr Siebeck.
Strack, H. L., and Gunter Stemberger. 1996. *Introduction to the Talmud and Midrash*. Translated and edited by Markus Bockmuehl. Minneapolis: Fortress.
Straub, Jürgen. 1998. *Erzählung, Identität und historisches Bewußtsein: Die psychologische Konstruktion von Zeit und Geschichte*. Frankfurt: Suhrkamp.

Strugnell, John. 1970. "Notes en marge du volume V des 'Discoveries in the Judaean Desert of Jordan.'" *RevQ* 26.7: 163–276.
Stulman, Louis. 2016. "Reflections on the Prose Sermons in the Book of Jeremiah: Duhm's and Mowinckel's Contributions to Contemporary Trauma Readings." Pages 123–39 in *Bible through the Lens of Trauma*. Edited by E. Boase and C. G. Frechette. Atlanta: SBL Press.
Sweeney, Marvin A. 2005. "King Manasseh of Judah and the Problem of Theodicy in the Deuteronomistic History." Pages 264–78 in *Good Kings and Bad Kings: The Kingdom of Judah in the Seventh Century BCE*. Edited by L. L. Grabbe. LHBOTS 437. London: T&T Clark.
Taylor, Charles. 1874. *The Dirge of Coheleth in Ecclesiastes Xii: Discussed and Literally Interpreted*. London: Williams & Norgate.
Thackeray, Henry St. J. 1928. *Josephus: The Jewish War, Books IV–VII*. LCL. Cambridge: Harvard University Press.
Thiel, Winfried. 1973. *Die deuteronomistische Redaktion von Jeremia 1–25*. WMANT 41. Neukirchen-Vluyn: Neukirchener Verlag.
Thiel, Winfried. 1981. *Die deuteronomistische Redaktion von Jeremia 26–45*. WMANT 46. Neukirchen-Vluyn: Neukirchener Verlag.
Thomas, Heath A. 2008. "The Liturgical Function of the Book of Lamentations." Pages 137–47 in *Thinking Towards New Horizons. Collected Communications to the XIXth Congress of the International Organization for the Study of the Old Testament: Ljubljana 2007*. Edited by Matthias Augustin and Hermann Michael Niemann. BEATAJ 55. Frankfurt am Main: Lang.
Thomas, Heath A. 2011. "Lamentations in the Patristic Period." Pages 113–19 in Parry and Thomas 2011.
Thomas, Heath A. 2013a. "A Survey of Research on Lamentations (2002–2012)." *CurBR* 12: 8–38.
Thomas, Heath A. 2013b. *Poetry and Theology in the Book of Lamentations: The Aesthetics of an Open Text*. HBM 47. Sheffield: Sheffield Phoenix Press.
Tiemeyer, Lena-Sofia. 2007. "Geography and Textual Allusions: Interpreting Isaiah xl–lv and Lamentations as Judahite Texts." *VT* 57: 367–85.
Timmer, Daniel C. 2007. "Small Lexemes, Large Semantics: Prepositions and Theology in the Golden Calf Episode (Exodus 32–34)." *Bib* 88.1: 92–9.
Tollington, Janet. 1993. *Tradition and Innovation in Haggai and Zechariah 1–8*. JSOTSup 150. Sheffield: JSOT Press.
Tombs, David. 2016. "Acknowledging Jesus as Victim of Sexual Abuse." Paper presented in a lecture at the University of Otago. Dunedin, New Zealand, July 20. https://mediastore.auckland.ac.nz/uploaded/project/CMS_ARTS/public/07-2016/8CC450E5BC7347AD90B4ED7FE51D607C.preview
Tooman, William A. 2011. *Gog of Magog: Reuse of Scripture and Compositional Technique in Ezekiel 38–39*. FAT II 52. Tübingen: Mohr Siebeck.
Tov, Emanuel. 1997. *Der Text der Hebräischen Bibel. Handbuch der Textkritik*. Stuttgart: Kohlhammer.
Tov, Emanuel. 2004. *Scribal Practices and Approaches Reflected in the Texts Found in the Judean Desert*. STDJ 54. Leiden: Brill.
Tov, Emanuel. 2012. *Textual Criticism of the Hebrew Bible*. 3rd ed. Minneapolis: Fortress.
Trible, Phyllis. 1978. *God and the Rhetoric of Sexuality*. OBT. London: SCM.
Tull Willey, Patricia K. 1997. *Remember the Former Things: The Recollection of Previous Texts in Second Isaiah*. SBLDS 161. Atlanta: Scholars Press.

Tull Willey, Patricia K. 1999. "Rhetorical Criticism and Intertextuality." Pages 156–80 in *To Each Its Own Meaning: Biblical Criticisms and Their Application*. Edited by S. L. McKenzie and S. R. Haynes. Louisville: Westminster John Knox.

Tull Willey, Patricia K. 2000. "Intertextuality and the Hebrew Scriptures." *CurBS* 8: 59–90.

Ueberschaer, Frank. 2012. "Die Septuaginta der Klagelieder: Überlegungen zu Entstehung und Textgeschichte." Pages 98–111 in *Die Septuaginta—Entstehung, Sprache, Geschichte: 3. Internationale Fachtagung veranstaltet von Septuaginta Deutsch (LXX.D), Wuppertal 22.–25. Juli 2010*. Edited by Siegfried Kreuzer and Martin Meiser. WUNT 286. Tübingen: Mohr Siebeck.

Ueberschaer, Frank. 2016. "Threnoi / Threni seu Lamentationes / Klagelieder." Pages 600–605 in *Einleitung in die Septuaginta. Handbuch zur Septuaginta / Handbook of the Septuagint 1*. Edited by Siegfried Kreuzer. Gütersloh: Gütersloher Verlagshaus.

Uehlinger, Christoph. 2013. "Klagelieder." Pages 614–26 in *Einleitung in das Alte Testament. Die Bücher der Hebräischen Bibel und die alttestamentlichen Schriften der katholischen, protestantischen und orthodoxen Kirchen*. Edited by Thomas Römer, Jean-Daniel Macchi, and Christophe Nihan. Zurich: TVZ.

Ulrich, Eugene. 2015. *The Dead Sea Scrolls and the Developmental Composition of the Bible*. VTSup 169. Leiden: Brill.

Van Dam, Cornelius. 2003. "Golden Calf." Pages 368–71 in *Dictionary of the Old Testament: Pentateuch*. Edited by T. Desmond Alexander and David W. Baker. Leicester: Inter-Varsity Press.

Van der Kooij, A. 2002. "The Textual Criticism of the Hebrew Bible before and after the Qumran Discoveries." Pages 167–77 in *The Bible as Book: The Hebrew Bible and the Judaean Desert Discoveries*. Edited by E. D. Herbert and E. Tov. London: British Library.

Van der Kooij, A. 2006. "Textual Criticism." Pages 579–90 in *The Oxford Handbook of Biblical Studies*. Edited by J. W. Rogerson and J. M. Lieu. Oxford: Oxford University Press.

Van Dijk-Hemmes, Fokkelien. 1993. "The Metaphorization of Woman in Prophetic Speech: An Analysis of Ezekiel XXIII." *VT* 43.2: 162–70.

Vermes, Geza. 2004. *The Complete Dead Sea Scrolls in English*. Rev. ed. London: Penguin Books.

Vice, Sue. 1997. *Introducing Bakhtin*. Manchester: Manchester University Press.

Weber, Beat. 2000. "Transitorische Ambiguität in Threni III." *VT* 50: 111–20.

Webster, Brian. 2002. "Chronological Index of the Texts from the Judaean Desert." Pages 351–446 in *The Texts from the Judaean Desert: Indices and an Introduction to the Discoveries in the Judaean Desert Series*. Edited by E. Tov. DJD 39. Oxford: Clarendon.

Weeks, Stuart. 2012. *Ecclesiastes and Scepticism*. LHBOTS 568. London: Bloomsbury.

Weiss, Dov. 2017. *Pious Irreverence: Confronting God in Rabbinic Judaism*. Philadelphia: University of Pennsylvania Press.

Westermann, Claus. 1990. *Klagelieder: Forschungsgeschichte und Auslegung*. Neukirchen-Vluyn: Neukirchener Verlag.

Westermann, Claus. 1994. *Lamentations: Issues and Interpretation*. Translated by Charles Muenchow. Minneapolis: Augsburg Fortress; Edinburgh: T. & T. Clark.

Whybray, Roger Norman. 1996. "City Life in Proverbs 1–9." Pages 243–50 in *"Jedes Ding hat seine Zeit..." Studien zur israelitischen und altorientalischen Weisheit, Diethelm Michel zum 65 Geburtstag*. Edited by A. A. Diesel, R. G. Lehmann, E. Otto, and A. Wagner. BZAW 241. Berlin: de Gruyter.
Wiesel, Elie. 1960. *Night*. London: MacGibbon & Kee.
Williamson, Jr., Robert. 2008. "Lament and the Arts of Resistance: Public and Hidden Transcripts in Lamentations 5." Pages 67–80 in Lee and Mandolfo 2008.
Williamson, Jr., Robert. 2015. "Taking Root in the Rubble: Trauma and Moral Subjectivity in the Book of Lamentations." *JSOT* 40.1: 7–23.
Wilson, Andrew. 2018. *Critical Entanglements: Postmodern Theory and Biblical Studies*. Leiden: Brill.
Wilson, Kelly M. 2012. "Daughter Zion Speaks in Auschwitz: A Post-Holocaust Reading of Lamentations." *JSOT* 37.1: 93–108.
Wischnowski, Marc. 2001. *Tochter Zion: Aufnahme und Überwindung der Stadtklage in den Prophetenschriften des Alten Testaments*. WMANT 89. Neukirchen-Vluyn: Neukirchener Verlag.
Wise, Michael O., Martin G. Abegg, and Edward M. Cook. 2005. *The Dead Sea Scrolls: A New Translation*. Rev. ed. San Francisco: HarperCollins.
Wolff, Hans Walter. 1984. *Anthropologie des Alten Testaments*. 4th ed. Munich: Kaiser.
Wright, Christopher J. H. 2015. "Lamentations." *IBMR* 39: 59–64.
Würthwein, Ernst, and Alexander A. Fischer. 2014. *The Text of the Old Testament: An Introduction to the Biblia Hebraica*. 3rd ed. Grand Rapids: Eerdmans.
Yee, Gale A. 2003. *Poor Banished Children of Eve: Women as Evil in the Hebrew Bible*. Minneapolis: Fortress.
Youngblood, Kevin J. 2004. "Translation Technique in the Greek Lamentations." PhD diss., The Southern Baptist Theological Seminary.
Youngblood, Kevin J. 2011. "The Character and Significance of LXX Lamentations." Pages 64–9 in Parry and Thomas 2011.
Zevit, Ziony. 2017. "Echoes of Texts Past." Pages 1–21 in *Subtle Citation, Allusion, and Translation in the Hebrew Bible*. Edited by Z. Zevit. Sheffield: Equinox.
Ziegler, Joseph. 1976. *Septuaginta. Vetus Testamentum Graecum: Auctoritate Academiae Scientiarum Gottingensis editum vol. XV Jeremias, Baruch, Threni, Epistula Jeremiae*. 2nd ed. Göttingen: Vandenhoeck & Ruprecht.
Zimmerli, Walther. 1979. *Ezekiel 1*. Hermeneia. Minneapolis: Fortress.

Index of References

Hebrew Bible/Old Testament

Genesis
1–2	121
1.2	121
1.17	285
1.31	121
2–3	192
2.7	121
3.24	130
4.10	117
6–8	110
12	147
12.7	20
12.10-20	110
14	47
14.6	47
15.5	20
16.7	47
19.23-25	30
20	110
21.14	47
21.20	47
21.21	47
26.6-11	110
36.24	47
37.22	47

Exodus
3.1	48
5.1	48
5.3	48
10.2	91
13.21-22	130
14.11-12	18
14.11	48
14.12	48
14.19-20	130
14.24	130
15.24	18
16.2-3	18
17.2-4	18
19	18
19.8	18
20.2-6	18
20.4	18
20.19	18
20.23	18
22.1	117
23.20	243
24.3	18
24.18–31.18	17
31	17
32–34	17, 19, 20, 25
32	17, 110
32.1	18
32.4-5	18
32.9-14	20
32.9-10	20
32.10	20
32.11-14	20
32.11	20
32.12	20
32.13	20
32.14	20
32.19	20
32.25-28	20
32.30-34	20
32.30	18, 20
32.31	18
32.32	18
32.33	18
32.34	18, 20
32.35	21
33.1-6	26, 27
33.1-3	26
33.2	21
33.3	21
33.4	26
33.5-6	26
33.7-11	26
33.12-17	20, 21
33.13	21
33.16	21
33.17	21
33.18-23	20, 21
33.20-23	21
34.5-10	20, 21, 25, 26
34.6-7	21, 28
34.6	63
34.7	18, 21, 28
34.9	18, 21
34.10-28	21

Leviticus
4.5-7	33
4.16-18	33
4.16	34
4.25	33
4.30	33
11–15	34
12	117
13	32
13.4-8	41
13.45-46	32
14.1-32	41
15	117
15.19-24	36, 117
16.14	33
16.16	33
16.19	33
17.13	117

18.25	34	19.10	117	*Ruth*	
18.28	34	20.18	61	1.6	200
18.29	34	21.1-9	83	1.8	199
20.9	117	22.5	61	1.13	197
20.22	34	23.16	61	1.20-21	197
		23.18 Eng.	61	2.2-3	197
Numbers		23.19	61	2.7	197
10	47	24.4	61	2.10-17	197
10.36	45	27.15	61	2.12	197
11.1	45, 52	28	56, 57, 64	3	197
13–14	51	28.13	64	3.1-4	197
13	47	28.22	64	3.7	197
13.25-33	53	28.28	232	3.9	197
14	48, 52, 53	28.30-33	64	4.11-12	197
14.2	48	28.32-67	57, 63	4.13	200
14.11	47, 51	28.37	64		
14.19	52	28.41	64	*1 Samuel*	
14.26-35	52	28.42	64	2.1-10	174, 203
14.28-35	47	28.44	64	6.8	126
14.35	47	28.47	64	16.1-17	203
14.39-45	51	28.50	64	20.20	177
14.40	48	28.52-57	64		
14.45	51	28.52	64	*2 Samuel*	
15.27-31	33	28.53-57	38	16.7	117
16.26	32	28.57	247	21.1	117
21	44	29.23	30	35.25	223
21.27-30	44	29.33-37	63		
		29.33-27	57	*1 Kings*	
Deuteronomy		30.1-10	65	5–6	183
2.9	44	30.1-5	57	8.1	76
4.25-31	65	30.2	65	8.15-21	73
4.26-27	57, 63	30.3	65	8.16	74
4.28-31	65	30.4-5	65	8.41-43	74
5.6-10	18	30.17-18	57, 63	9.1-9	74
5.23-24	130	32.10	130	11.26-40	74
7.25-26	61	32.16	61	11.36	74
12.5	74	32.35	149	14.25-29	78
12.11	74			15.4	74
12.13	74	*Joshua*			
12.31	61	10.20	126	*2 Kings*	
13.14 Eng.	61	19.29	126	3.19	126
13.15	61	19.35	126	6.17	130
17.1	61			6.28-29	78
17.3-4	61	*Judges*		6.28	247
18	228	9.15	148	8.19	74
18.12	61	19.25	37, 38, 91	10.2	126
19.8-13	83			12.17-18	78

2 Kings (cont.)		25.21	78	Job	
15.29	78	25.27-30	75, 80	2.10	105, 178
16.7-8	78			3.3	174
17.6	78	*1 Chronicles*		3.23	99, 105
17.9	126	15.29	234	4.18-19	178
18–19	77	28.1-10	128	5.4	178
18.1–20.19	76	28.4	128	5.8	178
18.8	126	28.5	128	5.16-18	106
18.13-16	78	28.6	128	5.16	178
19.20-34	76, 77	28.9	128	5.17	178, 179
19.21	75-7	28.10	128	5.18-27	178
19.22-28	76			5.18	178
19.31	75, 76	*2 Chronicles*		5.21	178, 179
19.34	76	17.19	126	5.27	179
21	127	31.21	234	6.4	174
21.1-16	82	35.19	234	7.11	235
21.7	74	35.20-27	256	7.17-18	171
21.10-15	74	35.25	173	8.2	178
21.13-14	82	36.12	223	8.3	106, 178, 180
21.13	127, 128	36.20	224		
21.16	83	36.21	223	8.20-21	178
23.24-27	83			9.2	176
23.26-27	74, 82	*Esther*		9.18	105, 175
23.26	83	1.20	196	9.34-35	174
23.29	256	2.7	196	10.1	235
23.32	82	2.9	196	10.16	104
23.37	82	2.15	196	11.2-3	178
24–25	5, 74, 78	2.16	196	11.13	179
24.2-4	82	2.17	196	11.15	179
24.2	78, 83	4.14	196	12.4	175
24.3	74	5.1	196	12.21	171
24.4	83	7.1	196	12.24	171
24.9	82	7.3-4	196	14.14	99
24.10-16	78	8.2	196	15.2-3	178
24.10-12	79	8.3	196	15.11-13	179
24.15	78, 79	8.5	196	15.14	176
24.19-20	82	8.7	196	16	171, 175, 177
25.1-7	50	9.13-14	196		
25.1-3	78	9.13	196	16.10	179
25.4-7	80	9.29-32	196	16.12-13	104, 177
25.4-5	50			16.19-21	177
25.5	80	*Ezra*		16.21	99
25.8-17	78	9	140	17.7	189
25.9	79			18.2	178
25.10	79	*Nehemiah*		18.5-6	176
25.13-21	81	9	140		

19	171, 175, 177	22	145, 146, 150, 151	74	148, 149, 181, 185, 187, 259
19.6-8	175	22.1-21 Eng.	146		
19.6	176, 180	22.2-22	146	74.1	143
19.7	176	22.22-31 Eng.	146	74.22	160
19.8	176	22.23-32	146	75	259
19.9	176	23	259	76	259
19.10-12	176	25	152	77	181
19.10	177	25.6	155	77.7	235
19.20	177	25.8	156	78	74
19.25	177	27.9	143	78.49	126
21.17	176	29	259	79	148, 149, 185
22.9	178	32	140		
22.23	179	32.16	156	79.6	144
22.26	179	34.9	99	80	148, 149, 185
25.4	176	37	152, 259		
28.28	34	37.23-25	165	86.15	144
30.29	49	38	140	87	259
33.19-30	178	38.2	126	88	149, 150
34.7	174	40.5	99	88.1-2	150
34.25	178	44	140, 142, 185	88.7 Eng.	143
34.36-37	179			88.8	143
35.9	176	44.17-22 Eng.	140	88.16-18	150
36.7-15	178	44.18-23	140	89	128, 143
37.11-13	178	46	130	89.20	128
37.23	178	48	130	89.39	128
42.7	181, 182	48.2 Eng.	148	89.46 Eng.	143
		48.3	148	89.47	143
Psalms		50.2	148	89.90	36
1.3	157	51	140	90	144
3.8	107	53	259	90.7-10	143
4	259	54.5	212	91.1	148
6	140, 142, 143	56.7 Eng.	144	93	259
		56.8	144	94.12	99
6.1 Eng.	142	59.13 Eng.	144	94.21	83
6.2	142	59.14	144	102	140
7.2	130	60	185	102.11	126
7.6 Eng.	144	68	259	103.15-17	110
7.7	144	69	259, 260	106.10	160
8.5	171	69.20	260	107.2	160
9–10	152	69.24 Eng.	144	107.40	171
9.5	108	69.25	144	108.11 MT	126
14	259	71	259	109.23	212
17.2	108	73	259	111	152
17.8	130			111.4	155
18	181			112	152

Psalms (cont.)		119.52	155	Ecclesiastes	
112.5	156	119.55	155	1.1	183, 184
119	7, 8, 152-7,	119.56	155	1.5-7	187
	159, 161-6,	119.57	156	12.1-7	8, 183-6,
	168	119.63	161, 168,		192
119.1-3	161		169	12.1	186, 192
119.1	154	119.64	156	12.2-7	186
119.3	154	119.65	156	12.2	187, 192
119.4	161	119.66	156	12.3	188, 189
119.5-8	161	119.67	167	12.4	188, 189
119.5	154	119.68	156, 162	12.5	190, 191
119.9	164, 167	119.71-72	156	12.6	188, 191,
119.53	216	119.71	156, 167		192
119.102	162	119.72	156	12.7	187
119.114	162	119.74	168		
119.12	162	119.75	167	Song of Songs	
119.120	159, 168	119.79	168	1.6	198
119.121-22	157	119.81	167	2.3–3.11	198
119.123	158	119.84	159	2.7	198
119.125	161	119.89-92	161	3.3	198
119.132	159	119.92	153, 166	3.4	198, 199
119.134	157	119.94	161	3.5	198
119.136	157, 159,	119.98-100	169	3.11	198
	165, 169	123.3-4	77	5.2-8	198
119.137	162	130	140	5.7	198
119.139	169	132	147	5.8-9	198
119.141	161, 169	132.11-18	148	5.10-16	198
119.145-46	158	137	281	6.1	198
119.145-160	167	137.7-9	78	6.9	198
119.149	158	143	140	7.10–8.7	198
119.150	159	145	152	8.1	198
119.151	159	145.7	155	8.2	198, 199
119.153	159	145.9	156	8.4	198
119.154	160			8.5	198
119.157	162	Proverbs			
119.158	159	1–9	188	Isaiah	
119.159	159	1.9	34	1.9	30
119.160	159	5.16	157	1.10-20	41
119.173	154	7.6	189	1.10	30
119.174	154, 162	9.10	34	2.9	190
119.176	154, 162	20.22	149	2.11	190
119.19	161	21.1	157	2.17	190
119.26	154	23.11	160	5.15	190
119.33	154	31.10-31	152	9.16	127
119.35	154	31.18	156	9.17 Eng.	127
119.49-50	167			10.25	126

13	127	50.4	107	8.18–9.1	102	
13.18	127	50.5	107	8.21	102	
13.19	30	50.6	106, 107,	8.23	102	
13.21	190		255	9.14	104	
14.1	127	50.8	107	9.16-20	115	
14.4	114	50.10	107	9.17	102	
14.12	114	51.3	128	9.19	185	
15	185	51.12	128	11.18–12.6	174	
16	185	51.17-23	91	11.19-21	226	
19.22	34	51.19	85	11.19	103, 226	
22.12	268, 276	52–53	108	11.20	103, 104	
22.24	102	52.12–53.5	255	12.1	226	
27.11	127	52.13–53.12	106, 108	13.14	127	
30.2-3	148	53.5	258	13.17	102	
30.22	117	54.10	127	13.22	37	
32.2	157	54.16	129	13.27	190	
32.14	190	55	92	14.17	102	
34.5-17	78	55.1-2	92	15.10	103, 226	
34.13	49	61.2	128	15.15	104, 226	
36–39	76	62.9	128	15.17	103, 226	
37.22	77	63	40	17.7	99	
38.10-20	174	63.1-6	39	17.15	226	
40–66	5	63.1	39	17.18	104	
40–55	128, 181	63.3-4	40	18.11	34	
40	88, 128	63.3	39, 40	18.18-20	226	
40.1-11	85	63.6	40	18.18	103	
40.1-2	134	64.5	117	18.20	232	
40.1	88, 128,	66.13	128	18.22	226, 232	
	181	a4.3	92	18.23	232	
40.6-8	110			20.7-9	226	
49	91	*Jeremiah*		20.7	101, 102,	
49.4	108	1	228		226	
49.13-26	89	1.18	126	20.9	226	
49.13	128	1.9	228	20.10	226	
49.14-26	90, 93	1.16	228	20.12	103, 104	
49.15	90, 93, 94,	2	48	20.14-18	109, 226	
	127	2.4-9	41	20.14-17	226	
49.21	93, 94	4.5	126	21.7	127	
49.22-23	95	4.28	125	23.9	228	
49.22	95, 96	5.14	126	23.14	30	
49.23	95	5.17	126	23.20	125	
49.26	95	6.7	37	25.10	188	
50–52	133	6.23	127	25.11	224	
50	104	6.25	191	26.1	228	
50.3	267, 276	7.1-15	228	26.7-24	31	
50.4-11	106, 108	8.11	102	27–28	103	

Index of References

Jeremiah (cont.)

Ref	Pages
28.10-11	103
29.1	225
29.4	225
29.10	224
30.12	38
30.15	38
30.24	125
31	127
31.29	67, 186
31.31-34	141
31.38-39	127
31.39	127
34.7	126
36.1	225
38	104
38.1-13	103
43.4	223
43.5-7	225
43.10	223
43.27	223
43.32	223
44	225
44.1	225
46.13	225
49.18	30
49.31	103
50.34	160
50.39	190
50.40	30
50.42	127
51 Eng.	225
51.12	125
51.31	223
52.6	246
52.11	80
52.12	249

Lamentations

Ref	Pages
1–5	222
1–4	152
1–2	6, 53, 97, 99, 100, 123-5, 128, 131-3, 135, 231, 254
1	4, 6, 19, 26, 29, 30, 37, 62, 87, 90, 97, 113, 114, 116, 117, 120-2, 139, 142, 198, 199, 210, 213, 264
1.1-18	208
1.1-11	22, 87
1.1-5	99, 259
1.1-2	272, 285
1.1	23, 29, 75, 95, 103, 104, 114, 190, 198, 210, 222, 223, 227, 245, 267-70, 272-4, 285
1.2	23, 53, 62, 87, 116, 128, 198, 210, 260, 272, 274
1.3	23, 78, 234, 286
1.4	31, 36, 116, 191, 254
1.5	18, 19, 22-4, 29-31, 56, 62, 64, 114, 139, 198, 229, 234, 260
1.6-9	259
1.6	23, 227, 270
1.7	23, 79, 119, 208, 234, 272, 286
1.8-9	23, 117
1.8	18, 23, 31, 56, 62, 116, 139, 229, 234, 260, 274
1.9	18, 23, 32, 36, 37, 56, 62, 65, 81, 87, 112, 128, 133, 198, 234, 260, 274
1.10-14	259
1.10-12	208
1.10	23, 75, 78, 79, 81, 119, 245, 250, 254, 264, 274, 286
1.11-21	87
1.11-16	62
1.11	23, 24, 62, 65, 92, 116, 119, 133, 208, 286
1.12-16	118
1.12-15	22, 26, 198
1.12	22-5, 38, 62, 65, 83, 147, 229, 234, 286
1.13	22, 79, 208, 226, 229
1.14	18, 19, 22, 56, 62, 79, 139, 179, 229, 260
1.15	22, 23, 75, 227, 252
1.16-17	134
1.16	24, 26, 62, 87, 99, 115, 119, 128, 274

1.17	22, 26, 36, 37, 62, 75, 87, 118, 128, 274		75, 83, 114, 126, 129	2.11-12 2.11	23, 24, 199 24, 75, 102, 115, 116, 184, 286
1.18-22	62	2.2-4	130, 131, 134, 135, 227, 254	2.12-15	259
1.18	18, 19, 23, 24, 26, 31, 37, 56, 62, 64, 79, 81, 107, 229	2.2	22-24, 36, 37, 62, 75, 126, 127, 131	2.12 2.13	24, 92, 184, 286 23, 25, 37, 38, 75, 126, 128, 227
1.19	23, 24, 26, 31, 92, 116	2.3	22, 37, 62, 77, 79, 129, 130, 134, 135, 229, 249	2.14	18, 19, 31, 56, 62, 63, 84, 132, 229, 263
1.20-22	18				
1.20	18, 19, 23, 26, 56, 62, 65, 87, 107, 133, 229	2.4	22, 23, 62, 119, 126, 130, 227	2.15-17 2.15-16	23 77
1.21-22	19	2.5-9	81	2.15	23, 75, 77, 116, 126, 253, 254, 264, 286
1.21	23, 26, 62, 83, 87, 116, 128, 134, 198, 274	2.5-7 2.5 2.6-7	36 22, 23, 37, 198, 208 22, 62, 75, 245, 254	2.17	22, 24, 37, 38, 62, 83, 125-7, 129, 134, 135, 163, 229, 267, 273, 277
1.22	18, 24, 26, 31, 38, 56, 62, 81, 116, 229	2.6 2.7-12	22, 31, 37, 62, 75, 81, 126, 132-4 184		
2	4, 6, 19, 30, 36, 37, 87, 90, 91, 97, 113, 114, 116, 117, 120-3, 125-35, 142, 147, 157, 198, 199, 249, 264	2.7-9 2.7 2.8-11 2.8-9 2.8	130 33, 36, 75, 116, 128 259 22, 130 22, 23, 62, 75, 79, 82, 126-8, 130, 134, 135, 227	2.18 2.19-22 2.19-20 2.19 2.20-22	23, 75, 79, 116, 126, 283 24 23, 24, 78 38, 91, 92, 184, 286 62, 115, 142
2.1-10	62	2.9-12	19	2.20	23, 24, 31, 37-9, 51, 64, 65, 75, 79, 81, 87, 91, 93, 94, 96, 133, 147, 198, 199, 286
2.1-9	22, 64, 198	2.9	22, 31, 75, 78-80, 132, 163		
2.1-8	19, 37, 63				
2.1-6	142, 229	2.10-11	131, 134, 135		
2.1-4	22, 87				
2.1-3	75	2.10	23, 75, 126, 129, 227, 272		
2.1	22, 23, 29, 35-7, 62,			2.21-22	83

Lamentations (cont.)		3.5	99	3.22	25, 26, 51, 98, 100, 156
2.21	22, 24, 37, 39, 62, 127, 134, 142, 164, 229, 286	3.6-9	175		
		3.6	232		
		3.7-9	176	3.23	27, 98, 107
		3.7	99, 105, 176	3.24	98, 100, 156
2.22	37, 39, 62, 92, 198, 229	3.8	23, 176	3.25-41	178
		3.9	99, 105, 176	3.25-39	97-100, 105, 109, 172, 255
3–5	133	3.10-13	99		
3	4, 6-8, 19, 24, 26, 51, 52, 63, 64, 80, 97-9, 101, 103-106, 108, 109, 133, 144, 146, 147, 150-3, 155-8, 161, 162-7, 170-82, 185, 202, 231, 249, 256, 260-2 280	3.10	22, 100, 104	3.25-30	63, 106, 108
		3.11-13	177	3.25-27	106, 156
		3.11	22, 99, 154	3.25-26	109
		3.12-13	22, 174	3.25	27, 100, 156, 178, 238
		3.12	104		
		3.14	101, 175		
		3.15	57, 100, 104, 105, 175, 233, 234, 252	3.26-27	179
				3.26	27, 167, 178
				3.27-28	103, 178
		3.16	22, 99	3.27	100, 162, 165, 167, 179
		3.17-21	99		
		3.18-19	100		
		3.18	80, 100, 155, 177	3.28-30	255
3.1-33				3.28	268, 269, 273, 277
3.1-24	97-101	3.19-21	166, 167, 230, 231, 233, 235		
3.1-21	98, 104, 106, 231			3.29	178
				3.30	106, 107, 178, 179, 255
3.1-20	31, 99, 100	3.19	98, 104, 155, 233, 234		
3.1-19	6				
3.1-18	22, 25, 62, 172, 178			3.31-33	63, 169, 230
		3.20	98, 234		
3.1-16	27	3.21-39	62	3.31-32	178
3.1-9	259	3.21-24	177	3.31	27, 178
3.1-3	232, 231	3.21	98, 155, 166, 238	3.32-34	234
3.1	9, 26, 97, 99, 153, 162, 164, 165, 171, 173, 174, 228, 231-3			3.32-33	31
		3.22-42	180	3.32	25, 27, 30, 63, 238
		3.22-39	56, 62		
		3.22-30	259	3.33-36	106
		3.22-26	162, 230	3.33	30, 144, 178, 281
		3.22-24	98, 106, 146, 167, 230, 233		
3.2-7	80			3.34-39	62
3.2	99, 107, 232			3.34-36	153, 168
		3.22-23	63	3.34	178
3.3	232			3.35-36	178, 180
3.4	22, 99				

3.35	159, 162, 163	3.55-62	145	4.4	78, 92, 95, 96
3.36	23	3.55-60	167	4.5	184, 210, 248
3.37-38	145, 178	3.55	87, 99, 158, 162, 238	4.6	18, 19, 25, 30, 56, 62, 75, 133, 199, 229, 248
3.38	63, 105				
3.39-40	52	3.56	23, 27, 107, 158, 238		
3.39	18, 19, 45, 52, 56, 63, 100, 145, 162, 179				
		3.57-59	107, 108		
		3.57	40, 87, 88, 158, 168, 238	4.7-9	30
3.40-47	97-100, 109, 172			4.9-10	23, 24, 78
				4.9	24, 92
3.40-46	158	3.58	87, 103, 159, 238	4.10	24, 30, 64, 75, 93, 94, 96, 102, 133, 199, 248, 286
3.40-42	80				
3.40-41	179	3.59-60	23		
3.40	51, 145, 162, 168, 179, 249	3.59	87, 159, 162, 163		
		3.60-63	27, 100	4.11-16	30, 31
3.41	179	3.60	103, 159	4.11	31, 79, 198, 229
3.42	18, 19, 25, 27, 56, 62, 81, 107, 162, 229	3.61	87, 103, 162		
				4.12-13	83
		3.63	23, 161	4.13-16	31
		3.64-66	100, 104	4.13-15	33, 39
3.43-45	27	3.64	18, 19, 56, 62, 162	4.13-14	40
3.43-44	62, 146			4.13	18, 19, 31, 32, 39, 56, 62, 83, 253
3.43	22, 24, 25, 229, 285	3.66	162		
		4–5	97, 231		
3.44	23, 105	4	4, 19, 30, 42, 50, 91, 92, 97, 133, 147, 148, 157, 208, 210, 213, 248, 249, 285	4.14-15	23
3.45	252			4.14	32, 39, 40, 184
3.48-66	97-100, 106			4.15	32, 37, 40
3.48	75, 100, 102, 157-9, 165, 199			4.16	33, 229
				4.17	133
				4.18	184
3.49-66	101, 108			4.19	50, 80, 156
3.49-51	169	4.1-10	30	4.20	9, 75, 79-81, 148, 255-8
3.49-50	23	4.1-6	259		
3.49	158	4.1-5	30		
3.50	65, 162, 238	4.1	29, 31, 114, 184, 227	4.21-22	62, 75, 78, 258
3.51	199			4.21	148, 199, 258
3.52-61	158	4.2	210, 227		
3.52-53	27, 100	4.3-5	23, 24	4.22	18, 19, 56, 75, 199, 227, 229, 230
3.53-62	208	4.3-4	24, 93, 94		
3.53-55	103	4.3	49, 75, 93-5, 199, 210, 245		
3.53	9, 129, 255				
3.55-63	80				

Lamentations (cont.)	5.19	65, 87, 229	24.18	119
5	8, 19, 50, 65, 97, 133, 147, 149, 150, 183, 185, 188, 192, 208, 213-15, 217, 218, 285	5.20-22	23, 63, 65, 280, 284	24.21	119, 131
		5.20	27, 186	24.23	119
		5.21-22	149	24.24	119
		5.21	27, 45, 87, 132, 149	24.25	131
				24.26-27	113, 120, 122
		5.22	27, 42, 52, 132, 149, 185, 222, 229, 284, 285	26.17	114
				33.26	35
				36	120
5.1-11	259			36.17	117, 120
5.1	23, 65, 87, 149, 185, 186, 213-15			37	120-2
				37.3	121
		Ezekiel		37.4	121
		3.26	116	37.7	121
5.2-18	215	4.1-7	116	37.9	121
5.2	64, 186, 213, 214	8–10	118	37.10	121
		8.6	36	37.11	121
5.3	23, 199	8.9	36	38.11	129
5.4	92	8.13	36	39.25	127
5.5	23	8.15	36	40–42	127
5.7	18, 19, 27, 56, 62, 67, 82, 83, 132, 229	8.17	36	40	127
		9.9	117	40.3	127
		16	112		
		16.38	112	*Daniel*	
5.8	23	18.2	67, 186	7.9	267, 276
5.9-10	64	18.21	34	9	140
5.9	50, 92	19	6, 113-17, 119-2	11.15	126
5.10	23, 24, 92, 213, 216, 217	19.4-5	114	*Hosea*	
		19.7	116	1–2	126
5.11	23, 183, 199, 234	19.9	116	1.6	127
		19.14	115	1.7	127
5.12	64, 191	21.31 Eng.	129	1.8	127
5.13	23, 188	21.36	129	2.3	127
5.14	190	22.2	35	2.6	127
5.15	186, 189-91	22.26	37	2.21	127
		22.31	126	2.25	127
5.16	18, 19, 27, 56, 62, 81, 176, 185, 229, 256	23	112	14.1	260
		23.36	35		
		24	6, 113, 116-19, 121, 122	*Joel*	
				3.19	253
5.17	186, 189			4.15	267, 276
5.18	75, 190, 224	24.1-14	118		
		24.13	117	*Amos*	
5.19-22	62, 65, 192	24.14	118	4.11	30
5.19-20	246	24.16	119, 131	5.8	187

5.16-17	187	2.4	129	24	253
5.16	185	2.8-9	129, 130	26.61	254
5.18	187	2.9	129, 130, 134, 135	27.19	253
5.20	187			27.24	253
5.21-27	41	2.10 Eng.	126	27.25	253
		2.12	130, 131, 134, 135	27.39-40	254
				27.40	254

Micah
1.8	49
3.11	41
4.14	107
7.9	108

2.13	131
2.14	126
4.2	191
6.9-15	132
8.1-5	131

Mark
15.29-30	253

Nahum
1.2-8	152
1.3	267, 276

8.4-5	134, 135
8.14-15	125, 126
9.9	126

Luke
1.46-55	203
19.41-44	263
19.41	263
23.27-31	263
24.25-27	252

Habakkuk
1.2	176

Malachi
1.2-5	78

John
1.14	253
2.19-21	265
2.19	254
2.21-22	254
4.24	257

Zephaniah
2.9	30
3.4	37

Tobit
1.4	203
1.12	203
1.13	203
2.2	203
3.7	203
3.16	203
5	203
6	203
12.15	203

Acts
8.23	252
12.3	187

Zechariah
1–8	132
1–2	6, 124, 131-4
1	128
1.2	132
1.3	133
1.4	132
1.6	125, 126, 134
1.12	126, 127, 133, 134, 224
1.14	126
1.15	132
1.16	127, 128, 134, 135
1.17	126, 128, 134
1.20-21 Eng.	129
2.1-4 MT	134, 135
2.3-4	129
2.3	129
2.4-5 Eng.	129

Romans
1.14	246
11	258

Ecclesiasticus
1.16	34
19.20	34
21.11	35
23.27	35
51.13-30	152

1 Corinthians
2.11	262
2.13	262
3.1-18	262
3.16-17	265
3.21-24	262
4.13	252
15.12-22	261
15.24-28	261

Baruch
1.3	223
2.2	247

NEW TESTAMENT
Matthew
5.38-39	255
11.9	243
23.35	253
23.37-39	253

2 Corinthians
6.16	265

Galatians		lines 2-3	212, 214, 215	7.148-49	250
4.25	258			7.161-62	250
		line 2	212	7.348	250
Ephesians		lines 4-5	215		
2.21	265	line 4	212, 215	CLASSICAL SOURCES	
		line 5	212-14, 217	Ambrose	
Hebrews				*Holy Spirit*	
4.1-11	46	line 6	212, 213, 215, 216	I.105	257
4.15	143				
		line 7	212	*On the Mysteries*	
Revelation		line 8	212	58	257
14.20	252	line 9	212		
19.15	252			Aphrahat	
		JOSEPHUS		*Select Demonstrations*	
MISHNAH		*Antiquities*		9	257
B. Bat.		10.79	244		
15a	245			Augustine	
		War		*Cat Lect*	
MIDRASH		1.1-30	247	7	258
Lamentations Rabbah		1.1	248		
Proem 24	269, 270, 275	1.3	246	*City*	
		1.11-12	245, 250	33	257
I. I, ss 1	267, 269-71, 273-7	5	245		
		5.19	245	*Reply to Faustus*	
III, 28-30 ss9	269	5.20	245	19.28	255
3.1	174	6	245, 249		
36.2	86	7	250	Basil	
		1.152	250	*On Spirit*	
TARGUMS		3.400	243	19.48	257
Targum Lamentations		3.402	243		
1	53	4.412-13	248	Cyril	
1.2	53	4.626	244	*Catechetical Lectures*	
2.20	39	5.184-237	245	34	257
		5.362-419	244		
QUMRAN		5.376-419	244, 247	Eusebius	
4Q179		5.392-93	244	*History of the Church*	
I ii 4	210	5.562	248	3.5-7	243
I ii 7	210	6.199-200	246		
I ii 9	210	6.208-11	248	Gregory of Nyssa	
I ii 10	210	6.217	249	*Against Eunomius*	
II 4	210	6.250	249	11.14	257
II 9	210	6.251	249		
		6.253	250	Hesiod	
4Q501		6.254	250	*Work and Days*	
lines 1-2	215	6.260	250	238-47	29
line 1	212-14, 217	6.266	250		
		6.267	250		

Homer
Iliad
1.50-52   29

Irenaeus
Demonstration of Apostolic Preaching
68   255

Justin
1 Apology
55   257

Rufinus
Commentary on the Apostles' Creed
19   257
27   256

Tertullian
Against Marcion
III   257

Index of Authors

Abegg, M. G. 210
Adorno, T. W. 150
Aitken, J. K. 170, 174, 175, 178, 181
Albertz, R. 228
Albrektson, B. 35, 56, 172, 221
Alexander, P. S. 268
Alkier, S. 11, 12
Allegro, J. M. 210
Allen, L. C. 149, 152, 220
Anderson, A. A. 273, 274
Archer, J. 227
Assmann, J. 65, 236
Avnery, O. 197

Baillet, M. 212, 216
Bakhtin, M. M. 2, 59, 64, 194
Balentine, S. E. 34, 35
Barbour, J. 184-86, 188-90, 192
Barstad, H. M. 224
Barthélemy, D. 131
Barton, J. 10, 11, 209
Bauernfeind, O. 246
Beal, T. K. 46
Begg, C. T. 245
Berges, U. 32, 35, 37, 100, 101, 109, 217, 219, 223, 227, 229, 232, 234, 240
Berlin, A. 286
Berlin, A. 7, 32, 33, 35, 39, 49, 50, 56-58, 86, 88, 92, 93, 96-98, 100, 104, 111, 118, 144, 170, 172-74, 178-80, 209, 210, 216, 219, 231, 232, 235-more-
Bernstein, M. J. 210
Bezzel, H. 97, 98, 104, 173, 226
Bier, M. J. 35, 59, 98, 141, 144, 163, 172, 181, 234
Blocher, H. 95
Boase, E. 18, 19, 56, 59-63, 83, 86, 87, 97, 100, 105, 141, 144, 150, 172, 229, 237
Boda, M. J. 75, 140

Bonhoeffer, D. 164
Borowski, O. 216
Bosworth, D. A. 24
Bouzard, W. C. 146, 178, 181
Boyarin, D. 11, 266, 276
Brady, C. M. M. 39, 53
Braitherman, Z. 10, 279
Brandscheidt, R. 174, 178, 179, 182, 229, 232
Brenner, A. 195, 198
Brenner-Idan, A. 198
Briggs, R. S. 44
Brooke, G. J. 207, 209
Brueggemann, W. 280
Buber, S. 166

Cameron-Mowat, A. 259
Carr, D. M. 1, 209
Carroll, R. P. 225
Cassiodorus 140
Chapman, H. H. 248, 250
Claassens, L. J. M. 115
Clines, D. J. A. 175, 176
Cohen, A. 11, 243, 244, 268, 270, 274, 275
Cook, E. M. 210
Cooper, A. 169
Creach, J. D. 168
Crenshaw, J. L. 35, 184, 200
Cross, F. M. 208

D'Elia, U. R. 54
Daube, D. 244
Davies, P. R. 207
Davila, J. R. 209, 216
Davis, D. R. 20, 21, 198
Day, P. L. 111
Deist, F. E. 217
Delkurt, H. 128, 129
Dell, K. J. 3, 181, 184, 185, 187, 188

Dempsey, C. J. 75
Derrida, J. 124
Dobbs-Allsopp, F. W. 17, 21-25, 35, 37, 38, 44, 58, 59, 62, 86-88, 91, 92, 100, 141, 142, 149, 172-74, 177-79
Driver, G. R. 217
Durham, J. I. 18

Enns, P. 18, 20, 21
Epstein, B. 166
Evans, P. S. 77
Exum, J. C. 197
Eynikel, E. 234

Feinstein, E. L. 33, 36
Feldman, E. 273-75
Fischer, A. A. 207
Fishbane, M. 3, 164, 207
Fitzmyer, J. A. 211
Flesher, L. S. 75
Fox, M. V. 184, 186-92
Frechette, C. G. 60
Frevel, C. 43, 217
Friedman, R. E. 201
Fuller, R. 131

Galvin, G. 197-200
Gane, R. 34
Garber, D. G. 111, 113, 115, 118
García Martínez, F. 210, 216
Garrett, D. A. 124
Gerstenberger, E. 219, 258
Gilbert, M. 184, 186, 187
Gitay, Y. 225, 235
Gladson, J. A. 168, 200, 202, 283
Gnuse, R. K. 244
Goppelt, L. 244
Gordis, R. 173, 174, 178
Gossai, H. 287
Gottlieb, H. 62, 80, 221
Gottwald, N. K. 19, 44, 56, 181
Gowan, D. E. 181
Grabbe, L. L. 224
Grant, C. A. 164, 183
Gray, R. 244
Green, B. 194, 195
Greenberg, M. 114
Greenstein, E. L. 20, 23, 24
Gruber, M. I. 199
Grudem, W. 2023

Häfner, G. 228
Halpern, B. 73
Handelman, S. A. 3, 266
Hanhart, C. 129
Hardmeier, C. 228
Harris, B. 87
Hauspie, K. 234
Hawk, L. D. 197
Hays, C. B. 209
Hays, R. B. 3
Heffelfinger, K. M. 88-90, 95, 96
Hendel, R. S. 207
Henze, M. 207
Herman, J. 59, 60, 114
Heschel, A. 289
Hillers, D. R. 17, 32, 35, 92, 93, 100, 155, 172, 173, 175, 217
Hinds, S. 165, 166
Hirsch-Luipold, R. 221, 223, 233
Høgenhaven, J. 210
Holladay, W. 37
Holquist, M. 194
Hope, V. M. 250
Horgan, M. P. 209, 210
Houck-Loomis, T. 280, 282, 284
House, P. R. 56, 124, 217
Houtman, C. 17, 18
Hubmann, F. D. 226

Inolowcki, S. 251

Jacobs, J. 242
Janoff-Bulman, R. 60
Janowski, B. 234
Janzen, D. 59, 61, 64, 67, 75
Jeremias, C. 129, 130
Jonker, L. C. 223
Joüon, P. 157, 158
Joyce, P. M. 45, 57, 66, 69, 111, 249, 259

Kaiser, B. B. 39, 87
Kartveit, M. 75
Kast, V. 227
Kauffman, J. 60
Kellner, M. 45
Kelly, J. R. 211
King, P. D. 212
King, P. J. 216
Klawans, J. 33, 36
Knoppers, G. 73

Körting, C. 210
Koenen, K. 98, 100, 107, 217, 233
Kosmala, H. 99, 165
Kotzé, G. R. 208, 215-17, 221, 229, 233
Kraemer, D. 269, 273
Krašovec, J. 280
Kraus, H.-J. 152, 217, 219
Kristeva, J. 2, 3, 118
Krüger, T. 184
Kühn, P. 269, 274
Kugel, J. 163
Kwon, J. J. 1, 171, 176
Kynes, W. 3, 171, 173, 176, 177, 179, 180, 184, 185

Labahn, A. 104, 142, 220, 221, 226-29, 231, 234
Lam, J. 32
Lambert, D. A. 35, 180-82
Lanahan, W. F. 23, 87, 196
Lange, A. 209, 211
Last Stone, S. 269
Léveque, J. 175, 177, 182
Lee, N. C. 178, 186, 262
Lemaire, A. 73
Leoni, T. 249
Levenson, J. D. 46, 165
Levine, B. A. 45
Linafelt, T. 22, 26, 37, 38, 53, 85-91, 94, 96, 97, 111, 112, 118, 120, 147, 150, 200, 269, 288
Lindner, H. 244
Lipton, D. 45, 57, 66, 69, 249, 259
Liss, K. 234
Longman, T., III 229, 234
Louth, A. 47
Love, M. C. 128, 132
Lundbom, J. R. 58, 61
Lust, J. 234
Lyons, M. A. 171

MacCormac, E. R. 235
Maier, C. M. 99, 111, 221, 223, 233
Mandel, P. 268
Mandolfo, C. 39, 59, 87, 110, 112, 118, 120, 180, 181, 194, 198, 269, 276
Marmur, M. 266
Mason, S. 248
McCarthy, B. R. 281

McCarthy, C.
McDaniel, T. F. 35
McKenzie, J. L. 86
Meek, R. L. 209
Melton, B. N. 40, 194, 195, 199, 202, 271, 280
Mensah, M. K. 164
Mettinger, T. N. D. 175, 176, 182
Meyers, C. 129, 198, 199, 202
Meyers, E. M. 129
Michel, O. 246
Middlemas, J. A. 97, 98, 106, 108, 109, 163, 164, 194, 195
Milgrom, J. 33, 34, 36, 44
Milik, J. T. 213
Miller, C. W. 59
Miller, P. D. 276
Mills, M. E. 183, 192
Mintz, A. 20, 23, 24, 56, 88, 267, 269, 270, 276, 286
Mirsky, M. J. 271
Moberly, R. W. L. 17, 18, 21
Moffitt, D. 253
Momigliano, A. 244
Moor, J. C. de 1
Moore, S. D. 1
Muilenburg, J. 86
Muraoka, T. 157, 158, 234, 238

Najman, H. 49
Nelson, R. D. 58, 61, 64
Neusner, J. 86, 166, 266, 268, 269, 272, 277
Newsom, C. 195
Nguyen, K. L. 151
Nicholson, E. 58, 65
Nurmela, R. 131

O'Connor, K. M. 24, 30, 31, 35, 38, 59, 61, 98, 102, 113, 141, 143, 147, 150, 151, 181
Olley, J. W. 77
Olyan, S. M. 273, 274
Owens, P. J. 25

Pabst, H. 210
Pardes, I. 194, 195
Parry, R. A. 51, 52, 145, 149, 151, 158, 163, 164, 168, 256, 259, 261, 264

Paschen, W. 35
Petersen, D. L. 128
Petitjean, A. 125
Pham, X. H. T. 274
Philip, T. S. 117
Pietersma, A. 233
Plank, K. A. 281
Pohlmann, K.-F. 226
Porteous, N. 80
Price, J. J. 247
Provan, I. W. 20, 32, 35, 52, 156, 163, 172, 176, 179, 181

Rah, S.-C. 196
Rainer, A. 57
Rashkow, I. 197
Reimer, D. J. 111
Renkema, J. 20, 24, 36, 40, 45, 50, 217, 219, 231, 232, 234
Reynolds, K. A. 160, 164, 168
Ricoeur, P. 91
Roberts, K. L. 89, 94, 95
Roth, J. K. 282
Rüsen, J. 227, 235, 238, 239
Rubenstein, R. L. 282
Rudolph, W. 31, 35, 217

Sänger, D. 234
Saebø, M. 80, 163, 172, 174
Sailhamer, J. H. 193
Salters, R. B. 35, 81, 145, 150, 152, 155-57, 163, 168, 173, 178, 179, 185, 217
Sanders, J. A. 46
Sarna, N. M. 18
Saxengaard, K. M. 200
Schipper, J. 82
Schmid, K. 177
Schreckenberg, H. 251
Schroer, S. 234
Schwartz, D. 247
Schwartz, S. 247
Scott, J. M. 224
Searle, J. R. 228
Seidler, V. J. 281
Seitz, C. R. 94
Seow, C.-L. 181
Seybold, K. 44, 129
Shafer-Elliott, C. 216
Sherwood, Y. 1

Shields, M. E. 111
Smith Landsman, I. 60
Smith, J. Z. 152
Smith-Christopher, D. L. 57, 111, 116
Sommer, B. D. 85, 98, 211
Spilsbury, P. 245
Stager, L. E. 216
Staubli, T. 234
Stead, M. R. 123, 124
Stemberger, G. 268
Stern, D. 269, 275
Stevens, W. 30, 41, 42
Stiebert, J. 21-25
Stone, T. J. 193
Strack, H. L. 268
Straub, J. 238
Strugnell, J. 210
Stulman, L. 55, 59, 68
Sweeney, M. A. 82

Taylor, C. 186
Thackeray, H. St. J. 247, 249
Thiel, W. 228
Thomas, H. A. 4, 31, 38, 39, 45, 87, 98, 100, 101, 143, 146, 173, 221, 256, 270, 271
Tiemayer, L.-S. 86, 90
Tigchelaar, E. J. C. 210, 216
Timmer, D. C. 26
Tollington, J. 129
Tombs, D. 264
Tooman, W. A. 165
Tov, E. 207, 212, 221
Trible, P. 89, 93, 94, 196, 199
Tull Willey, P. K. 85, 88-91, 95, 98, 106-108, 133, 181

Ueberschaer, F. 221
Uehlinger, F. 219, 223, 234, 237
Ulrich, E. 207

Van Dam, C. 18
Van Dijk-Hemmes, F. 111
Van der Kooij, A. 207, 209
Vermes, G. 210, 216
Vice, S. 194

Weber, B. 99
Webster, B. 210, 212

Weeks, S. 183
Weigold, M. 209, 211
Weiss, D. 271
Westermann, C. 56, 97, 105, 164, 172, 173, 217
Whybray, R. N. 188
Wiesel, E. 38, 282
Williamson, R. Jr. 280
Wilson, A. 10
Wilson, K. M. 284, 286
Wischnowski, M. 227
Wise, M. O. 210

Wolff, H. W. 234
Wright, C. J. H. 141
Würthwein, E. 207

Yee, G. A. 111
Yona, S. 199
Youngblood, K. J. 221, 222, 226, 231, 233

Zevit, Z. 209
Ziegler, J. 221, 230, 233
Zimmerli, W. 114, 119

www.ingramcontent.com/pod-product-compliance
Lightning Source LLC
Chambersburg PA
CBHW052143300426
44115CB00011B/1504